John Frederick Smith, Georg Heinrich August von Ewald

Commentary on the Prophets of the Old Testament

John Frederick Smith, Georg Heinrich August von Ewald

Commentary on the Prophets of the Old Testament

ISBN/EAN: 9783337037581

Printed in Europe, USA, Canada, Australia, Japan

Cover: Foto ©Lupo / pixelio.de

More available books at **www.hansebooks.com**

COMMENTARY

ON THE

PROPHETS OF THE OLD TESTAMENT,

BY THE LATE

DR. GEORG HEINRICH AUGUST VON EWALD,

Professor of Oriental Languages in the University of Göttingen.

Translated by

J. FREDERICK SMITH.

VOL. V.

ANONYMOUS PIECES, HAGGÁI, ZAKHARYA, MAL'AKI, YONA,
BARÛKH, DANIEL.

WILLIAMS AND NORGATE,
14, HENRIETTA STREET, COVENT GARDEN, LONDON;
AND 20, SOUTH FREDERICK STREET, EDINBURGH.
1881.

INDEX TO VOL. V.

III.—PROPHETS OF THE LATER PERIOD.

B.—To the End of the Captivity—*continued*.

		PAGE
4.	An Anonymous Prophet (Jer. l.—li.)	1—18
5.	The same Anonymous Prophet ("Isa." xxxiv.—xxxv.)	19—23
6.	An Anonymous Prophet ("Isa." xxiv.—xxvii.)	23—34

C.—In the New Jerusalem.

1.	Haggái	36—44
2.	Zakharya	44—70
3.	Mal'akhi	70—86

APPENDIX.

Prophetic Aftergrowths in the Kanon.

1.	Collectors of Oracles	87—89
2.	Prophetic Writers of Legends. Book of Yona	89—107
3.	The New Prophetic Authors	
	1. Barûkh	108—137
	Epistle of Yéremyá	137—152
	2. The Book of Daniel	152—324
	Index to the Prophetic Writings in this Work	325

ERRATUM.

Page 64, line 13, read *offshoot* for *shoot*.

III. PROPHETS OF THE LATER PERIOD.
B.—TO THE END OF THE CAPTIVITY.

4. AN ANONYMOUS PROPHET.
"JER." CH. L., LI.

THIS lengthy piece against Babel cannot be placed earlier in point of time than in the series which we are now considering, although it is most closely connected, according to Vol. III., p. 87 sq., with the book of Yéremyá as it is at present arranged. In fact, it contains many utterances, turns of thought, and ideas which are the same as Yéremyá's, and, indeed, its entire plan is such as he adopts; and inasmuch as Yéremyá is in the habit of repeating himself on occasions, this fact might at first sight create a prepossession in favour of his authorship. However, Yéremyá repeats himself upon a larger scale than is here the case, and in his repetitions does not become untrue to himself. But in this piece Yéremyá's peculiarities are perceptible only in certain passages, although they are numerous, and the repeated passages are often completely recast and altered.* As far, therefore, as the style of Yéremyá appears here, it must be considered as artistic copying and imitation, which had in this case to be the more close inasmuch as this piece was intended to be considered really a work of this prophet's.—On the other hand, where new thoughts and expressions occur in the long piece which are quite foreign to Yéremyá, it there approximates quite as decidedly to the

---

* As l. 2, 29; li. 27, compared with Jer. iv. 16. Numerous particulars have been mentioned previously in Vol. III.

pieces of this later period. We see Babel already threatened immediately by Kyros. Moreover, the view of Babel as of a totally corrupt kingdom, to which there is no longer the possibility of escaping the final overthrow; this indignation against the Chaldean tyrants, which had evidently only grown so intense and even prophetically violent by the lapse of time; and this public summons addressed to all fellow countrymen yet living in Babel to flee from the hopelessly doomed city and to return to the Holy Land, whither, indeed, some individuals appear already to have returned, l. 28; this unveiled designation of the Medes and other northern nations as the mortal enemies of Babel, and open mention of the immediate ruin of this city as certain—all this is as foreign, indeed repugnant and impossible, to Yéremyá as it is peculiar and necessary to the pieces of this period. It is doubtful whether Yéremyá even once, xxv. 26, really wrote ששך instead of בבל, with the alphabetical order of the letters reversed;* but this author not only repeats this name, li. 41, in quite other circumstances, inasmuch as there was nothing further to fear from Babel, but he also uses the new, more enigmatic name, formed in the same way, לֵב קָמָי, "the heart of my enemies," instead of כשדים, li. 1, comp. vv. 24, 35; indeed he forms similar enigmatical transcriptions of Chaldean names, l. 21, so that it is observable how great the advance in such matters had been since Yéremyá's days. Entirely new words, not found before the time of Hézeqiél and still later writers, are סָגָן, פֶּחָה, li. 23, 28, 57, גִּלּוּלִים, l. 2,† בַּדִּים as "false prophets," l. 36; nor does הֶחֱרִים, to ban, curse, l. 21, 26; li. 3, occur more than once

---

* It was originally mortal danger undoubtedly which led the exiles in Babel to deceive the rulers of the country with such ingenious alphabetic puzzles: but in this piece they are evidently no longer employed from this motive, but simply because the habit of using them had grown very general, even when nothing more was desired than a poetic variation of a proper name.

† The word is here rendered by *dolls*, as it may perhaps be considered, when derived from גלל in the sense of to *roll up*, as a nickname of this kind for idols; previous to Yéremyá only Lev xxvi. 30; Deut. xxix. 16.

in Yéremyá's writings, xxv. 9, but frequently in Hézeqiél's. And with every desire to retain the outward peculiarities of Yéremyá, it appears that even the headings, l. 1; li. 59, have received another form than Yéremyá would have given them. On the other hand, if we consider the great resemblance of l. 27; li. 40 with "Isa." xxxiv. 6 sq., of l. 39 with "Isa." xxxiv. 14, of li. 60 sq. with "Isa." xxxiv. 16, and many other particulars of the same kind, the opinion is formed, and it can hardly be wrong, that the author of the piece which follows this wrote this longer piece first, and then that somewhat later after Babel had been taken, upon another occasion.*

The author lived, as may be gathered from some of his expressions, l. 5 (*hither*, *i.e.*, to Ssion), and li. 50 (remember Jerusalem *from afar*), neither in Babel nor in any foreign land, but in the Holy Land itself, probably as a descendant of those who had never gone into exile. The movements of the Medes against the kingdom of Babel had begun, and Babel itself had been already seriously threatened, but the desired conquest and destruction was delayed on account of the unusually strong and ingenious fortification of the great city; contradictory reports were rife, the tyranny still continued to hold sway in another form, and the courage of many an exile who had already rejoiced at the prospect of its immediate fall sank once more, li. 45, 46; moreover, probably some lethargic ones amongst them appealed to Yéremyá's exhortations to composure, ch. xxix. Precisely this appeal to Yéremyá, which was then inappropriate, appears to have really been the immediate occasion which led our anonymous prophet to make this recast of this word of Yéremyá, and not without just reason: as Yéremyá, according to ch. xxv., had at least distantly threatened a Divine investigation and punishment to the Chaldean kingdom, and as his name had such weight amongst the exiles that they trusted him before all the prophets of that age,

* Comp. with regard to this event and the piece under notice *History of Israel*, V., 46 sq. (IV., 61 sq.)

it appeared to him both proper and effective to now make a more particular application to present circumstances of the threats which Yéremyá had uttered from a distance, and which had since approved themselves in the event as true prophecy, by letting Yéremyá speak as he would be compelled to do in the present state of affairs, when he would see the fulfilment of his own words. This is a resuscitation of the older prophet in an altered time, an instruction as to the way in which his words, which were already perversely applied, ought to be understood in the present time: and it was shown above, Vol. III., p. 87 sq., in what way an entirely new revision of the whole book of Yéremyá for the use of that period was connected with this fact. Accordingly, many of Yéremyá's peculiar words and ideas receive insensibly an entirely different reference, such as would be more intelligible to this later time; for instance, northern nations continue still to be spoken of here as the instruments of Divine punishment, but they are no longer the nations whom Yéremyá had in his mind, the Chaldeans, but, on the contrary, their enemies, the Medes; and Nabukodrossor is spoken of as if he still lived, l. 17; li. 34, simply because he has become the symbol of the Chaldean rule, comp. "Isa." xxiii. 15, but it may be seen from li. 31, that the king who was then actually reigning was not a hero like Nabukodrossor, but a weakling.

The origin of this piece is very interesting. As the first two pieces explained above, Vol. IV., pp. 233-244, show that prophetic voices in Babylonia itself understood the Divine call of the age, and as the work of the great anonymous prophet, *ibid.*, pp. 245-354, shows that this call was clearly re-echoed by one of the most powerful of these voices in Egypt, so we see in the pieces before us that neither was there wanting to this age upon the sacred soil of Palestine itself, though now it lay desolate, a true prophet; and although many might at that time in opposition to the new prophet appeal from simple love of fame to the words once uttered by Yéremyá, we see here one of these prophets labouring and speaking just as Yéremyá would certainly have laboured and spoken had he been then living. An additional circumstance of great interest is that this prophet, living in the Holy Land itself, had at that time evidently no knowledge whatever of the great work of the prophet in Egypt, a peculiarity which we shall not find in the next piece. The similarity with the words, "Isa." xlviii. 20; lii. 11, is in this piece manifestly after all simply accidental.

The author, however, finds it needful to show how it was possible for this piece, which is by its essential character intended for exiles only, to reach Babel during Yéremyá's life-time. To do this he avails himself of a historical reminiscence. People must at that time have been still in some way aware of the fact that the king Ssedeqia had in the fourth year of his reign made a kind of journey of homage to Babel to his patron Nabukodrossor; as this is narrated, li. 59, it has the appearance of being quite historical, and may have been taken almost verbatim from an older work, so little ground is there to regard the event as in itself doubtful; on the contrary, see the notes on ch. xxvii., xxviii. To this historical reminiscence our author adds the invention, that Yéremyá gave to Ssedeqia's travelling marshall, Seraya (also without doubt a person who was still remembered historically), this long discourse, that he might read it when occasion offered to the exiles at Babel; and as Yéremyá likes to introduce symbols at the end of his discourses, it is here also narrated in the postscript, li. 59-64, that Seraya received at the same time the charge to cast a stone into the Euphrates in confirmation of the certainty of the fall of Babel, comp. Ex. xv. 5.—When once the writing of the book in Yéremyá's name has been presupposed, the further carrying out of that intention, as above described, in the only way in which it was possible, is only a necessary consequence, as is also the case with the further imitation of Jer. ch. xix., for instance. It has also been shown at greater length in the *Jahrbücher der Bibl. Wiss.*, III.,

p. 316 sq., how useless it is to try to think of Yéremyá himself as the author of the piece in the strict historical sense.

The long piece itself, l. 2—li. 58, deals with its subject-matter in a very loose and languid manner; without any strict arrangement or incisive brevity the discourse can only by degrees reach its conclusion: in this respect also it is like the following piece from the same time. Still, a certain degree of arrangement is by no means absent. It falls into ten strophes of the kind used by Yéremyá; the first three of these form the first main section of the entire piece, the four middle ones the second section, the next three the last, while each of these three main sections has at the commencement an energetic exhortation to battle against Babel. In other respects, in the first of these three sections, l. 2-28, the reference to the necessary redemption of Israel predominates; in the second, l. 29—li. 26, the emphasis of the whole antithesis between Babel, Yahvé, and his spiritual instrument Israel; in the third, li. 27-58, the more particular description of the condition of Babel at that time.

l.

1   The word which Yahvé spake concerning Babel, concerning the land of the Chaldeans, by the prophet Yéremyá:

1.

1. Announçe ye among the nations, and proclaim ye and raise a sign, | proclaim ye deny not and say "Babel is taken! | Bel is ashamed Merodakh is dismayed, her images are ashamed her dolls are dismayed; || for there advanceth against her a nation from the north, | it will make her land into a desert, so that there is no inhabitant therein, | both man and beast flee go!"—In those days and in that time (saith Yahvé)—the sons of Israel will come they and the sons of Yudah together, | they will go on weeping, and Yahvé their
5   God will they seek; || for Ssion will they ask, hitherward their faces: | "come ye and join yourselves unto Yahvé, for an everlasting covenant not to be forgotten!" || As lost sheep was my people, their shepherds caused them to stray through rebel-

lious mountains, | from mountain to hill they went, forgot their resting place; || all who found them devoured them, and their oppressors said "we are not guilty," | because that they sinned against Yahvé the pasture of salvation, and the hope of their fathers Yahvé. ||—Flee ye forth from Babel, and from the land of the Chaldeans withdraw ye, | and be as he-goats before the flock! || for behold I arouse and bring up over Babel a community of great nations, | (from the north country —from there they get ready against her, from there will she be taken) | whose arrows are as those of a skilful hero, who
10 returneth not home for nothing; || and Chaldea will be a spoil, | all that spoil her will be satisfied, saith Yahvé. ||

2. Although ye rejoice, although ye exult ye plunderers of my heritage, | although ye leap like a calf through the grass, and neigh as stallions : || yet your mother is greatly ashamed, she that bare you is abashed ; | "behold the last of the nations, a desert a waste and steppe !" || because of Yahvé's displeasure

1. As in the first section it is specially the necessary redemption of Israel which is to be dwelt upon as the reason for the overthrow of Babel, the discourse hastens immediately after the suitable opening, vv. 2, 3, to the description of the fair time soon to arrive, when the exiles of all tribes will in rivalry hasten to Ssion to a new and eternal covenant with Yahvé, vv. 4, 5, since the enemies of the nation were only on that account able with such small pains, as if they had done nothing reprehensible, to finish their work of destruction, that it went astray, misled by its guides, like sheep by careless shepherds, to the rebellions, *i.e.*, idolatrous, mountains (that is, as they were formerly called, the *Heights*, the seats of idolatry), and lost the refreshing pastures of true prosperity, the hope of the fathers (Ps. xxii. 5, 6), the true God, vv. 6, 7. But now, since Babel must succumb to its successful enemies, let not Israel be slow to make use of its freedom! vv. 8-10. Ver. 3 after ix. 9; vv. 4, 5 after xxxi. 9 sq.; xx. 11; xxiii. 40; as to הָלוֹךְ, ver. 5, which must be an *imperat.* according to the context, see § 226 *c.* Ver. 6 the *K'thib* שׁוֹבָבִים is quite correct, נְוֵה צֶדֶק, ver. 7, is altered from xxxi. 23, ver. 9 at the end from 2 Sam. i. 22. The brief, pointed resumption of a member of the sentence by the construction וְעָרְכוּ, ver. 9 (comp. ver. 14) according to § 357 *a* is a favourite usage with this author, comp. li. 58, 64 ; and that the accents must then be altered follows as a matter of course.

2. Although the individual Babylonians, the devastators of the Holy Land, may still live so luxuriously and licentiously, ver. 11 (comp. li. 38, 39, and v. 8; viii. 16), their native city Babel, otherwise the first of all nations (Num. xxiv. 20), will nevertheless be now deeply humiliated and generally

she will not be inhabited, will become a wilderness altogether, |
everyone that passeth by Babel will be astonished and hiss at
all her punishments. ‖ —Get ye ready against Babel round
about all ye bowmen, shoot at her spare not an arrow: |
because she hath sinned against Yahvé! ‖ shout aloud over her
round about "she hath surrendered, | her foundations have
fallen, her walls are destroyed!" | because it is Yahvé's
vengeance take ye vengeance on her, as she hath done do ye
unto her! ‖ cut ye off from Babel the sower, and the sickle-
holder at harvest-time! | before the sword of destruction let them
return every one to his people, and flee every one to his land! ‖
—A scattered lamb is Israel, which lions drove away: | first
the Assyrian king devoured it, and now at last Nabukodrossor
king of Babel hath rent it. ‖ Therefore thus saith Yahvé of
Hosts Israel's God: behold I visit the king of Babel and his
land, | as I have visited the king of Assyria, ‖ I bring back
Israel into its pasture, that it may feed on Karmel and
Bashan, | and on the mountain of Ephráim and Gilead its soul
may satisfy itself! ‖ In those days and in that time (saith
Yahvé) will Israel's iniquity be sought for but in vain, and
Yuda's guilt without being found: | because I pardon whom I
reserve. ‖

3. "Against the land *Double-Defiance*—advance against it,
and against the inhabitants of *Wrathwich*, | slaughter and ban

dishonoured by Yahvé's righteous punishment, vv. 12, 13, after xix. 8; xlix. 17. Only be courageous against Babel, which is already before Yahvé devoted to destruction; be courageous ye warriors, ye heralds, ye exiles! let her sowers and reapers be destroyed (Babel having, as is well known, many gardens and fields within the immense circuit of its walls, Plin. *Hist. Nat.* xviii. 17), in order that all hope of obtaining commonest necessities may fail her! vv. 14-16. As formerly the first devourer (the Assyrian) of the lamb of Israel, which was so miserably scattered, acc. ver. 6, fell, so shall the Chaldean now fall, in order that the Community may in the peaceful possession of the Holy Land, finally attain the long-promised Messianic age! vv. 17-20. If the pointing דָּשָׁא, ver. 11, were correct the sense would be, "leapeth as a young threshing heifer," after Hos. x. 11; but the vocalisation דָּשָׁא, which is most natural, is all that is required, inasmuch as פֻּנָה can, like הָלַךְ, be construed immediately with the object, § 282 *a*. *She hath surrendered*, ver. 15, lit. given her hand, to be manacled if the conqueror chooses.

3. And as soon as ever this command is heard from above, to advance with sword and anathema against the country *Double-defiance* (really Aram-

after them (saith Yahvé), and do altogether as I have commanded thee!" || Hark war in the earth, and great ruin! || O how is the hammer of the whole earth hewn and broken! | O how is Babel become a desolation among the nations! || I laid nets for thee, and thou wast taken also Babel, quite unawares; | wast found and captured, because thou hadst struck at Yahvé! ||
25 —Yahvé hath opened his store and brought forth the weapons of his indignation: | for a work is it which Lord Yahvé of Hosts hath in the land of the Chaldeans. || Come ye against her ye last ones also, open her granaries, | thresh her as sheaves and ban her, let her have no remnant! || slaughter all her bullocks, send them down to the butchery! | woe unto them for their day cometh, the time of their punishment. || Hark fugitives and escaped ones from the land of Babel, | to announce in Ssion the vengeance of Yahvé our God, the vengeance of his temple. ||

Naharáim, the land of the *double-river*, Mesopotamia), and the city *Punishment* (the city deserving punishment, Babel, but with a reference to the actual name פקוד, Ezek. xxiii. 23), Babel falls into ruins, the heavy hammer which smote the whole earth is itself dashed in pieces, nor can the kingdom which entered into the most bitter antagonism to Yahvé deliver itself by all its arts and stratagems in conflict with higher wisdom, vv. 21-24. If she has desired war against Yahvé, he has now in turn brought forth against her, as from the hidden celestial arsenals, all the weapons of his wrath, Job. xxxviii. 23, and her barns shall also be now broken into, the masses of people which are crowded together in her shall be threshed amid anathemas, like sheaves fetched from the barns, her potentates slaughtered like fat sacrificial animals, vv. 25-27, and already the victory may be proclaimed to Ssion from afar, ver. 28. Comp. "Isa." xxxiv. 9; with regard to the figures taken from *threshing*, see *History of Israel*, III., 150 (III., 203 sq.). סַל, ver. 26, *to draw out* may mean to *thresh out*, when sheaves are spoken of. מְקֵץ like מְקָצָה li. 31.

2.

1. Call ye to Babel archers all bowmen, beleaguer her round about, let her have no escape, | repay her according to her work, altogether as she hath done do to her: | because she was
30 haughty towards Yahvé, Israel's Holy One! || therefore will her youths fall in her streets, | and all her warriors perish in that day, saith Yahvé. || I come against thee thou haughtiness! saith the Lord Yahvé of Hosts, | for thy day is come, the time of thy punishment; || and haughtiness stumbleth and

falleth, with none to raise him up, | and I kindle a fire in his forest, that it may devour everything around him. | —Thus saith Yahvé of Hosts: oppressed are the sons of Israel together with the sons of Juda, and all their bondlords hold them fast, refuse to let them go: || their strong redeemer, Yahvé of Hosts his name—he will indeed plead their cause, | in order to make the earth shake, and the inhabitants of Babel 35 to tremble. || Sword against the Chaldeans! saith Yahvé, | and against Babel's inhabitants and against her princes and her wise men! || Sword against the boasters, that they become foolish, | Sword against the heroes, that they become dismayed! || Sword against her horses and her chariots, and against all the hirelings that are in her, that they become women, | Sword against her treasures, that they be plundered!|| Sword against her waters, that they be dried up! | for it is a land of idols, and by the scare-images they let themselves be befooled. || Therefore wild cats will dwell with wolves, yea ostriches dwell in her | and never more will she abide, nor flourish 40 from generation to generation; || as God destroyed Sodom and Gomorrah and its neighbours, saith Yahvé, | no man will dwell there, nor a son of man sojourn in her.

1. The last strophe has thus already prepared for the chief subject of the second section, namely, the description of the whole antithesis between Babel and the true God. Accordingly the criminal haughtiness with which Babel defies Yahvé is at once brought forward very prominently, vv. 29-32; ver. 30 from xlix. 26; ver. 32 b from xxi. 14, according to which it is better to read בְּעָרוֹ, the reading retained by the LXX, instead of בְּעָרָיו *in his cities*, although it is true that li. 43 the *cities* of the land are spoken of. With regard to עֵת פקדתיך, ver. 31, comp. Vol. III., p. 122.—In more definite language the discourse proceeds: because it continues to oppress the Israelites and to refuse to liberate them, the true deliverer will rise on their behalf with the convulsion of the whole world, and the great sword (the divine punishment) shall smite the Chaldeans and everything in which they place their hopes, the *boasters* also, *i.e.*, the false prophets, Isa. xlix. 25, and the costly *water*-conduits, upon which a great part of the security of the immense city depended (li. 13, 32, 36, 37; Isa. xiv. 23; Herod. I., 178 sq., 185 sq.), since Babel chooses with such infatuation to be befooled by *scare-images*, *i.e.*, idols, nonentities (התחלל as li. 7; xxv. 16); so that there arises a horrible wilderness where now the rich city appears in her splendour, vv. 39, 40, like "Isa." xxxiv. 14-17 and Jer. xlix. 18. Inasmuch as the sword in the long enumeration vv. 35-38 is evidently each time repeated with a purpose, and must not be taken in the material sense, but has been adopted from such a usage as xlvii. 6, it is neither well nor needful to adopt

2. Behold a people cometh from the north, | a great nation and many kings bestir themselves from the utmost ends of the earth : || bow and lance they hold, are cruel and without compassion, | people whose voice roareth like the sea, and who drive upon horses, | prepared as a man for war against thee thou daughter of Babel! || the Babylonian king hath heard the rumour of them, and his hands hang down, | distress hath laid hold on him, trembling like her that travaileth. || Behold, as a lion will it come up out of the pride of Jordan to the pasture of rock : | in a moment will I tear them down thence, and appoint over it whoever is chosen! | for who is like me and who will arraign me ? and who is that shepherd who would
45 stand before me ? ||—Therefore hear Yahvé's counsel which he hath determined concerning Babel, and his thoughts which he hath thought concerning the land of the Chaldeans : | surely men will seize them those weak sheep ; surely the pasture will be shocked at them ! || at the voice " Babel is taken !" the earth
li. is shaken, and the cry is heard among the nations. || Thus
1 saith Yahvé : behold I stir up against Babel and against the inhabitants of Aedlach the spirit of destruction, || and send forth against Babel winnowers who winnow her and empty her land, | because she is come upon round about in the day of evil. || " Here let the archer draw his bow, and there let the harness be put on, | and spare ye not her brave ones, ban ye her whole army !" || and the slain fall in the land of the Chaldeans, | and those thrust through in her streets. ||

instead of it the punctuation of the Massôra, חֹרֶב, *drought!* ver. 38 ; on the contrary, the entire construction also continues the same as in the previous verses. The frequent reference

2. If it is desired to know more particularly than is told vv. 3, 9 *with what instruments* Yahvé executes this determination regarding Babel, hear what follows : barbarous northern armies come against it, vv. 41-43, (from vi. 22) under a daring leader, ver. 44 ; thus the great overthrow is unavoidable, the spirit of destruction which Yahvé arouses against Babel calls the most barbaric warriors to their feet, and as

to Israel and Yuda at the same time, vv, 4, 20, 33 ; li. 5, is in imitation of Yéremyá's habit, ch. iii ; the *hirelings*, or smaller vassal-princes, ver. 37, from Jer. xxv. 20, 24, Vol. III., p. 223 sq.

soon as he commands them to use their weapons the Chaldeans fall as vanquished on all sides, vv. 45—li. 4. It is here surprising to see how vv. 41-43 have been transferred hither with certain more or less necessary changes from vi. 22-24 and vv. 44-46 from xlix. 19-21. *Aedlach*, li. 1, in imitation of the Hebrew inversion of *Chaldea* (כשדים), which is mentioned in the same connexion vv. 24, 35;

5   3. For Israel is not bereaved and Yuda of his God Yahvé of Hosts, | but their land is full of guilt on account of the Holy One of Israel. || Flee ye out of Babel, and save every one his soul, perish not in her iniquity! | for it is a time of vengeance for Yahvé, recompense payeth he to her. || " A golden cup was Babel in Yahvé's hand, intoxicating the whole earth ; | of its wine nations drank, therefore nations became mad : || is Babel suddenly fallen and broken ? | bemoan her, take balsam for her pains, perhaps she will be healed !" ||—" We sought to heal Babel yet she was not made whole, leave her that we may go every one to his land ! | for her punishment reacheth to heaven, and riseth up even to the clouds ; || Yahvé hath
10 brought out our justification, | come and let us recount in Ssion the deed of Yahvé our God !" ||—Polish the arrows, fill the quivers, | Yahvé hath stirred up the spirit of the Median kings, because against Babel his plan is to destroy it : | for it is the vengeance of Yahvé, the vengeance of his temple. || Towards the walls of Babel raise the banner, | strengthen the watch, set watchmen, prepare the outlookers : | for as he hath planned so doeth Yahvé what he hath spoken against the inhabitants of Babel. || Thou that dwellest by abundant waters, thou that dost abound in treasures : | thine end is come, thy gains have ceased ! || Yahvé of Hosts sweareth by his soul : | though I have filled thee with men as with locusts, nevertheless the trampling-song is sung before thee ! ||

although by the inversion of the letters in the Hebrew the satirical meaning could be found, that the words *the heart of my enemies*, i.e., of my bitterest enemies, formed the best circumlocution for the Chaldeans. It is better, on account of the figure of the winnowing, rejection, and emptying to read זָרִים instead of זָרִים, *barbarians*, ver. 2 ; the last member ver. 2 c is very similar to Ps. lv. 19. It appears from the connexion that the twice-repeated אֵל, ver. 3, cannot be the preposition ; neither would the negative אַל supply any sense ; we must therefore look upon it as an adverb of place, related to the Aram. חַל and חֲלָא, § 103 *f*. The verb יְתָעֵל from the Aram. עֲלַל, acc. § 121 *a ad fin*.

3. For this is precisely the great advantage of Israel, that its God never dies, and therefore his punishment as it now hangs over Babel cannot fail : let Israel flee quickly therefore from all partnership with her ! vv. 5, 6. After all, Babel was formerly simply an instrument of the divine justice against the nations which were then guilty, ver. 7, after xxv. 15, 16 : now that she herself falls, to the surprise of all, pity might be felt for her and the desire to help, as in other cases of misfortune, ver. 8. But if any voice should be raised with such thoughts, vv. 7, 8, another and better instructed voice is at once

15   4. He who created the earth by his power, who holdeth the world by his wisdom, | and by his understanding stretched out the heavens, || when he thundereth there is a roaring of waters in heaven, and he draweth up vapours from the end of the earth, | lightnings unto the rain he maketh, and bringeth the wind out of his chambers. || Too stupid is every man to know that : every smelter is ashamed before the graven image, | because his molten-work is a lie and no spirit therein; || vain are they, the work of error, | at the time of their visitation they perish !|| Not like these is Yaqob's portion, but the Creator of the Universe* is he, | and the stock of his inheritance is named Yahvé of Hosts. ||—A hammer art thou
20   unto me, weapons of war : | and so I hammer with thee nations, and destroy with thee kingdoms, || and hammer with thee horse and rider, | and hammer with thee chariot and driver, || and hammer with thee man and woman, and hammer with thee old and young, | and hammer with thee youth and maiden, || and hammer with thee shepherd and flock, and hammer with thee husbandman and yoke, | and hammer with

raised in opposition to it, crying that experience teaches that with the best intention she cannot be assisted, and that great care must be taken not to get involved in her ruin, which must be rather reverenced as a salutary manifestation of divine righteousness, vv. 9, 10. Be always armed and on the watch therefore against Babel, whose fall is finally determined by Yahvé, vv. 14, 15 ; neither do all the scientific water-fortifications, the numerous exacted treasures, the innumerable hosts of people, avail her anything ! as is said vv. 13, 14, only in another way than above l. 35-38.—הֵידָד, ver. 14, the winepress-cry, the treading-cry, but as is quite evident here, after xxv. 30, the cry of the sanguinary treading of the battle, ver. 33. Instead of the unintelligible אֹמַר, ver. 13, it is probably better to read שָׁבַת after "Isa." xiv. 4.

4 And to finally bring into greatest prominence the antithesis upon which everything here depends : who is Yahvé in reality, who is Israel, who is the Chaldean ? Yahvé, if it is desired to describe him further, is the only true God, with whom the gods of the Heathen cannot be distantly compared, vv. 15-19 (from x. 12-16, only ver. 19 the meaning has been somewhat altered, though not for the better). The true community is as such invincible, while she herself gradually subjugates all that oppress her : the true Israel is like a hammer in Yahvé's hand, by means of which he can beat to pieces everything, even the Chaldeans, vv. 20-24. And although Babel may be

---

*˙Germ. *vom All*. Comp. III., p. 141, and *Die Lehre der Bibel von Gott*, III., p. 4.—Tr.

thee governors and commanders; ‖ I repay Babel and all the inhabitants of Chaldea all their evil | which they have done in
25 Ssion before you, saith Yahvé. ‖ —I come against thee thou mountain of destruction (saith Yahvé), which destroyed the whole earth, | and stretch out my hand against thee, roll thee from the rocks and make thee a burning mountain, ‖ so that there shall not be taken from thee a stone for a corner nor a stone for foundations, | but everlasting ruins wilt thou be, | saith Yahvé. ‖

as great as a mountain, yea as a fire-mountain (volcano) destructive to the whole earth, even the highest fire-mountain may at a sign from Yahvé crumble to pieces and as it were burn itself up, so that there remains nothing in its place but a wide desert, vv. 25, 26. This is the mutual relation of these three! The figure of *corner-stones* seems to indicate the intention of expressing the exact opposite of Ps. cxviii. 22.

3.

li.
27 " Set up a banner on the earth, blow the trumpet among the nations, | consecrate against her nations, call against her the kingdoms Ararat Minni and Ashkenaz, | set over her a war-captain, let steeds charge like bristling locusts! ‖ consecrate against her nations, Media's kings governors and commanders, | with the whole land of his dominion!" ‖ Then the earth shook and writhed, | because against Babel Yahvé's thoughts rose up, to make Babel's land a desert without any
30 inhabitant; ‖ Babel's heroes ceased to fight, remained in the castles, their power was spent, they became as women; | her dwellings were set on fire, broken were her bars; ‖ one runner runneth against the other, and one messenger against the other, | to tell the king of Babel " his city is wholly taken, ‖ the fords are occupied, and the outworks burned with fire, | and the warriors struck with dismay." ‖ —For thus saith Yahvé of Hosts Israel's God : the daughter of Babel is as a threshing floor when it is trampled : | yet a little—and the harvest time cometh to her. ‖ " Nabukodrossor king of Babel devoured us mangled us,* put us forth as an empty vessel; | swallowed us as a dragon, filled his belly with my dainties,

---

* Ewald keeps up the figure in the second verb by rendering it *zerkaute uns, chewed us to pieces.*—Tr.

35 thrust us out: ‖ my wrong and my body be upon Babel!" let the township Ssion say, | "and my blood upon the inhabitants of Chaldea!" let Jerusalem say. ‖ Therefore thus saith Yahvé: behold I plead thy cause, and take vengeance for thee, | and dry up her sea, and parch up her spring, ‖ so that Babel becometh stone-heaps a haunt of jackals, a desolation and emptiness without an inhabitant. ‖

2. Together they roar as lions, | growl as young lions: ‖ if they are heated I will prepare their feast and make them drunken | in order that they may rejoice—and sleep an eternal

1. Since the third section is confined more particularly to the locality of Babel, the imagination first projects a somewhat vivid picture of the method by which Babel must be captured according to the requirements of its position. As soon as at a given sign the numerous northern nations, with war-horses bristling with armour like locusts, rush as if consecrated (Isa. xiii. 3) to the holy war, vv. 27, 28, the earth trembles, the Babylonian heroes are in a state of inexplicable helplessness, the conquest begins, and one messenger of evil tidings after another runs to the Babylonian king, vv. 29-32: all this a description like the earlier one, Nah. ii. and iii. For, the higher voice proclaims, Babel has already become as a threshing-floor prepared for threshing, and soon the proper harvest-time arrives when it will be used, as was more particularly described above, l. 26, ver. 33, comp. iv. 14; l. 26. Babel must fall, if for no other reason, on account of its cruel conduct towards Israel, which the Chaldean quietly devoured, and then after it had been completely devoured, rudely cast it away like an empty vessel and thrust it into exile, so that its flesh and blood, its whole life, may bitterly complain to Yahvé against him,

vv. 34-37. Ver. 32, אֲגַמִּים is obscure, it is true: still, it is evident that the usual meaning, *swamps*, does not suit the idea of burning with fire; it is more likely that we have quite a different word, which the ancient Arabic lexicons explain as a kind of castle, in this case therefore probably an outwork. The accents have this time unfortunately damaged the forcible figure ver. 34, comp. Ps. xiv. 4. The phrase ver. 35 is simply extended from the ancient form Gen. xvi. 5; in other respects, comp. Ps. cxxiv. 1 sq. The word הֲרִידָנוּ is intended most likely to signify *he emptied us*, from רוּד = לוּחַ, bright, clean, empty: but הֲדִי suits the context better. — *Sea and spring*, ver. 36, is equivalent to everything, but it has reference to the splendid streams which served both to increase the trade and the strength of the fortifications of the city, vv. 13, 32, 42 and l. 37, 38. Ver. 35, *Jerusalem* is addressed just as "Isa." xxi. 10; xl. 9 and in other prophets of this period notwithstanding that it was then in ruins. Instead of שְׁרֵקָה, *hissing*, ver. 37, it is almost certain that this author had in his mind the Aram. שְׁרִיקָה, *emptiness*.

2. It is true the Babylonians are full of reckless pleasure and wild delight,

ver 38, comp. l. 11: but precisely in this inebriation of joy the intoxication

40 sleep never awaking, saith Yahvé; ‖ I will bring them down as lambs to the slaughter, | as rams with he-goats. | —" O how is Lebab taken, and the praise of the whole earth captured! | O how is Babel become a desolation among the nations! ‖ the sea is gone over Babel, | with the roaring of its waves she is covered; ‖ her cities are become a desolation, a land of drought and a steppe of land, | so that no one dwelleth in them, no son of man passeth through them." ‖ And I visit it upon Bel in Babel and draw what he swallowed out of his mouth, that nations may no more flow unto him : | nevertheless
45 Babel's wall falleth! ‖ — Go forth out of her my people, and save every one his soul | from the heat of the anger of Yahvé! ‖ and lest your heart faint and ye fear for the rumour heard upon the earth, | and because in the year cometh this rumour, and in the following that, and violence is upon the earth, tyrant upon tyrant! ‖—Therefore behold days come that I visit upon the stone images of Babel, | and her whole land will be dried up, and all her slain fall within her; ‖ then heaven and earth and all that is in them shout for joy over Babel, | that from the north the desolaters come unto her, saith Yahvé : ‖ " Babel must fall as well, O ye slain of Israel ! | as on account of Babel fell the slain of the whole earth." ‖

of death surprises them the sooner, so that partaking of the meal of the divine punishment they fall like sacrificial animals into the eternal sleep, ver. 39, comp. l. 27; Ps. lix. 16; lxxvi. 6; Isa. xxi. 5. Already the elegy on the fall of Babel, which was once the praise of the whole earth, may be struck up; Babel, which is inundated by hostile armies as Pharaoh was formerly by the waves of the sea (ver. 56; xlvi. 7, 8), becomes a desolation for ever, vv. 41-43 : the idol Bel must fall, whose temple attracted so many visitors and donors of the richest offerings because it was richly adorned by booty taken from all nations of the earth ; and whatever may yet be done to hinder it, it is certain that the famous walls of the city will fall, as is said in one closing word of great brevity and emphatic force, ver. 44, comp. ver. 58. Therefore flee ye members of the true Community before the dangers become too great, and above all do not suffer yourselves to be alarmed by the rumours which are always so contradictory in this confused time, or by the continued delay of deliverance, vv. 45, 46 (an utterance historically very remarkable !): the more confused the times continue to be, the more certain and glorious is the redemption which comes from Yahvé; and as certain as martyrs from all nations fell on account of Babel must now Babel also fall (hear that, ye martyrs of Israel!) vv. 47-49. Lebab, ver. 41, is only an imitation of the Hebrew *Sheshak* made by an alphabetic inversion, as ver. 1.—Ver. 43, the second אֶרֶץ is better connected with the foregoing member.—בָּ, ver. 44, is in this

50   3. Ye that have escaped the sword, go ye stand not! |
remember from afar Yahvé, and let Jerusalem come into your
mind! || "We are ashamed that we heard the reproach, | shame
hath covered our face that barbarians came upon the sanctuaries
of Yahvé's house!" || therefore behold days come (saith Yahvé)
that I visit upon the stone images, | and in all her land the
slain will groan. || Though Babel ascend to heaven, and though
she fortify her towering height : | from me desolaters will go
forth into her! saith Yahvé. || —Hark a cry from Babel | and
55 great ruin from the land of the Chaldeans! || for Yahvé will
desolate Babel, and destroy from her the proud voice; | and
though her waves roar as many waters, the noise of their sound
be given forth, ||yet there cometh over her over Babel a desolater,
and her heroes are taken, their bows split in pieces : | for a
God of recompense is Yahvé, he doth repay; || and I make
drunk her princes and wise men, her governors and commanders and heroes, so that they sleep an eternal sleep never
awaking, | saith the King called Yahvé of Hosts. || —Thus saith
Yahvé of Hosts : the broadest walls of Babel—laid bare will
they be, and her highest gates burned with fire : | *that nations
weary themselves for vanity, and peoples for the fire—for that
labour!* ||

The word with which the prophet Yéremyá charged Seraya
son of Nêriya son of Machseya, when he went with Ssedeqia

connexion, Germ. *doch, nevertheless,* acc. § 354 a. בָּא, ver. 46, acc. § 351 b,	with regard to the repeated הַשְׁמוּעָה, see § 360 c.
3. Once more, ye survivors, return to Ssion, forget not in the distance Yahvé and the holy city! ver. 50, comp. Ps. cxxxvii. 5, 6. And in reality the exiles are already heard praying, with tears of shame at their previous contempt of themselves and the holy place, ver. 51 : wherefore, on the other hand, the most definite promises proceed from Yahvé regarding proud Babel, vv. 52, 53, with ver. 53 comp. Isa. xiv. 12. Already is heard the loud noise of the inundating enemies which come to stop all loud defiant noise in Babel as executors of the will of Yahvé, vv. 54, 55 :	yes, certainly, as truly as Yahvé is the righteous awarder, the destroyer comes upon Babel, which is suddenly paralysed, although it is still like a sea roaring with wild noise (acc. ver. 38), and as if by the intoxication of the divine punishment its mighty men fall into the eternal sleep, vv. 55 b—57, comp. ver. 39 ; and, to compress everything into one word : Babel must fall, in spite of its ingeniously constructed walls and gates, in order that the oracle of Habaqqûq's, ii. 13, that the work built upon wrong, though it may be by means of the sweat of great subjugated

60 king of Yuda to Babel in the fourth year of his reign (and Seraya was camp-prince), and Yéremyá wrote all the evil which should come upon Babel in a book, all these words which are written concerning Babel: then said Yéremyá to Seraya: when thou comest to Babel, then see and read all these words, and say: "Yahvé thou hast spoken concerning this place to destroy it, | that there be not in it an inhabitant neither man nor beast, | but eternal desolations shall it be!" || And when thou hast made an end of reading this book, thou wilt bind a stone thereto and cast it into the midst of the Euphrates, and say: Thus will Babel sink under and not rise, | from the evil which I have spoken concerning her—therefrom despair! ||

nations, never lasts, ver. 58. The particle כִּי, ver. 53, like l. 11, acc. § 362 b; ver. 55 b (where the division of the verse is not suitable), there is, moreover, a continuation of it with וְחָמוּ.—It cannot be denied that the long piece closes very appropriately with that oracle from Habaqqûq, which quite suits the context.

Vv. 59-64. Inasmuch as the last words of ver. 59 undoubtedly are intended to indicate the reason wherefore, amongst so many other princes, i.e., courtiers, it was only this Seraya who went in a special way with the king on his visit to Babel, it follows that the official name, שַׂר מְנוּחָה, *prince of the rest*, or of *the night encampment*, which does not occur elsewhere, must signify pretty much *travelling marshal*; as filling such an office he was indispensable; comp. with reference to him, *History of Israel*, III. 272 (III. 372).—Ver. 61, *look and read*, that is, seek a good opportunity for reading; ver. 62 is a brief extract of the entire foregoing piece. It is at all events the case that פְּרָת already stands here thus alone without נהר for the Euphrates, and the author may have understood the name in this sense in ch. xiii. also. —Comp. Vol. III., 153.—The word וְיָעֵפוּ receives a somewhat different application, ver. 64, from the oracle of Habaqqûq, ver. 58: but the younger prophet was free to do this.

We have almost the same supposition in the closing words of this piece as at the close of the book of Daniel. The divine words shall not merely come as a curse over the city, just as they are read aloud over it, but the small book also shall be cast with the heavy stone of the curse into the river, as if to ascertain whether it will perhaps in the future come once more to light. And as a fact it is indeed in the best sense still there, and well deserves to have its place beside the book of Yéremyá, although it is only one of the earliest re-echoes of many of his words and thoughts.

The last words, *thus far Yéremyá's words*, do not date from an earlier hand than that of him who still later added ch. lii., comp. Vol. III. 90.

5. The same Anonymous Prophet.

"Isa." xxxiv, xxxv.

This small piece of the same prophet's dates from a somewhat later time, already like an echo of the joyous portion of the thoughts of the great piece, "Isa." xl.—xlviii. It is as if he had only just read that great piece, xl.—lxiii. 6, and had been so deeply inspired by its high and encouraging thoughts, and particularly by the closing oracle concerning Edóm, lxiii. 1-6, that his own powers of production were aroused, and carried away by the first impression of those lofty words he wrote this piece. The only new element in the piece is, strictly speaking, simply the further elaboration of that threat against Edóm. Before the end of the first strophe, xxxiv. 1-7, the discourse, which threatens great commotions of heaven and earth as about to come over all nations, turns very soon to Edóm alone, continues with it in the second strophe, vv. 8-17, and not before the last, ch. xxxv., presents with pure joy, as an antithesis to it, Israel's liberation from the captivity. In the description of the desolation of Edóm, the author transfers to this new relation the figures which were used xiii. 2—xiv. 23 at first of Babel, as if at that time the hatred of Babel had already been turned aside more to Edóm, inasmuch as in the return closer contact with Edóm as a fact became necessary; comp. Ps. cxxxvii. In that case the piece would be written between 538 and 536 B.C.

It is certain that the great anonymous prophet did not thus copy himself; moreover, the author who is here discoverable has not a few peculiarities in language and figures by which he distinguishes himself sufficiently from the author of xl.—lxvi. Still, it is very remarkable that many things in ch. xxxv. almost word for word remind one of Isa. xxxii, xxxiii., ver. 2, like xxxiii. 6; ver. 3 from xxxiii. 9; vv. 4-6 from xxxii. 4-6; xxxiii. 23, 24; whilst, on the other hand, it is impossible in

2 *

every respect to separate ch. xxxiv. from ch. xxxv., since what is announced in xxxiv. 7, is completed ch. xxxv. We must therefore suppose that this later author, full of the new thoughts uttered in ch. xiii., xiv., xl.—lxvi., connected his small piece with the earlier piece, Isa. xxviii.—xxxiii., in some such way as we have before observed in the case of ch. xii. and xxiii. 15-18, Vol. I. 95. The ancient piece of Yesaya's, ch. xxviii.—xxxiii., may thus have been afresh brought into circulation at that time; and thus the younger prophet, reviving the ancient book by means of this addition, might speak, xxxiv. 16, of a *book of Yahvé*, as is further explained in the *Jahrbb. der Bibl. Wiss.*, VII., p. 75.

xxxiv 1.

1 Come near ye nations to hear, and ye Heathen give heed! let the earth hear and her fulness, the world and all its springings! ‖ For displeasure hath Yahvé upon all the nations, and indignation upon all their host; | he hath banned them devoted them to the slaughter, ‖ and their smitten are stretched at length, the smell of their corpses cometh up, | and mountains melt with their blood; ‖ all the host of heaven rotteth, and as a book the heavens roll together, | all their host withereth away —as a leaf withereth away from the vine, and as the withering
5 of the figtree. ‖ —For drunken in heaven was my sword: | now will it descend upon Edóm, and upon the nation of my ban unto judgment, ‖ a sword Yahvé hath that is full of blood, it is soaked with fat, | with the blood of lambs and hegoats, with the kidney-fat of rams : | for Yahvé hath a sacrifice in Bossra and a great slaughter in the land of Edóm, ‖ and wild buffaloes sink down with them, and bullocks with mighty ones, | their land is drunken with blood, and their ground soaked with fat. ‖

1. All nations must hear this prophetic voice, because in the present great commotion of the world all are alike threatened by an outbreak of divine wrath, which must be felt not only by men as they fall by thousands in the battles, but before which the powers of heaven also totter and the firm welkin is rolled together in alarm like a scroll just opened but immediately let go, vv. 1-4. The sword which is appointed to execute the divine judgments, already invisibly brandished in heaven and dropping as in anticipation with the blood of fat offerings, must now descend upon

2.

For Yahvé hath a day of vengeance, | a year of recompense for Ssion's cause : ‖ and its* brooks turn into pitch its ground into brimstone, | and its land becometh burning pitch ; ‖ night 10 nor day is it quenched, for ever its smoke goeth up, | from generation to generation it goeth waste, for all time no one shall journey through it, ‖ and pelicans and hedgehogs take possession of it, heron and raven dwell therein, | and thereon is laid the line of desolation and the weight of emptiness. ‖ Its freemen—none are there who proclaim the kingdom, | and all its princes come to nothing; ‖ and its palaces get overgrown with thorns, nettles and thistles are in its castles, | so that it becometh a pasture of jackals, an enclosure for ostriches, ‖ and wild cats light upon wolves, and one hegoat meeteth another; | there only hath the night spectre repose, and findeth for herself 15 a resting place; ‖ there the arrowsnake maketh a nest and layeth, broodeth and hatcheth in her shadow, | there only vultures gather one to the other. ‖ Seek from Yahvé's book and read, no one of these faileth, neither the one nor the other is missing : | for His word hath commanded it, and His spirit hath gathered them, | and He hath cast it to them as a lot, and his hand hath allotted it to them by line : | for ever will they possess it, through all time dwell therein. ‖

Edóm to satiate itself upon those who are really guilty, and the overthrow of the magnates and potentates of this land is like a fat sacrificial meal which is prepared for Yahvé in that land, vv.

5-7. Such passages as Jer. xlvi. 10 ; Ez. xxxii. 5-7 ; xxxix. 17 sq., were evidently present to the author's mind : the strong word *to ban (sacrare),* vv. 2, 5, reminds us of Ḥézeqiél.

2. In order to explain this more particularly, it is sufficient to say that now the great day of compensation and redemption for all the oppressed, accordingly, for Ssion especially, is coming : and Edóm, as bearing the chief guilt with respect to Ssion, must be punished most severely, be destroyed by fire, as Sodóm once was in order that it may, like Sodóm, bear for ever the warning marks of such a judgment of fire, and be for all times laid waste and inhabited only by animals of the desert ; Yahvé will measure it afresh in order to apportion it to new inhabitants, but he will thereby apportion it to desolation, to primitive chaos (Amos vii. 7, 8) vv. 8-11. The magnates who hitherto ruled Edóm as the domain of their prey, and lived luxuriously in palaces, will all vanish with the latter, in order to make room for wild beasts

---

* *i.e., Edóm's.*

xxxv   3.

1   The desert and waste will be glad, | so that the steppe exulteth and blossometh as with lilies; || it will indeed blossom and exult, yea exult and rejoice, | Lebanon's glory is given to it, the magnificence of Karmel and Sharon: | théy will see Yahvé's glory, the magnificence of our God. || Strengthen ye slack hands, and tottering knees make ye firm, || say to those of affrighted heart "be strong fear not! | behold your God, vengeance cometh God's recompense, hé will come to
5   help you!" || —Then will blind eyes be unclosed, and deaf ears opened; || then will the lame man spring as the hart, and the tongue of the dumb shout for joy: | for in the wilderness waters burst forth, and rivers in the steppe, | and the mirage becometh a pool, the dry land springs of water. || In the pasture where jackals crouch, the inclosure for reed and rush, || there will there be a high road and a way, and a holy way will it be called, trodden by no one unclean, | and as He goeth the way for them, even the unwise will not go wrong; || no lion will be there, and the mightiest of the beasts will not tread it, not
10   to be found there; | so they walk redeemed, || and Yahvé's ransomed return and come to Ssion in jubilation, with eternal joy upon their heads; | gladness and joy will they obtain, grief and sighs flee away. ||

of all kinds, as well as monsters and ghosts of the desert, vv. 12-15; certainly all such goblins will be found there, since Yahvé himself has so willed, and has apportioned this land to the wild beasts as their possession: let this very oracle, this book of Yahvé's, be a witness of this for future times, vv. 16, 17. Thus this prophet, ver. 16, refers almost like Isa. xxx. 8 to his book as a witness for the future: but it can be observed that he imitates this custom of earlier prophets without having publicly uttered the same truth as they had done. It is also evident that the simpler conceptions of the beasts and monsters of the desert, xiii. 20-22; xiv. 23 are present to the author's mind as he here describes them in a more developed form, and the two classes of land and bog animals which were then kept distinct are here less fittingly thrown together in one description. The *Lâlith*, or *Lîlith*, acc. § 36 *b*, *i.e.*, the *night-spirit*, is related to the other female goblin, Prov. xxx. 15. Comp. *Dichter des A. B.* II. *a*, p. 257.

3. But while Edóm is thus laid waste, all that land through which Yahvé's march from Babel proceeds, and where Yahvé takes up his residence, will rise all the more gloriously from its desolation, xxxv. 1, 2, after xl. 3, 4; lii. 8; therefore be of good courage, ye men of Israel who have been so long bowed down, vv. 3, 4. Then, when once Yahvé's mighty salvation rises, as

indeed it soon will shine forth, will the weak also in Israel feel that they are suddenly as it were made whole, inasmuch as the miracles of the march of Moses through the desert will be repeated; and a powerful, holy hand will protect the homeward march of the newly redeemed people to its ancient holy land, vv. 5-10. We have here still plainer reechoes of much from "Isa." xl. sq.; on ver. 10, however, comp. the comment on li. 11.

---

xxxiv. 16. פיו must undoubtedly be read instead of פי, acc. § 311 a; the first person is used of Yahvé in the whole piece only xxxiv. 5.

It is evident that with בנוה, xxxv. 7, a new sentence and verse commences, the discourse in the two next short members bringing together the desert and the bog, desert animals and bog plants, just as xxxiv. 11-14, so that בוה and חציר must correspond to each other just as xxxiv. 13; we can in that case read בְּוֵה. In ver. 8 also the accents mislead in the case of והוא למו. With regard to ישׁשׁום, ver. 1, see § 91 b.

6. AN ANONYMOUS PROPHET.

"Isa." ch. xxiv.—xxvii.

According to all indications we are brought here to a still later time than by the last of the previous pieces and by the appendix "Isa." lxiii. 7—lxvi. Of the first enthusiasm of those days there is not much more to be perceived; on the contrary, acc. xxvi. 14-19, although the new Jerusalem was again rising from its ruins, it had already become painfully perceptible that the new settlement would not satisfactorily go forward, and continued to be very deficient in strength and numbers. Now, inasmuch as there are plainly very definite and pointed references to the complete overthrow of the strong and luxurious city of tyrants, *i.e.*, manifestly Babel, xxv. 1-5, 11; xxvi. 5, 6; xxvii. 10, 11, it might be thought that the conquest of Babel by Dareios Hystaspis, when it was for the first time thoroughly destroyed, was meant. However, descriptions of the devastation of an already conquered city are frequently somewhat exaggerated, especially by a prophet who, like ours, was living far from Babel, evidently in the Holy Land itself. When everything has been considered, my present opinion is that the piece belongs to the time when Kambyses was making preparations for his Egyptian campaign. After the fall of Babel, which is here pre-supposed as complete, fresh world-storms of a severe character were threatening, xxiv. 1-20; the Egyptian campaign must have appeared very specially dangerous to the Holy Land, as Kambyses was moreover, according to the book of Ezra, very unfavourable to the new settlement; and while for this nothing could be so desirable as peace, xxvi. 3, 12; xxvii. 5, in order that it might collect and confirm its energies, that campaign threatened, even with merely a march of barbarous soldiers through Jerusalem, lamentable plundering and devastation, xxiv. 1-3, 13, 16.—It was at this time that the prophet, although he foretells the approaching world-calamity with great agitation, knows nevertheless that at last nothing else can proceed from all such storms but the victory of good, ch. xxiv. and xxv. 6-11 (which verses must have been misplaced by an early error in copying), in three strophes; and after he has introduced the people praying to Yahvé in its distress, as is becoming, and has shown it how it ought now to pray, xxv. 1-5, 12; xxvi. 1-13, in four quite poetical strophes, he closes with his own mediatorial word, which is prophetic of good, xxvi. 14—xxvii., in three strophes.—The discourse affects very strong and frequent paronomasiæ, and generally graphic and figurative language: in this respect this prophetic writer is like no other. Further, the verse in the lyric description of the threatening storms, xxiv. 1-20, is often triple membered, which can have a beautiful effect. However, it is everywhere observable with all this that the prophet puts together his verses and strophes more as mosaic-work from earlier thoughts and verses. The beautiful words, xxv. 6-8; xxvii. 9, 12, 13, are very plainly borrowed from earlier oracles now lost, xxv. 6-8 (probably vv. 10, 11 also), perhaps from a prophet of the seventh century, xxvii. 9, 12, 13 from Yesaya. Where the prophet writes in his own manner, such a great similarity with "Isa.," ch. xii. appears that the author of that short addition to Yesaya's sixth book was probably the same writer that appended this longer piece without a name to the book of Yesaya, ch. i.-xxiii.

1. *Prophecy of the Universal Judgment.*
Ch. xxiv., xxv. 6-11.

The first two strophes prophesy, in great agitation and a kind of fear such as is foreign to the earlier prophets (ver. 16), a general devastation, caused also by greedy, plundering warriors; nevertheless, inasmuch as the approaching world-catastrophe is closely connected with the sin of men, as if it is intended to serve the purpose of violently destroying the sin by Yahvé's wrath, the hope is also held out of the glorious time which shall follow that destruction, which, described with Messianic images, remains exclusively predominant in the third strophe.

1.

xxiv.
1 Behold Yahvé will spoil the earth and despoil it, | overturn its face and scatter its inhabitants, || so that it will be as with the people so with the priest, as with the servant so with his lord, as with the bondswoman so with her mistress, | as with the buyer so with the seller, as with the lender so with the borrower, as with the creditor so with the debtor; || spoiled spoiled is the earth and plundered plundered! | surely Yahvé spake this word. ||—The earth withereth and wasteth, the world withereth away wasteth, wither away the exalted folk of the
5 earth; || since the earth is profaned under its inhabitants, | because they transgressed the laws, overstepped right, broke the eternal covenant: || therefore a curse cankered the earth, and they who dwell therein suffer punishment, | therefore the inhabitants of the earth are burned up, and few people will remain.||—The must withereth, the vine withereth away, all the glad of heart moan; || silent is the mirth of the tabret, the noise of the jubilant resteth, silent is the mirth of the harp, || singing they drink not wine, bitter is the mead to its
10 drinkers; || the desolate town is laid in ruins, every house is

shut up without entrance, ‖ lamentation over the wine resoundeth without, all joy hath fled away, the mirth of the land is banished : ‖ there is left in the city desolation, and to ruins the gate is smitten. ‖

2.

For so will it be in the midst of the earth, amid the nations : | as at the olive-beating, as at the gleaning when the grape-gathering is done ! ‖ There are indeed loud voices and jubilation, | "on account of Yahvé's majesty exult ye from the west ! ‖ therefore in the east countries glorify Yahvé, by the coasts of the sea the name of Yahvé the God of Israel !" ‖ from the skirt of the earth we heard songs "fame to the righteous !" | but I say O famine to me famine to me ! O alas for me ! | robbers do rob, and the robe robbers do rob !* ‖ panic pitfall and preytrap† be upon thee O inhabitant of the land ! ‖ for he that hath fled from the loud panic falleth into the pitfall, and he that ariseth from the midst of the pitfall is taken by the preytrap ! ‖ For the windows from out of the height open, and the foundations of the earth tremble ; ‖ shattered

At the very commencement, the approaching devastation which will make high and low, rich and poor, equal, is alone brought forward, vv. 1-3 (the mention of the priest in such a way being very indicative of the age of this prophet) : but immediately the higher truth also appears, that only because the earth is desecrated and corrupted by the very burden of her debts, as it were,

the fire of a divine curse burns up her inhabitants, vv. 4-6, and, amid the fellow-suffering of the entire visible creation, all the joy which was formerly often so boisterous will flee from the land which is falling into ruin, vv. 7-12. The figures of wine and joy from Joel, ch. i. —For, the discourse proceeds with new energy in the

second strophe, certainly a complete depopulation will be made in Palestina, which will spare or leave scarcely anything, ver. 13 after Isa. xvii. 6. It is true that now from the end of the earth (i.e., from Babylonia) many poetical-prophetic solicitations are heard to praise Yahvé, both in the West (in Palestina) and in the East, as now directly victorious and

leading his people (the righteous) to victory : but this prophet is unable to join in such jubilation, as he anticipates for the immediate future nothing else than frightful devastation by barbarous warriors, vv. 14-16 ; for his part, he must, with Yéremyá xlviii. 43, 44, prophesy for this time endless calamity which none can escape, inasmuch as nothing less is impending than a second

---

* Or more literally, "cozeners do cozen, and the covering cozeners do cozen away."—Tr.

† Comp. Vol. III., p. 209.—Tr.

shattered indeed is the earth, dashed dashed in pieces is earth, convulsed convulsed is earth, || stagger stagger will the earth like a drunken man, and be swayed to and fro like a hammock, | her transgressions will weigh her down, and she will fall to rise no more. ||

3.

But then on that day will Yahvé visit the host of the height in the height, | and the kings of the earth upon the earth, | they will be gathered together as prisoners into the dungeon, and imprisoned in the prison, | and only after long years released :|| and the pale one will blush and the burning one turn white, | because Yahvé of Hosts reigneth upon mount Ssion and in Jeru-
xxv. salem, | shining in majesty before his Elders. ||—And Yahvé
6 of Hosts will make ready for all the nations upon this mountain a feast of fat things a feast of lees, | of marrowy fat things and refined lees ; || and he destroyeth upon this mountain the thick veil which veileth all the nations, | and the woof which is woven over all the peoples, || destroyeth death for ever, | and Lord Yahvé wipeth away tears from all faces, | and his people's reproach he removeth from the whole earth ! yea, Yahvé hath spoken it. ||—Then it is said on that day : "behold there is our God, in whom we hope that he may help us, | there is Yahvé in whom we hope : let us rejoice and be glad in
10 his help !" || For Yahvé's hand will rest upon this mountain, | but Môab will be crushed on his ground like strawheaps in the dunghill water, | and if he spread forth his arms therein as the swimmer doth in order to swim, | yet he layeth low his pride together with the joints of his hands. ||

Noachian chastisement and destruction of the earth, which is so heavily oppressed by its burden of sin, and is therefore swaying to and fro before the divine wrath-blast like a hammock driven hither and thither by the wind vv. 17-20. Ver. 18 *ad fin.* after Gen. vii. 11; viii. 2. But, the

third strophe begins in quite another strain : then precisely (after the wickedness has been destroyed by such a world-catastrophe) Yahvé will hold the great judgment over the wicked powers of heaven and earth, but will himself be, as it were, visibly enthroned by the sanctuary at Ssion in his brightest glory in the restored ancient theocracy, vv. 21-23. Yes, precisely Ssion will then witness the great spectacle of all the nations of the earth resting around it as the table of the noblest and most refreshing food (sacrificial food), and seeking there the true, *i.e.*, spiritual, satisfaction, ver. 6 (like Matt. viii. 11 ;

Rev. iii. 20); and the similar spectacle, of all the nations which are now so troubled and overwhelmed with calamity, before whose face there is as it were a thick veil drawn from anxiety and confusion (2 Sam. xv. 30), then suddenly here recovering sight and gladness by means of a higher light, by means of the true life, that is, which is also the true joy, and which Yahvé appointed for Israel primarily because it had suffered and endured the most, vv. 7, 8. Then hope in Yahvé is never again wavering, when it is seen how firmly Yahvé sustains Ssion, and how, on the other hand, proud Môab finds such a filthy end upon the battle-field, as it deserved according to its habits, Gen. xix., in vain applying its arts at the last moment in order to remain as it is, vv. 9-11. The figure used of Môab, vv. 10, 11, is not nice; however, it must be remembered, in addition to the earlier legend, Gen. xix., that in the seventh and sixth century Môab, like Edóm, was nothing more than an example of incorrigible rebellion against Yahvé; this rebellion will still in the end, with its material arts, remain true to its own nature, will seek to save itself from the abyss by swimming with the strong joints of its hands without any reformation, but all in vain.— Vv. 21, 22, notwithstanding the brevity of the description, we already see quite the same new conception of the kinship of the great celestial and terrestrial powers of evil, comp. xxvii. 1, and of the confinement of the devil with his associates, as we have Rev. xix., xx., Jude ver. 6; 2 Pet. ii. 4.

Ver. 14, it is certainly more correct to read the *imperat.* אָרִים and צָהֳלוּ, and means according to the context the *regions of light*, *i.e.*, in the East; ver. 16, בְּגַד must be taken in its usual meaning precisely on account of the paronomasia, especially as ver. 16 refers back to vv. 13, 1-3. רָזִי, ver. 16 after Isa. xvii. 4.

The construction, ver. 22, would be most easy if we might read אֲסֻפָּת in *st. constr.*

2. *Prayer of the Community.*
Ch. xxv. 1-5; xxvi. 1-13.

Each of the four strophes of the prayer of the nation consists of seven long members, or short verses, just like the lyric, xiv. 4 sq. A vivid remembrance of the great overthrow of the city (Babel), which can never again rise from her ruin, makes itself felt through the first three strophes as the starting-point of this prayer and the reason for further help through Yahvé: not until the fourth and last strophe is this reference dismissed.

1.

xxv.
1   Yahvé my God art thou: I exalt thee I praise thy name, |
       that thou didst wonders, distant decrees are fidelity faithful-

ness! | for thou turnedst for them the city into rubbish, the fortified castle into ruins, | the palace of barbarians so that it is no more a city, never again to be built. ‖ Therefore mighty people honour thee, the city of tyrannical Heathen feareth thee, | because thou wast a defence to the bowed down, a defence to the unfortunate in his distress, | a refuge from the storm a shade from the heat, when the snorting of the tyrants is as a storm to the wall. ‖

2.

As heat in drought thou puttest down the noise of the barbarians; | as heat by the clouds' shadow bringeth he low the song of the tyrants, | and the high fortress of thy walls hath he sunk down laid low hurled to the earth to the dust. | At that day will this song be sung in the land of Yuda :

> We have a strong castle, salvation give walls and moat ;
> open the gates that a righteous nation which keepeth faith may enter !"

Firm is the hope : peace peace wilt thou confirm!
because men trust in thee. ‖

12
xxvi.
1

3.

Trust in Yahvé for evermore! for in Yah Yahvé is an eternal rock; ‖ for he hath humbled those proudly enthroned, the strong city he layeth low, | layeth it low unto the earth, hurleth it into the dust, ‖ the foot treadeth it down, the foot of

In the first strophe, vv. 1-4, Yahvé is praised just because this marvellous devastation furnishes a proof, first, that the most distant counsels of Yahvé and such as seem impossible of execution, are nevertheless in the end always accomplished in such a way as is to be expected from the faithful God (for Babel's overthrow had already been foretold by Yéremyá), and, secondly, that he is the strong defence of the helpless when the hot snorting wrath of the tyrants breaks loose against them like a tempest against a weak wall, comp. xxviii. 2.—Yea, the second strophe, xxv. 5, 12; xxvi. 1-3, accordingly continues, because it is now seen how Yahvé humbles the proud exultation of the tyrants (Chaldeans), and hurls the proud fortress of the Chaldean into the dust, in the future a festive multitude singing joyous songs will travel to the temple full of confidence in Yahvé, believing that they possess in Yahvé and his sanctuary a better fortress than Babel was, xxv. 5, 12; xxvi. 1-3, comp. lx. 18; Ps. cxviii. 19, 20, these passages probably being taken for imitation.—Therefore, the third strophe, vv. 4-8, goes on, let Him be trusted as in all time so at present, let Him be trusted, who is not only mighty but also judges men according to the same righteousness which man must set the poor, the steps of the oppressed. ‖ The path for the righteous is straightforwardness: straight weighest thou the track of the righteous, ‖ and for the path of thy judgments— O Yahvé we wait for thee! | unto thy name and unto thy memorial is the desire of the soul. ‖

4.

With my soul I desire thee in the night, and with my spirit within me I seek thee: | for as soon as thy judgments get to the earth, the inhabitants of the world learn righteousness; ‖ 10 if the wicked is pardoned he doth not learn righteousness, in the land of equity he committeth wrong and seeth not Yahvé's majesty. ‖ Yahvé exalted is thy right hand—they behold it not: | let them behold (and be ashamed) the zeal of thy people, and the fire of thine enemies let it devour them! ‖ Yahvé, thou wilt ordain peace for us: surely thou also gavest us all our benefactions: ‖ Yahve our God, other lords than thou rule over us: thee only do we praise, thy name! ‖

before him and imitate in his daily walk; the righteous (*i.e.*, the true Community) desire nothing but judgment from Him, a revelation of his righteousness at the present time.—But, the fourth strophe, vv. 9-13, concludes, this judgment is now most intensely longed for in order that the enemies of Yahvé, who have been as it seems too long unchastised, may not through longer forbearance too grievously sin against Israel; may He, from whom Israel declares that it receives all its benefits, and whom it resolves alone to serve, bring peace instead of the devastating war!

The מ of מעיר, xxv. 2, it might seem better to omit as in the way: but attached to שפתה as שמתה, it furnishes a good meaning, acc. § 315 *b*.— As ver. 5 *b*, the address to Yahvé changes into the third person, it cannot be surprising that the tyrant himself should be immediately addressed, ver. 12, though this is done only in a rapid transition of the thought.—תצר, xxvi. 3, must be derived from יצר, in accordance with the corresponding השבת, ver. 12, which gives rise to one of the paronomasiæ which are so frequent in this prophet.—Ver. 9 after Ps. xvi. 7; ver. 11 *b* after 2 Kings i. 10 sq.; ver. 13, שמד is simply explicative of בד.

3. *Final explanation.*

Appearing now as mediator between the Community thus praying and its eternal Lord, the prophet in the first strophe refers to the manner in which the present calamity is to be borne with true believing patience; in the second strophe he turns his glance to the salvation of the future, which is, nevertheless, certain; and in the third he concludes, not without casting a backward glance even here at Babel, which has now fallen, all his joyous promises to the Community.

1.

Dead men do not live again, Shades do not rise again : | therefore visitedst thou and destroyedst thou, and madest to
15 perish every remembrance of them. || Thou addest to the nation, O Yahvé, thou addest to the nation glorifyest thyself, | widenest all the borders of the land! || Yahvé! in distress they sought thee, | a charmed circle of defence was thy chastening unto them; || as one with child who is about to give birth, who in her pains laboureth and crieth, | so were we trembling before thee O Yahvé! || we were with child we laboured: when we had given birth it was wind; | unto salvation we wrought not the earth, neither were inhabitants of the land born! || O that thy dead men might live again, my corpses rise again! || Awake and shout for joy ye inhabitants of the dust! | for quickening dew is thy dew, and the earth will give birth to
20 Shades! || —Go my people into thy chambers, and shut thy doors behind thee, | hide thee a little while, till the indignation passeth over! ||

The prophet appearing as mediator after this prayer of the nation (comp. ver. 16), in the first instance, ver. 14, advances the proposition, that past times, the dead who cannot rise again, and accordingly the earlier Israelites, who were really destroyed on account of their sins, must not be grieved about. But at the same time the prophetic truth also remains valid, that Yahvé is the eternal augmenter of the nation, in whom the diminished and weakened nation must continue to hope, ver. 15 ; in the exile, accordingly, in the great distress, the nation full of true patience and resignation prayed to Yahvé, finding in their sufferings nothing but Yahvé's chastisement, yea, as a woman in travail is in alarm, the nation trembled, praying full of profound fear, before Yahvé, vv. 16, 17 ; and indeed the painful crisis of the exile was as the time of birth-pangs (Hos. xiii. 13) : but unhappily it now appears that they had passed through their birth-throes in vain; now that the exile is past the fruit of the birth-pangs will not show itself, the Holy Land remains without prosperity, without children (*i.e.*, without numerous inhabitants, comp. lxvi. 7, 8); is *that* then part of the divine purpose? O certainly not! O that, on the contrary, He whose word is like reviving dew, would call forth the dead of the Holy Land from their dust and grave, that Ssion might again become as

2.

xxvii.
1

For behold Yahvé will come up out of his place to visit the guilt of the inhabitant of the earth upon him, | and the earth discovereth her deeds of blood, and no longer concealeth her murdered ones. ‖ At that day will Yahvé with his sword the cruel and great and strong one visit the monster the fleet serpent, and the monster the ringed serpent, | and slay the dragon which is in the sea. ‖ At that day of the lovely vineyard sing ye thus:

> I Yahvé am its keeper, every moment I water it,
> lest a visitation come upon it night and day I keep it;
> wrath I have not; should I get thorns and thistles,
>   with war would I walk through them! would kindle
>   them at once,
>   unless they laid hold of my protection,
>   they made peace with me,
>   peace they made with me!

In time to come Yaqob will take root, Israel will blossom and bud forth, | and they will fill the face of the kingdom of the world with fruits. ‖

richly peopled and as prosperous as in David's time! vv. 18, 19, after Ezek. xxxvii. And before the first strophe closes an answer is sent back from heaven such as can be given in response to such a prayer from both the nation and the prophet: the wrath, *i.e*, the world-catastrophe threatened xxiv. 2-20, will indeed come, yet let Israel

second strophe, in the world-storms after all it is only the righteous avenger of old barbarities who appears; happy therefore the nation which has no bloodguiltiness to answer for, ver. 21; the three monsters which lay waste the world alone have to fear, xxvii. 1 (comp. li. 9; Ezek. xxix. 3, *et al.*, probably an allusion to united Medo-Persia and

maintain composure, withdraw itself a little while into its chambers, until it goes over without reaching it! ver. 20; and a small nation, such as Jerusalem at the commencement of its restoration, can easily hide itself more quietly from such world-storms.—For, the prophetic discourse goes on to explain, in the

Egypt, comp. Ps. lxviii. 31 from the same period); and on the same day when this great universal judgment is completed, may sound forth songs of praise upon Ssion, the fair vineyard, which (as will then be generally known) Yahvé carefully guards and cultivates: he who is not full of anger but really a gracious God, but who,

3.

Did he smite it then as him who smote it, | or is it slain as its slayers? || —driving her forth sending her away, thou didst contend with her; | he thrust her forth with his rough blast on the day of the storm. || Therefore by this is Yaqob's guilt atoned for, and this is the whole fruit of the removal of his sins, | when it maketh all altar stones as shivered brimstones, so that the idol-groves and sun-cones may arise ro
10   more. || —For the fenced city is alone, a tract cast out and forsaken like the desert, | there calves feed and lie down, and consume its branches; || when its shoots are dry they are broken, women come set them on fire : | for it is not a nation of understanding, therefore its creator compassionateth it not, and its former is not gracious to it. || "And on that day will Yahvé beat out from the ears of the Euphrates unto the brook of Egypt, | and ye will be gleaned one by one ye sons of Israel! || And on that day the great trumpet will be blown | and those who were lost in the land of Assyria come and the outcasts in the land of Egypt | and do homage to Yahvé upon the holy mountain in Jerusalem." ||

should thorns and thistles, *i.e.*, barbarous enemies (comp. 2 Sam. xxiii. 6, 7) desire to approach this vineyard, would in a moment set on fire and wholly consume these dry thistles by simply passing through them, unless

Indeed, Israel is after all, the last strophe begins, not by far so seriously smitten, or even slain, as is the Chaldean who smote it, or even desired to slay it, in the exile, ver. 7 : on the contrary, a simple thrusting of the unfaithful Community into the exile was all he did on the day of punishment, ver. 8, the same idea as l. 1-3 ; hence the simple removal of the idols (which the nation now after the exile really put away) is all that he also requires to reconcile him, ver. 9. Whilst Babel, on account of the folly of its inhabitants,

these enemies should be converted to peaceful intentions and seek the true protection, vv. 2-5, after v. 6, 7 ; x. 17: yea, Israel will in the future flourish again ! ver. 6.

remains an eternally waste place, where flocks pasture (v. 17), and dry brushwood for breaking off and burning grows, as in the desert, vv. 10, 11, the Heathen who now occupy the Holy Land will be as easily driven out of it as the chaff is carried away by the wind from fine threshed corn, but the Israelites living in the Holy Land will not only be preserved (as the grains of such corn are carefully and one by one picked up), but also all those who are scattered in foreign lands will be gathered to them. Vv. 12, 13 refer back to xxvi. 15, 19.

The *perf.* xxvi. 15 acc. § 223 *b*.
As xxvi. 16 צָקוּן can be read and be derived from צוּק like לָצוּן, and may also be construed with the בְּ of the foreigoing בַּצַּר, it might be conjectured that לְחַשׁ should be read

instead of לָחַשׁ: *in the distress was "thy chastisement" whispered by them,* or, they whispered in prayer that the distress was only thy chastisement, accordingly to be borne patiently; as indeed this prophet particularly likes such brief insertions, comp. xxiv. 16; xxvi. 3; Jer. l. 46. Still, an easier course is to compare צָקוּן with Eth. *saquan,* or, rather with Eth. *saquen,* which as regards its formation is still better: as this word can signify an inclusive paling or ring, we obtain in this passage the figure of a magic circle out of which the man that is put within it cannot pass (comp. חָמְעַגֵּל, *History of Israel,* V., 398 (IV., 519), as if the divine chastisement and distress had at that time drawn round them the magic circle of true fear and of prayer out of which they must thus learn not to pass.—On חָבִי, ver. 20, see § 224 *c*; ver. 21 like Job. xvi. 19.—xxvii. 2 read חֶמֶד. Ver. 7 it appears on all considerations much better and not too strong to read הָרְגִיו as *part. act.* On סַאסְאָה, ver. 8, as it is best punctuated, see § 88 *d.* לְאַחַד אַחַד ver. 12, is κατὰ ἕνα ἕκαστον, one by one, so that not a grain remains ungleaned. It is quite evident that vv. 12, 13 and ver. 9 are Yesaianic as regards language and matter; ver. 9 transfers us to a time when the removal of the idols appeared of itself sufficient as a *fruit* or consequence of an inward reformation.*

---

* In his last work, *Die Lehre der Bibel von Gott,* Vol. III., p. 444 *note,* the author adds to his commentary on the above piece the following: " The words xxvii. 10, 11, as well as vv. 9, 12, 13, may have been cited from a work of Yesaya's by the writer; the words have quite the same ring as xxxii. 10-14; xxx. 9, 19; ix. 16; v. 17; and the *strong city,* ver. 10, can in that case be Jerusalem in Yesaya's own sense. Perhaps the words xxv. 6-8, 10, 11 also are from the eighth century and by Yesaya himself."—Tr.

C.—IN THE NEW JERUSALEM.

The hope of a restoration of Jerusalem was fulfilled; a new temple shall arise, the endeavour shall be made also to form some kind of state. In such circumstances there appear prophets again after the manner of ancient times, who once more lay aside the reserve of anonymity and write in their own names with an exact specification of dates. This revival of the ancient form of prophetic literature followed in consequence of the public labours of the prophets in a new body politic. The first years of the reign of king Dareios moreover were calculated to excite the prophetic activity to attempt everything which was possible in order to further the progress of the good cause in the restoration of Jerusalem. The Persian kingdom, as we now know more particularly from the Dareios inscriptions of those years, once more underwent the most violent convulsions: and there is plain allusion to such general world-storms in Hag. ii. 6, 21, 22; Zech. ii. 1-4. According to Zech. i. 12, it immediately recurred very vividly to the memory, that seventy years would soon have fled since the destruction of Jerusalem, and Yéremyá's prophecy concerning a Messianic prosperity after seventy years appeared possible of much more complete fulfilment now than under Kyros.

But it is in vain that the Shades desire to live again: we behold the power of prophecy irrecoverably decline and die, and these feeble endeavours in the new time simply prove that the genuine ancient prophecy could not be reproduced, and that that revival in the anonymous pieces at the end of the exile was destined to remain the last fair afterbloom of the ancient noble stock. Two causes co-operated to promote this final decay: the publicity and freedom of national life, this sound and vigorous root of ancient prophecy, very soon wholly disappeared again under the Persian rule, and Mal'akhi has already ceased to follow Haggái and Zakharya by writing as a public man; and at the same time the letter of the ancient law and the spiritual timidity connected therewith became predominant in the Community, whilst only one of these two causes would have been of itself sufficient to produce the essential ruin of the ancient prophetism. Accordingly there were strictly speaking only the two prophets Haggái and Zakharya who ventured once more to labour both in speaking and writing exactly like the ancient prophets, as is also briefly related of them Ezra v. 1.

1. HAGGÁI.

The unexpected hindrances put in the way of the building of the second temple, which had been begun with the greatest hope (Ezra iii.), enkindled the prophetic zeal of Haggái to lift up in the new Jerusalem as it arose from its ruins the voice of the ancient prophets. His five discourses, which are written down with the exact date of each, all belong to three months of the same year, and were without doubt shortly after their delivery committed to writing by him when their happy effect began to show itself and the small, weak Community prosecuted the work of building with fresh zeal, Ezra v. 1. Probably Haggái belonged to the few, once mentioned by himself, ii. 3, who had seen the first temple, and accordingly willingly resigned his further prophetic activity, after fresh zeal for the great work had been revived, to the younger prophet Zakharya, who begins to speak almost exactly at the point where Haggái leaves off.

Still, it must be granted that we do not here again hear the high power of the voice of the ancient prophets of Jerusalem; the general oppression under which the nation suffered in those times weighs upon Haggái also in his capacity of prophet, his style is sensibly more depressed and meagre, his handling of his subject lacks the combination of compression and fulness which is met with in the earlier prophets. And as the entire national life of the people was then only just seeking in the best way possible to recover itself somewhat from complete disorganization, the external features of Haggái's language even bear visible traces of the endeavour to recover once more the purity of the ancient language, and yet at the same time it departs in many peculiar usages from its older and established form in an important degree, e.g., in the expression פָּמֹהוּ כְּאַיִן, ii. 3, instead of which the ancients would have said more simply הוּא כְּאַיִן *it is as nothing;* in אֵין אֶתְכֶם, ii. 17, instead of אֵינְכֶם, as if it were no longer enough to subordinate the pron. suff. immediately to אין; and in the construction מִהְיוֹתָם בָּא, ii. 16. In all these peculiarities one may also see signs of the advanced age of this prophet, as other prophetic writers about that time, and particularly his immediate successor Zakharya, affect quite different linguistic characteristics. Many lyrics from this first period of the dissolution of the noble past and the commencement of an entirely different age, present linguistic peculiarities of a most marked character, comp. *Dichter des Alten Bundes*, I. b, p. 378 A.

1. *Exhortation to promote the building of the temple.*

Ch. i. 1-11.

As the zeal of the inhabitants of the new Jerusalem, who were it is true still few in numbers and in necessitous circumstances, had slackened in the prosecution of the work of rebuilding the temple, Haggái shows to them the folly of excessive care with regard to their own comfort, inasmuch as, after all, the material comfort of the individual without any respect to things of universal import and the direction of labour and toil to higher ends, cannot be attended by any divine blessing (comp. from the same time Ps. cxxvii.). And a sign from heaven itself seemed to confirm this. For in the years immediately preceding, when this selfish tendency and anxious care for their own bread had become predominant, the yield of the fields was after all far below their expectations and increasingly painful scarcity oppressed all: as if Yahvé himself intended still more plainly and as it were in anger to prove to those who thus already knew that they were under condemnation, how little the individual is able perforce to seize prosperity by such care and haste. This is accordingly insisted upon twice, vv. 5, 6, and vv. 7-11, comp. Ps. lxvii.

i.
1   In the second year of Dareios the king in the sixth month, on the first day of the month Yahvé's word came by Haggái the prophet to Zerubabel the son of Sh'altiel the governor of Yuda and to Yosua the son of Yôssadaq the high priest saying: ‖ Thus saith Yahvé of Hosts in these words: | these people say, "it is not a time to come, a time for the house of Yahvé to be built." ‖ But Yahvé's word came by Haggái the prophet saying: ‖ Have ye yourselves time to dwell in your
5   finely wainscoted houses, | while this house lieth waste ? ‖ Now therefore, thus saith Yahvé of Hosts: | give heed thereto how it fareth with you ! ‖ ye have sown much, of ingathering there is little !—ye eat but it serves not to satisfy, drink but it serves not to drinking enough, clothe you but it serves not to warm you ! | and he who hireth himself, hireth himself for a slit purse ! ‖ - Thus saith Yahvé of Hosts: | give heed thereto how it fareth with you ! ‖ ascend the mountain that ye may bring wood, and build ye the House, | that I may have pleasure therein and feel myself honoured ! saith Yahvé. ‖ Ye hope for much and behold it comes to little, and if ye gather it in into

In addition to the two heads he could at the commencement, i. 1, just as well as i. 12, 14; ii. 2, 4, have mentioned the rest of the people, as he evidently intended them also: but he is here content to name those two only as the principal men of the Community. It is moreover observable that at the beginning particularly, vv. 1-3, the style is more than usually cumbrous; although Haggái generally likes to mention his prophetic commission twice, i. 12, 13. The expression *the rest of the people* has plainly in these passages quite another reference and sense than in Zech. viii. 6, 11, 12.

the house then I blow it away! | wherefore? saith Yahvé of Hosts: "because of my house that lieth waste, whilst ye run 10 every one into his house; || therefore unto you heaven refuseth of the dew, | and the earth refuseth her produce, || and I called a drought upon the earth and upon the mountains, upon the corn and upon the must and upon the oil and upon whatever the earth bringeth forth, | and upon the men and upon the cattle | and upon every labour of the land." ||

Ver. 2. *These people* (as Isa. vi. 9) say, when they are summoned, It is not the time to come! that is, to the site of the temple, to work there, vv. 9, 14; ii. 4; the second member explains this further. And in reality Haggái was on that account compelled to address the people at a new moon, because they probably came together to the site of the temple at no other time during the whole month.—Ver. 5 and vv. 7, 8, ver. 6 and vv. 9-11 correspond to each other in such a way that both the admonition to be more attentive to their own circumstances and therefore more active with regard to higher purposes, and the explanation of those circumstances are more exhaustive and lengthy in the second reference to them. The present condition of the people is, that they sow and hope much but reap little, and even what is reaped is soon as if blown away, that the blessing is absent both from above and from below. This condition they ought to lay to heart and to perceive that their past course of self-seeking does not really profit them, they ought to take part in the higher work, *e.g.*, to go or send to the mountain, *i.e.*, Lebanon (Ps. cxxxii. 6), to fetch suitable cedar wood for the decoration of the temple, since what was first fetched, acc. Ezra iii. 7, might not be sufficient.

סובנים, ver. 4, the art. is intentionally omitted; the לוֹ in לוֹ חַם, ver. 6, comes from the phrase לִי חַם, § 294 b.

מִטַּל, ver. 10, we have the Greek genitive with verbs of giving and refusing; dew was not altogether withheld, but sufficient had not fallen.

2. *Its effect.*

As this discourse did not remain without effect and the whole nation exhibited a will to work, Haggái added the same day some further words of divine encouragement and favour, vv. 12, 13. And as a fact they began the interrupted work with new zeal, and for this purpose assembled together on an appointed day, the 24th of the same month, vv. 14, 15.

Then hearkened Zerubabel son of Sh'altiel and Yosua son of Yôssadaq the high priest and all the rest of the people to the voice of Yahvé their God and unto the words of Haggái

the prophet, as Yahvé their God had sent him, and they feared before Yahvé; and Haggái the messenger of Yahvé spoke with the message of Yahvé to the people saying: I am with you! saith Yahvé.—Thus Yahvé stirred up the spirit of Zerubabel son of Sh'altiel governor of Yuda and the spirit of Yosua son of Yôssadaq the high priest and the spirit of all the rest of the people, so that they came and did work in the
15 house of Yahvé of Hosts their God on the four-and-twentieth day of the sixth month, in the second year of Dareios the king.

3. *The Messianic hope of the temple.*

Ch. ii. 1-9.

As therefore the building of the temple was thus zealously prosecuted, it was all the more painfully observable how great was the lack of sufficient means to decorate the temple in a worthy manner. The largest portion of the new inhabitants of the land were poor, the rich appear to have remained more in foreign countries, and the dawn of the Messianic age, for which hope had been so strong towards the end of the exile, still seemed as if it would not come. Nevertheless Haggái here inspires the labourers with a higher courage, and points them to a better time when even Foreigners and Heathen will lay aside their present coldness and indifference toward Yahvé's kingdom, so that the temple-edifice, just commenced with such meagre resources, will be even more magnificent than the former one.

ii.
1   In the seventh, on the one-and-twentieth of the month, came Yahvé's word by Haggái the prophet saying: Say now to Zerubabel son of Sh'altiel the governor of Yuda and to Yosua son of Yôssadaq the high priest and to the rest of the people thus: Who is there among you yet surviving who saw this house in its former splendour? | and how do ye see it now? is not the like of it as nothing in your eyes? ||—Yet now—be brave Zerubabel! saith Yahvé, and be brave Yosua the son of

Yòssadaq the high priest, and be brave all people of the land and work ye! | for I am with you, saith Yahvé of Hosts, || by
5 that word which I covenanted with you when ye came out of Egypt and my spirit stood in your midst: | fear ye not! || For thus saith Yahvé of Hosts: yet one little while is it | and I shake the heavens and the earth, the sea and the dry land, || and I shake all the nations, so that the high treasures of all nations may come: | then I fill this house with splendour, saith Yahvé of Hosts. || Mine is the silver and mine the gold, | saith Yahvé of Hosts; || greater will be the latter splendour of this house than the former, saith Yahvé of Hosts, | and in this place will I put peace, saith Yahvé of Hosts. ||

A thing which is so small and humble at its commencement as this edifice may well appear to you as really nothing! must here, ver. 3, be said to those who are prone to doubt. But courage they can and must take, and bravely give themselves to the work which is now necessary, if they only remember the similarly feeble and depressing commencement of the foundation of the nation of the covenant and the similar divine exhortation not to yield to human fear, vv. 4, 5: the passage of which they are reminded is from the history of the covenant, Ex. xx. 20. For soon, vv. 6, 7, comp. vi. 21, 22, will the universe and will the nations lose their present inactivity and coldness, and the *choice treasures of all the nations*, e. g., of the rich Babylonians, Zech. vi. 8, 10-15, shall come to the temple: for if they come they bring also plentiful gifts by which the splendour of the temple is increased; and at all events if Yahvé desires this splendour, he will certainly bring it, vv. 8, 9. The comparison ver. 8 like Job xlii. 12.

For the phrase כְּמַֽעַט כְּאַיִן, ver. 3, taken rather from common life, comp. § 105 b: it is found exactly in this form here only.

For the אֶת, ver. 5, in a broken sentence, see § 329 a. It might also be conjectured that some such word as *remember!* were understood here, after the manner of broken sentences, comp. Zech. vii. 7: however, it is sufficient to take the words as a reference almost in the form of an oath to the ancient sacred utterance. Haggái calls to mind the power of the *Spirit of God* in those times under Moses in the same way as the great anonymous prophet "Isa." lix. 21; lxiii. 11.

אַתָּה, ver. 6, may be added to מְעַט in order to intensify the meaning, as in the English phrase *but one minute* (Germ. *noch éine minute!*), comp. something similar Isa. xxix. 17; x. 25. This could be done the more easily if מְעַט really signified a definite very small portion of time and in that way was treated as a fem.

With regard to חֶמְדַּת, ver. 7, comp. *History of Israel*, V., p. 111 (IV., p. 145).

4. The true sacrifice.

Ch. ii. 10-19.

Soon after this some, those perhaps who had for a long time brought considerable offerings, appear to have complained of the continuance of the times of distress and therefore the uselessness of their offerings. In opposition to this Haggái shows that both in conformity with the nature of the case, vv. 11-14, and the testimony of history, vv. 15-19, none of the past offerings had been the genuine acceptable ones, and that only from this time forth, with the newly kindled and lasting zeal, the divine blessing could be expected.

10 On the four-and-twentieth of the ninth, in the second year of Dareios came Yahvé's word by Haggái the prophet, saying: Thus saith Yahvé of Hosts: | Ask now the priests for instruction in these words: || if one beareth consecrated flesh in the skirt of his garment and toucheth with his skirt the bread and the broth and the wine and the oil or any meat whatsoever, is it consecrated? | Then answered the priests and said "No!" || And Haggái said: if one unclean from some one toucheth all that, becometh it unclean? | Then answered the priests and said, "It doth!" || and Haggái answered and said: So is this people and so this nation before me, saith Yahvé, and so is all the work of their hands; | —and that which they
15 there offer is unclean. || —And now, bethink ye then from this day and backward, | before one stone was laid upon

As regards the nature of the case, vv. 11-14, let the priests themselves, who gain such a preponderating respect in the community, give the decision as to it in accordance with their ancient sacred principles! As the healthy man coming to a sick one does not make him well by his simple presence, but will be probably himself infected by him, so neither can holiness according to ancient Mosaic laws externally communicate itself by mere contact (Lev. vi. 20, A.V. ver. 27), and no offering which an unclean man brings is made pure and good by the simple presentation of it upon a pure altar; on the other hand, the uncleanness spreads over everything which it touches, and if a man who is unclean from having touched something impure, e.g., a dead body, touches any material thing, it is rendered unclean (Num. xix. 11-22, comp. *Antiquities of Israel*, p. 198 sq. (169 sq.). Therefore a man must himself first be pure if he will expect that all that he begins and gains and offers before God shall be deemed pure and good; and because the nation as a whole is at present still another in Yahvé's temple : ‖ as often as one came to a corn-heap of twenty [measures], there were ten, | came to the wine press to draw fifty buckets, there were twenty ; ‖ I smote you with parched-corn and with yellow-corn, and with hail all the work of your hands : | and yet ye were not good towards me ! saith Yahvé. ‖ Bethink yourselves then from to-day and backward, from the four-and-twentieth day of the ninth to the day when Yahvé's temple was founded bethink you : ‖ was there then still the seed in the barn, and even the vine and the fig and the pomegranate and the olive-tree did not bear ! | From this day will I bless ! ‖

unclean, its toils and labours, *e.g.*, in the field, as well as its offerings, continue to lack true purity and honour before Yahvé. There, ver. 14, *i.e.*, upon the provisional altar near the temple, Ezra iii. 2.—The same conclusion is obtained with greater particularity by a reference to the entire history of the last years since the return of these exiles into the midst of the ruins of Jerusalem and the commencement of the erection of the temple : a thought which is here worked out twice, vv. 15-17 and vv. 18, 19. All along there was painful deficiency : a corn-heap from which twenty measures of threshed corn might from its size be expected, yielded after it was threshed only ten measures, a pressfat where, to judge from the vineyard to which it belonged, fifty buckets might be expected yielded only twenty ; there was scarcely left in the barn the seed for the new year, and even the fruit-trees did not bear, the heavens were unfavourable to husbandry (ver. 17 from Amos iv. 9), comp. with what was said above i. 6-11, and thereby the proof was given that offerings and offerers were still unclean ; whilst the nation for a long time refused to acknowledge this and to show repentance ! From this time forth only, since the fresh zeal no more slackens, will the blessing begin to come !—Thus everything is clear as soon as the fact is not overlooked, that this discourse quickly followed those of ch. i. and during the continuance of similar circumstances.

The unusual phrase מִהְיוֹתָם בָּא, ver. 16, must be understood so that it as well as the following בָּא is a *part.*, the *part.* used together with הָיָה according to § 168 *c*, and מִן as in מִדֵּי indicates the commencement of a point of time, § 337 *ad fin.*, while the force of דֵּי in this instance is found in the *part.* with היה ; the sing. and plur. are used acc. § 319 *a*.

Ver. 17 וּבַבָּרָד should be connected with a following member in opposition to the accents, and it is not in the quotations from Amos.—As regards אֵין אֶתְכֶם, see § 262 *d ;* and as regards אֶל in such a phrase § 217 *c*.

5. *Joyous message to Zerubabel.*

Ch. ii. 20-23.

To Zerubabel, on the other hand, the zealous head of the Community, the man of David's house and the hope of his time, with whom Messianic hopes were associated, Haggái spoke on the same day a few words of simple comfort and promise:

20   And Yahvé's word came once more unto Haggái on the four-and-twentieth of the month saying: Say unto Zerubabel the governor of Yuda thus: I shake soon the heavens and the earth, ‖ and overthrow the throne of kingdoms and destroy the strength of the kingdoms of the Heathen, ∣ I overthrow the chariot and its driver, so that the horses come down with their drivers, one by the sword of another! ‖ On that day, saith Yahvé of Hosts, will I take thee Zerubabel son of Sh'altiel my servant, saith Yahvé, and regard thee as the signet-ring; ∣ for in thee have I delight! saith Yahvé of Hosts. ‖

Vv. 21-22 the arrival of the Messianic time is described pretty much as in vv. 6, 7, and Zech. xiv. 12, 13.—*Take thee and regard thee as the signet-ring* i.e., preserve thee as the most precious gem, from Cant. viii. 6.

2. ZAKHARYA.

It is only in a few respects that Zakharya differs from Haggái. His longer book, ch. i.—viii., deals with more subjects, although the chief subject in his case also is the erection of the temple. His language has already grown firmer and more precise, in outward form it is again more like the earlier language; of later irregularities it has in common with Haggái not much more than the use of the accusative particle את at the commencement of unfinished sentences, vii. 7; viii. 17; Hag. ii. 5. According to all appearances he was younger in years than Haggái: as though he belonged to a new age, he constantly refers back to the earlier prophets and their utterances, and admonishes his hearers not to become like their forefathers, i. 2-6; vii. 7-14; viii. 14; the distinctive characteristic of the new as compared with the older time, that which mainly agitates and determines the new time, is expressed much more plainly in Zakharya than in Haggái; he has particularly the most cheerful views and the most exuberant hopes of the present and the future. Further, a youthful, very luxuriant, and active imagination distinguishes this prophet and is the cause of a peculiarity which completely separates him from Haggái and constitutes the chief portion of his book —the presentation of a series of very artistically arranged and clearly drawn visions. And the fact that in the employment of representations of divine things he even goes far beyond the innovations introduced by Hézeqiél, becomes, indeed, the author of a new kind of prophetic vision, is another proof that he had obtained his education in Eastern parts of the world. Comp. *History of Israel*, V., 183 sq. (IV., 237 sq.) An innovation of importance for that day is the introduction by this prophet of the use of the Aramaic names for the months, comp. *Antiquities of Israel*, p. 456 sq. (Eng. Trans., p. 345 sq.)

The book contains three pieces arranged as in Haggái exactly according to their dates. But of the three pieces the second is essentially the most important portion of the entire book, where the prophet endeavours to bring together in a great series of visions all the hopes, wishes, and forebodings of that memorable sacred year of the reign of Dareios; the first piece is a brief general admonition, serving as a preface; the third was occasioned by an entirely different matter and was written two years later.

I. *Preface.*

Ch. i. 1-6.

Would that the new Israel which is now being formed may

be a better nation, having taken warning from the great example of the past! The fathers, who did not hearken to the ancient prophets, recognized the lesson of the past too late, they are no more, neither are the prophets immortal and may perhaps soon wholly cease to appear (as in fact was the case): their words only have been found valid and remain eternally valid: would therefore that the new Israel might seek salvation from them alone!—It is as if in these few words the whole spirit which henceforth actually guided the new nation to the most conscientious observance of the ancient religion found expression.

i.
1   In the eighth month, in the second year of Dareios, came Yahvé's word to Zakharya son of Bérekhyá son of 'Iddo the prophet, saying:
Yahvé hath been angry with your fathers, yes angry! || Therefore say unto them: thus saith Yahvé of Hosts "Turn ye unto me," saith Yahvé of Hosts, | "that I may turn unto you!" saith Yahvé of Hosts. || Be ye not as your fathers to whom the former prophets cried saying "Thus saith Yahvé of Hosts, turn now from your evil ways and from your evil deeds!" | but they heard not and listened not unto me, saith
5   Yahvé. || Your fathers—where are they? | and the prophets—will they live for ever? || only my words and laws, which I commanded my servants the prophets, have they not overtaken your fathers, | so that they came to themselves and said "Like as Yahvé of Hosts thought to do unto us according to our ways and according to our deeds, so hath he dealt with us!" ||

How profound is the foreboding question, *will the prophets live for ever?* and how accurately it touches the real truth of the matter, almost contrary to what was desired! ver. 5. It is really as if this young prophet, precisely at the same moment when he undertook the bold venture of labouring in Jerusalem in his day like one of the old prophets, had been seized by the more overwhelming presentiment that the higher conditions for such an undertaking were still wanting and were not again to be supplied.

II. *The seven visions.*

Ch. i. 7—vi. 8.

All that the prophet in other respects desires and hopes for his time he presses into a most highly artistic series of visions, which as forming a connected whole must be conceived as making up a long dream. When that moment comes upon a prophet that his spirit, as wholly absorbed in the divine spirit and lost to all the outward world, simply lives in the new representations and thoughts with which that spirit floods his, he then lies as in a state of sleep though in the most vivid dream. Zakharya longs most intensely to see a new and better day arise for the kingdom of God: at present it is for that kingdom dark night; he accordingly falls at evening into the long, most varied, and equally vivid dream of a night when he feels himself surrounded and elevated by simply celestial forms, places, symbols and voices, when it becomes clear to him near the divine throne how out of all the confusion of the dark time gradually a new bright day, and one more according to the divine purpose, will arise, and when he only wakes up to announce to his friends what he had seen of this unfolding of a better coming day and of the conditions of this Messianic future. A dream permits the most vivid and varied unfolding of new and surprising phenomena, which pass before the eye in such a way that the dreamer often does not himself know at once what they are. But in this case the interpreter of the symbols is no longer Yahvé as in the case of Amos, Vol. I., 194 sq., but the prophetic spirit, conceived here as a person, or as one of the principal angels, and called *the angel that spoke with me;*[*] this angel knows Yahvé and his mind, intercedes with him for others, utters his commands and prophecies, so that at times Yahvé himself interchanges with him, iii. 2; in some passages where he shows greater independent activity, he is called also

---

[*] Comp. on this דִּבֶּר־בְּ, § 217 *f.* 3; in the fourth book of Ezra we still meet with *loqui in* . . . . bearing this force, even in the Vulgate (*i.e*, at third hand).

the *angel of Yahvé*, i. 12 ; iii. 1-6; comp. Vol. IV., p. 13 sq. In addition to him other higher or subordinate angels appear, just as the symbol in each case requires. The most important thing is that the seven highest spirits, or eyes of Yahvé, are already introduced into the symbolic representations as well-known beings, ch. iii. and iv. (comp. *History of Israel*, V., 184 (IV., 239); in fact the sacred number seven determines for our prophet the order and arrangement of all his visions, for with great art he brings forward a well-arranged series of exactly seven visions, which passed by in a night and as in one long dream from evening to morning, i. 8; vi. 1-8. The first three describe the present condition of the new Jerusalem, and, which is of much greater importance, how it is to be helped and what a glorious Messianic future is before it; the fourth and the fifth confine themselves in similar sense to the two heads of the kingdom at that time, already mentioned by Haggái; but the sixth and the seventh set forth in symbols the fact that only a completely purified and sanctified land can supply the first condition of the prosperity of the Messianic age; until the last, reverting to the commencement, describes how all this sevenfold vision which had been seen in one night begins really to find fulfilment with the morning of a new day. While, therefore, two double visions are placed together after the first three, and these double visions are followed by a single one as a conclusion, we have the groups of three and four within the whole number of seven. Comp. the article in the *Theologische Studien und Kritiken*, p. 347 sq., as far back as the year 1828.

On the four-and-twentieth of the eleventh month, that is the month Shebát, in the second year of Dareios, came Yahvé's word unto Zakharya son of Bérekhyá son of Iddo the prophet saying :

These words yield a meaning only when they are taken as the heading of the entire piece following. What the *word of Yahvé* is which is mentioned in it as the chief matter, the reader may find from the whole of the following narrative.

(I.) 1. *Evening. The indolent repose of the present world.*

Ch. i. 8-17.

With the approach of night (and of the dream) there arrive from the four quarters of the world at the celestial palace, whither the spirit of Zakharya feels itself translated, all the angels which have during the day roamed in chariots and on swift horses over the whole earth, in order to announce what they had seen to their chief and through him to Yahvé. Comp. Job i. 7, 8, a description which is present to the mind of our prophet in all these visions. As they then announce that they had found the state of the whole earth that day also quite motionless and indifferent, and the high angel, shocked thereat, has put in his intercession to Yahvé for a speedy alteration, there are then heard gracious promises of the awakening of a higher zeal upon the earth also amongst the nations, of the completion of the temple and of the desired salvation—these promises being the real object of the vision; comp. the same Hag. ii. 6, 7, 21, 22.

I saw by night and behold a man* standing among the myrtles by the tent, and behind him bright-red brown and grey and dark-red horses; || then said I "what are these, my lord?" and the Angel that conversed with me said to me, "shall
10 I show thee who these are?" || and the man who stood between the myrtles answered and said: these are they whom Yahvé hath sent to go to and fro through the earth! || —Then they answered the Angel of Yahvé who stood among the myrtles and said: we went to and fro through the earth, | but behold the whole earth is still and quiet. || So the Angel of Yahvé answered and said: O Yahvé of Hosts, how long hast thou no pity for Jerusalem and the cities of Yuda, | against which thou hast been angry even seventy years! || But Yahvé returned the Angel who spoke with me good words, | comfortable words; || so the Angel that conversed with me said

---

* *riding upon a bright red horse*

unto me: cry thou, saying: Thus saith Yahvé of Hosts: | I
15 cherish a great zeal for Jerusalem and for Ssion; || and great
wrath against the inactive nations, since I was only a little
wroth, but they helped for evil. || Therefore thus saith Yahvé:
I turn to Jerusalem with compassion, my house will be built in
her, saith Yahvé of Hosts, | and a measuring line will be
drawn over Jerusalem. || Cry yet, saying: thus saith Yahvé of
Hosts: my cities will yet overflow with good, | and Yahvé will
yet compassionate Ssion, and take delight in Jerusalem! ||

The points which are here left obscure with regard to the number and significance of the horses and their chariots and drivers are sufficiently cleared up by the corresponding final vision, vi. 1-6: it is intended that there shall be four kinds of horses, with different colours corresponding to the four quarters of the heavens, red for the bright east, brown, or black as they are called ch. vi., for the dark north, grey for the west, spotted dark-red for the south (as similar symbols occur in the *Qirq Vezîr*, p. 42, 14 sq., Hauch's *Nordischer Mythol.*, p. 72 sq.) But Zakharya observes particularly a *man*, as at first he appears to be no more than a man, but who afterwards more and more plainly proves to be an exalted Angel: he has charge over these chariots, whose drivers daily speed through the whole world with their fleet chargers, in order to carry in the morning the divine commands into it and returning at evening to report its condition in the celestial palace. Now their chief already stands *among the high myrtle trees* prepared to receive them at the celestial tent, which denotes the dwelling of Yahvé according to the type of the Mosaic tabernacle, the trees standing before the two mountains or hills which surround this celestial palace in some such way as the two principal mountains of Jerusalem; but they are called *brazen*, vi. 1, just as the firmament is often conceived by the ancients as of metal, Gen. i. 6. The prophet's own Angel is a different one from him, and to his own Angel he always turns when he requires information, inasmuch as he is always prepared to assist him when it is necessary, iv. 4, 5, 13; vi. 4, and it is at the desire of the prophet's Angel that the former Angel explains who the riders are, vv. 8-10. It is true that a guide of this kind does not appear again in vi. 1-6; but in the passage before us he is very plainly distinguished from the Angel of the prophet by the entire description of him and the tone in which he is spoken of.—As soon as all the riders, having arrived in due order, have made their report to their chief regarding the present condition of the earth, ver. 11, the intercession of the prophetic Angel commences, ver. 12, and after he has received a gracious answer, ver. 13, he expounds it aloud to the prophet in order that he may proclaim it to the earth, vv. 14-17. The Heathen, ver. 15, deserve divine wrath, because having been seventy years before summoned by Yahvé to assist in the chastisement of Israel, they did not chastise it a little as Yahvé desired, thereby helping for good, but immoderately, contrary to the divine intention, helping for evil, Isa. x. 5 sq. *The measuring line*, ver. 16, shall be drawn over Jerusalem, *i.e.*, it shall be completely re-built, as at present it still lies for the most part in ruins, all this being further explained, ii. 5 sq.

In order to understand the symbols, it becomes necessary above everything to recognize the fact that the words *riding upon a bright red horse,* ver. 8, mar the lucidity of the description at the very commencement, and can only have been added from a misconception by an early hand. At most, pre-supposing their genuineness, this Angel would have to be conceived as the driver of the first chariot, that coming from the east, he also speaking and acting for the others. However, the prophet does not see him dismounting from his horse, but on the contrary all the horses and chariots are *behind him, i.e.,* waiting for him as their overlooker, *the bright red* horses also. Neither can there be any doubt that one of the four names of colours has been lost from ver. 8, namely, acc. vi. 3, אֲמֻצִּים (the same as חָמוּץ)

"Isa." lxiii. 1, or acc. vi. 3 more fully בְּרֻדִּים אָ), which might easily drop out before וַאֹמַר: the *brown* ones may very well interchange with the *black* ones, vi. 2, but the south (for the order goes by the east and north) requires its *spotted dark-red* ones. When then the four chariots are pulled up, acc. vi. 1, at the valley between the two mountains, this chief and mediator with regard to them stands farther to the front in the direction of the divine *tent* (מִצְלָה, Arab. *mizhallah*), accordingly by the forecourt where high myrtle-trees are placed, comp. *History of Israel,* III., 245 (III., 334). We may therefore retain the reading הֲדַסִּים without adopting the alteration of the LXX, הָרִים, *mountains,* vi. 1.—The words of the Angel, ver. 9, are best taken as interrogative: meanwhile he gives a sign to the higher Angel which he understands.

2. *The future of the great empires.*

Ch. ii. 1-4 (A.V. i. 18-21).

The promises of the first vision have only excited but not satisfied the desire to know *how* they are to be fulfilled: the second and the third visions now satisfy this desire completely. As regards the Heathen empires of all four quarters of the world, as far as they occur here again from the previous vision, and which still continue to impede the true divine kingdom, the prophet beholds in a plain symbol their destruction, the cutting down of their four proud horns by four still stronger smiths, vv. 1-4; as regards the new Jerusalem as the seat of the true divine kingdom, he beholds in the third vision, which is more closely connected with the foregoing one on account of its kindred subject-matter, the vast proportions upon which it shall be rebuilt at the express command of Yahvé, and generally the form which it will assume, vv. 5-9 ; and the divine voice, having thus once begun to speak freely, goes on in less restrained form to explain both that stern truth with regard to the Heathen and its consequences, vv. 10-13, and this joyous one concerning the future Jerusalem, vv. 14-17. In this way every thing assumes an excellent form : towards the end the joyful divine promises which follow from both visions are combined.

Then I lifted up mine eyes and saw, and behold four horns. ‖ So I said to the Angel that conversed with me : what are these? and he said to me : these are the horns which have scattered Yuda Israel and Jerusalem. ‖ Then Yahvé caused me to see four smiths, ‖ and I said : what come these to do ? then he spake, saying : those horns which scattered Yuda in such wise that no man lifted up his head, these came to terrify them, to cast down the horns of the nations which lifted up the horn against the land of Yuda to scatter it. ‖

ii. 1-4. Horn, power, empire : but the number four remains in conformity with the previous vision ; whether at that time there existed four great empires corresponding to the four quarters of the heavens, is of very little importance ; there is a playful interchange of figure and thing prefigured at the end, ver. 4. *In such wise*, ver. 3, that no one raised his head, could look up unhindered, comp. i. 15.—The fact that Israel stands between Yuda and Jerusalem, ver. 2, completely accords with my note on Ps. lxviii. 27.

3. *The future of Jerusalem.*

Ch. ii. 5-17.

5   Then I lifted up mine eyes and saw and behold a man holding a cord for measuring ; ‖ then said I : whither wilt thou go ? and he said unto me : to measure Jerusalem, to see how great its breadth and how great its length. ‖ And behold the Angel that conversed with me appeared, and another Angel appeared over against him ‖ and said unto him : run speak to that youth saying : countrywise will Jerusalem lie, on account of the multitude of men and cattle therein ; ‖ and I will be to her, saith Yahvé, a wall of fire round about, | and splendour will I be within her ! ‖—Hear hear and flee ye from the land of the north ! saith Yahvé, | for like the four

winds of heaven have I spread you out, saith Yahvé ; ‖ O save thee Ssion, | thou citizeness daughter of Babel ! ‖ For thus saith Yahvé of Hosts : | (after honour hath he sent me to the nations which spoiled you, | for he who toucheth you toucheth the apple of his eye !) ‖ yea, behold I wave my hand over them that they become a spoil to those who serve them, | and ye know that Yahvé of Hosts hath sent me. ‖—Sing aloud and rejoice daughter of Ssion ! | for behold I come and dwell
15 in thy midst, saith Yahvé, ‖ and many nations join themselves to Yahvé in that day, and become to me a people ; | so I dwell in thy midst and thou knowest that Yahvé of Hosts hath sent me to thee ! ‖ Then will Yahvé take Yuda for his inheritance upon the holy ground, | and still have pleasure in Jerusalem. ‖ —Be silent all flesh before Yahvé ! for he bestirreth himself from his holy dwelling. ‖

The young Angel who appears, vv. 5, 6, comp. ver. 8, supposes that as a subordinate servant the time has now arrived for him simply to measure and determine the future circumference of Jerusalem, the measure of it being unknown to him. But when he has only just appeared, a far higher Angel, after he has learnt the particulars from Yahvé, cries to the prophet's Angel, as he approaches him, that he must supply the younger Angel with the divine measurement: the new and reformed city shall on account of its populousness have no limited measurement, but (as is the case with all the largest cities of the earth) shall extend itself indefinitely after the manner of villages, without fixed walls and gates ; neither has it any need of material walls, since Yahvé, enthroned above it in majesty, in fire and splendour after Ex. xl. 38 ; Isa. iv. 5, 6, will both protect and glorify it.—When the Heathen kingdoms shall thus fall, let the numerous Israelites who still live scattered throughout them flee in time from them and assemble themselves at the place where their arrival is so ardently desired, in the Holy Land ; particularly let the numerous wealthy Israelites in the north, in Babylonia, flee ! "Isa." xlviii. 20 (the addition of the four winds, ver. 10 b, is clear only as an explanation of vv. 1-4). They may do this without fear, vv. 12, 13 : a sign from Yahvé is sufficient to make the degenerated conquerors the prey of those who are oppressed by them, and this Angel has himself the commission to summon the Heathen to give back the captives, and he will execute his mission with honour ! *After honour, i.e.*, in order to receive honour, not in vain, without effect, Ps. lxxiii. 24.— Let Ssion, on the other hand, vv. 14-17, rejoice, receiving early the fulfilment of these promises ; the Heathen will yet turn to her God and be mingled with the ancient Community, "Isa." xiv. 1, 2 ; "Jer." l. 5, Yahvé will still be enthroned in her with all splendour ; and already he arouseth himself for this from the celestial palace, let all flesh therefore be still before him ! after Sseph. i. 7 ; Hab. ii. 20.

As in all pieces of Zakharya voices particularly of the anonymous prophet explained Vol. IV., 224-354, are audible as those of his immediate precursors, so also the appeal to Ssion-Babel, ver. 11, *i.e.*, the great Yudean community which still continued to prefer to dwell in Babel, reminds us very much of the mighty voice of "Jer." ch. l., li., which only carried out further what is heard here as a subsequent echo.

(II.) 4. *The High-priest's dignity and prosperity.*

Ch. iii.

Of the two chief men of the community of that time, to whom the next two visions are devoted, the High-priest appears to have then been persecuted by either an actual or threatened accusation in the Persian court; a defamation and persecution of this kind may be discerned as underlying this vision, the whole manner and conception of the narrative pre-supposing it. For the prophet beholds him acquitted in a solemn session before the celestial judge in spite of the accusation of Satan: and if he is acquitted there, what accusation can harm him upon earth? After this has been symbolically represented, vv. 1-5, the good Angel promises to the innocent High-priest before him further protection, and, which concerns him very closely, the arrival of the Messiah with the completion of the temple, vv. 6-10.

iii.
1   Then he showed me the High-priest Yosúa standing before the Angel of Yahvé, whilst the accuser stood at his right hand to accuse him; || but Yahvé said to the accuser: Yahvé rebuke thee thou accuser, and rebuke thee Yahvé who hath pleasure in Jerusalem : | is not this a brand plucked out of the fire? || And whereas Yosúa was clothed in dirty garments and stood before the Angel, || he replied and spake to those that stood before him saying: take away the dirty garments from him! and he spake to him: behold I remove thy guilt
5   from thee and clothe thee in festive array! || and he spake: let them set a pure tiara upon his head! | So they set the pure tiara upon his head and clothed him with the garments, whilst Yahvé's Angel yet stood by. ||—Then Yahvé's Angel certified

to Yosúa saying: ‖ Thus saith Yahvé of Hosts: if thou walkest in my ways, and if thou keepest my charge in charge, | then wilt thou also judge mine house, thou also keep in charge my courts, | and I give thee passages between them that stand here. ‖ Yet hear Yosúa the High-priest, thou and thy friends that sit before thee, | (for they are men of omen): surely I bring my servant *Offshoot*! ‖ For behold the stone which I lay before Yosúa—upon one stone seven eyes!— | behold I will engrave its writing, saith Yahvé of Hosts, and put away the guilt of this land in one day; ‖ in that day, saith Yahvé of Hosts, ye will invite one the other | under a vine and under a fig-tree! ‖

The description vv. 1-5 follows completely the usages of ancient courts of justice. Before the representative of Yahvé, who in ver. 2 is even called Yahvé himself in the brevity of the narrative, as the sitting judge stands the accused and on his right, in the place of honour, the accuser before God, the Satan, who maintains rightly or wrongly that he has discovered something in the High-priest deserving of accusation. But the supreme judge immediately discerns the groundlessness of the charge and how unjust it is so early again to violently assail a man who has moreover only just escaped from the greatest peril, from the exile (from Amos iv. 11); with the name of the Righteous One and the friend of Jerusalem he bids therefore the Satan to hold his peace, and as a sign of his complete acquittal he orders pure shining garments such as are usual in the case of accused persons of high rank to be given to the accused instead of the dirty ones which an accused person wears when on his trial, Rev. vi. 11. In this change of garments, as is fitting, the friends of the accused, the subordinate priests, who attend and surround him as clients, are to be employed; ver. 4 they are called "those who stand before him," those surrounding him, waiting for his commands, as is said again ver. 7; those sitting before him, ver. 8, that is not here but in the Community, where all sit.—But the Angel, having already risen from the judgment-seat, now lingers quite calmly in order to explain the divine purposes concerning this man who has been thus acquitted. First, as regards the immediate event, ver. 7, Yosúa shall, if he is himself only faithful to Yahvé and fills the office entrusted to him according to the intentions of its donor, be in turn protected by Yahvé, always remain as judge and supervisor in the temple, freely going in and out amongst his servants in the discharge of his functions (not again to be accused). But the Messiah, ver. 8, will soon come, the servant of Yahvé who is here briefly and disguisedly named *Offshoot*, after Jer. xxiii. 5, comp. vi. 12; and precisely the present friends of the High-priest shall be witnesses of this promise, men of the foretoken and of the future, as certainly as they are now there will the Messiah come, they shall therefore by their existence and life point to this great future, Isa. viii. 3. 4 ; Ezek. xii. 5 sq. Yet Yahvé himself gives a still higher sign, ver. 9 : the stone which he herewith holds before Yosúa as a model, a wonderful stone, upon which are engraved seven eyes (and the seven eyes are the symbol of the seven highest spirits, Rev. i. 4, it is therefore a marvellous stone toward which divine love and care is itself wholly directed, as it were all the seven highest spirits, or eyes of Yahvé, iv. 10, as a sign of which to him all these seven eyes are engraved)—that stone he will himself some day really adorn with this his inscription (just as a stone which is built into the gable receives at last its decorative inscription) and display it as the crowning and gable-stone of the temple, so that from that place where the completed temple shines forth with these seven eyes, toward which all divine love and care is directed, sin flees far and wide, as is immediately further explained, ch. v.; that will be the Messianic age! ver. 10 after Mic. iv. 4. The brief and rapid mention of the stone and the seven spirits receives further explanation in ch. iv.

As regards the figures which appear in this scenic piece, the immediate subordinate officials and friends of the High-priest, who naturally stand on both sides, on the right and left, *before him* in this trying situation as true clients, are so expressly mentioned, vv. 4, 7, for the further reason that they are here so necessary and significant as witnesses, acc. ver. 8.—It is true that it has been foolishly and obstinately supposed that the dirty garments, vv. 3-5, are intended to signify that Yosúa had committed the sin of marriage with a harlot; as Justin Martyr, *Dialogues*, ch. cxvi, explains this, manifestly following a prevalent opinion of the Jewish schools of his time, founded upon Ezra x. 18: but such an idea is not worthy of serious refutation. It is, on the contrary, the custom of Persian courts, which Zakharya has before his mind in his description of the court of justice, just as in the case of the picture of the imperial messengers in their arrival at and despatch from the palace, i. 8, 9, it is the Persian imperial post which is present to his imagination.

Instead of וְאָמַר, ver. 5, it is necessary to read וַיֹּאמֶר; and as a matter of course מַהְלְכִים comes from a sing. מַהְלָךְ *passage; passages*, are here, however, *functions*, according to the well-known phrase of *going in and out, i.e.*, to transact public business.

The reason why Zakharya here and vi. 12 denominates the Messiah *Offshoot* with such brevity, and unintelligibly, as the name is here used, is explained in the *Geschichte des Volkes Israel*, V., p. 146.*

---

* The explanation referred to in this untranslated volume of the *History of Israel* is as follows:—" Zech. iii. 8; vi. 12: the abbreviated name *Offshoot*, used of the greatest shoot or new youthful hero whom men expected, probably owes its origin not simply to the artistic language of the time, but also to an intentional avoidance of the name '*David's* Offshoot,' inasmuch as the name David, remarkably enough, never occurs in Haggái and Zakharya; a fact which is intelligible from *History of Israel*, V., 110 sq. (IV., 144 sq.)"—*Tr.*

5. *The dignity and prosperity of the secular and the ecclesiastical chief.*

Ch. iv.

While the correlative piece to the previous one does special honour to Zerubabel, it also treats of the two chiefs both together again. An exceedingly brilliant symbolic picture presents itself, so that the prophet (although in a dream) is, as it were, awakened out of the dream, ver. 1, and his attention cannot be directed with sufficient intensity to what he sees, vv. 4, 5. It is a chandelier branching up into seven lights, being the symbol of the seven highest spirits, or of the eyes of the one Yahvé as they travel through the world: where the chandelier therefore presents itself (and its idea is derived from the Mosaic sanctuary, Ex. ch. xxv.), there all the activities of divine providence and love meet together, there the spirit is present and ready to help; and thus Zerubabel, trusting in the spirit of Yahvé, not in material power, and protected by Him, will complete his great work, the erection of the temple, in spite of all obstacles. But at the same time the prophet beholds by the side of this sevenfold lamp two olive trees, particularly two branches of them climbing aloft close by its side: thus the two chiefs, like Anointed ones appointed to do great things, stand together most closely and intimately with Yahvé and his spirit, are his nearest servants and also most immediately enlightened and guarded by him. This is added at the end, vv. 11-14, after what concerns Zerubabel has been explained at length in the middle of the piece, vv. 6-10.

iv.
1   Then the Angel that conversed with me turned and wakened me as one who is awakened out of his sleep, || and spake to me: what seest thou ? then I said: I saw and behold a chandelier all gold and an oil-vessel on the top of it; and its seven lights on it, and seven pipes for the lights which are on the top of

5   it; ‖ and two olive trees beside it, one at the right of the oil-vessel and one at the left. ‖—Then I answered and spake to the Angel that conversed with me, saying: what are these, my Lord? ‖ and the Angel that conversed with me answered and said to me: knowest thou not what these are? I said: No, my Lord! ‖ then he answered and spake to me, saying: This is Yahvé's word to Zerubabel, saying: | not by power and not by might, but by my spirit! saith Yahvé of Hosts; ‖ who art thou great mountain? before Zerubabel thou becomest a plain,] so that he bringeth the top-stone amid the acclamations " grace grace unto it!" ‖ And Yahvé's word came to me saying: ‖ Zerubabel's hands have founded this house, and his hands will finish it, | that thou mayest know that Yahvé
10 of Hosts hath sent me to you: ‖ for whoever mocked the weak beginnings of the day, they will rejoice and see the plummet in Zerubabel's hand: | these seven are Yahvé's eyes, roving through the whole earth. ‖—Then I answered and spake to him: what are these two olive-trees at the right of the chandelier and at the left? ‖ and I answered yet again and said to him: what are the two olive branches which are beside the two golden pipes which pour the gold from themselves? ‖ then he said to me thus: knowest thou not what these are? I said: no, my Lord! ‖ so he said: these are the two sons of the oil, | which stand before the Lord of the whole earth! ‖

The application to Zerubabel is not completed in a single utterance, but needs two: not by mere human force (Job xxxiv. 20), but by my spirit! learn this, in the first place, from those symbols! nevertheless, before Zerubabel, who is faithful to this principle, on that very account every great mountain will become a plain, every difficulty will vanish, so that he actually brings the headstone of the temple, already mentioned iii. 9, under the loud acclamations, as it is put on, "grace, grace let this stone have for ever!"—Still more plainly it is then said, vv. 8-10: he who laid the foundation-stone will also put on the top-stone; those who may have ridiculed the day when the temple was founded amid poor beginnings, would still with joy behold the top-stone, adorned with its inscription in lead (Job xix. 23), in the hand of Zerubabel, comp. iii. 9: this is precisely the meaning, as is here added at the end, of the number seven which occurs in the two symbols, that in and from this place all highest spirits will be at work!—At the first question, ver. 11, no answer follows, because it is too general, observing which the prophet immediately put it more definitely, ver. 12, namely, what the two branches, which are attached to the two extreme pipes on the left and right, signify? for there are only two single persons, two branches of the trees, who are concerned. *Gold*, ver. 12, *i.e.*, golden light. *Sons of the oil* for *anointed ones*, with an allusion to the olive-trees.

The present reading ver. 2 would cause the great departure from the pattern of the ancient temple-chandelier, Ex. xxv. 31-39, that here with the increasing significance of the number seven every pipe from the oil-vessel to the light would be multiplied by seven: for this there is no reason apparent; and accordingly the second שִׁבְעָה should be omitted with the LXX. Moreover, גֻלָּה, ver. 2, should be read without Mappiq, as the suff. is here unnecessary, while the word ver. 3 and elsewhere has always the feminine ending.

צַנְתֹּר, ver. 12, is manifestly only the common name for the same thing which is called a *thing to pour with*, ver. 2. It is clear enough that *the two pipes*, ver. 12, are those of the seven which stand to the beholder most to the right and left.

(III.) 6. *The cleansing virtue.*
Ch. v. 1-4.

The two following visions unfold at greater length the sentence which had been so briefly and rapidly uttered, iii. 9 *b*: in what way, as soon as holiness has gained a firm and indestructible basis, the unholiness and impurity must entirely disappear from the Community; this is in reality the fundamental condition under which alone holiness as outwardly established can bring the hoped-for prosperity. From holiness in any of its forms there ought always to go forth a purifying virtue for the final destruction of evil in whatever forms it shows itself: so the prophet here beholds how even the simple holy word, when it becomes a curse, works as the destroyer of evil, just as the ancients narrate so much about the effective force of this curse when really spoken by a holy mouth (comp. *Antiquities of Israel*, p. 20 sq. (15 sq.). And such words of blessing or of cursing had at that time been already written down in sacred books, Deut. xxvii. sq.; with less difficulty therefore our prophet here beholds a great book-roll flying, and learns what its rapid flight through the land signifies and whom it will infallibly strike.

v.
1 Then I turned myself lifted mine eyes and looked—and behold a roll, flying; || and he said to me: what seest thou? I said: I see a roll flying, its length is twenty cubits and its breadth ten cubits. || Then he said to me: this is the curse which goeth forth over the face of the whole land! | for every one that stealeth is driven out hence like it, and every one that sweareth is driven out hence like it; || and I cause it to go forth, saith Yahvé of Hosts, that it may enter into the house of the thief and into the house of him that sweareth falsely by my name, | that it may remain in his house and destroy it with its timber and stones. ||

Ver. 3, 4: as quickly as thou seest it fly, shall every one who sins, whether with the hand or with the mouth, be driven, literally emptied, from the Holy Land; and in the future also the contents of the book, its curse, will irresistibly force its way into his house in order to destroy it totally. *Who sweareth*, ver. 3, is indeed more definitely explained ver. 4, but in fact any kind of swearing may so easily degenerate, and most men who swear swear falsely; comp. similarly Ecc. ix. 2.

7. *The vanishing wickedness.*

Ch. v. 5-11.

But if this cleansing virtue continues to operate, wickedness itself must finally disappear from the land. As a wild animal, at length imprisoned in a cage, is got rid of, as an incorrigibly immoral woman is at last driven by force from the land amid general scorn and mockery, so the prophet here beholds wickedness already shut up in its narrow prison, vv. 5-8, in order that it may be quickly brought thence into close keeping, where long since all evil spirits dwell and appear able to dwell for a long time to come ("Isa." xxxiv. 14), unto Babylonia, which had at that time the general significance of a counterpart of the Holy Land, vv. 9-11.

5 Then the Angel that conversed with me appeared and said to me: Lift up now thine eyes and see, what is this appearance? ||

then I said; what is it? he said: this cask which appeareth! and he said: this is their spectacle in the whole land! ‖ And behold a leaden cover was lifted up, and there was a woman sitting in the midst of the cask; ‖ and he said: this is wickedness! and threw her back into the cask and threw the leadweight upon the top of it. ‖—Then I lifted mine eyes and looked ǀ and behold two women appeared with wind in their wings, and having wings like the wings of storks; they lifted up the cask between heaven and earth. ‖ Then I said to the Angel that conversed with me: whither do they carry the cask? ‖ and he said to me: to build for it a house in the land of Shinear, in order when it is finished to leave it there in its place. ‖

Ver. 6: *their spectacle*, *i.e.*, indefinitely (§ 294 b), the spectacle of people generally in the whole land, which all may behold as a warning example, in the form in which it must here raise itself somewhat and show itself after the cover (also called a stone of lead on account of its weight) has been lifted somewhat. עֵינָם, lit. *their eye*, their gaze, that which they much like to see, and then pretty much the same as θέατρον 1 Cor. iv. 9, comp. *Dichter des A. Bs. Ia*, p. 71; the word is very similar and the entire description Nah. iii. 6. See also a very similar appearance in Tod's *Rajasthan*, tom. 2, p. 688, and *Journ. As.* 1844, II., p. 99. The reading of the LXX עֲוֹנָם, *their sin*, in this connexion, even of the words of the sentence, supplies no sense whatever.—The two women, ver. 9, appear merely to preserve the similarity of the figure, in order to drive away the woman. Instead of the strongly Chaldaic הֲבִיאֹתָה we might also read וֶהֱבִיאֻהָ: but that this is not necessary is shown § 131 *d*.

8. Conclusion. The new morning.

Ch. vi. 1-8.

But dreams and visions of the long night approach their end, the morning draws near. Accordingly the prophet beholds the same Angels with chariots and fleet horses whom he saw in the first vision at evening arriving at the celestial palace, from their flight through the earth, but this time as they are about again to start on their way through the earth. And he beholds them this time ready to roam through the earth with Yahvé's new commissions, which have been already explained in the previous visions; everything which had been previously proclaimed as the divine word and will they shall begin from the new morning and henceforward to execute as they again take their way through the earth; they have thus presented themselves before Yahvé, ver. 5, in order to receive his behests. And there is one divine behest to which special prominence must be given (which at that time belonged to the most eager desires): in order that the Israelites in the north, in Babylonia, wrought upon by the spirit, may quickly catch higher courage and purer zeal, the Angels which wend their way thither shall leave there the spirit of Yahvé, ver. 8, comp. ii. 10, 11, and this Zakharya shall proclaim as he has beheld it.

vi.
1   Then I turned myself and lifted up mine eyes and looked—and behold four chariots came forth between the two mountains, and the mountains were mountains of brass; || in the first chariot were bright-red horses, in the second chariot dark horses,|| in the third chariot grey horses, and in the fourth chariot dark-red spotted horses. || Then I answered and said to the Angel
5   that conversed with me: what are these, my Lord? || and the Angel answered and said to me: these are the four winds of heaven, going forth after they have presented themselves before the Lord of the whole earth; || whereon the dark horses, they go forth to the land of the north, and the grey go forth to the west, and the spotted go forth to the land of the south. || Then the bright red went forth and sought to go to speed through the earth; then he said: go ye speed ye through the earth! and they sped through all the earth. || Then he called me and spake to me saying: behold, those which go forth to the land of the north, they leave my spirit in the land of the north! ||

When the four chariots, ver. 5, are interpreted as the four winds of the heavens, that can mean simply, they hasten as rapidly into all four quarters as the four winds, as if the four wind-angels were the drivers of these chariots. Ver. 6 only three are mentioned, because the direction of the fourth follows as a matter of course; but this fourth, the one going to the east, is in return for the omission desirous to be the first to start, ver. 7, as becomes the chief wind, waits impatiently for the command to start; and as soon as this is given, they all rapidly drive off, each into his quarter. Ver. 6 אֶל־אַחֲרֵיהֶם is lit. *towards behind them*, i.e., to the west; *spotted*, ver. 6, stands briefly for *spotted-red;* but instead of אָמֹץ, ver. 7, which acc. "Isa." lxiii.1, 2, signifies something different, we must here read אָדֹם, after ver. 2 and i. 8. The connexion of the whole scene also shows that יֵצְאוּ must be read twice in ver. 6 instead of יָצְאוּ.—It is clear that the words concerning the *spirit*, ver. 8, must be interpreted in the sense indicated above, ii. 10, 11, and further below on vv. 9 sq.: a phrase such as Ezek. v. 13 is quite foreign to this passage; yet one may prefer to read חָכִי instead of חֲמָתִי.

If the series and position of the visions, which are brought quite to a close with the eighth, are conceived as regards their mutual relation according to the following scheme:

1. 2. 3.
4. 5.
6. 7.
8.

—it becomes evident that the eighth is intended simply to close the completed series of seven.

Appendix. The confirmation.

Ch. vi. 9-15.

And as a fact about the same time a small event occurred which might be deemed the first confirmation of this hope with regard to the new zeal of the north: three Israelites came to Jerusalem from Babel with rich presents and were hospitably received in the house of Yosia the son of Ssephanya. At that moment it seemed to the prophet as if it were commanded him in a continuation of his dream, as a representative of the nation, to take these presents into his charge in such a way that the most worthy use should be made of them according to the intentions of Yahvé. Two crowns shall be made of one portion of the great gift for those two worthy chiefs, not merely as crowns of honour to adorn the heads of the highly deserving men, but also as a foretoken of their future Messianic exaltation, which was previously similarly anticipated, ch. iv. But inasmuch as this Messianic age has not yet arrived, the crowns shall be provisionally placed in the temple as a memorial of the donors and their host, ver. 14. Thus many will soon follow their example and all that is hoped-for be fulfilled, ver. 15.—Whether that which Zakharya beheld as a suitable divine sign for this age was actually carried out, is quite another matter : there is simply set forth symbolically what is conformable to the divine mind and what the prophet might do accordingly.

10   And Yahvé's word came to me saying: ‖ thou shalt take from the exiles, from Cheldai, from Tóbia, and from Yed'aya—so that thou comest in that day, comest into the house of Yosia the son of Ssephanya whither they are come from Babel, ‖ and takest silver and gold and makest it into crowns, and settest them upon the head of Zerubabel and the head of Yosúa the son of Yòssadaq the High-priest, ‖ and sayest to him thus; Thus saith Yahvé of Hosts, saying : | "behold a man called *Shoot*, and under him it will shoot forth, and he will build the temple of Yahvé ; ‖ yes *he* will build Yahvé's temple, yes *he* will bear splendour, and sit and rule upon his throne; | and Yosúa will be priest upon his throne, and counsel of peace will be between both!" ‖ And the crowns shall be for Cheldai Tóbia and Yed'aya, and to the favour of the son of Ssephanya
15   as a memorial in Yahvé's temple. ‖—And those far off will come and build at the temple of Yahvé, that ye may perceive that Yahvé of Hosts hath sent me unto you ; | and then if ye hearken not unto the voice of Yahvé your God . . . .

That vv. 9-15 forms simply an appendix to the previous part of this book appears not only from the subject-matter, which is only a continuation to ch. iv., but also very plainly from the character of the words. Ver. 9 is like iv. 8, and vii. 4 ; viii. 1, 18, but not like the commencement of an entirely new piece, as i. 1, 7 ; vii. 1. Further, in the phrase ver. 15 b plainly the same Angel continues to speak, who speaks throughout these visions, ii. 12, 13. 15 ; iv. 9 ; nor is the expression *on that day*, ver. 10, clear, unless the whole is looked upon as still a presentiment dream. The style is at the beginning, ver. 10, somewhat clumsy : but apart from that, the piece contains evident mistakes : ver. 10 חלדי and ver. 14 חלם are plainly intended to be the same name ; ver. 15 the conclusion is clearly wanting, if the real meaning of the words is attended to ; and ver. 11 זרבבל וברֹאש, is wanting ; ver. 13 the name Yosúa has been omitted before פֹּחֵן, inasmuch as the direct address of ver. 12 is properly addressed in the first instance to Zerubabel as the higher of the two, and only with the words והיה כהן alludes to Yosúa. But that both are intended and the crowns are not both to be put upon one, is equally apparent from the words at the close, ver. 13, as that from the force of all the words, vv. 12, 13, as far as והיה כהן the direct address of the two must necessarily be addressed to Zerubabel according iv. 7-10. Comp. similar anticipations Jer. xxxiii. 17-26. —*Under him*, everywhere where he goes, it will flourish and shoot forth; flourishing himself the Messiah makes everything flourish that his foot touches; comp. *Hes. theog.*, 194 sq.; *Tabari*, according to Dubeux, I., p. 79 sq.—To bear *splendour*, *i.e.*, the crown.

I leave the above interpretation of this piece substantially just as I gave it in 1828 and in 1840, without any further reference to the numerous misconceptions which it has since been attempted once more to bring into it. It is possible that somewhat early some things in this piece were struck out, because the Messianic hope in Zerubabel was not fulfilled.

III. *Decision with regard to fast days.*

Ch. vii., viii.

An inquiry was sent to the temple, whether the days of humiliation and fasting in commemoration of the destruction of Jerusalem ought to be kept up? On the one hand, it seemed as if they might be discontinued, inasmuch as the compulsory exile was at an end and Jerusalem was gradually rising from its ruins; on the other hand, their retention seemed better, since the new settlement in the Holy Land had to contend with so many difficulties, the larger number of the exiles had not yet returned home, and the times, so distressing and unfavourable in many ways, were far from the expected Messianic prosperity. Many people of position, *e.g.*, priests (vii. 5) in connexion with the temple, evidently inclined to the dark view, since in general the sullen consideration of the course of events became from this time prevalent in the nation, which was, as it seemed, always vainly hoping for the Messiah. But Zakharya once more rises to the full power and dignity of the ancient prophetic spirit, and relying upon the divine perception of the nature of all feasts and other human customs, vii. 4-14, and upon a better estimate of the present and future, viii. 1-17, furnishes the infallible decision not only with regard to the particular question proposed, but also with regard to all similar questions, viii. 18-23. The three sections into which the piece naturally falls are correctly divided by similar headings; this heading, in the case of vii. 8, is, on the other hand, incorrect, and only to be explained as an early error. Inasmuch as the second section may easily be divided into two strophes, we may consider that we have altogether four strophes.

vii.
1 And it came to pass in the fourth year of Dareios the king that Yahvé's word came to Zakharya, on the fourth of the ninth month, in Kislev :—for they of Bethel, Sharésser and Régem-Mélekh and his people, sent to seek the favour of Yahvé with these words to the priests which were at the house of Yahvé of Hosts and to the prophets: "Shall I weep in the fifth month with abstinence, as I have done so many years?" Then came the word of Yahvé of Hosts to me saying:

1.

Say to all the people of the land and to the priests thus:
5 When ye fasted with mourning in the fifth and in the seventh, and these seventy years— | have ye then fasted me? || or though ye eat and though ye drink: | is it not ye who eat and ye who drink? ||—(Know ye) not the words which Yahvé proclaimed by the earlier prophets, when Jerusalem was inhabited and secure and its cities around it, | and the south and the plain was inhabited? || "thus saith Yahvé of Hosts, namely: | judgment of truth judge ye, and love and compassion practise ye towards one another; || and widow and orphan, stranger and helpless do not oppress, | and evil

Vv. 2, 3 form a parenthesis : the inquiry had come to the new temple through a deputation from the people at Bethel, of whom the two most important only are here mentioned by name, and the deputation could not well appear in the temple without presents and offerings, comp. viii. 21, 22. The earlier temple was destroyed in the fifth month, 2 Kings xxv. 8-10. As regards the similar days of mourning mentioned ver. 5 and viii. 19, comp. Jer. ch. xli.; 2 Kings xxv. 21 sq.; Jer. lii. 6, 7; 2 Kings xxv. 1 and *History of Israel*, V., 22, 114 (IV., 30 sq., 149).

1. Have ye perhaps by your fasting fasted *me*, *i.e.*, compelled, necessitated, macerated me? does bodily compulsion compel the spirit? Thus Zakharya, with a bold but plain turn of language, once more takes up the Hebrew word for *fasting* and construes it with the accusative of the person whom the fast, the compulsion, affects; and in the translation this construction has been imitated.— Or, on the other hand, when ye eat and drink on festive occasions or at other

towards one another meditate not in your heart!" ‖ But they refused to give heed and put forth a rebellious shoulder, | and their ears they dulled not to hear, ‖ and their heart they made as a diamond, not to hear the doctrine and the words which Yahvé of Hosts sent by his spirit through the earlier prophets: | so there came great displeasure from Yahvé of Hosts, ‖ and as he called and they heard not, | "so shall they call and I not hear!" said Yahvé of Hosts, ‖ "and I will whirl them over all the nations which they know not!" and the land became desolate behind them, so that none passed on and none turned, | and the pleasant land was made a desolation. ‖

viii. 2.

1 And the word of Yahvé of Hosts came saying: Thus saith Yahvé of Hosts: I am jealous for Ssion with great jealousy, | and with great indignation am I jealous for her! ‖ Thus saith Yahvé: I return unto Ssion and dwell in the midst of Jerusalem, | so that Jerusalem shall be called the city of faithfulness, and the mountain of Yahvé of Hosts the holy mountain! ‖ Thus saith Yahvé of Hosts: there will yet old men and old women dwell in the streets of Jerusalem, | each holding his

times, do ye think that ye gratify *me*, that I share pains or pleasures of sense? vv. 5, 6. O, no; do not imagine that you can influence me by this or by fasting and a complaining mood! ye make that a chief matter, but I must show you how little things of that kind are meritorious before God! Have ye then not heard what a few but necessary general commands Yahvé caused to be given to the people by the prophets in the noblest times? They are the principal things, that which Yahvé in reality requires, and amongst them there is not even the mention of fasting,

2. But now a new and better time commences for those for whom the terrible lessons of former times cannot have been sent in vain: this is the true view of the present, and as certainly as now in this important time the

vv. 7-10; and if the nation of earlier times had fulfilled these few great requirements and bent its shoulders to this easy yoke, they would have remained prosperous always: but they hardened themselves against them, and so all kinds of calamities and punishments came just as they had been threatened, all the misery of the exile! vv. 11-14. Vv. 13, 14 the language becomes very cursory, the threat being made the more vivid and forcible by the introduction of the original words, and its fulfilment being then immediately also described in similar words.

Community takes a new form may a prosperous Messianic future be expected. Thus the prophet repeats here in the first instance, viii. 1-8, in various forms almost the same glorious hopes which he had already

5 *

staff for great age; || and the streets of the city will be filled with boys and girls, | playing in her streets. || Thus saith Yahvé of Hosts: when it seemeth marvellous to the remnant of this people in those days, | will it also seem marvellous to me? saith Yahvé of Hosts. || Thus saith Yahvé of Hosts: behold I save my people from the land of the rising, | and from the land of the setting of the sun, || and bring them that they may dwell in the midst of Jerusalem : | then they will be unto me a people and I will be unto them God in truth and righteousness! ||

3.

Thus saith Yahvé of Hosts: let your hands be strong, ye who hear in these days these words from the mouth of the prophets, | who have been since the house of Yahvé of Hosts, 10 the temple, was founded to be finished! || for before those days there was no value for man and no value for beast, | he that went out or came in had no peace from the oppressor, and I delivered men one to another: || but now I am not as in the former days unto the remnant of this people, saith Yahvé of Hosts, || but the seed of peace, the vine will yield her fruit, and the earth will yield her produce and the heavens their dew, | and I cause the remnant of this people to possess all that; || and as ye were a curse among the nations, house of Yuda and house of Israel! so will I save you that ye may become a blessing; | fear not, let your hands be strong! || For

expressed, i. 14, 16; ii. 14-17 and elsewhere; Jerusalem which is at present so thinly populated, where undoubtedly after the depopulating storms of the exile so few aged people were living, will still be filled with old and young inhabitants, "Isa." lxv. 20; and though such promises may appear to contemporaries as too marvellous, the prophet correctly perceives that according to the divine purpose they contain nothing impossible, after Gen. xviii. 14. Ver. 3, after Isa. i. 21. Accordingly, the further exhortation follows,

3. vv. 9-15, only be courageous and fearless, ye who have such promises in this important time! for although formerly, in the times of the Chaldean rule in Palestine, the life of man and beast was valueless, no security in business, universal disorder, ver. 11, henceforth an entirely new state of things shall arise, the reconciliation between Yahvé and the nation shall be dominant, the vine, the plant of peace, iii. 10, as its sign, shall without interruption bear its fruit for the reconciled nation, vv. 11, 12, from Hos. ii. 23, so that in the same degree as they were formerly a curse amongst the nations, *i.e.*, were as cursed by Yahvé an object and example of the curse amongst men

thus saith Yahvé of Hosts: as I determined to do evil to you when your fathers provoked me, saith Yahvé of Hosts, | 15 and I repented not: || so have I in these days contrariwise determined to do good to Jerusalem and the house of Yuda; fear ye not! || These are the words which ye shall do: | speak ye truth one to another, truth and judgment of peace judge ye in your gates, || and let none think evil against another in his heart, and an oath of lies love ye not! | for all that is what I hate, saith Yahvé. ||

4.

And the word of Yahvé of Hosts came unto me saying: || thus saith Yahvé of Hosts: the fast of the fourth and the fast of the fifth, and the fast of the seventh and the fast of the tenth, shall be to the house of Yuda joy and gladness and happy 20 feasts! | but love ye truth and peace! || Thus saith Yahvé of Hosts: it will yet be that nations and inhabitants of many cities come, || and the inhabitants of the one go to another saying " let us go continually to gain the favour of Yahvé!" and " to seek Yahvé of Hosts will I also go!" || thus many nations and powerful peoples come to seek Yahvé of Hosts in Jerusalem and to gain Yahvé's favour. || Thus saith Yahvé of Hosts: in those days it will be that ten people from all tongues of the nations lay hold of — | that they lay hold of the skirt of a Yudean saying " let us go with you! for we heard that God is with you!" ||

also, they now become a blessing, ver. 13, from Gen. xii. 2; "Isa." lxv. 15: he who formerly executed his threat without alteration will also execute this promise without diminution, vv. 14, 15. He does not require much on their part as the condition of this salvation: they are the few well-known great commandments, vv. 16, 17, comp. vii. 9, 10.

4. From these two suppositions it follows clearly that according to the divine intention all mourning - feasts ought henceforth to be changed into bright and cheerful days—if the nation does but fulfil the above condition! ver. 19. Without doubt, the fair days will yet come when amongst the Heathen themselves the noblest rivalry arises to learn to know Yahvé and his doctrine from the first source at the right place! vv. 20-23, from Isa. ii. 2-4 combined with Isa. iv. 1.

vii 6, the double כי must be understood acc. § 362 b, the antithesis and emphasis of the language being only thus brought out.

viii. 6, it might be supposed that החם stood for הָאֵלֶּה, *these:* but this supposition is as little allowable here as ver. 10, inasmuch as Zakharya will certainly not have confounded these fundamentally different ideas in his language. We may however perceive that his language is here, as elsewhere in his book and particularly in this piece, ch. vii., viii., somewhat compressed and strained, and the sense more fully expressed would be: if it appears to the reduced remnant of the people now living (who are precisely on account of their small numbers much inclined to doubt such promises of a far more glorious age as yet to arrive) impossible that *then in those days* anything of that kind can take place.

Ver. 9, it might be thought that אֲשֶׁר refers, contrary to the accents, not to the prophets but to those who are addressed. But manifestly Zakharya does not intend himself and Haggái exclusively, but also many other prophets who had laboured since the commencement of the new settlement in the year 536 B.C. Accordingly the accents are correct, and *those days,* ver. 10, are those of the years before that great new period. Only we must then read מִיָּמִים with the LXX instead of בַּיָּמִים.

At the close, ver. 17, he meant to say: *all this* (accusative) *I hate,* but in the midst of the sentence the more extended and lively division of the sentence by means of the relative construction is introduced, as vv. 20 and 23.

3. MAL'AKHI.

It is remarkable how greatly this small book, which as the latest closes the entire series, differs even from the two which precede it, as regards those matters of outward form even to which the eye is first attracted in the case of books. While the two previous books contained particulars with respect to the names of their authors and the times when they laboured, after the manner of the books of the older prophets, information in both respects is absent from this book, just as was the case with those fly-sheets of the time of the Chaldean rule, Vol. IV., p. 225—Vol. V., p. 34; and the small book which now follows might itself be looked upon as another example of such fly-leaves. For the times in which the public labours of prophets appeared once more under the Persian rule possible in the ancient manner, very soon passed away; and so far the endeavour of Haggái and Zakharya to bring back the influential labours of the earlier prophets had been in vain. It appeared only too soon that the new Jerusalem was no longer adapted for such labours; and here once more only was there revived one of those fly-sheets which had been customary before Haggái and Zakharya.

Particular notes of times are not found in this prophet: still, it follows from general indications that he probably did not write until some fifty years after Haggái and Zakharya. The exile already lies in the distant past and is not referred to at all; the temple had at that time been long finished, and the priests possessed not merely the preponderating authority with regard to it, but had thereby already acquired a kind of arrogance and covetousness which continued to develop itself increasingly in the course of the fifth and fourth centuries, and ended with the establishment of a fully-developed hierarchy, i. 6—ii. 9; iii. 3, 4. The new Jerusalem had arrived at a tolerable condition of order and repose, although it might be but weak: the lofty enthusiasm, however, of the days of the redemption from the exile had long ago passed away. Since those who conscientiously adhered to the regulations of the Pentateuch, as they were already interpreted with painful scrupulousness, notwithstanding did not live to see any great and splendid times, and the ancient Messianic promises appeared quite to fail to arrive, as a consequence, on the one hand, a dangerous indifference as to moral distinctions and the entire ancient religion had already arisen, and, on the other, a decidedly querulous life along with the arrogance and the unbelief of others, ii. 17—iii. 18; in short, we already meet here, as in the similar book of Ecclesiastes, the germs, though as yet in an undeveloped stage, of the three great divisions which arose in the heart of the ancient religion and continued to grow more marked in the subsequent centuries. Moreover, the important question regarding mixed marriages had already been proposed, ii. 10-16, which 'Ezra and Nehemya had so violently decided most likely not long before.

In opposition to the perversities and misconceptions of this time, we find here that it is still not too late for a prophet, under impulses like those of ancient times, to lift up the voice of Yahvé of Hosts ; this prophet, like one of olden times, does not scruple (although probably himself a priest) to call the priests also to a strict account ; and he is still able to utter many a vigorous word such as would be worthy of previous prophetic times. Still, on the whole, the power is not at all equal to the will, and it is quite plain that the prophetic office was completely declining. For there is not the slightest proof that the prophet had also spoken in public upon his subjects, although they concern solely the public conduct of his fellow-countrymen, and although he himself lived in Jerusalem. The ancient prophetic phrases appear again, but the subject-matter is never treated as if the author had previously exhaustively handled it in an oral discourse, and as if his book were the reflexion of what he had publicly spoken. On the contrary, the style of colloquy and of the didactic manner of the schools makes itself felt here as an entirely new phenomenon, inasmuch as the discourse presents a short proposition, then brings forward the doubtful questions which could be raised in objection to it, and finally answers these questions at length. Instead of public life, therefore, we see that the life of the schools and learning had already become predominant ; and in this book the two different manners, the ancient prophetic and the modern dialogistic manner, are still found together, but the prophetic manner is preserved almost as by way of tradition and imitation. Moreover, apart from this unusual combination of two distinct manners, the style and language has retained a good degree of beauty and smoothness, when the late age is considered, quite unlike what we find in the somewhat later book of Ecclesiastes.

Another feature, connected with the powerful influence of the learning of the schools, and one which forms an entirely new characteristic of this last prophet, is the nature of the general arrangement and division of the book. For the author brings together the various matters on which he has to speak under certain principal truths and brief propositions, which he prefers also to place in an incisive form at the head of his discussions; thus the special matters which he has to handle appear simply as applications and inferences. This is really more like a learned essay, more of a book than a spoken discourse; and no earlier prophet arranges his work by following various leading propositions of this kind. We find here three propositions concerning God according to which the whole book is arranged, the first portion of it considering Yahvé as the loving Father and Lord of His people, i. 2—ii. 9, the second as the only God and Father, ii. 10-16, the third as the eternally unchangeable, absolutely Righteous One and the final Judge! With this arrangement the conclusion, at all events as treating of the eternal Judge, can be quite in the elevated manner of the older prophets. Moreover, each of these three portions is carefully divided into strophes, an artistic form in which this latest prophet follows the custom of previous times; the strophes belong to those of medium size, but their size is no longer so strictly measured.

The mention of one or more prophets of that time, still so frequent in the case of Haggái and Zakharya, is not found in this prophet at all. Even the word itself does not occur, save that the author, as if clearly conscious of the complete extinction of prophetism in his age, points to the reappearance of a prophet Elias, iii. 23, comp. ver. 1.

But though our prophet, therefore, caused his flying-sheet to go forth without his own name, the hand which connected it with the collection of smaller pieces of various prophets distinguished it with decisive ingenuity, after the word iii. 1, as the work of a man who was truly called מַלְאָכִי, inasmuch as this name may signify not only *my Messenger*, or God's Messenger, but also the Latin *Angelicus*. Comp. Vol. I., p. 100. We shall most likely never be able to discover the real name of the author. As he is so perfectly familiar with the priests, as regards all their weaknesses and excellences, and also gives evidence of possessing a highly learned education and shows that noble frankness which is the inimitable mark of lofty spirits, we might think that he was 'Ezra himself, since he undoubtedly belonged to his time. This small book would be certainly worthy of 'Ezra: but on the other hand his famous name would surely have remained attached to the book, if it had really been written by him. And so far as we are concerned, no reason exists why we should not call the prophet, who is really like an angel, by that name with which the hand of the writer of the heading of the book has already distinguished him. Comp. the remarks made on a late occasion in the *Gött. Gel. Anz.* 1865, p. 1722 sq.

i.
1   Oracle of the word of Yahvé to Israel by Mal'akhi.

1. *Yahvé the loving Father.*

Ch. i. 2—ii. 9.

Yahvé is the loving Father and Lord of Israel: Israel ought therefore to meet him with love and esteem, and most of all the priests, who are still more closely bound to him by the ancient prerogatives, ought to do this. But it is the exact opposite of this which the present priests do: they who are only able by the same spiritual power and work which once distinguished their fathers to maintain their dignity and vocation, now give false, one-sided doctrine according as they are paid, ii. 8, 9, and refuse, having become arrogant and luxurious, to receive the sacrificial loaves, probably somewhat coarse and mean, which the poorer people offer, whilst they themselves, when they are obliged to present sacrifices, do not at all scruple to bring the worst animals, i. 7-14. Such conduct does not flow from love and esteem of Yahvé, but is, on the contrary, the evidence of the slighting of his love. After the prophet, therefore, has in the first of the five strophes established the principle of the love of Yahvé for Israel by brief reference to history, he shows in the four subsequent strophes the sins of the priests against this truth; how they even seek their own ends with the temple sacrifices, i. 6-10, which is all the more infatuated inasmuch as the fear of Yahvé is now spreading more and more amongst all the nations of the earth, i. 11-14; accordingly the divine threat must come upon these priests, ii. 1-4, which have strayed so far from their noble original model, from that which Levi was at the first, ii. 5-9.

1.

I love you! saith Yahvé; ask ye "wherein hast thou loved us?" | —is not 'Esau the brother of Yaqob? saith Yahvé: and yet I loved Yaqob! || and 'Esau I hated and made his mountains a desolation, and his inheritance for jackals of the wilderness. || When Edóm saith "we are smitten down, yet let us again build up the desolations!" thus saith Yahvé of Hosts: they will build but I pull down, | so that they may be called the border of wickedness, the people which Yahvé curseth for
5 ever! || and your eyes will see it, | while ye say "great is Yahvé beyond the border of Israel!" ||

1. The prophet deems a historical proof, which was precisely at that time capable of being most easily understood, sufficient to establish the principle which he really intends. The difficulties between Edóm and Israel are well-known, which had broken out again with new and bitter acuteness, since Jerusalem had begun to be restored (*History of Israel*, V., 80 sq. (IV., 105 sq.)). Many things since the destruction of Jerusalem might lead to the false idea that Edóm and not Israel was the nation preferred by God: and yet the opposite must be maintained. For if the entire history of Edóm be compared with that of Israel, as well as the ancient prophecies regarding both nations, Gen. xxvii. 39, it is seen that Edóm was both less favourably placed from the earliest times, having had assigned to it a barren, uncultivated land, and had subsequently remained without any true and lasting prosperity, and in addition is incapable of attaining higher culture; for if they imagine that they have for once improved their position (just as Israel now has higher ambitions, notwithstanding the desolation of the exile, and this not without some result), the fruitlessness of their efforts will nevertheless soon be manifested before the eyes of Israel itself, because the Edómites lack the firm foundation of genuine fear of Yahvé, and with that all profounder wisdom and judgment. Here, therefore, there must have been wanting from earliest times the strength which makes the true community prosperous and never suffers it

2.

A son honoureth a father, a servant his lord : | yet if I am a father, where is my honour ? and if I am a lord, where is my fear ? saith Yahvé of Hosts unto you priests, despisers of my name ! | Say ye "wherein have we despised thy name ?" ||— presenting upon mine altar defiled bread ! | say ye "wherein have we defiled thee ?"—in your saying "Yahvé's table is defiled !" || and when ye present a blind (animal) for sacrifice, is it not evil ! and when ye present a lame and sick one, is it not evil ! | offer it now to thy governor—will he be gracious to thee ? or show regard to thee ? saith Yahvé of Hosts. || Therefore seek ye now the favour of God that he may be merciful unto us ! | —from your hand is this come to pass—will he
10 show a regard for you ? saith Yahvé of Hosts ; || would that there were but one among you, that he might shut the doors, that ye lighten not my altar for nought ! I have no pleasure in you, saith Yahvé of Hosts, and a gift I receive not from your hand with favour. ||

entirely to decline and perish: a thought which is incontestably true when understood from a general point of view, although it must be allowed that it is here expressed with some exaggeration under the influence of the decided national feelings which obtained a firmer hold with the progress of time. Still, the general principle remains, that a community which in accordance with historical fact is conscious of something higher and eternal at work within it, must also recognize therein the more particular traces of the love of Yahvé, the work of which once commenced in the community and may still further perpetuate itself in its consequences.

2. The priests who are here aimed at, in rapid transition, have, it is true, no idea that they depise Yahvé's name, ver. 6 : but they despise it by the simple fact that they themselves as people of impure intentions nevertheless bring sacrifices, which must on that very account be impure and repugnant to Yahvé, Hag. ii. 12-14 ; but if that oracular utterance is still too lofty and unintelligible for them, so that they ask whereby they had then really defiled Yahvé (and his sacrifices), the prophet can tell them with greater particularity: thereby that they look upon what, it may be the poor offer, as too bad, as defiling the sacred table, and refuse to eat of things which they ought to eat according to the law ; while, on the other hand, they do not look upon it as evil if they choose the worst and most illegal animals when they are obliged to present sacrificial animals ! But even a human lord, whom men approach with petitions and prayers for help, does not accept such bad offerings ; how much less will Yahvé ! although they pray to him, it will be in vain ! since their hand practises such deeds of evil intention (the parenthesis, ver. 9) ;

3.

For from the rising of the sun even to his setting is my name great among the nations, and everywhere is incense and sacrifice offered to my name even pure gifts, | yea great is my name among the nations, saith Yahvé of Hosts. || But ye profane it, | in that ye say "Yahvé's table is defiled, and its fruit contemptible is it to eat it!" || and ye say "behold what loathing!" and ye push it away, saith Yahvé of Hosts, but ye bring the stolen and the lame and the sick: | yet if ye bring the gift, shall I receive it with favour from your hand? saith Yahvé. || But cursed is he that defraudeth and there is in his herd a male but he voweth and sacrificeth a blemished female to the Lord! | for a great king am I, saith Yahvé of Hosts, and my name is feared among the nations. ||

4.

ii.
1   Therefore unto you this commandment cometh ye priests! || if ye hear not and if ye lay it not to heart to give honour to

it might even be better wholly to close the temple, in order not to burn the lights by the altar to no purpose:

the favour of Yahvé cannot be felt here!

3. As many Israelites remained all along amongst the Heathen, and the conversion of the Heathen began at that time to be more common on that very account, the prophet was able very properly to point these priests to the growing esteem in which the religion of Yahvé was coming to be held even beyond the limited confines of Jerusalem. What a contrast! whilst the worship of Yahvé increases everywhere and does not therefore in the least depend on you, ye priests of Jerusalem, ye despise him by such a contempt of the produce, *i.e.*, of the food or sacrifices of the sacred table, as if it were something to eat which caused you great trouble and loathing, your-

selves bringing bad, illegal sacrifices: can Yahvé look with pleasure on such sacrifices? No, he whose religion does not in the remotest degree depend on Jerusalem and the favour of its priests, must curse every form of deceit practised with sacred things! ver. 14. — As regards the words vv. 11, 12, which are so often incorrectly understood, comp. the refutation of the perverse Papal view in the *Jahrbb. der Bibl. Wiss.*, VIII., p. 161 sq. Equally without foundation is the opinion that the prophet supposes that the worship of *Ahura-Mazda*, or that of *Zeus*, was the same as that of Yahvé; such an idea could never occur to a prophet of Yahvé, even in the age of Mal'akhi.

4. Therefore hear ye this commandment, which it is all the more necessary

I should lay upon you that I am more closely connected with you than with my name, saith Yahvé of Hosts : | then I send upon you the curse and I curse your blessings! | and I have already cursed them, because ye lay it not to heart. ‖ Behold I rebuke unto you the arm, | and scatter refuse upon your faces—the refuse of your feasts, that it may draw you to itself! ‖ that ye may know that I sent forth unto you this commandment, | since my covenant was with Levi! saith Yahvé of Hosts.

5.

5   My covenant was with him life and peace, and I gave him fear so that he feared me, | and before my name he humbled himself; ‖ doctrine of truth was in his mouth, and wrong was not found in his lips : | in peace and in uprightness he walked with me, and many he brought back from guilt. ‖ For the lips of a priest keep knowledge, and doctrine is sought from his mouth, | for he is the messenger of Yahvé of Hosts. ‖ But ye are turned aside from the way, ye have caused many to fall by the doctrine, | ye have corrupted Levi's covenant! saith Yahvé of Hosts : ‖ therefore I also make you contemptible and despised to all the people, | in proportion as ye keep not my ways, and are partial in doctrine. ‖

the laity, according to the ancient institutions and laws (Ex. xxxii.—xxxiv.), that I have with you a special covenant, the substance of which implies that the one side may always strictly remind the other of his duties or hold out the threat of the punishments which necessarily follow the violation of the covenant. Ye pronounce blessings, best wishes, in the community, under the supposition that what ye bless is also blessed by me; but if ye continue to act as in the past, so that ye also bless merely with the mouth, in heart are estranged from me, I pronounce the curse with your blessing, and have already pronounced it! ii. 1, 2. Yea, that ye may observe the seriousness of this threat, I will with rebukes dry up the arm which ye raise to bless with such intentions, and throw in your faces the filth or offal of your feasts and sacrificial animals (Ps. cxviii. 27), that it may draw you into association with it, since ye dissolve your association with purity and holiness!

5. How glorious was the time formerly when this covenant of Yahvé with Levi continued to exist unviolated! It was life and peace, nothing short of that, which Yahvé desired to give them by means of this covenant, and really gave them as long as they were true to it (as it were the articles of this covenant), and genuine fear (religion) given to them, like every celestial gift, by Yahvé, and kept by them, was on their side the bond of the covenant; thus they supplied the model of perfect priests, true teachers and reformers of the nation, just as the priest is meant to be as the messenger and represen-

tative of God among men, vv. 6, 7; comp. Ecc. v. 6. But by departure from the eternal path, by false or even one-sided (party) doctrine, which favours the rich in preference to the poor, and thus by the misguidance of many, ye have spoilt that covenant, and accordingly ye must also be surrendered to public contempt in so far as (or exactly in proportion to the state of the case) ye have become degenerate. The words ver. 6 have great similarity with "Isa." liii. 9, 12.

The words i. 4 are historically very important, inasmuch as they furnish, according to all indications, the earliest evidence as regards the inroads of the Nabatheans and the check of the Edómite people by them, comp. *History of Israel*, V., 350 sq. (IV., 458 sq.).

i. 13 the *Athnach* ought to be placed before the second וְהֵבֵאתֶם.

ii. 3 זֹרֵעַ must, according to the connexion and the structure of the members of this verse, be read with the LXX Vulg. instead of זֶרַע. The far more unusual *the arm*, and not *your arm*, is intentionally chosen here; the latter would have naturally suggested the arm of man in the ordinary sense, which is not what is here intended.

The thought of ii. 4 is also somewhat unusual, where it is said that they shall be thus punished (1) in order that they may perceive that God has really said the above words i. 6–ii. 1; and (2) *because his covenant was* (originated) *with Levi*, in that God has commanded them in the Pentateuch, as may very well be said, to remember and never to forget that his covenant is intended to be with Levi in a special sense, and in the manner in which it was concluded with this tribe, לִהְיוֹת neither in this connexion of the sentence acc. § 237 c but acc. § 217 d *ad fin*. Hence this thought is continued vv. 5, 6.

ii. 5 וָאֶתְּנָה must be read with LXX Vulg. instead of וָאֶתְנֵם.

ii. 9 כְּפִי אֲשֶׁר signifies *according to the proportion in which*, or *just as it must be inasmuch as ye.* . . . .

2. Yahvé the only God.

Ch. ii. 10-16.

The prophet now applies the highest principle of the unity of the creator to a matter which caused at that time much disquiet and a good deal of injustice, the matter of mixed marriages. We know from the books of 'Ezra and Nehemya with what inflexible logic the leaders of the people at that time punished the mixed marriages and commanded all those which had been concluded to be dissolved without exception. Neither can this prophet justify such marriages with heathen women, inasmuch as they violated the good old custom of the patriarchs and might by too close contact with heathenism become dangerous to Mosaism. On the other hand, however, he rejects with great earnestness all thoughtless separations, by which it so often happened that absolute wrong was done by the husband to the weaker party, so that the women often went away from the temple bitterly weeping; and if such separations may at that time have not been infrequent generally, they nevertheless become still more frequent on account of that merciless command to send away all heathen-born women, in pursuance of which it could easily happen that such women as were gradually giving up their heathenism and turning to the temple at Jerusalem were also sent away. This severe word concerning the inadmissability of any separations is that which is really original and important in our prophet's utterance: woman also, as created by the same God (Job xxxi. 15), has equal rights with the man, and a marriage once concluded is for all time sacred, that is the great doctrine which occupies the second strophe, vv. 13-16, exclusively, after the first has more by the way disapproved of the formation of mixed marriages.

1.

10 Have we not all one father? hath not one God created us? | wherefore shall we be unfaithful to one another, to profane the covenant of our fathers? || —Yuda became unfaithful, and abomination has been wrought in Israel and in Jerusalem, | in that Yuda profaned Yahvé's sanctuary which he loveth, and marrieth the daughter of a strange God. || May Yahvé cut off unto the man that doeth this race and representative from the tents of Yaqob | and one who may present a sacrifice to Yahvé of Hosts! ||

1. The commencement points immediately to the wrong committed by the divorces and is specially resumed again ver. 15: but as early as the last member of ver. 10, where the covenant of the fathers with Yahvé is mentioned, the discourse makes the transition to the preliminary observation which is further explained exclusively, vv. 11, 12. The marriage of heathen wives is also unfaithfulness towards the sanctuary which Yahvé loves, that is, the Community which is loved by Yahvé, acc. i. 2, and is sacred to him, acc. Ex. xix. 6, with its marriage which is sanctified by Yahvé, acc. ver. 15: whoever does that, may Yahvé exterminate his family, that none of his descendants may sacri-

2.

But this ye do further: the covering Yahvé's altar with tears, with weeping and groaning, | so that there can be no more regard unto the sacrifice, nor an acceptable thing taken at your hand! ‖ Say ye "wherefore?" | —because Yahvé hath been witness between thee and the wife of thy youth to whom thou becamest unfaithful, though she is thy companion and the wife of thy covenant! ‖ and hath not one created them, and doth not the whole spirit belong to him? and what doth the One seek? a seed of God! | therefore take heed for your spirit's sake, and be not unfaithful to the wife of thy youth! ‖ For he who from hatred breaketh wedlock, saith Yahvé Israel's God,— he covereth with cruelty his garment, saith Yahvé of Hosts: | so take heed for your spirit's sake and be not unfaithful!

fice for him again! almost as the Hindoos wish that a bad man may have no son or grandson to bring the funeral sacrifices.

2. If you are doubtful at first sight what is meant when it is said, ye cover with tears the altar, so that the divine mercy itself cannot bear to look toward a place which must be the witness of such groans of the cruelly persecuted unfortunates, I will tell you more plainly: they are the groans of the women who flee to the altar, driven thither by your unfaithfulness, whom ye thrust out of the marriage relationship although the covenant of marriage is not simply binding like any other contract, but is also a sacred contract, made before Yahvé as a witness, which cannot therefore be arbitrarily dissolved! vv. 13, 14. And has not then *one*, one and the same God (plain enough after, ver. 10, comp. an equally brief reference, Job xxxi. 15) created them, the woman no less than thyself, so that husband and wife are equal before him, and the husband may not proceed arbitrarily against the wife? and does not the remnant of the spirit, *i.e.*, the whole spirit (Zeph. i. 4), belong to this one God, even after death, so that the smallest part of it cannot be withdrawn from its accountability to him and his punishment Ecc. xii. 7)? and what does this one God require?—seed of God, *i.e.*, children begotten to his glory in holy matrimony, an object which is hindered by divorce. Accordingly the prophet properly admonishes the husbands repeatedly, to be on their guard with *their spirit*, because by this unfaithfulness the spirit also becomes guilty before God, spiritual well-being also is ruined for all time; for whoever from hatred, from mere passion, should put his wife away, would cover with cruelty *his* own *garment, i.e.*, that which is next to him, that which surrounds him with the protection of his garment, *i.e.*, his own wife.

ער וענה ver. 12 is understood, manifestly with great suitability to the sense, by the Pesh. and Targ. of *son* and *grandson*; as a fact several derivatives from the Arab. root *gharra* signify boy, child; עֶבֶד is then as *witness* probably equivalent to descendant, child, and the whole phrase a proverbial one of undoubtedly very ancient origin like בֵּין וְנֶכֶד, Job. xviii. 19. The Vulg. translates much less appropriately *magistrum et discipulum*. The collocation of the two words was made the more common on account of the similarity of their sound, and the similarity has been reproduced as far as possible in this translation.*

Ver. 16 the vocalization שֹׂנֵא and שַׁלַּח is better: *he that hateth by putting away*, acc. § 280 a, comp. Zech. vii. 3, which we can express in another way by saying, he that hating, or from hatred, putteth away, divorceth his wife. —A genuinely popular phrase is *his garment for his wife*, comp. Ovid, *Heroides*, XVI., 222, and *Koran, Sûr.* ii. 183.—*For the sake of your spirit*, acc. § 217 f. (3): for your spirit is thereby imperilled, its existence is really at stake in this matter. The variation in the use of the indefinite *thou* and *one* (Germ. *man*) in the same sentence even, ver. 15 b, is also a popular form of speech: the apodosis thereto is all the more emphatically expressed, on account of the parenthetical clause, by the word וְכִסָּה.

3. Yahvé the final unchangeable Judge.

Ch. ii. 17—iii. 24.

Those things which the prophet has further to say and to censure, he connects with the idea of Yahvé as the Righteous One and the Judge. There are particularly three sins against the truth of the divine righteousness which he has to lay to the charge of the whole nation: (1) the careless confounding of the moral ideas of good and evil, a peril into which very many easily came during this century, when they waited in vain for the fulfilment of the Messianic promises and the threatened general judgment; comp. *e.g.*, *Ecclesiastes;* (2) dishonesty as regards the temple, many refusing the tithes and other offerings, *e.g.*, the first-fruits, which were due according to the Pentateuch, on the false plea that the times were too unfavourable; (3) the complaining, discontented temper of many who though they observed outwardly the laws still looked with envy upon the prosperity of the proud, comp. Ps. lxxiii. In opposition to all these perversities, the prophet points to the eternal righteousness and to the certainty, how-

---

* The author's adaptation is: "*Gezeugten und zeugen.*"—Tᴿ.

ever things may seem, of a final judgment. Still, as if he observed that between the lofty height of this final judgment and the increasingly faint-hearted and unprophetic condition of those times there existed a wide impassable chasm, the prophet anticipates that a resuscitated Elias must go before the Lord (Yahvé) when he comes to judgment, in order to prepare the way by powerful teaching and a reconciliation of the restless and divided hearts—the plainest sign that prophetism is now conscious of its own extinction. This reference to the future, which is partly threatening and partly consoling, becomes the sole thought of the last of the four lengthy and symmetrical strophes, after those three perversities have been expounded in the first three; the book therefore closes at all events completely in the prophetic manner.

1.

Ye have wearied Yahvé with your words! Say ye "whereby have we wearied him?" | by your saying: "everyone that
iii. doeth evil is good in Yahvé's eyes, and in them he taketh
1 pleasure: or where is the God of judgment?" ‖ Behold I send you my messenger, that he may clear the way before me: | and unexpectedly will come unto his temple the Lord whom ye seek, and the Messenger of the covenant whom ye take pleasure in behold he cometh! saith Yahvé of Hosts. ‖ But who will bear the day of his coming, and who is he that standeth when he appeareth? | for he is as the smelter's fire and as the soap of the fullers; ‖ there sitteth a silver smelter and refiner —and he refineth the sons of Levi and purifieth them as gold and silver, | that they may be unto Yahvé offerers of sacrifices in righteousness, ‖ that the sacrifice of Yuda and Jerusalem may be pleasing to Yahvé as in the days of old and as in the
5 earlier years. ‖ So I come near to you to judgment and become a ready witness against the magicians and against the adulterers and against the false swearers, | and against those who oppress the hireling's hire, widow and orphan, and put down the stranger and fear not me! saith Yahvé of Hosts.

---

1. The *messenger of the covenant,* of the covenant between me and you,
iii. 1, whom I send to you on account ii. 4; Ps. lxxiv. 20: who this is,

2.

For I Yahvé have not changed: | but ye sons of Yaqob—have ye not altered? || From the days of your fathers have ye turned aside from my laws and have not kept them: | return unto me that I may return unto you! saith Yahvé of Hosts: || Say ye "wherein shall we return?]"—doth then a man rob God that ye rob me? | say ye "wherein have we robbed thee?"—in the tithe and the tribute! || With the curse
10 are ye cursed, and me will ye rob? | all ye people? || bring the whole of the tithe to the store-house, that there may be victuals in my house, and prove me now herewith! saith Yahvé of Hosts, | whether I do not open to you the windows of heaven and pour you out a blessing till there is no more room! || Then will I rebuke for you the devourer that he may not destroy unto you the fruit of the earth, | neither shall the vine in the field fail unto you, saith Yahvé of Hosts; || and all the nations will congratulate you, because ye will be a land of delight! saith Yahvé of Hosts.

when more particularly considered, is said vv. 23, 24; it is the returning Elias, regarding whom a good deal must have been said at that time in a book which has been lost, and in which he was spoken of as the gentlest and kindest messenger of God, notwithstanding the fact that he was invested with great power; he could accordingly be here briefly referred to as the messenger whom *they delight to see;* he was undoubtedly spoken of at some length in that book for the first time as one who should *go before* the final judge and prepare the way for him; comp. *History of Israel*, IV., 113; V., 178 (III., 590; IV., 230; V., 168). Thus the expression *whom ye seek*, *i.e.*, almost equivalent to *ye miss*, which is explained from ii. 17, does not mean the same as the expression *whom ye take delight in.*—But the Lord, when he really comes to the last judgment, most rigidly separates (after Isa. i. 25) all the bad elements of the multitude, the bad priests too (to refer once more retrospectively to what was said at greater length in the first section), so that then better sacrifices than now will be brought, vv. 2-4. Thus, in no other way, does he come to judgment, he who as omniscient is at the same time the ready witness against every kind of unrighteousness, ver. 5, comp. ii. 14.

2. The dishonesty as regards the temple is so much the more infatuated as the land is already unfruitful enough as if it were afflicted by the divine curse (comp. Hag. i. 5 sq.; ii. 14 sq.): is it intended in some way to force the divine mercy by robbing the temple and withholding legal dues? but Yahvé changes not, remains always the righteous God, ever ready to help also: it is Israel only that is really changed, and becoming more

3.

Your words are hard upon me! saith Yahvé; | Say ye "what have we talked over against thee?" || —ye say "it is vain to serve God! | and what profit is there that we watched his ward and that we walked mournfully before Yahvé of Hosts? ||
15 and so we congratulate the haughty; | they that work unrighteousness have nevertheless prospered! they have tempted God and nevertheless escaped!" || — But they that feared Yahvé once talked to one another | and Yahvé gave heed and listened, and a book of remembrance was written before him for those that feared Yahvé and thought upon his name! || they will be unto me, saith Yahvé of Hosts, in the day which I prepare for a possession, | that I may spare them as one spareth his son who serveth him; || then will ye contrariwise see what is the difference between the righteous and the unrighteous, between him that serveth God and him that serveth him not. ||

4.

For behold the day cometh burning as an oven, | and all the

disobedient to him has also grown continually weaker and frailer: therefore try Yahvé, if ye desire to try him, rather with sincere conversion and with the performance of the demands of the law, then he on his part will give you prosperity, not withhold from you the

3. Ye use among yourselves, not intending Yahvé to hear it, grievous and hard words against him, imagining that it was in vain ye had observed with mourning and fasting and bending the knee before him (Zech. vii., viii.) everything which he had in the Pentateuch prescribed for you to observe; ye imagine that it were better to congratulate the wicked, proud, unrighteous men and to follow their example, since they, notwithstanding their wicked doings and their tempting God thereby, were prosperous and in security! But the prophet has, on the other hand, ver. 16,

4. For that strict day of trial certainly draws near! ver. 19, comp. vv.

celestial blessing, with his rebuke, *i.e.*, by threat, keep from you the devourer, *i.e.*, the locusts, and cause the vine, the symbol of peace, to become fruitful, so that foreigners even observe that the divine approval rests upon this laud.

listened to the retired conversations of the devout, and knows that the secret thoughts and words of theirs are not forgotten by a Higher One, but have been written to their honour and their reward in an imperishable memorial volume (Ps. lvi. 9): such people will at the great day of judgment be treated by Yahvé as by a father even outwardly and visibly, after Ex. xix. 5, as his possession, *i.e.*, his house, his family and children, ver. 17; then ye fools will see the immense difference between the just and the unjust which ye now desire to overlook, ver. 18.

2, 3; Isa. v. 24. Then will the sun of righteousness, which is now darkened

haughty and whoever wrought unrighteousness will be stubble, and the day that cometh setteth them on fire, saith Yahvé of Hosts,—so that it leaveth them neither root nor branch. ||
20 Then unto you that fear my name the sun of righteousness will arise, bringing healing in his wings; | and ye go forth and leap like calves of the stall, || and tread down the unrighteous, surely they are dust under the soles of your feet | in the day which I will prepare, saith Yahvé of Hosts. || —Remember ye the doctrine of Moses my servant | to whom I committed on Horeb concerning all Israel laws and judgments! || Behold I send you Elias the prophet | before the great and terrible day of Yahvé cometh : || he will turn again the fathers' heart to the sons, and the sons' hearts to the fathers, | lest I come and smite the earth with the ban ! ||

to so many, rise in full splendour, bringing to the faithful in his rapid flight (Zeph. i. 18) also the healing of all wounds, so that they, having been quickly invigorated and emboldened, irresistibly conquer, vv. 20, 21 and Zech. ix. 15, 16.—Observe only the condition, forget not your duty, ver. 22: those who do their best Yahvé himself will assist by the mission of Elias, comp. ver. 1, who must restore domestic peace, in order that the arrival of the judge may result in the general welfare and not the general condemnation and punishment, in order that a new, reformed Community may be possible ?

---

iii. 6 פְּלִיתִי must be a new verb formed from פְּלָא, *two kinds*, or *sorts*: the latter itself is, as the Ethiopic *keľé* shows, a common possession of the ancient Semitic languages and merely a variation of שָׁנָה, inasmuch as in it also, as is proved § 267 b, *note*, the idea *two* is derived from that of splitting or separating. The sentence is interrogative, as ii. 15, and the translation *have ye not altered?* is intentional, with a view of expressing the unusual Hebrew word.

עַד־בְּלִי־דַי iii. 10 literally until it no longer suffices, *i.e.*, until there is no more space for the blessing, just like Zech. x. 10.

Ver. 16. אָז, acc. § 354 a, undoubtedly expresses the complete antithesis to vv. 14, 15, but it expresses this in the purely prophetic manner, in the form of new vision which has suddenly come upon the speaker, and here particularly inasmuch as the prophet is able not only to see the most varied things one after another, but also to *hear* them ; comp. the remarks in Vol. III., 148, on Jer. xi. 18.—Of course they who fear God, even in the severe distress of the time, secretly talk over with each other quite different matters from those which the prophet censured above, vv. 12-15.

APPENDIX.

Prophetic Aftergrowths in the Kanon.

Although the mighty ancient tree of Hebrew prophetism had fallen completely into decay, it had nevertheless sent its roots too deep into the life and especially the literature of the nation, and it had been too full of the energy of true life, to permit it to suddenly disappear without some new aftershoots. Many of these later after-shoots start up indeed very soon with peculiar luxuriance and form a distinct kind of literature; they survive also until after the second destruction of Jerusalem, and find their way unobserved even into the territory of Christianity. But inasmuch as a new loftier spirit, such as could meet the needs of the later age, did not at the same time constitute the vital energy of the majority of these offshoots of the ancient tree, they remained, notwithstanding all the luxuriance of their growth, mostly but sapless and feeble scions, which lived simply upon the sap of the old underground roots; they have more of the nature of merely learned imitations and purely literary essays, called forth by the lofty power of the books of early prophecy, but not springing like these from really active and public prophetic life; and thus they only furnish in general the proof that the flourishing period of true prophetism in this community had long been passed, and that no art and skill in imitation could bring it back again. At the same time, they occupy by no means all the same level; and some of them, at all events as respects the deepest tendencies of their spirit, attain something of the elevation and greatness of the ancient prophetic books. It is not consistent with the limits of this work to examine the whole of these aftergrowths: we can only briefly describe their nature and various classes, particularly with reference to those pieces which have come down to us in the Kanon of the Old Testament. With a view to this we will explain the books of Yona and Daniel at length, and for special reasons take the book of Barûkh as well.

1. *The Collectors of Oracles.*

We have previously, Vol. I., pp. 85-106, examined the manner of the collection of prophetic writings, which was done principally towards the time of the decay of the original prophetic power, and seen how at that time the finest pieces from the older and larger books were put together in new books. It only remains for us now to say that such collectors had certainly themselves always preserved some kind of prophetic feeling and tact, as the last of the long line of prophets. This is quite natural in the case of such arts and literatures: the ancient epic songs, for instance, were probably in the case of all early nations reduced to order by the last epic poets, and the first collectors of the early Arabic lyrics, *e.g.*, Abu-Temmam, were themselves, to some extent, good poets. And we may perceive clearly from certain indications that in this way the earliest Hebrew collectors of oracles were still conscious of a certain prophetic vein within themselves, and still preserved sufficient confidence to work on in the spirit of the great earlier prophets. For it has been before shown, Vol. I., p. 95, that the collector of Isa. i.—xxiii. took the liberty to make his own prophetic continuation of the oracle of Yesaya at the close of each half of that collection; and to the same collector we probably owe also (see *supra* p. 24 sq.) the following original piece, xxiv.—xxvii., which he desired to add as an appendix. Again, the author who (see *supra* p. 1 sq.) wrote the piece Jer. l., li. quite in the style of Yéremyâ, is at the same time the reconstructor of the entire book of Yéremyâ, as if he believed himself to possess prophetic power enough to make the book more productive for his contemporaries. Indeed, if it is established (see *supra* p. 3) that this same later prophet also wrote the piece "Isa." xxxiv., xxxv., we might venture to accept, somewhat more confidently than we have done above, Vol. III., p. 89, the opinion that he also had already proposed the transference of the oracles of Yéremyá concerning foreign nations to the end of the book in order to be able thus more easily to add his own piece, l., li., as an appendix; for in the same way as he would in that case have appended also the extract from the national records, lii., to the book of Yéremyá as a closing piece, he would have enlarged the genuine piece of Yesaya's, xxviii.—xxxii. (xxxiii.) not only by his own continuation, xxxiv., xxxv., but also have concluded the whole with the similar extract from the national records, xxxvi. —xxxix. The last conjecture would, it is true, be more evidently attested if the formula of transition עד הנה דברי ישעיהו were found after Isa. xxxv. as well as after Jer. li. ; still, I do not think I ought to completely suppress an idea which has frequently forced itself upon me. It is conjectured above, Vol. I., p. 100, that the book of the so-called Minor Prophets was closed by Mal'akhi's own hand. And thus in any case the principle is established, that one of the first of the aftergrowths of ancient prophetism led to the collection and rejuvenating of the more important earlier pieces, and that the last prophets of the ancient type themselves present to us this transition into an entirely different age.

2. *The prophetic writers of Legends. Book of Yona.*

1. It has often been shown earlier in this work how much the literary prophets recount of their own personal history, sometimes at length and at other times by way of mere reference, so that every larger book of a prophet furnishes also the best idea of his true life. Nevertheless, what a prophet wrote about himself was always undoubtedly but a small

portion of all the things he experienced, or of what his contemporaries narrated concerning him, since it was precisely the life of an ancient prophet which always found its true object in the light of perfect publicity and in the midst of the most stirring national movements. Moreover, the most ancient prophets wrote but little or nothing in any shape. Accordingly it follows that a great number of oral stories and histories about prophets might just as well as other popular traditions and legends be collected, grow up and receive fresh forms, be preserved through many generations, and travel far through various times and vicissitudes; and inasmuch as the most characteristic tendencies of the ancient nation found their expression in the prophetic life, it was exactly the legends of the prophets which would become in the times subsequent to Davîd the most important and finest portion of all national stories. When, however, a series of such legends were collected by an able editor simply for the sake of the story, a great example of which is preserved in the Books of the Kings in the case of the stories of Elias and Elisha, it is not that kind of literature which we are here concerned with. We must remember that a legend about prophets might be revived and be newly shaped with greater freedom in the same spirit in which it first arose, *i.e.*, under the influence of prophetic thoughts, in such a way that it would serve the author simply as pliable material for the elaboration of his own principles. At the time of the decadence of every independent literature there is found (as we should now say) such a novelistic treatment of stories and legends. We need here only refer to the Hindoo *Kathâ-sarit-sâgara* and to the *Thousand and One Nights*. The course of ancient Hebrew literature is distinguished from that of the other ancient literatures not as regards its form, but only as regards its subject-matter and its higher prophetic tendencies. At a time when prophetism inevitably approached its decadence, a great quantity of prophetic legends existed amongst the Hebrews, coming the more into the foreground in proportion as the public labours of the prophets became more a thing of the past. It is easy to imagine that this superabundance of legendary narrative at such a time produced at length a desire to collect and recast it : at the same time many of the prophetic truths, which had formerly been uttered with such energy, produced still such abiding effects that they also sought in the fresh revival and presentation of these legends to obtain complete utterance. Thus the last prophets themselves were able to be the inaugurators of this late after-growth of prophetic literature.

2. We possess a pretty early and at the same time very excellent example of this kind in the *Book of Yona*. Examination shows, it is true, that this little book forms in itself a perfectly intelligible and complete piece of narrative : yet the feeling is soon obtained that a multitude of similar pieces, containing narratives from the lives and uncommon fortunes of other ancient prophets, might exist in addition to this, and that this small series of historical pictures and legends might easily be worked up into a much larger series. For it is surely very unlikely that an author should intend to write simply these few prosaic words (I mean in times when literature had not yet split itself up into the fritters of leaves for the day and hour as in the present day), and it would be as easy to take a piece out of the *Arabian Nights*, or out of the *Kathâ-sarit-sâgara*, and place it by itself as this small narrative piece, now in a separate form and received into the Book of the Twelve Prophets which is in other respects so very dissimilar. Plainly, however, as this piece, which is now unique in the Old Testament, has been taken from a larger series of similar pieces and belongs to an entirely new branch of literature, it is no less clear that its object is not to present a simple narrative of Yona's life and labours, whether it be from historical memory or from legendary story ; or, if that were its intention, why does the narrative leave its hero quite alone by the withered bower near Nineveh, so that the reader does not

at all comprehend what became of Yona even immediately afterwards, whether or not he all along continued to stay full of bitter feelings in the open field near Nineveh.

As a fact it is quite impossible, from the sources of history concerning Yona which are now open to us, to say more definitely what and how much the author received through earlier tradition, and with how much freedom he himself then treated his materials in detail. We see from 2 Kings xiv. 25 nothing further than that this Yona, son of Amittai, was really an early prophet of the time of 'Amôs, or a little earlier, and belonged like Hoséa to the Northern kingdom. From this accidentally preserved reference to him and the much later legends which underlie the descriptions of this book, we may make highly probable conjectures. We may conclude that this prophet, so uncommon as regards his antique features, was in his whole character a genuine successor of Elias and Elisha, as the greatest prophets of the Northern kingdom; that his life passed through almost equally unusual vicissitudes of marvellous exaltation, victory, and glorification, and of flagging zeal and despair, and on that account passed into the region of national legend equally early with the lives of Elias and Elisha. We must, finally, allow the possibility that as prophet of the Northern kingdom he stood in some close relation with Nineveh, in some such way as the Books of the Kings place the labours of Elias and Elisha in close connexion with the kingdom of Damascus. But ways and means of penetrating further this historical obscurity are no longer at our command.

Still, this much is apparent from the style and character of the little book which now perpetuates the prophet's name, from the failing end of the story, and (which is the most decisive thing) from the true meaning of the whole book, namely, that the author beheld in the legendary material which was ready to his hand simply a given medium for presenting in an attractive form a prophetic truth which lived in his own heart. The one task which we have here to perform is to correctly seize this meaning of the whole book and with it the prophetic truth taught by the piece: and this little book is so transparently clear and at the same time brings such a noble truth to light that to accomplish this task is no less possible than remunerative.

We see (1) the prophet shrinking from the divine commission to preach repentance in Nineveh: he has indeed heard the plain voice of higher duty, but because the execution of the commission appears to him difficult and dubious (iv. 2), from human doubt and hesitation he fails to obey and thus falls into a first sin such as is least excusable in a prophet of all men. But it is in vain that he endeavours to flee into the most distant and obscure regions of the West (Ps. cxxxix. 9) instead of going to the East: in the midst of his flight the terrible voice from above overtakes him with all the more overwhelming force; for it seems it was his intention, as he remained persistent in his obduracy, to get as far from that voice as he could, and so laid himself to sleep as soon as he had got on board a ship: but all to no purpose, and as the lot then falls upon him as the guilty person, he resigns himself to the inevitable and is cast into the sea. But the sailors, although people worshipping various and accordingly heathen Gods, as they witness Yona's punishment, become all of them suddenly changed men, give Yahvé alone the glory—and are saved. Thus the proof is for the first time given that true fear and repentance bring salvation from Yahvé.—(2) Yona meanwhile finds, after he appears to have been wholly lost, an unexpected protection and as it were a final respite in the belly of a sea-monster which has swallowed him alive: and as one who has thus marvellously been spared, amid extreme peril, for another day of grace, he is really at last moved, as by this miracle itself, to sing from a full heart a hymn of praise to Yahvé, he gives the glory to him to whom it is due,—and is saved; a second time the fundamental thought is proved. The fact that the figures of the fine hymn, ch. ii., and the entire historical basis which it in the strict sense presupposes, do not suit the position of Yona as described in the story, and that there is no allusion in it to the sea-monster, shows that it is only an insertion here by the author, and must accordingly itself belong to an earlier age, as is stated in the *Dichter des Alten Bundes.*, I a., pp. 155-157. At the same time, our author's selection of this lyric was appropriate in so far as it was intended only in general to be the hymn of a man who had been already rescued from the depths of the sea, although he had not yet returned to the peace and repose of his native land.—(3) Now no longer resisting the will of Yahvé, Yona really executes manfully his onerous commission : and even the Ninevites at last, before it is too late, ascribe to Yahvé the glory and are saved, and for the third time the same fundamental truth is confirmed.

After a threefold confirmation of the same truth in the case of the most different kinds of men—the rude sailors, Yona the prophet of Yahvé, the thousands of luxurious Ninevites,—the narrator might well come to an end : but inasmuch as he has not yet explained the ultimate basis of the truth in Yahvé himself and his nature, he proceeds to join, in the same somewhat loose manner in which all the three sections, like so many short easily separable narrative pictures, are connected together, a fresh incident to those which have gone before. This is the brief story, ch. iv., which first throws a clear light upon all that has preceded. This story makes evident the supreme divine love as the true and necessary basis of the above redemption of the penitent of all classes without exception; but the story also, inasmuch as it introduces Yahvé as the teacher who is yet higher than the prophet, treats its material with extraordinary skill, since it enables the reader to perceive that such and not a different thing must the divine superiority be whenever it manifests itself. At first Yahvé's reply to the complaining Yona is merely the question, whether then he is really so very angry ? Not a word of rebuke in the strict sense: it is enough that he has observed this conduct of Yona, he permits him for a time to have his own way without any proper explanation, and to do what he likes, but meanwhile eternal wisdom, which embraces all things and continues its work, has unobserved taken him captive in his weak and sinful self-love, and when, after this has been destroyed, the divine wisdom again asks him whether he is really so very angry, this is not done without immediately, with all sublime superiority and certainty, shaming him by reference to the eternal truth of the divine love itself.

If the thought which it is intended to establish in the whole of the four sections of this piece had not already been established as regards its ultimate foundation, the loose thread of the narrative might easily have been in this way continued by further use of Yona's history. But everything finds in it a satisfactory conclusion, and we are quite content to leave Yona by his bower.—Moreover, as may be supposed, many other subsidiary truths, in addition to the principal truth, may be derived from any narrative of this kind: we may gather from it what the true prophet of Yahvé ought not to be; we may prove from it that people of all callings and religions are equal before the divine love and forgiveness: but neither the latter nor the former truth is presented by the author as the primary principle of his narrative.

There is no difficulty in the way of the supposition that the little book was written in the course of the sixth, or at the beginning of the fifth century: the conclusion, ch. iv., particularly has still genuinely prophetic characteristics, and is moreover a masterpiece of description of rare excellence; for although passages like 1 Kings xix. 4, sq., may be present to his mind, how far he surpasses them! It appears, on the other hand, from the manner in which he speaks of Nineveh as a marvellous city which had long ago perished, iii. 3, that he did not write before its overthrow. The narrative is perfectly simple, too, and makes no claim to have been written by Yona himself.—

But the Hebrew of the book has peculiarities; and we cannot ascribe these peculiarities of language and of style simply to the fact that we have a later author before us. On the contrary, they are as a whole to be traced to the fact that popular and national stories generally presented linguistic and stylistic features, differing from those which are customary in written books. The legends about Elias and Elisha which were received into the Books of Kings also bear linguistic peculiarities (comp. *e.g.*, *History of Israel*, IV., p. 86 (III., p. 553), although in detail they differ again.from those of this book. From this, however, no further inference can be drawn than that we have here an author from whom nothing further has been preserved.

The Story of Yona.

i.   1.

1 And Yahvé's word came to Yona son of Amittai saying:
2 "Arise, go to Nineveh the great city, and preach unto her
3 that their wickedness is come before my face!" But Yona arose to flee to Tarshish from before Yahvé, went down to Yaphô and found a ship which was bound for Tarshish: so he gave the fare thereof and took ship therein to go with the
4 people to Tarshish, fleeing from Yahvé. But Yahvé cast a mighty wind upon the sea, and a great storm arose in the sea
5 so that the ship threatened to go to pieces. Therefore the seamen began to fear and cried every one to his God, and they threw the freight which was in the ship into the sea to ease themselves; but Yona had gone down into the hold of the ship had
6 laid himself down and was sound asleep. Then the captain of the ship came near and said to him "wherefore sleepest thou so sound? arise call upon thy God, if so be the God may deign
7 to remember us that we perish not!"—Then they said one to the other "come and let us cast lots, that we may know on whose account we have this evil!" So they cast lots, and the
8 lot fell upon Yona. Then said they unto him "tell us now on whose account have we this evil? what is thy business and whence comest thou? what is thy country, and of what kind of nation art thou?" and he said unto them "I am a Hebrew, and Yahvé the God of heaven I fear who hath created the sea

10 and the dry land ...." Then the men began to feel great fear and said unto him "why hast thou done this?" For the men had discovered that from before Yahvé he sought to flee,
11 because he had declared it to them. So they said unto him "what shall we do that the sea may hold its peace before us? for the sea groweth more and more stormy;" and he said unto them "take me and throw me into the sea, that the sea may hold its peace before you! For I know that for my sake this
13 great storm is upon you."—Then the men strained hard to put back to land, but were not able, for the sea grew more
14 and more stormy. So they called unto Yahvé and said "we pray thee Yahvé! let us not perish for the sake of the soul of this man, and lay not innocent blood upon us! surely thou Yahvé—as it pleaseth thee thou doest!" and they took
15 Yona and threw him into the sea. Then the sea abated its
16 fury: but the men felt great fear before Yahvé, brought sacrifices to Yahvé and vowed unto him vows.

The wickedness of the great city *has come before God's face*, has become too great to permit God to further let it go on: Yona perceives that, and a distinct voice of God seeks to urge him, in spite of all the difficulties which he will thereby have to encounter, to go to the city and *preach unto it* the things which he as a true prophet had to preach to it. These difficulties (as appears from the slight hint given iv. 2) are found most of all simply in his human, overstrained reasonings. He supposed that either the hundreds of thousands of Nineveh would not be converted, and then his heavy labours would have been in vain. Or, if the more improbable case is put that they are converted, then the divine punishment, with which he shall threaten them if they should not be converted, will, after all, by virtue of the mercy of Yahvé, which is so well known to him, not be carried out, and then his prophetic reputation will suffer. These are vain reasonings such as very naturally overtake and involve in their meshes even the best educated and apparently most gifted men in presence of a great, onerous, but unavoidable task. — But whoever, like Yona in his day, becomes unfaithful to a clearly recognized divine will, simply from fear lest he should have to encounter too many difficulties, that man too often falls all the lower in proportion as his position was high: thus an irresistible feeling urges Yona to go so much the further from Nineveh, as if the further he was from Nineveh he could the more easily escape the terrible voice of Yahvé as it reminded him of his duty; so he seeks to go to the most distant West, and embarks upon a Phœnician ship which is bound thither. The city Yaphô had as early as the times of the Judges fallen again into the hands of the Phœnicians,[*] and appears here also a city in which they

---

[*] Comp. the addition, which I published in the *Gött. Gel. Anz.*, 1868, p. 142 sq., to my interpretation of the large Sidonian inscription.

ruled and where the crew which had to row and steer the ship were taken from the Heathen.

Yona appears here as the opposite of an 'Amôs (comp. Vol. I., p. 143 sq.), and does not even remember what is said with such unsurpassable truth Ps. cxxxix. 9. Thus the man, who as prophet ought to have better known what was his duty, must be reminded of his grievous violation of it by an unlooked-for occurrence. A violent storm arises out in the open sea, the ship is on the point of being wrecked: but while every one of the crew, consisting of men of various heathen nations and religions, being in the mortal peril suddenly overcome by a deeper religious feeling, calls upon his own special deity for help, Yona is lying fast asleep in the cabin into which he had retired before the storm; so that the captain* himself is compelled to go below to wake and bring on deck the strange man who has long been missed by the whole crew who are all on deck under the open heaven.†

The reason why he is called on deck in haste by the crew and in their name by the captain, is that it has already been agreed, that if all prayers are of no avail against the growing rage of the storm, and every single man on the ship has prayed in vain to his particular God, then the last means of appeasing the Gods which seems left to them, according to ancient custom, must be resorted to. In that case it must be discovered by the lot who the really guilty person is, and he must be cast into the sea as an acceptable offering it may be to some God for the salvation of the rest. The way in which all this is here described shows clearly that it was an ancient sacred custom which was made use of on the ship when all other means failed. It is all the more remarkable that the seamen of that time, as appears with equal clearness from the following description, vv. 7-15, nevertheless themselves felt doubt whether the lot always fell upon the guilty one: thus enlightened therefore were this heathen crew in their day even, and these doubts were naturally most numerous when they saw a man selected by the lot from whose appearance and history anything so bad could not be suspected. This is their feeling with regard to Yona. For he, already most profoundly terrified by the sudden awakening from the deep sleep in which he had expected to find complete repose, and by the unexpected sight of the horrible storm as well as of all the men who were waiting for him, the only one that yet failed, is by all this snatched as by a fearful wrench from his spiritual still more than from his physical slumber, beholds himself smitten down by the thunder of the divine wrath as none of his fellow-passengers, and in the same moment feels that he is an entirely different man from what he had just appeared to be to the seamen and from their ideas of him. As soon therefore as the lot has fallen on him, a totally new and strange scene

---

* That is the force of רַב הַחֹבֵל, lit. *head-steersman*, the two words more closely connected acc. § 287 c.

† Whoever apprehends the sense of the whole story will easily perceive that according to it Yona cannot have gone below while the storm was raging, in order then to go to sleep and thus bid defiance to what he foresaw was coming: in that case he would appear not as a timid man but as a knavish prophet, which he is not and does not show himself to be in the course of the narrative.

commences in the midst of this confusion and storm from above and below: the Heathen will not believe that he is the guilty person, beg him to tell them *on whose account* they have this evil, inasmuch as they cannot imagine that they have it on his account,* they inquire nevertheless more particularly with regard to all his circumstances, vv. 7, 8. But he is now, as we have said, a god-fearing man again and without any reserve, because he has undergone an inward change and become sufficiently altered to tell them everything; and the great prophet stands then before these Heathen, as not one of them had expected, as a sinner against his God! For even these Heathen have at once perceived what a grievous sin, furthermore against the only almighty and true God, who was probably known to them by distant report or intuitively recognized, Yona has committed by his resistance of the divine will; and they have also perceived that on that account the storm of this God has fallen upon the ship :† accordingly they ask him, *how he could do that*, vv. 9, 10, delay at first and ask what they are to do with him, vv. 11, 12, try with utmost effort,‡ even after he has requested them to consider him as the guilty one, to steer the ship to land, ver. 13, and not until this last means also has proved itself vain do they resolve to do to him as he had requested of them, even then when they do it first in fear and trembling calling upon the true God not to punish them if they cast an innocent man into the sea, and only silencing their last scruples by openly confessing that they know well *that he doeth what he will*, can accordingly either destroy them all in a moment by the utmost increase of the storm if they should treat an innocent man as guilty, or save them if the contrary be the case.§

When they saw realized what they had just conceded the possibility of, ver. 14, but had considered as most unlikely, when the rage of the storm ceased in a moment and a calm arose, what are we therefore to think? was the first feeling of these seamen, who had hitherto been so rude and untaught though so quick to feel the divine both in man and in the world without,

---

* Accordingly the question *on whose account have we this evil*, ver. 8, is quite correct, and by no means to be omitted as is the case in some early MSS. It seems also as if the author himself wished not to repeat it quite *verbatim* from ver. 7: as if the seamen themselves employ a somewhat more elegant language in Yona's presence, they say בַּאֲשֶׁר לְמִי instead of בְּשֶׁלְּמִי, comp. ver. 12 and § 222 c.

† It is self-evident from the connexion and meaning of the earlier narrative that the words of Yona to the seamen are here, ver. 9, given only in an abbreviated shape, that is, they do not add the sequel which every reader can supply from vv. 1-3; otherwise everything would have to be repeated from vv. 1-3, which the narrator very properly considers superfluous for attentive readers, but to which he nevertheless points back at the end of ver. 10 for the sake of the general perspicuity of the discourse.

‡ This must be pretty much the force of חָתַר, ver. 13, as the LXX already correctly perceived: and from the signification of *breaking in, penetrating (instare)* that of *endeavouring with every power* may very well be obtained.

§ As regards the *two perfects*, ver. 14, comp. §§ 357 b, 360 b.

and who at least in this moment of mortal danger had become so profoundly religious. *One* moment, and they saw that that man in whose guilt before his God they would not believe was really guilty, that therefore that God also whom they had learnt to know through him and this occurrence could and really did so severely punish his own distinguished servant, in brief, they perceive what Yona himself ought to have perceived and known long before them and from the very first. If they were previously more and more agitated by fear before the Unknown and Mysterious One into whose presence they had been brought, they are now, after they have come to know Him as far as they are able to know him *from greatest fear* of him, moved by the profoundest feeling of true religion, and immediately attest this by *sacrifices*, which they bring to him as they are able at the moment, and by *vows* of still larger ones to be brought in the future ; and thus Heathen become better worshippers of the true God than the prophet was as yet.

ii.
1 Then Yahvé appointed a great fish, to swallow Yona : and
2 Yona was in the fish's belly three days and three nights.—But
3 Yona prayed unto his God from the fish's belly, and said :

1.

I called out of my distress unto Yahvé : he answered me ;
    out of the heart of Hell I cried : thou heardest my
        voice !
5 For a whirlpool cast me into the heart of the seas, and the
    current encompassed me round,
  all thy breakers and waves passed over me :
5 then said I " I am cast forth before thine eyes !"
  still I shall look again — unto thy holy temple !

2.

Waters had surrounded me even to the life, the deep encom-
    passed me round,
6   seaweed wrapped around my head ;
7 unto the bases of the mountains I went down,
  bars of Hell were closed upon me for ever :
then thou didst raise from the pit my life,
  O Yahvé my God !

3.

8 When my soul grew dark unto me I remembered Yahvé :
  and unto thee my prayer entered into thine holy
    temple.

9   They who heed vain idols forsake their graciousness:
10   but with loud thanks I will sacrifice to thee,
         I will pay that which I vowed!
         Salvation is Yahvé's!
11   Then Yahvé commanded the fish, and it vomited Yona
                    upon the dry land.

Yona appears now to men wholly lost. But though this appears to be the case, still at the first moment when he was aroused from his profound spiritual sleep as by a celestial though wrathful violence, he had again become at the same time an entirely different man, had confessed his guilt even before Heathen men in that terrible moment, yea, had himself desired the whole vehemence of the final punishment to fall upon him. Thus though he has sunk down into the awful depths, it is still as one who has already been inwardly regenerated: and thus a divine deliverance is possible for him even in the midst of these depths; and that he, thus swallowed by a mighty fish, is conscious even in its belly that he is alive, becomes for him the commencement of another possible deliverance. This he now perceives even in the midst of this doubly awful depth, and instead of an elegy concerning the dark, mysterious God, such he had previously been tempted to sing, he strikes up a joyous song of praise and thanksgiving concerning the Redeemer, like those converted Heathen who had thrown him overboard, yet a song as definite, clear, eloquent, and deep in feeling as was to be expected from a true prophet and an old servant of Yahvé. And a single word from Him to whom he has once more come quite near suffices to deliver him from his provisional place of rescue and set him on the dry land and once more in the sunlight.

This is the story, which would have been wholly impossible if legends of similar miraculous deliverances from the jaws of the sea and its monsters had not long before our narrator been in circulation not only in other seaboard countries, but along those long-stretching coasts of Phœnicia, which were almost without harbours and so difficult to navigate. These legends were used by our narrator so as to work in with the fundamental thought of all his narrations, and yet his story is incomparably superior to them all. The base and earthly elements are ennobled by the breath of the Divine in its purity, and things material and monstrous are transformed by contact with the light of the Immortal.*

But the hymn of praise itself plainly comes from another who had himself only shortly before suffered the greatest perils in the sea; and having at the time of writing been saved therefrom, he vowed in future to present his further thanks in the temple if possible. His own horrible experience of such

---

* A host of more or less similar myths, reaching back into the earliest times, may be found amongst all such nations, comp. *e.g.*, Philo's *Opera*, II., p. 465 sq.; Burnouf's *Introduction à l'hist. du Bouddhisme*, p. 316 sq.; *Journ. as.* 1859, II., p. 512; also the German story of *Ortnit*.—But in so far it is remarkable that reminiscences of the name of Yona and memorials of him are to be found in several places of that long coast-line, see Osborne's *Palestine*, p. 137.

extreme perils in the depths of the sea is the principal feeling of the lyric which makes itself felt in the vivid description: accompanying this horror is the feeling of deep inward joy that deliverance has been sent from the true God in order that life may henceforth be more completely devoted to His graciousness. That these two feelings both find such suitable expression in the lyric, was no doubt the motive which led our narrator to adopt it; and he was able to borrow it from some existing collection of lyrics. It is as improbable that he himself wrote it as it is incapable of proof that it is a song of the ancient prophet himself.*

---

* Comp. as to the lyric itself the *Dichter des A. Bs. Ia.*, p. 155 sq.† It is already said there that the lyric occupies a place between Pss. xviii. and xlii. : from the former it borrows some phrases, but is itself, on the other hand, imitated by the author of Ps. xlii. 8, because this author already uses a phrase in a metaphorical sense which is purely original in the poet before us. Moreover, the poet of Ps. xxxi. borrows in vv. 7, 23 some clauses from ours; and the temple which the poet of our lyric has in his eye is probably that at Jerusalem, judging from the analogy of the other lyrics of this kind.

† For the sake of completeness, the exposition of this lyric, referred to in the author's work on the Poets of the Old Testament, has been inserted. "The poet had been delivered from mortal peril in the sea, comp. Ps. cvii. 23 sq. A historical supposition of this kind is necessary, because the figures are too definite and are too exclusively directed to circumstances of that kind to suffer them to be interpreted in a merely general way of some great mortal danger, as in Pss. xviii. and xlii., of which two lyrics the first must have been present to the mind of our poet, and Ps. cxxiv. also. Having been rescued from the greatest peril, he here strikes up a hymn of thanksgiving, calm in tone, measured in style and arrangement, the poet being full of the joyful hope to be able at length to behold the temple, and there amid offerings to pay his vows, a hope which he here expresses. It is, however, the thought of having been miraculously brought from the gates of the under-world once more into the light of the upper world by Yahvé's grace, which takes such possession of the poet's soul that each of the first two strophes commences with the description of the danger, and closes with the description of the deliverance, both marvellous facts, particularly the first—the danger—being gradually more completely described until there is nothing more to be said. It is only in the third and last strophe, which once more begins with the fundamental matter of the first two, that the poet looks around him with a somewhat freer and wider glance ; ver. 10 carries out further what was previously hinted at ver. 5 b.—Each of the three strophes of this lyric plainly falls into six verse-members, which in the first strophe are all long members, but in the next two get shorter towards the end.

"Ver. 5. ואני before אמרתי expresses, it is true, primarily an antithesis : however, as the antithesis makes itself felt in the *following* clause where אך is equivalent to the Latin *verum*, it becomes on that ground a restriction, that is, has the force of our 'indeed,' 'it is true' (Germ. *zwar*). This modification of the particles by their place and relation is not rare in Hebrew.

"Ver. 7. *The bases of the mountains at the bottom of the sea, where earth*

3.

iii.
1 Then came Yahvé's word again to Yona, saying "Arise, go to Nineveh the great city, and preach unto it the preaching which
3 I will speak unto thee!" Then Yona arose and went to Nineveh according to Yahvé's word. But Nineveh was a
4 divinely great city, three days to go through. So Yona began to advance through the city one day's length, preached and said
5 "Yet forty days, and Nineveh will be overthrown!"—Then the people of Nineveh believed on God, proclaimed a fast, and put on mourning-garments from their greatest to their least.
6 And the thing came unto the king of Nineveh: he arose from his throne, put off his state-robe, put on a mourning-garment and sat in ashes, then caused to be proclaimed in Nineveh and
7 said "By command of the king and his magnates, &c., man and beast, herd and flock, shall not taste anything, neither shall
8 browse nor drink water, man and beast shall be covered with mourning-garments; and men shall call upon God with fervour and every one shall turn from his evil way and from the wrong
9 with which they act! It may be God will turn and have pity, turn from the fierceness of his wrath that we perish not!"—
10 Then God saw their doings, how they had turned from their evil way: so God had pity at the evil which he had spoken to do unto them, and did it not.

If Yona now receives the same commission of his Lord again, it is understood that, in the frame of mind in which he now is as a regenerated prophet, he gladly obeys it. All his former doubts have disappeared, and at this moment seem as if they could never again come back. He permits himself, too, to be borne more unreservedly than before by the flight of divine inspiration; simply what *God will speak to him*, ver. 2, must and will he speak as prophet in the immense city; as, indeed, what he now preaches to it, ver. 4, is quite different from what was said formerly, i.2. Nor is it impossible that the word which would be the correct one for to-day should to-morrow in altered circumstances undergo an important change; and if the task which Yona

---

and hell separate. It seems necessary to regard שאול instead of הארץ as the original reading, comp. also ver. 3 and Job xvii. 16; if the present reading were correct, בעד would have to be understood in its other meaning: the earth's bars (trammels) were *behind* me, *i.e.*, I was free from them, as having my place already in the lower world. Yet this meaning would be ill-expressed and ambiguous.

"Ver. 9: *their graciousness*, favour, the divine power of love which could alone save them, and which is nevertheless originally so near to all men that it can be called *their graciousness*."—Tr.

has to perform is immensely difficult, he has himself in the meantime grown with its growth, and is able, therefore, to speak otherwise than it would have been best to do previously.—However, before this altered word of God is itself announced, the narrative, ver. 3, suitably refers in a few words to the immense size of that city which then *existed*, whilst at the time of the narrator it scarcely remained as a shadow of its former greatness. Its magnitude cannot be more briefly and at the same time more adequately described than in the words: *it was a divinely great city*, an expression taken from the language of the people, like the Arabic *lillāhi 'l-kāilu, divine is he that composed thus*, Hariri, p. 9 sq., comp. *Jahrbb. der Biblischen Wiss.*, X., p. 50. In the more dignified language of the prophets and poets, and, indeed, of the historical writers, of the Old Testament, such an expression is not found: at most it is only the language of the people which tolerates expressions less consonant with the stricter nature of the true religion; it is all the more noteworthy that a similar proverbial phrase, Gen. x. 9, has been preserved as from that region, "as Nimrod, a hero of the chase before Yahvé," *i.e.*, almost like *mehercle*, or our *by God*, as little more than an asseveration.—When it is further added that Nineveh was *a space to go through in three days*, this refers more particularly to the manner in which Yona acted in the city, acc. ver. 4: the historical significance of this is explained in the above *Jahrbb.*, p. 50 sq.

The announcement which Yona now preached in Nineveh, that it will be overthrown within forty days (unless it is converted), has plainly a much more decisive, urgent, and threatening tone than what he would at first have said, acc. i. 2; and it may be readily conceived with what urgent admonitions the prophet enforced this announcement: and this may also be seen from the nature of the royal proclamation, ver. 9, which is manifestly intended to cite important words from the prophet's call to repentance.—The immediate effect of the fresh vigour and power of his preaching appears also in the fact, that before he had proceeded through half the city, before he had got as far as the middle of it, all the inhabitants were overtaken by the most earnest and deepest repentance, and even the king, overpowered by this irresistible impulse of the spirit, *together with his magnates* (as at an imperial diet) publishes a public summons, in conformity with this feeling, to hold a general day of humiliation. It is simply in accordance with ancient custom that this day of fasting and humiliation is also to be observed by all the cattle which are in the possession of men, and that at least the nobler animals which are received more into the society of men, such as horses and the like, shall be covered like men themselves in mourning garments: we have no reason to suppose that the prophet desired all this should be done just as it is here described, but that the king commanded it thus in agreement with ancient sacred customs of his kingdom. Herod. ix. 24 narrates something similar of the Persians. Moreover, it also follows from the nature of the case, without special mention of it, that the general public fast which is thus proclaimed is intended to last only *one day*: in the case of the people of Israel also * a fast

---

* This is put more strongly here than in the *Antiquities*, p. 111 sq. (96 sq.).—*Tr.*

was always thought of as lasting but one day.*

We know as a fact from other sources that among the ancient nations of those countries days of profound humiliation frequently interchanged with the most luxurious life and feasts of wildest joy, as this was most plainly seen in the worship of Tammûz, acc. Vol. IV., 59sq. How greatly, moreover, feeling changes in great cities, and at times even the most serious feeling of repentance will become prevalent, is a phenomenon with which we are sufficiently familiar in our own day and experience both in Europe and America. A true Hebrew prophet of the time when these prophets had often produced the most powerful effects, both in their own land and far beyond its limits, was able to become also in Nineveh the man of the day. It is true, our narrator is himself unable to maintain that that conversion in Nineveh was very lasting. For that it takes place far too rapidly even for such a city, and it assumes too little the form which had been long sacred in Israel. It is to be observed, too, that our narrator, although he cites the penitent words of Joel ii. 14, nevertheless does not like in this case, vv. 5-10, even to speak of God as Yahvé, as if that were only a very general and new acquaintance with divine things which had come to the people of Nineveh, and not even such an acquaintance as had come to the seamen previously, i. 9-16. Still, it could be, nevertheless, the commencement of a lasting amendment ; and that such a great city should only once begin with one mind to really perceive its ancient errors, is of itself a great thing. Acordingly it obtains for this time forgiveness from God, ver. 10.

4.

iv.
1 Then that seemed very evil to Yona, and he was angry and
2 prayed to Yahvé and said " O surely Yahvé ! is not this what I thought as long as I was in my own country ? therefore fled I beforehand to Tarshish, because I knew that thou art a God gracious and merciful, long-suffering and of great kindness
3 and willing to grieve for the evil ! And now Yahvé, take then
4 my soul from me, for to die is better for me than to live !"—
5 Then said Yahvé " art thou so very angry ?" And Yona went out of the city and fixed his abode to the east of the city, made himself a bower there and fixed his abode under it in the
6 shade, till he should see what would happen in the city. Then

---

* The לֵאמֹר, ver. 7, in the course of the royal proclamation is remarkable ; we must look upon the words *according to the pleasure of the king and his magnates* as forming the heading ; then the titles of the king and his magnates might have followed at length ; but in order to come at once to the chief point, which is indicated by לֵאמֹר, all those titles are left out. We see here the transition to the לֵאמֹר in the great Sidonian Inscription, line 2, and to the Syriac abbreviation therefrom *lam*.

Yahvé God appointed a Ricinus: which grew up above Yona to be to him a shade over his head, to give shade to him against his evil mood; and so Yona rejoiced over the Ricinus
7 exceedingly. But God appointed a worm whilst the next dawn was rising: which smote the Ricinus so that it withered;
8 and when the sun rose, God appointed a stinging east wind: then the sun smote upon Yona's head so that he fainted and wished that his soul might die and said "to die is better for
9 me than to live."—Then said God unto Yona "Art thou so very
10 angry on account of the Ricinus?" and he said "I am very angry even unto death." But Yahvé said "*Thou* wast sorry on account of the Ricinus for which thou didst not toil and which thou didst not make grow, which was of a night and died
11 in a night: and *I* shall not I be sorry on account of Nineveh the great city, wherein are more than twelve ten thousand men who do not know the right from the left and much cattle?

The primary truth has now been taught three times, a truth which is presen ed about the same time by the last prophets (Hag. i. 12, 13; Mal. ii. 5) as one of the highest: Yona had had opportunity of recognizing it, not only in the cases of the rude seamen and of the polished Ninevites, but also in his own case; and at all events he had long since overcome all fear of mere men as regards the Heathen also. But, on the other hand, he had not yet overcome human vanity, which is apt to make itself most conspicuous when, as in the case of Yona, great results have been achieved. So he must again pass through the school of God himself, in another way than formerly, and yet in one not less humiliating for him. What further comment is necessary has been given above.—The picture of despair of life, which is here so vividly drawn, and in the case of this prophet of the kingdom of the Ten Tribes, reminds us very much of Elias, who may be considered Yona's great prototype, 1 Kings xix. 4: but the picture is more lofty in the case of Elias as suited his character.—Moreover, as regards all these final delineations of the story, it must not be forgotten that they are meant to be simply great strong strokes for large frescoes. It is in conformity with this painter's manner that the *Qiqayon*, or Ricinus, which by us also usually grows with its broad leaves uncommonly high and rapidly, but in those regions still more quickly, is called *the child of a night*, Germ. *einnächtig*, just as Greeks and moderns speak in like manner of *ephemeral* things.* Of peculiarities of language the following should be observed: (1) חֵיטָב, vv. 4, 9, answering exactly to the Syriac *ṭôbh* in the sense of *very*; (2) חֲרִישִׁית, ver. 8, instead of which חֲרִישִׁית must be read; the latter word, as the same in its root with

---

* How much of a far bolder character later writers ventured to say in such instances, may be seen in the *G.* תענית, fol. 23, and with respect to Muhammed in *Burckhardt's Travels in Arabia*, II., p. 213.

חָרָס, Syriac ch*e*ras, and formed like אֱלִי, Zech. xi. 15, may very well signify that which is of a rough, scraping, and stinging nature. The language assumes a more exalted and poetic form in ver. 6, in the description of the object which God had with the Ricinus as regards Yona in his condition calling for twofold commiseration, namely, "that it might be to him a shade above his head, and give him shade also from his (self-provoked, spiritual) evil."

It has been further shown in the *History of Israel*, IV., 123, 128 (III. 602, 609) how certainly Yona was a historical prophet; this later narrative also, which is so modest and yet so exceedingly ingenious and profoundly suggestive, supplies evidence of his vastly impressive and daring labours. His name appears to have been common in northern Palestine and to have been abbreviated from יוֹנָן, *i.e.*, *Doveman*; the Syrians call him *Yaunān*, and this name is found Luke iii. 30.

3. *The New Prophetic Authors:*

(1) *of the simpler kind.*

In the last place, although these centuries become less and less prophetic, they are still very fruitful in new works of prophetic art and learning. For there was still no want of times when the stimulus of the prophetic word could produce as beneficial effects as in the genuinely prophetic centuries; as, indeed, particularly the Makkabean period approached once more almost the elevation of the days of Yesaya by its profound awakening of all noble national energies. Neither could there be an absence of minds who, as they looked back upon the ancient prophetic models, were strongly conscious in themselves of the need there was to work prophetically for their contemporaries, and to enkindle their higher courage; and though public prophetic speech had long since been wholly laid aside, they were still free to use literary imitation of the power of the ancient prophetic word, and this was all the more zealously adopted as the last instrument for the production of a similar effect.

But as such imitations are altogether called forth, sustained, and completed by the overwhelming power of the ancient written models, it appears as if their authors were almost all of them unable to write save under the name and guise of the earlier prophets. We saw in the piece Jer. l., li. (*supra*, p. 1 sq.) the first and at the same time the only example which we have yet met with of one of these oracles under feigned names; however there were special circumstances which might have caused that anonymous prophet to write in Yéremyá's name rather than any other. But later the production of books of this kind under the name of an earlier prophet or saint became simply an art, a custom in literature in the employment of which both the author and his readers mutually met each other's necessities: for if the former in his later, increasingly feeble and confused time was conscious of receiving purer impulses and attaining higher elevation by means of his profound studies and descriptions of the region of sublime antiquity and of a great prophetic name, on the other hand, his readers also preferred most to hear such voices which might seem to be sounding into their low days from an antiquity held sacred and revered by all.

Still, with this tendency of post-prophetic literature, it is rare again that a book is written in the simple manner of the earlier prophets, as is the case with the book of Barûkh and the Epistle of Yéremyá in the Apokrypha; and for various reasons it appears to us that the first of these deserves precisely at this point to be explained at length.

The Epistle of Barûkh.

Bar. i. 1—iii. 8.

This epistle, as I before showed elsewhere,* was written during the last period of the Persian rule, as the communities in and around Jerusalem were becoming more restless and

---

* *History of Israel*, V., 206 sq. (IV., 266 sq.). By this subsequent examination I have simply perceived further (1) that the Epistle, though substantially complete with i. 1—iii. 8, has yet been somewhat mutilated at the end, and (2) that the remainder must have been a distinct book of somewhat later date; as this will be shown below in detail.

disaffected towards the existing rule, and, on the other hand, the communities in the east were fearing and perhaps had actually experienced therefrom great injury both to themselves and the cause of the true religion generally. The eastern communities had hitherto sustained, with at the same time great independence, a close relation to those of the west, as long as they were under the same government: it was not until the rule of the Ptolemies, Seleukidæ, and Romans that this relation was gradually dissolved. It is not surprising therefore that when the western communities became more restless towards the supreme rule, those of the east, which were nearer to the seat of it, should experience, or at all events dread, much to their disadvantage in consequence. As now Yéremyá had formerly written a letter to the community in Babel on account of disaffections of this kind (Vol. III., p. 235 sq.), a prophetic writer in the eastern communities at that time thought he could best counteract the folly going on in Jerusalem by means of the earnest voice of a similar epistle, which, written at some time by Barûkh, was intended by the great community in Babel for the community in Jerusalem. The epistle was thus simply appended to the book of Yéremyá, as we can still see from the form of its commencement, *And these are the words of the little book which Barûkh wrote:* for no book complete in itself could begin thus; and this edition must have then been preserved in Egypt particularly, where it became the basis of the Septuagint version, and was in this version subsequently enlarged by a few additions of a similar nature.*

Yéremyá was never, according to historical reminiscences, himself in Babel. Neither have we any trace of Barûkh ever being there without him. Nevertheless, our author might suppose that

---

* The history of the book of Yéremyá, which was brought down a long way in Vol. III., p. 87 sq., is accordingly in this way continued further.—This view is further confirmed by the fact that in the LXX the book of Barûkh follows immediately and only then the book of Lamentations, a book which, from its introductory words in the LXX, might easily have been subjoined to the book of the Kings.

Barûkh had also in addition to the men there mentioned, ver. 3, gone as bearer of the epistle, Jer. ch. xxix., to Babel to read and explain there Yéremyá's epistle; and if he further adopted, acc. Jer. li. 59, the fourth year of Ssedeqia's reign as the year of his journey thither, he might very well go on to fix *Sivan*, *i.e.*, the last spring-month of the following year, as the term of the return home. It was simply in accordance with this chronology that he then assumed that the epistle written by Barûkh was read by him before the whole Babylonian community on the seventh of that month, *i.e.*, on a *Pentecost* day, which had been converted into a day of mourning, the community sanctioning it in such a way that they altogether adopted it as expressing their mind. But the author aptly further connects therewith, acc. i. 6-13, another twofold assumption. First, the community is supposed to have arranged for a collection of voluntary offerings on that day, that is of money which it was intended Barûkh should take with him to Jerusalem in order that he might there for that money present the necessary sacrifices of all kinds for the community at Babel; thus should the sacrifices and prayers meet here and there, having been presented in both places for the same object! Second, the temple vessels made of silver are supposed to have at the same time been given to him to convey to Jerusalem, the same silver vessels which King Ssedeqia (who was in Babel in the fourth year of his reign, acc. Jer. li. 59) had had made in place of the golden ones carried off by Nabukodrossor, and exactly after their pattern; a supposition of the historical value of which we know nothing. But as the final preparations for the journey must have been somewhat delayed in this way, it is easy to imagine that the departure might be postponed until after the tenth of the month, acc. ver. 8.

When, however, the community at Babel immediately in this manner explained at the outset to the community in Jerusalem, that they had appointed Barûkh bearer of this epistle and of this twofold gift for the temple, and in what sense they desired a common religious life and prayer, they took occasion, as in merely a continuation of this explanation, to communicate the great prayer of penitence and petition which Barûkh had drawn up and they had adopted, adding the request that this prayer might thenceforth be read in Jerusalem likewise on every feast and solemn day, i. 14. This long prayer has not indeed the usual opening at the commencement, ver. 15, but simply because it has been previously introduced by the foregoing words, vv. 10-13; however, it proceeds quite naturally and in such a way that it could not be more perfect in its peculiar manner. All mere supplication of the divine mercy is useless as long as the person has not put himself in the right relation to God, *i.e.*, recognized with the utmost clearness and sincerity his own sins and defects, both general and special, which have precipitated him into his present misery; and as this holds of every individual it must also hold of the entire nation. It is only from the deep earnestness of penitence that the stream of joyous petition for mercy springs heavenward. When accordingly this prayer, taking a wider review of the whole past history of the nation, has shown in a first strophe, i. 15—ii. 10, in general the suppliants' own unworthiness with a true humiliation of their own pride, then in a second and third, ii. 11-23; 24-35, with equal profundity and special reference to the present case, in a fourth, iii. 1-8, the power of believing petition for new mercy and salvation grows more and more in strength and inwardness; and it cannot be denied that therewith the plan of the prayer has been properly worked out.

It is true enough that the prayer is, after the manner of these late writers, very lengthy; simply by reference to passages of the Scriptures and their quotations so extended. Still, it cannot be denied that it is full of the genuine prophetic spirit and can be considered a model of an earnest and profound penitential prayer. The best proof of this is supplied by the book of Daniel, in which it is already, as we shall soon see, made use of as such a model. Its plan and execution, too, in four strophes, are quite suitable; and as that part of it which might be considered its proper introduction is woven into a first strophe of the whole book, we may properly suppose that the whole book has five strophes. It is, in the last place, easy to understand why the author borrows his phrases mostly from the book of Yéremyá. It is in other phrases, however, that we recognize all the more plainly his real age, as will be shown more particularly at i. 11, 12.

Inasmuch as the little book, as was above said, was according to all indications widely circulated from the very first only by means of Yéremyá's book in the form of an appendix to it, it is not difficult to understand how we come into the possession of it only from the hand of the same Greek translator by whom the book of Yéremyá appears translated in the LXX.* For the earliest history of the little book this is not without its importance. For as the book of Yéremyá was undoubtedly translated rather early into Greek, we perceive from that fact also that this little book of Barûkh must have been appended at a comparatively early date to it, and must have been looked upon as a genuine book of Barûkh's, at all events in the copies of Yéremyá's book which were in use in Egypt.

Nevertheless, if a serious endeavour is made to understand accurately this little book now preserved only in the Greek tongue, it is soon perceived that it has a very corrupt text, which particularly shows *lacunæ* in many places. Some of these errors go no further back than the Greek translation, and need not be charged to the translator himself, but only to later hands. But others were manifestly found by the Greek translator himself, and he was unable to rectify them. They are, however, all dealt with one by one below: neither would

---

* The proof of this has been previously given in the *History of Israel*, V., 208 (IV., 268): however, it is here also needful to bear in mind that this proof when taken more strictly extends only to the larger half of the present book of Barûkh, *i.e.*, only to iii. 8.

it be possible rightly to appreciate the little book as a whole, in its true value and its simple art, if these textual errors were not carefully observed. As regards the book generally, however, we must here observe, that a complete and clear conclusion to the little book is now wanting. It is true the petition in the last strophe, iii. 1-8, is by no means one that is broken off in the middle; for the strophe is manifestly intended to be shorter as compared with the rest, because the whole prayer consists of a series of strophes of diminishing length, like a genuine lamentation in perfect conformity with the principle discussed in the *Dichter des A. Bs. Ia.* p. 148 sq. The closing strophe therefore has in itself suffered scarcely the loss of a few words. At the same time, it might very well be observed at the end as a complete close of the little book, that this epistle was actually read constantly at that time in the synagogues of the Holy Land as is desired i. 14.

If this little book lacked thus early a distinct ending, it was all the more easy for the piece without a heading, iii. 9—v. 9, to get attached to it. This piece may now be reckoned as the second smaller half of the book of Barûkh, but in point of age, subject, and purpose, as well as art and execution, it was originally a different piece, and though its original language was also the Hebrew, it must have fallen, to judge from its Greek, into the hands of an entirely different translator. This smaller but intact book is distinguished greatly from the *little book* (Βιβλίον i. 1, 14) of Barûkh by the fact that it is translated into good Greek, and has also been handed down free from any serious errors.

But to these two appendices, soon made into one, to the book of Yéremyá as it circulated in Egypt, was subsequently added further the epistle of Yéremyá which is in many editions reckoned as the sixth chapter of Barûkh, though it had not even a Hebrew original.*—Our present book of Barûkh, inas-

---

* Comp. *History of Israel*, V. 479 sq. (IV., 625 sq.).

much as it has come with its five chapters to be looked upon as a connected whole, might be more correctly named 1 *Barûkh*, to distinguish it from a 2 *Barûkh*, a book which has been completely rediscovered,* and from a 3 *Barûkh*, a little work now likewise rediscovered and published,† but which owes its origin to the hand of a Christian. It is true that the Syrian church reckons as 1 *Barûkh* what we have here named 2 *Barûkh* and our much older book as 2 *Barûkh*, but this arises simply from the fact that the former was a much longer book when it came into the Syrian Kanon.

1.

i.
1   And these are the words of the book which Barûkh wrote, son of Nêria son of Maasaya son of Ssedeqia son of Hasadya son of Chelqia in Babel in the fifth year on the seventh of the month
2   . . . . ‡, | before the time when the Chaldeans took Jeru-
3   salem and burned it with fire. || And Barûkh read aloud the words of this book unto Yekhonya son of Yoyaqim king of Yuda and unto all the people as many as came to the Bible §, |
4   unto the mighty ones and the kings' sons and unto the elders and unto all the people from the little to the great, to all who
5   were dwelling in Babel and by the river Sûd; || and they wept and fasted and prayed before the Lord, collected money
6   as the hand of each was able, | and they sent him to Jerusalem to
7   Yoyaqim son of Chelqia the son of Shalôm the priest and to the priests and all the people as many as were found with him
8   in Jerusalem: || (in that he received on the tenth of Sivan the vessels of the house of the Lord which had been carried away out of the temple to take back as silver ones into the land of
9   Yuda, | which Ssedeqia son of Yosia king of Yuda had caused to be made after Nabukodrossor king of Babel had led away prisoners to Babel Yekhonya and the princes and the chief men and the mighty men and the common people from Jerusalem

---

* See on it *Gött. Gel. Anz.* 1867, p. 1706-16.
† In Dillmann's *Chrest. Aeth.* (Leipzig, 1865).
‡ *Sivan* has here been omitted acc. ver. 8.
§ That is, to a place where the Bible is publicly read and prayer offered to God.

10 unto Babel), ‖ and said " we have sent unto you money : | so buy ye with the money whole burnt-offerings and sin-offerings and incense and make ye it a presentation and present ye it
11 upon the altar of the Lord our God, ‖ and pray ye for the life of Nabukodrossor king of Babel and for Baltasar's life his son, | that their days may be as the days of heaven upon
12 earth! ‖ And the Lord will give us strength and enlighten our eyes, | that we may live under the shadow of Nabukodrossor king of Babel and under the shadow of Baltasar his

1. The situation described vv. 1-9 cannot be correctly understood until two emendations have been made. (1) Ver. 2. The name of the month, which had most likely already disappeared from the manuscript of the translator, must be restored from ver. 8, and then πρὸ τοῦ καιροῦ must be read instead of ἐν τῷ καιρῷ. From the simple fact that *Babel* is spoken of it was evident that the chronology which is used in the book of Hézeqiél was here intended ; accordingly everybody knew that in the fifth year of this chronology Jerusalem had not been destroyed, as is indeed presupposed in all that follows. If, moreover, our author lived in Babel, we can suppose that the mode of reckoning time which is used in the book of Hézeqiél was still kept up in his day ; although this cannot be inferred from the recently discovered Crimean inscriptions (comp. *Gött. Gel. Anz.*, 1866, p. 1246 sq.), it is still in itself possible. — (2) Ver. 4 we must read with the Pesh.* " in Babel *and* by the river Σούδ :" for the situation of Babel needed no further definition ; but that they who did not dwell too far from Babel also assembled for that great feast, was not a superfluous observation. The name of this river is at present obscure, it is true ; and the orthography of the Pesh. *ssūr* does not help us. But if the district which the Arabs call or *as-sawād* (Abulfeda, p. 52, 307, ed. Reinaud), derived its name at first from one of the numerous rivers of southern Mesopotamia and is here meant, its locality would suit here very well ; and if our author lived in those eastern regions, he would accordingly know this district well. — (3.) αὐτὸν must be inserted after ἀπέστειλαν, this αὐτὸν as well as that of ver. 8 referring to Barûkh, for it follows from the manner of the enumeration of the men in ver. 7, that this *sending*, ver. 7, is not intended to refer as ver. 10 to the money mentioned ver. 6.

The ancestors of Barûkh, as far back as the fifth generation, are met with here only : the father and grandfather are also found Jer. xxxii. 12, and these two are the same as those of Seraya, " Jer." li. 59, as if this travelling attendant of the king had been a brother of Barûkh's. Still, we have no good reason to doubt that our author could still have been in possession of reliable ancient sources for such information. —On the other hand, the name of the high-priest at that time, Yoyaqim, ver. 7, must acc. 1 Chron. v. 39-41 (A. V. vi. 13-15) be based upon some confusion : it was a later high-priest

---

* We follow this version as edited by Lagarde, *Libri V. T. apocryphi syriace* (Leipzig. 1861).

son, | serve them many days and find favour before them. ||
13 And pray ye for us to the Lord our God because we have sinned against the Lord our God and the wrath and anger of
14 the Lord turned not from us even to this day, | and read ye this book aloud which we have sent unto you that it may be proclaimed in the house of the Lord on feast days and on holidays, so that ye say : ||

2.

15 To the Lord our God be righteousness, but to us shame of

that bore this name (comp. *History of Israel*, V., 123 sq. (IV., 160 sq.¹), and his name was later very popular (as the book of Judith shows).

The expression δεσμώτας, ver. 9, shows not only that the words were taken from Jer. xxiv. 1 ; xxix. 2, although with great freedom, but also that the Hebrew מֻצְעָר is rendered by the same translator by the, to us, very obscure word δεσμώτας. It is probably intended to signify bundle-bearers in the sense of lictors (*fasces*), as the Pesh. (into which the τεχνίται also have been received after it from these passages) render it by *dachshē* (comp. the Syriac *Protev. Jacobi*, ch. xxi. 23) ; but this sense of this Greek word does not suit the connexion, and the author undoubtedly understood the Hebrew word which he adopted here differently ; we have, however, given a very vague rendering of it above.

The words ποιήσατε μάννα (a corruption of μαναά, *i.e.*, מִנְחָה), ver. 10, must signify *let it be consecrated for a sacred gift* by means of the prescribed temple rites.

The prayer for Nabukodrossor and his son Baltasar, vv. 11, 12, must be understood as in conformity with the custom which reigning monarchs have of having prayers offered for themselves and their immediate successor.

2. In the confession the *man of Yuda and the inhabitants of Jerusalem* only

This presupposes that Nabukodrossor had at that time appointed a son of this name to be his successor; and this is evidently the same supposition as is met with in the book of Daniel, ch. v., where Belshassar is described as the son of Nabukodrossor, and at the same time the last king of his stock and of his nation. We may also very easily conceive that this had become a customary supposition towards the end of the Persian period by means of later popular narratives. The LXX, moreover, both here and in the book of Daniel, confound the name Bêlteshazar, Dan. i. 7 sq., with the name Bêlshazar, Dan. ch. v.— But evidently the chief emphasis is here to be laid upon the words vv. 12, 13, that is, upon the desire that God may grant, both to the communities in Babel and (as appears from ver. 11) to those in the Holy Land, the needed strength and enlightenment to avoid all inclination to rebellion ; for if this desire is particularly necessary for the communities in the Holy Land, those in Babel are none the less unwilling to show superiority to them, but rather with a consciousness of their errors and calamities gladly accept for themselves the intercession at Jerusalem, ver. 13.—It follows from their antethesis to the feast days that the ἡμέραι καιροῦ, ver. 14, are the Sabbath days.

(a phrase so frequent in Yéremyá) are mentioned at first, i. 15, with reference

face now at this time, | to the man of Yuda and to the
16 inhabitants of Jerusalem, | to our kings and our princes, and
17 to our priests and to our prophets and to our fathers, || for the
18 things in which we have sinned before the Lord and were disobedient unto him and hearkened not to the voice of the Lord our God | to walk in the commandments of the Lord which he
19 gave before our face. || From that day in which the Lord led our fathers out of the land of Egypt and until to this day we were disobedient to the Lord our God | and too careless to
20 hearken to his voice : || so there clave unto us the evils and the curse which the Lord delivered to Moses his servant on that day when he led our fathers out of the land of Egypt to give
21 us a land flowing with milk and honey | now at this time. || And we hearkened not to the Lord our God according to all the
22 words of the prophets whom he sent unto us, | and walked
ii. every one in the thought of his evil heart, to serve other gods,
1 to do what is evil in the eyes of the Lord our God : | so the Lord executed his word which he spake concerning us and concerning our Judges which judged Israel and concerning our kings and princes and concerning the man of Israel and of
2 Yuda, | to bring upon us great evils which never happened under the whole heaven as they happened in Jerusalem, |
3 according to that written in the Law of Moses that we should eat every one the flesh of his son and every one the flesh of his
4 daughter ; || and he made them subject to all the kingdoms round about us, | to be a shame and a desolation among all the

---

to כַּיּוֹם הַזֶּה* *as it is to-day*, i.e., with reference to the present time : but as the discourse is about to pass in review the whole of the ancient history from the moment when God gave his Law *before our face*, after Ex. ch. xix.-xxiv.,the kings and princes,as well as their contemporary priests and prophets and *fathers*, *i.e.*, the rest of the ancestors, are immediately, vv. 16-18, connected with them. For with vv. 19, 20 the discourse begins more definitely to explain how the curse of God upon the rebellious, which was in those early times (for there were always such) pronounced by Moses, acc. Lev. xxvi. 14 sq ; Deut. xxviii. 15 sq., is being fulfilled ; which is then shown more and more clearly in the long sentence, ver. 21—ii. 5, also with reference to the work of Moses as continued by the true prophets, particularly as regards the most terrible of all the divine curses and evils, Lev. xxvi. 29 ; Deut. xxviii. 53, because Jer. xix. 9 had similarly spoken of it. The whole of the long general confession, i. 15—ii. 5, which

---

* Ewald takes כַּיּוֹם הַזֶּה here and in Jer. as meaning simply *now, at present*. Comp. Vol. III., 223.—Tr.

5 nations round whither he scattered them, ‖ and they came down beneath and not up above, | because we sinned against the Lord our God not to hearken to his voice. ‖
6 To the Lord our God be the righteousness, but to us and our fathers the shame of face now at this time! ‖ As the Lord
7 spake all the evils concerning us which came upon us, | but
8 we did not entreat the face of the Lord that every one might turn away from the thoughts of his evil heart: ‖ so the
9 Lord watched over the evils and brought them upon us, | because the Lord is righteous with respect to all his works
10 which he commanded us, | but we hearkened not to his voice to walk in the ordinances of the Lord which he gave before our face. ‖

3.

11 And now, O Lord God of Israel, | thou who leddest forth thy people out of the land of Egypt with mighty hand with signs and wonders and with great power and high arm and madest
12 thee a name now at this time: ‖ we sinned we offended | we did wrong, O Lord our God, against all thy righteous laws! ‖

of itself occupies a whole strophe, consists, therefore, essentially of three sentences only, the last of which is the longest: but the substance of it is gathered up with all the greater point at the close, ii. 6-10. And here at the close the peculiar phrase, *God watched over the evils, i.e.*, he did not forget or overlook those evils which had long been threatened, *and brought them*, therefore, at the right time *upon us*, is intentionally thus borrowed from Jer. i. 12; xxxi. 28; xliv. 27. From Yéremyá also are taken the phrases ὡς ἡ ἡμέρα αὕτη, i. 15, 20; ii. 6, 11, 26, and that of the *reproach and desolation* (שַׁמָּה

would have been better translated *astonishment*) *among all nations round about*, ii. 4; iii. 8; on the other hand, the phrase ii. 5 is from Deut. xxviii. 43.—It remains only to observe that ὧν, i. 17, depends quite correctly, though indirectly, on αἰσχύνη, ver. 15, comp. *Jahrbb. der Bibl. Wiss.*, IV., p. 77. The expression *the curse which he prescribed to Moses*, i. 20, may signify, in a brief way of speaking, that he prescribed it to him to pronounce; it does not seem necessary to suppose that the words required to complete the sense have been lost from the text.

3. It is manifest that after this glance at the divine punishments threatened in the Law, and the disobedience shown towards the ancient prophets, the general confession, ii. 11, 12, must begin again with new fervour; but inasmuch as the petition for mercy also begins and is sus-

tained by its various reasons, beginning three times with growing urgency and becoming thereby more and more conscious of its reasons, vv. 13, 14, 15; 16-19, the discourse is, at the same time, purposely conducted so that, as the last and most forcible reason, the present

13 Let thy wrath turn away from us, because we are left only few
14 among the nations whither thou didst scatter us! | hear O Lord our prayer and our petition and save us for thy sake, | and give
15 us favour before the face of our captors, || in order that the whole earth may know that thou art the Lord our God, | that thy name is called upon Israel and his race! || O Lord, look down from
16 thy holy house and give heed unto us, | and incline O Lord
17 thine ear and hear! || open thine eyes and see! | because the dead in the lower world whose spirit is taken from within
18 them will not give praise and righteous due to the Lord, || but the grieving soul and the pride which goeth along bowed and fainting, | the failing eyes and the hungry soul will give thee
19 praise and righteousness, O Lord! || Because not upon the just claims of our fathers and our kings do we support our prayer
20 before thy face, O Lord our God, | . . . * Because thou hast sent down thy wrath and anger upon us when thou spakest by
21 thy servants the prophets: | "Thus saith the Lord: bow ye your shoulder and serve the king of Babel, that ye may thus remain upon the land which I gave to your fathers! || but if
22 ye hearken not to the voice of the Lord to serve the king of
23 Babel, | I will cause to cease from the cities of Yuda and outside Jerusalem the voice of joy and of gladness, the voice of the bridegroom and bride, | and the whole land will become a desolation before its inhabitants!" ||

calamity simply is brought forward inasmuch as it has been caused by disobedience to the word of Yéremyá urging quiet submission to foreign rule, vv. 20-23. The whole of this strophe is occupied with this order of thought, but because everything thus issues in the final and most serious reason existing in the Heathen of the present time, it is said at once incidentally, ver. 14, *give us favour before our captors*, the powerful lords who keep us in exile, and into whose power thou hast now delivered us on account of our sins. As reasons for divine compassion we find urged with increasing cogency:—(1) that there are so few of them left in their wide dispersion, ver. 13, after Jer. xlii. 2 and Ezra ix. 15;—(2) because it must after all be desired that the God of the community of the true religion, and so this religion itself, should not be wholly misunderstood, ver. 15, after Jer. xiv. 9, and many later passages of the Psalms; —(3) because according to Ps vi. 6; lxxxviii. 11-13, those who are already dead cannot praise God (and how near is the whole community of Israel to its final dissolution at the present time! comp. iii. 4), but, on the other hand, the prayer of praise and thanksgiving from humbled pride and a contrite lowly heart

---

* Some such clause as *but upon thy mercy*, &c. has been omitted here.

4.

24 But we hearkened not to thy voice to serve the king of Babel : | so thou didst execute thy words which thou spakest by thy servants the prophets, that the bones of our kings and
25 of our fathers should be removed from their place : ‖ and now are they cast out . . . * ‖ to the heat of the day and to the cold of the night and die in evil hardships, by famine and
26 sword and by sudden death ; ‖ and thou madest thine house whereupon thy name was called as it is now at this time, | on account of the wickedness of the house of Israel and of the

must be acceptable to God, vv. 17, 18, after "Isa." lvii. 15 and similar passages ; and because the community is now conscious of being in this state of mind, there follows—(4) the further reason, that they do not base *their prayer before God* upon any such thing as the *deserts of their famous fathers and kings*, ver. 19 ; to which is finally added, vv. 20-23, as has been already explained, the last reason and the most weighty, inasmuch as it concerns most deeply the present time. The words, vv. 21-23, are from Jer. xxvii. 11, 12, 17, at all events as regards their substantial meaning, and xxv. 9-11, taken together with vii. 34 ; xxxiii. 10, 11 : but instead of simply quoting Yéremyá's name as authority, in prophetic style it is more suitable to refer them to the prophets generally ; indeed, they already stood in *the Book*, i. 3, *i.e.*, in the Kanon of the Law and the Prophets. The same thing occurs again, ver. 24.—Ver. 18 καὶ τὸ must be read for ἐπὶ τὸ ; otherwise no sense can be got, and this emendation is demanded also by the structure of the verse-members, there being here four sub-members to two principal members. The Pesh. seeks another way out of the difficulty.—Ver. 19 according to the correct reading τὸν ἔλεον ἡμῶν we have simply an erroneous translation of תְּחִנָּתֵנוּ. Moreover, in this verse some words are wanting, as is indicated in the translation.

4. As now a rebellious feeling towards the government has been just mentioned as the immediate and most efficient cause of the present distress, in agreement with i. 11, 12, the confession may begin afresh from this immediate and most burning sin with new fervour, in order, together with a public confession of this sin, to confess with equal publicity that with it are connected all the present serious evils, the ruin and desecration of the graves of great kings and fathers of old, ver. 24, the leading away of the nation into captivity so that, exposed on the way to the great heat by day and the great cold by night, they died off by all kinds of cruel death, ver. 25, and the present lamentable condition of the temple itself, ver. 26. In fact, the discourse with these words, vv. 24-26, does not forsake its assumed date so far that with them allusion is made to the time subsequent to the destruction of the temple : for the words, ver. 24, may

---

* There is wanting in the text : *of their graves ; and thy surviving ones are exposed*

27 house of Yuda.— ‖ And yet thou didst deal with us, O Lord our God, only after all thy kindness and after all thy great
28 compassion | even as thou spakest by thy servant Moses in the day that thou commandedst him to write thy Law before
29 the sons of Israel, saying ‖ "if ye hearken not to my voice, then surely this great and numerous swarm of people will become very small among the nations whither I will scatter
30 them, | because I know that they will not hearken to me because it is a stiffnecked people. ‖ —Yet they will bethink themselves in the land of their homelessness and know that I
31 am the Lord their God : | so I will give them a heart and ears
32 which hear, and they will praise me in the land of their
33 homelessness and remember my name, ‖ will turn away from their stiffneckedness and their evil deeds | if they remember
34 the ways of their fathers who sinned against the Lord. ‖ Then will I lead them back into the land which I swore to their fathers to Abraham Isaak and Yaqob, and they will rule over
35 it, | and I will multiply them that they may not be too small; ‖ and will establish with them an everlasting covenant that I will be to them a God and they to me a people, | and I will no more drive my people Israel from the land which I gave them.

very well refer to a violation of the graves which occurred at the first conquest of Jerusalem by Nabukodrossor's army (*History of Israel.* IV., 263 (III., 792, VII., 533)), just as here it is brought into connexion with Yéremyá's words as their fulfilment, viii.1 sq., the words themselves having been spoken long before the event. The disasters referred to ver. 25, and described acc. Jer. xiv. 12; xxxii. 36; xxxviii. 2, could very well befall those led away captive who would be exposed to the heat and cold; and the condition of the temple, alluded to ver. 26, need be nothing more than that unworthy one of its plunder presupposed above, i. 8, 9. But after ἐξεῤῥιμμένα, ver. 25, as was above indicated, some words have been lost through copyists' errors, and it was the Greek text in which the omission arose. On ἀποστολή,

ver. 25, comp. the *Jahrbb. der Bibl. Wiss.*, IV., p. 77.

The transition to believing supplication is made gradually by two stages, vv. 27-30a, 30b-35. Instead of complaining over these most recent great disasters, there is seen in their infliction simply a mark of the divine goodness, inasmuch as with them nothing occurred but what had before been threatened in the Pentateuch as the necessary consequence of the transgressions, so that it is therefore the merciful God who manifests even thereby his mercy in that he foretells to his people all the consequences of their sins in order that they may take warning and not afterwards complain when they follow, vv. 27-30a. For when it is further added that the same God who thus beforehand declares the consequence of

iii.   5.

1   O Lord Almighty, Israel's God! | a soul in straits and a
2   spirit crieth to thee of troubles : || hear Lord and have mercy,
3   because we sinned before thee! || Surely thou art enthroned
4   for ever, and we are perishing for ever! | O, Lord Almighty
    Israel's God, hear now the prayer of the dead of Israel, and of
    the sons of those who sinned before thee, | who hearkened not
    to thy voice our God, so that the evils clave to us! || Re-
5   member not the unrighteousnesses of our fathers, | but
6   remember thy hand and thy name at this juncture! || Surely
    thou art the Lord our God, and we will praise thee O Lord! |
7   surely for this cause thou didst put thy fear in our hearts and

their sins to his people none the less assures them of his Messianic favour if they, as he desires and hopes from them, having taken warning from the chastisements of his love, turn to him in true faith and true repentance, vv. 30 b-35, there is then nothing further in the way of this believing prayer for salvation and the flow of true petition to Him, as we then immediately find this petition in the following strophe.—It is accordingly quite as it should be when the quotation of the ancient words of the curse, vv. 28-30a pass immediately into those of the Messianic promise, vv. 30b-35, as if first the one and then the other passage were read aloud from a Sacred Scripture. And really we might suppose from the reference ver. 28 that all these passages were meant to be from the Pentateuch. The remarkable thing is, however, that although the words of the threat ver. 29a begin like Lev. xxvi. 14 ; Deut. xxviii. 15, those that follow are not found in our Pentateuch, while those of the promise, vv. 30b-35, are met with much more in Yéremyá, Hézeqiél and other prophets than in the Pentateuch. As a fact, the threat, ver. 30a, is found almost verbatim "Isa." xlviii. 8. We must, therefore, here bear in mind the great freedom with which everything " Biblical " was in such cases made use of and handled at that time. For in this respect also our author is in close relationship with similar writings of the period, comp. the observations *History of Israel*, I., 130, 178 (I, 190, 257).— It is only needful to add, that instead of προσταγμάτων, ver. 33, other manuscripts have the better reading πραγμάτων, since the passage Ezek. xx. 25 does not belong here.

5. Thus the perfectly calm, believing petition follows, with three fresh starts, iii. 1, 4, 8, and based (1) upon the general weakness of men as compared with the Eternal, iii. 1-3 ; (2) upon the condition of those who are already like completely annihilated people, like already dead members of that Community which was in reality prepared by God to praise and call on him in true fear which he himself had placed in their heart, and which now just as he desires prays to him in deepest and sincerest repentance, vv. 4-7 ; (3) upon the peculiar circumstances in which they have now to lead so difficult a life

to call upon thy name that we should praise thee in our homelessness! ‖ Surely we turned away from our hearts all the unrighteousnesses of our fathers, who have sinned before thee! ‖—

8 Behold we are to-day in our homelessness whither thou didst scatter us | for a reproach and for a curse and for a penalty according to all the unrighteousnesses of our fathers, who have rebelled from the Lord our God! ‖

among the Heathen in consequence of the sins of their forefathers, ver. 8, and it is not until this point is reached that the consciousness of the actual circumstances of contemporaries of the author most clearly breaks through all artificial veils.—It is at the very commencement, ver. 1, very well said *a soul in straits and a spirit* of that kind, that is, which was sufficiently described ii. 18.

—Who *the dead of Israel* are in this connexion is plain from ii. 18; we have in addition such previous passages as Ps. cxliii. 3; Lam. iii. 6; "Isa." xxvi. 19; lix. 10, but particularly xli. 14, where our author probably punctuated מֵרֵי.—The petition itself concludes something like Ps. lxxxix., and it cannot be said that it leaves anything essential unsaid.

A prophetic Liturgy on the basis of the Law.

Bar. iii. 9—v. 9.

We might thus most briefly and most distinctively name this piece which has been appended to the book of Barûkh, and which has already been referred to, *supra*, p. 113 sq. Though belonging to the late times, it is still a fairly prophetic piece, substantially of the same kind and plan as the small book of Habaqqûq, Vol. III., 27 sq.; it owes its origin to a similar occasion, and is based like this small book upon the Law; but nevertheless as regards its spirit it is exceedingly unlike it, inasmuch as it is almost three centuries later and belongs to a period of the ancient nation of such a totally altered character precisely as regards its spirit.

In direct contrast with the book of Barûkh, which we have just expounded, this piece is, as regards its pretentions, perfectly simple and unartificial, not having been written in the name of another or an older prophet; and inasmuch as it was designed, by a writer who was probably otherwise but little known, to be used at a public service of humiliation in the temple at Jerusalem, it has been preserved in the same unpretentious form in which it was written without any further note or heading. Jerusalem had at that time been taken by force of arms by a powerful enemy, and deprived of many of its inhabitants by forcible deportation; thus much appears to be certain from iv. 10, 24, 26; v. 6. The captive transports were all, or at all events most of them, carried away into a distant city, iv. 32, which prided itself on including within it very many different nations, iv. 34, and which was nevertheless very unlike the great cities into which captive Judeans had formerly been carried in a similar way, iv. 32, comp. iii. 10. By the latter no other cities can be intended than those known to everyone—Nineveh, Babel, and the rest in the east: we must therefore here understand quite another great city whither the main stream of the captives of war, or of other violent means, flowed at that time. We are the less able plainly to recognize the conqueror himself and his own nation inasmuch as the distant nation which proceeded in this pitiless manner, iv. 15, 16, is described simply in accordance with the earlier language, Deut. xxviii. 49, 50. It seems therefore as if very free scope were here given for conjecture: and we might be bold enough to suppose the conquest of Jerusalem by Pompeius and the deportation of many captives to Rome at that time was the event intended. However, there are here no details at all pointing to that time; on the contrary, people in Jerusalem were then still looking above all towards the east as the region in which most of the chief communities are whose banishment was most deplored in Palestine, iv. 36, 37; v. 5; and the west receives only subordinate mention, v. 5, as the direction in which many had also been scattered. The condition of things, therefore, was still substantially the same as it was under the Persian rule; but for the reasons already mentioned we cannot here suppose a Persian conquest is intended.

On the other hand, everything agrees well with the supposition that the conquest of Jerusalem by Ptolemæus I. in the year 320 B.C. is the historical background of the piece. The circumstances of this conquest in detail are but little known, but we know that Jerusalem then suffered severely and was compelled to submit to the loss of a large number of captives, who were transported chiefly to Alexandria : * this city, which, although still so new, had rapidly and powerfully risen by a confluence of people from the most various nations, is that which is intended iv. 32. This is also confirmed by another circumstance. In this book the divine wisdom is referred to as the one highest possession of Israel, which must remain inalienable and in respect of which no other nation can compare with her, and this divine wisdom is treated as identical with the sacred Law, iii. 9—iv. 1. It is true, indeed, that this view remains the same in Israel during the next centuries also, and finally obtains its noblest development in the Alexandrine Philo. But we find here, together with this view, that Israel is compared with other nations which laboured to find out wisdom and obtained great fame in the search; and whilst at a later date than that named above the Greeks must necessarily have also been mentioned, we find here, iii. 22, 23, it is only the Phœnicians and Arabians who are named. In the year 320 B.C. that was still quite natural in Jerusalem : Greek wisdom was then a wholly unknown thing there, whilst the very next half-century brought about the well-known great change in this respect.

Another proof for this date is found in the meaning and the plan of the piece itself. For we have here still not merely the simple, genuine, ancient religion of Israel in the form which was possible in that age, but also a piece of prophetic art in its genuine form, such as was very well possible in those times, but which was later on lost beyond restoration. Divine

---

* All that is at present known of this event is collected in the *History of Israel*, V., 225 sq. (IV., 290 sq.). We might now raise the question whether the Psalms of Solomon belong to this period.

consolation shall be administered in that dark day of mourning for the community, the best that prophetic thoughts and prophetic art can administer; a public solemnity shall therefore be observed in the temple, in which all people may take part. But this consolation shall not be based upon the ancient Messianic promises simply, as if it were enough to repeat them in a new form and clothed in some new style of art. The community has not fallen into this most recent misery without fault of her own: and is not the fact that she has lain so long under the yoke of foreigners partly a consequence of her continued want of perfect energy and sincerity in her own true religion? In this religion Israel possesses a divine wisdom which no other nation has been able by utmost effort to obtain; it is identical with the contents of the sacred Law, in the form in which this was received since 'Esra's time. In its religion Israel must grow much more steadfast than it has been hitherto: it may then hope for new prosperity in accordance with ancient promises. But this is above all the business of the individual members of this nation, of men personally and of each separate community; or is it of any avail to be perhaps angry, if not with God himself, yet with Jerusalem, *i.e.*, the whole community, including all that belongs to it and the true religion taught by it? That is really now done by so many, iv. 8.

With this fundamental thought as its basis, a small drama is here unfolded, such as may be performed at occasional solemnities of public worship. The prophet comes on the scene admonishing Israel, reminding it of its incomparable, eternal possession, but also reminding it of its unfaithfulness towards God and towards Jerusalem, *i.e.*, the community, and thus introducing the words of this mother, now in such deep sorrow, to her neighbouring cities as to her children, iii. 9— iv. 9*a*. Thus the noble, now so profoundly humiliated, mother herself begins to speak, addressing her neighbouring cities and then her numerous children of the dispersion also, bewailing the sins of her children, bewailing their exposed condition and helplessness, and yet hoping and exhorting all her children to have true hope, iv. 9*b*—29. But at this point a Higher One himself begins to speak, comforting her also and renewing all the ancient Messianic hopes, iv. 30—v. 9. The whole drama unfolds itself in symmetrical strophes of medium length, but, corresponding to the nature of a mourning solemnity, in such a way that the number of them grows successively less with each great member of the drama; the first section has five, the second has four, and the third three. The art of the mourning and penitential poem is therefore at this late period still that of the best poetry of the ancient literature, see *Dichter des Alten Bundes*, Ia, p. 148 sq.

The entire piece is not merely very artistic, and at the same time purely Hebrew, but it is also in style in the highest degree refined, the sublime passages from "Isa." xl.—lxvi. particularly, then the book of Job and the existing book of Proverbs, being present to the mind of the prophet-poet. Still, nearly all that we have here is but an echo from such earlier and grander books: the only new thing strictly speaking is the view of the relation of Wisdom to the sacred Law. With all this, the Greek of the book is so good that we might be tempted to look upon it as its original language, did not certain errors and obscurities of the Greek show that it is after all but a translation.

I. *The Prophet.*

1.

i.
9   Hear Israel commandments of life ! | attend ye to understand
10 discretion ! ‖ What is it Israel ? what that thou art in the
11 land of the enemies, waxedst old in a strange land, | wast
     alike polluted with the dead, counted with those of Hades ? |
12 —Thou forsookest the fountain of wisdom ! hadst thou walked
13 in the ways of God, thou wouldst dwell in peace for all time ! ‖

14 Learn where is discretion, where is strength, where is understanding, | in order to know therewith where is length of
15 days and life, where is light of eyes and peace! || Who found
16 the place of her, and who entered into her treasures? || Where are the princes of the nations and the rulers of the beasts upon
17 the earth, | who played with the birds of heaven, and heaped up silver and gold wherein men trust, and there is no end of their possession? ||

2.

18 Yes who built* and were anxious for silver, and there
19 is no sufficiency of their works: | they vanished and went
20 down to Hades, and others arose in their place. || Younger men saw the light and settled upon the earth: | but the way of knowledge they knew not, neither did they understand her
21 paths; | nor did their sons lay hold of her, they remained far
22 from the way of them. || Neither was she heard in Kanáan, nor
23 seen in Thaeman; | also the sons of Hagar who search into understanding, who are upon the earth the merchants of Madyan and Thaeman the narrators of myths and the searchers into understanding— | but the way of wisdom they knew not, nor did they remember her paths. ||

3.

24 O Israel, how great is the house of God and wide the place of his possession, | great and hath no end, high and immea-
25 surable! || There were born the giants famous from of old, having
26 become very huge, understanding war: | not these did God choose, nor gave he to them the way of knowledge; | and they perished because they had no discretion, perished on
29 account of their heedlessness. || —Who ascended up to heaven
30 and took her, and brought her down out of the clouds? | who passed over the sea and found her, and will carry her off as
31 choice gold? || There is none who knoweth her way, or who considereth her path: | only he who knoweth all things knoweth her, discovered her with his understanding. ||

4.

32 He who prepared the earth for endless time, filled it with

---

* The author translates τὸ ἀργύριον τεκταίνοντες *die auf das silber baueten.*— Tr.

33 four footed beasts of burden; | he who sendeth forth the light
34 and it goeth, called it and it obeyed him with trembling; || and
the stars shined at their watch-posts and rejoiced, | he called
them and they said "here we be!" | shined with rejoicing unto
35 him who made them: || this our God (another will not be
36 taken account of beside him!)—discovered all the way of
knowledge and gave it to Yaqob his servant and Israel his
37 beloved. || Afterwards she was seen upon the earth, and her
iv. conversation was among men. || This is the book of the ordi-
1 nances of God, and the Law which endureth for ever; | all who
keep it may live, but they who forsake it will die. ||

5.

2 Return Yaqob, and lay hold of her, | walk towards the
3 shining before her light! || give not to another the honour, | and
4 all the things profitable to thee to a strange people! || Happy
are we Israel that the things pleasing to God are known to
us. || —Take courage ye my people, thou incense-offering
Israel! | ye were sold to the nations not for destruction:
because ye angered God were ye given over to the adver-
saries; || for ye provoked him who formed you, sacrificing to
demons and not to God, | forgot him who brought you up the
eternal God, and grieved her also who nourished you Jeru-
salem; || for she saw the wrath which had come upon you
from God and said:

I. The first word, *Hear, Israel!* is evidently selected in this form because at that time it was a favourite custom to open certain solemn addresses in the synagogues with Deut. vi. 4: but here words are immediately added from such passages as Prov. iv. 1, 22, 23; xv. 31, because it is intended to speak specially of wisdom. From this opening, however, the discourse comes rapidly in its first strophe to the proof of the fact, that the true wisdom must be wanting to the nation because it has been already so long dragging along its existence among the *dead*, *i.e.*, such as were without the true pure life mentioned ver. 9, *i.e.*, among Heathen and under their rule, itself as it were dead and polluted by the dead, vv. 10-13, that wisdom being wanting to it which was certainly not to be found among the ancient powerful rulers of the Heathen, inasmuch as it is one with the power of true religion and true life, vv. 14-17.—If the ancient native land of Israel is here called a *foreign* land, ver. 10, we need not be surprised at this at a time when the most utterly foreign nations and rulers marched over its soil, as if it were entirely lost to Israel; and the nation was indeed at that time, as regards a large and noble portion of it, not in its own land in any sense, and this fact must be specially borne in mind, according to iv. 31, 32 and the whole meaning of this piece, in the case of this expression which is used at the very opening of the discourse. The phrase, ver. 10, *what is it Israel, what that thou* . . . seems like an echo from Prov. xxxi. 2.—That so much importance is ascribed, ver. 16, to the power of the kings over *animals*, is explained by the fact that in those times war-horses decided everything : with these royal quadrupeds, which are therefore alluded to again ver. 32, are thus associated, ver. 17, the *birds* with which the kings *sport*, the falcons and similar birds of the chase.

In the next four strophes ((2) vv. 18-23 ; (3) vv. 24-31 ; (4) ver. 32—iv. 1 ; (5) iv. 2-9 *a*) the climax in the unfolding of the thought is gradually reached in the last but one of them, while in the last and fifth of the whole section, the exhortation commenced above in the first is more forcibly presented : thus vv. 18-23 the above glance at the vanity of all endeavour after wealth and wisdom, as it has been shown in all times in the case of the Heathen, is further pursued ; then in vv. 24-31 the same glance ranges still further over the whole extent of ancient and modern history and the various efforts of the races of mankind, in order, in vv. 32—iv. 1, to show, in its highest survey, that true wisdom is with God alone, but that Israel has an incalculably precious share of it in his Law ; and in the last strophe, iv. 2-9 *a*, we have a powerful return to the exhortation, which it was the aim of the section to supply. Such is the simple course of the thoughts of the great prophetic discourse ; and it is impossible not to see that there is something very complete in this arrangement in five strophes. The opening of the second strophe, vv. 18, 19, is at once highly rhetorical, a greatly interlacing sentence which, notwithstanding great difference in minor respects, corresponds fully in the structure of the various clauses to the previous one vv. 16, 17. The words *and there is no* ἐξεύρεσις [Germ. *gefinde*] *of their works* particularly are placed in the sentence exactly like the words *and there is no end of their possession*, ver. 16; but the words themselves are, as far as the Greek goes, very obscure, and the sense of them is first discovered when it is remembered that they are only an inaccurate translation of a phrase like וְאֵין מְצָא, *and there is no sufficiency of their works*, in which case they answer completely to the last member, ver. 16; comp. with regard to מְצָא the note on Ps. xxxii 6, *Dichter des A. Bs., Ib*, p. 66.* There are three successive generations described vv. 18-21, but only in the most general sense ; but it is said all the more appropriately that *the sons* also of the later generation did *not lay hold of wisdom*, inasmuch as it is *per se* becoming that the sons should take up what the older people left unfinished. The reading αὐτῶν after ὁδοῦ need not be changed into αὐτῆς if the word is only referred to τρίβους, comp with regard to the possibility of דֶּרֶךְ נְתִיבוֹת, Prov. xii. 28.

The order of time is then, ver. 23, followed by that of place : neither the

---

* The note is : " A chief portion of the emphasis falls upon לְעֵת מְצֹא, *at a time of reaching to* (מְצֹא, *to reach to, to suffice*, Num. xi. 22), *i.e.*, at the time when the aim, the object, can still be attained, therefore at the suitable, right time, like the Latin *aptus*, from Sansk. *áp, to reach*, ἱκανός, the LXX correct in point of sense ἐν καιρῷ εὐθέτῳ."—*Tr.*

Phœnicians on the west nor the Arabians, famous as zealous inquirers after wisdom, on the east, found her. But since the Arabians here intended were at the same time famous as indefatigable traders, and as such probably then more so than the Phœnicians, whilst wealth is here spoken of as well as wisdom, vv. 16 sq., they are thus further described as by way of correction: *who are upon the earth* (read ὅι ἐπὶ τῆς instead of οἱ) the famous *merchants of Madian and Thæman*, and as Thæman is undoubtedly here and ver. 22 taken from Job iv. 1 ; vi. 19, so the men of Madyan are placed with them after Gen. xxxvii. 28 and other passages. For it cannot be doubted that Μεῤῥάν is simply from מִדְיָן or מְדָן by an error in reading on the part of the Greek translator ; the town Merane (from Pharan*) on the Red Sea, in Pliny, *Nat. Hist.*, VI., 32, as well as its inhabitants, *Maranitæ, Diod.*, III., 43, and *Strabo*, XVI., 4, is foreign to this passage, where only famous names of ancient times are appropriate.—It is in the highest degree noteworthy that they are then in the second member, before they are reverted to again as *inquirers after wisdom*, also further quite briefly extolled as *the* well-known μυθολόγοι, *narrators of myths and legends* (*sagenerzähler*) ; this undoubtedly refers to a literature of legends and stories, much read at that time, and which spread from this people over the whole earth, a precursor of the later *Thousand and One Nights*, and of which we probably still find remnants in Oriental books, without knowing or surmising that they owe their origin ultimately to this source. This entire description, ver. 23, is for us at present all the more important, inasmuch as it certainly treats of the power of the Nabathean people which was then recently acquired, comp. *History of Israel*, V., 351 (IV., 458 sq.), only that our prophet-speaker avoids the mention of this new name.

In the new and more extended glance into *the House of God, i.e.*, the great world (after "Isa." lxvi. 1 ; Ps. civ. 3 *a*), which begins with greater vivacity, as if to complete the historical review, reference is before everything made to the Giants of the primæval world, well-known from Gen. vi. 4, who as such immense combatants stood most in need of wisdom, and yet found such a miserable end on account of their *lack of counsel*, vv. 26-28. It is impossible that this short description can have been taken simply from the few words Gen. vi. 4, although they also are here used *verbatim* in part; without doubt there existed before the Book of Henokh writings in which the histories of the primæval world had been dealt with, particularly from a belligerent point of view, comp. the remarks in *History of Israel*, I., 380, note (I.. 514 sq. *anmerk*), and the *Abhandlung über des Aeth. B. Henókh entstehung sinn und zusammensezung* (*Gött.* 1854), p. 77 sq. In Philo Henokh is very often the model of reputance, as *de praemiis*, c. iii., where he is not named but intended ; the way in which he is described, *de Abrahamo*, c. iii. sq. and c. ix., manifestly following elaborate writings, is particularly surprising.—But so much the more rapidly does the discourse pass at the end of this strophe, vv. 29-31, to the proof of the fact, that indeed according to all history genuine wisdom is to be found only with God himself as the creator of the world ; and here the words and thoughts Deut. xxx. 12, 13 and those of Job xxviii. 12 sq. ; xxxviii. 15 sq., are

---

* Comp. *History of Israel*, II., 189 (II., 267).—*Tr*.

completely blended together, whilst at the same time, according to the connexion of the whole discourse, it is only these words from Job which primarily belong here, which were previously discernible, vv. 15, 20, and which are carried further to their purest elevation in the following strophe, iii. 32—iv. 1. And yet the thoughts in their highest elevation are here little more than a combination of the words of Job xxviii. 23 sq.; xxxviii. 7, 19, 35 ; that each of the stars has its *watchpost*, ver. 34 ; Sir. xliii. 9, 10, is only a further carrying out of the words " Isa." xl. 26, which our author must have found ready to his hand in a writer of the interim. But the rapid transition to the *Book of the Law* as, so far as regards its subject-matter, like this wisdom, inasmuch as those who follow it obtain *Life*, and therewith the highest good of wisdom, is all the more surprising. particularly after the God of Israel has been so strictly pointed to vv. 15, 36 *b*, in an insertion in addition to the words of Job, as excluding all heathen gods. Still this transition is prepared for and also explained by the thought, ver. 37, that this wisdom, after it had been committed to Israel in early times as intended for it, *afterwards* (that is, through Moses and as in visible form) *appeared upon the earth and had its conversation among men*, as if it was thereby intended to refer what is said of wisdom Prov. viii. 31 particularly to the historical life and work of Moses.

It is undoubtedly this idealization of the Law, treasured in such an eloquent discourse, which secured for the whole piece its preservation, inasmuch as it fell in with a fundamental principle which grew exclusively prevalent in the course of the next centuries. But after the discourse, iv. 1, has reverted with the mention of *life* to one of its first words, iii. 9, in the last strophe, iv. 2-9 *a*, it makes for its goal with all the fuller sails—to exhort and comfort exclusively. The consolation seeks to make itself felt, vv. 5, 6 : and here appears, in the affectionate address, an appellation — μνημόσυνον Ἰσραήλ — which occurs nowhere else, and which in the Greek form is wholly unintelligible. We must suppose that it is only a translation of אִפְרַת יִשְׂרָ' *thou incense-offering Israel* (comp. *Antiquities*, p. 62 (51)) : thus a bold speaker or poet might before our author, on a proper occasion, denominate that nation whose whole life (and therefore itself in a certain sense) ought to be continually a sweet odour for the true God or a sweet-smelling sacrifice for him ; and ramifications of this phrase taken from sacrificial usages remain to us, 2 Cor. ii. 15 ; Phil. iv. 18.—However, the exhortation must here prevail : with it the discourse begins, vv. 2, 3, and to it it immediately comes back again with an easy transition, vv. 6 *b*-9 *a*. The nation of that time is charged with two things : (1) that it *sacrificed to the Demons and not to God*, ver. 7, or, which amounts to the same thing, *gave to another* (God) *its honour and its profitable things, i.e.*, its property, *to a foreign nation*, ver. 3 : phrases which are mutually explanatory and point to the fact, that many members of the nation exhibited a questionable inclination to Heathen habits, which is intelligible enough when it is remembered that the great ruling power of the world was at that time always Heathenism. Of an entirely different kind is (2) the charge that the nation as it had *forgotten* God its father and *nourisher* (after Deut. xxxii. 6 sq.) by that first sin, so it had *grieved Jerusalem* (the Community, Church) as its spiritual mother by despair of the true religion, of its power and its institutions. Thus far more than in the magnificent representations of "Isa." xl.—lxvi., particularly of ch. liv., lx., in which our author's mind fully revels, does Jerusalem already appear here as a being of celestial nature, hovering high above the separate communities and their members (her children), as the high mother-church associated with God himself, who, though for the moment most deeply afflicted and bitterly lamenting, nevertheless still more bears in her loving heart the fortunes of her children. She foresaw that great misery which now fell upon her children, but which she could not avert because of their own sin, ver. 9 *a*, and she notwithstanding desires to comfort her despairing children and to teach her unthankful ones, but in the first instance precisely as the exalted mother she turns rather to her younger sister-churches, *i.e.*, to the several Synagogues outside the capital, only entreating their compassion, and not till afterwards does she gradually turn also to her individual children who are now by force carried away and dispersed. We have here already the outlines of the constitution of the Church which were soon after further developed by Christianity; although the *daughters of Ssion, i.e.* the towns in the country, Ps. xlviii. 12, form thus early a transition to this conception. And after the last words, vv. 8, 9 *a*, have thus as by a bound conducted to this point, then follows

II. *Ssion*.

1.

10 Hear ye neighbouring cities of Ssion! God brought upon me great mourning! | for I saw the captivity of my sons and daughters, which the Eternal brought upon them! || Surely I nourished them with joy, but sent them away with weeping and mourning. || Let no man rejoice over me the widow and forsaken of many: | I was desolated because of the sins of my children, because they turned aside from God's Law and knew not his judgments, | nor walked in the ways of the commands of God, nor trod the paths of discipline in his righteousness. ||

2.

14 Come hither Ssion's neighbour cities! and remember the captivity of my sons and daughters which the Eternal brought
15 upon them! || For he brought upon them a nation from afar, a shameless and strange-tongued nation, because they rever-
16 enced not any old man nor pitied a youth, | and carried away the beloved ones of the widow and deprived the lone woman
17 of her daughters. | —But I—what can I do to help you? |
18 surely he who caused the evils will save you out of your
19 enemies' hand! || Go your way children, go your way, | surely

20 *I* was left desolate, ‖ took off the garment of peace, and put on the sackcloth of my misery! | I will cry to the Eternal in my days! ‖

3.

21 Take courage take courage ye children, make complaint to God, and he will deliver you out of the tyranny out of the
22 hand of the enemy! ‖ Surely I hope in the Eternal for your salvation, | and joy came to me from the Holy One at the mercy which will shortly come to you from the Eternal your
23 saviour; ‖ surely I sent you forth with weeping and mourning, | but God will restore you to me with joy and gladness
24 for ever. ‖ For just as now Ssion's neighbouring cities have seen your captivity, | so will they shortly see the salvation by your God, which will come upon you with great glory and brightness of the Eternal. ‖

4.

25 Children, endure steadfastly the wrath came from God upon you! | 'the enemy persecuted thee—and thou wilt shortly see
26 his destruction and tread upon their necks." ‖ My delicate ones travelled rough ways, | were taken away as a flock robbed
27 by enemies: | take courage children and make complaint unto God! surely there will be remembrance of you by him who
28 brought it on you. ‖ For as your thought was to go astray from
29 God, ten times turn ye to seek him: | surely he who brought the evils upon you will bring upon you everlasting joy with your salvation. ‖

II. The voice of this exalted mother herself, as she in the first two strophes entreats her younger sisters for their compassion and desires to call them to her, but in the last two, as if she had herself grown more courageous again, turns to her own children who had been by force carried off to exhort them to have courage. She feels that she is a *widow, forsaken, alone*, after figures which are from "Isa." liv., li. 18, and other passages of the great book of the great anonymous prophet, which is present to our author's mind particularly from this place onwards: thus in the first strophe, vv. 9 *b*-13, she refers specially to that which most closely concerns her, her own helplessness after the deportation of her children, though she knows that they are certainly not innocent; in the second strophe, vv. 14-20, she refers principally to the barbarity of the enemy. Both strophes begin quite suitably with the wish, that the younger sisters, the πάροικοι (*dwellers by*, smaller neighbouring cities) might come to comfort her, not to express pleasure at her condition: but just this mention of the mighty, barbarous nation in the second strophe, ver. 15, 16, forms the transition: if she cannot help her *sons and daughters* who have been thus carried off, if she is compelled in her helplessness and deep mourning to proclaim to them that they must for the present only go whither the enemy transports them, she nevertheless knows that it is only the same God who sent these evils upon them who can once more help them, and only to him will she also turn, vv. 17-20.

But after she has turned to Him, calm and collected, she is now able in the second half of this discourse to directly exhort these her children also to have that divine courage with which she feels herself filled afresh, to exhort them to all endurance in misery and to point them to the Messianic prosperity. But when at the end of the third strophe, vv. 21-24, she once more takes a glance at the sister-cities whose compassion had been besought, she does not forget in either strophe, amid all the words of comfort which she addresses to her own children, to remind them also of their own guilt and the duty to eradicate this in the proper way, and mentions this at the beginning of the first strophe, ver. 21, and again at the end of the second, vv. 27, 28. The strong expression *to tread upon the necks*, ver. 25, is here simply quoted from Deut. xxxiii. 29 in accordance with an interpretation of the word בָּמוֹת which must have then been popular in the schools and is also found in the LXX, whence this translator might take it.

III. *An Angel.*

1.

30 Take courage Jerusalem! | comfort thee will he who named
31 thee. | Miserable are they who did thee injury and rejoiced at
32 thy fall, | miserable the cities which thy children served,
33 miserable she which received thy sons! || For as she rejoiced at thy fall and exulted over thy corpse, | she will mourn over
34 her own desolation; || and I will take from her the fame of mother of nations,* | and her proud boasting must become
35 mourning: || for fire will come upon her from the Eternal for long days, | and she will be inhabited of Demons for most time. ||

2.

34 Look about thee to the East, Jerusalem, | and behold the joy which is coming to thee from God: || behold thy sons come
37 whom thou sentest away, | they come gathered together from
v. East to West—by the word of the Holy One, rejoicing in the

---

* Ewald renders πολυοχλία *völkermutter*, comp. his interpretation of the verse *supra*, p. 124.—Tr.

1 glory of God! ‖ Put off Jerusalem the garment of thy mourning and injury, | and put on the adornment of the glory from
2 God for ever! ‖ cast round thee the robe of righteousness before God, set as a mitre on thy head the glory of the
3 Eternal! | surely God will show to everything under heaven
4 thy brightness! ‖ surely thy name will be called of God for ever "Peace of Righteousness" and "Glory of Piety."

3.

5 Arise Jerusalem and take thy stand upon the height and look about thee towards the East, | and behold thy children gathered together from the setting of the sun to its rising by the word of the Holy One, rejoicing at the remembrance of
6 God! ‖ For though they went out from thee on foot driven by enemies, | yet God will bring them in unto thee with glory
7 borne as in the throne of the king. ‖ Surely God commanded that every high mountain and the everlasting hills should be made low, and the ravines should be filled up unto the level of the earth | in order that Israel may go along safely under the glory of God! ‖ yea the trees also and every sweet-smelling tree made a shade for Israel by God's command! ‖ For Israel's God will lead them with rejoicing in the light of his glory,] with the mercy and righteousness from him. ‖

III. It might be supposed that the neighbouring cities, thus forcibly summoned to sympathy and friendly approach, would speak the words of comfort to the mother in accordance with her wish : but there is nothing in these words themselves which definitely points to this. It is true that God is here generally spoken of as if he were not himself speaking; still, since He himself once, iv. 34, also speaks in an entirely new and highly significant oracle, it is best to suppose that these words of comfort are spoken by an exalted Angel, and this supposition is the most suitable on other grounds.

The thrice repeated exhortation to Jerusalem, after "Isa." ch. lx. ; li. 17 and similar passages, to rise from her mourning, forms of itself the commencement of each of the three strophes, the first of which appropriately directs the glance particularly to the capital of the enemy, the second to Jerusalem, the third to her children who are sometime to return. The fact that at the mention of the future of the hostile capital, ver. 35, the words about the Demons allude to "Isa." xiii. 21, 22, is not sufficient to prove that by that capital Babel is intended. For in general the quotations from earlier prophecies here are very free, just as in the words v. 7-9 very many are a re-echo from "Isa." ch. xl. sq., and then when it is said all these things are to come to pass *by the word* or *the command of the Holy One*, iv. 37 ; v. 8, we have nothing more than general references to those prophecies. It remains to note some

APPENDIX, 3. 1.—THE GREEK YÉREMYÁ.

further defects in the translation : (1) *comfort thee will he who named thee,* iv. 30, is too short and would have in Hebrew a longer and weightier form הַקֹּרֵא לְךָ בְּשֵׁם; thereby is intended probably the name in the passage, which is supposed to be known, " Isa." lx. 14, or Ezek. xlviii. 35, although here below also, v. 4, two names are added.—(2) ὡς θρόνον,

v. 6, can only be explained if כְּבָבָא stood in the original ; for the figure is manifestly based on the simpler one of " Isa." xlix. 22, 23, and is made stronger only so as to correspond to the increasing elevation of the Messianic hope. Owing to the obscurity of the Greek, ancient readers and translators greatly stumbled at the passage ; and Pesh. translates simply *upon a throne*.

The Greek Epistle of Yéremyá.

(Bar. ch. vi.)

We insert at this place this piece also, which acc. p. 113 was in many manuscripts closely connected with the book of Barûkh. It has characteristics resembling the prophetic writings, and must have been much read in the times immediately preceding the birth of Christ and in those immediately following it. But it owes its origin like all these pieces simply to the Greek Bible when it had become Christian.

This piece brings together, as in a last desperate attempt, everything that could be said in these later times by way of warning against idolatry, or rather almost simply by way of ridicule of idols. What Yéremyá himself had said on this subject, ch. x., may have seemed to later people in the Hellenistic age as no longer quite adequate: so a Hellenist undertook by this piece afresh to lift up the voice of Yéremyá to meet the wants of his time, as if the ancient prophet had only sent this epistle by way of warning after those who were destined after the first Chaldean conquest of Jerusalem to be carried to Babel and whither they were already on the way: for that this first Chaldean conquest is intended here can no more be doubted than in the case of the book of Barûkh. And it is as if the man who here ventures to renovate a Yéremyá-voice desired to collect as in one *fasciculus* everything that was scattered in the earlier writings, such as Jer. ch. x., "Isa." xl.—xlix.; Ps. cxv., in ridicule of the idols, in order to speak with sufficient effect to tell upon his contemporaries in that later age. It is, however, remarkable that in doing this our author not only repeats with new skill and aptly puts together, as other later authors had done, the oracles of the earlier books, but he also treats the subject in as new and as independent a manner as was very well possible in his late age. Some things are here but an echo from Yéremyá and other earlier writings; but the working out of the subject is new in character and manner, and in this respect sufficiently independent.

That is to say, the most characteristic feature of this piece is nothing other than the evident combination of two completely different literary elements. As a genuine Hellenist the author is, on the one hand, an orator and oratorical writer quite of the Grecian type, loves the Grecian style, which is rhetorically redundant, ornate with flowers of rhetoric, and loving triumphs of artistic effect; he also himself writes Greek on his own account, and ventures to make the ancient and venerable Yéremyá even to speak afresh in this rehabilitation. On the other hand, he has after all been tolerably intimately initiated into the spirit of the ancient Hebrew manner of speaking and writing, and cannot forget that it is his design here to make the voice of an ancient prophet deliver afresh its mighty accents. It is from the combination of these two exceedingly different elements of discourse and language that this piece has taken the form it has; and nowhere else does this mixture of such fundamentally different elements manifest itself so plainly as in it.

The first thing to observe in this respect is, that the author is no longer able to bring his discourse to the elevation of the genuine prophetic style; it lacks the poetic rhythm of the verse-members, and the beautiful symmetry which characterizes prophetic writing. Indeed, Greek rhetoric, the object of which is to quickly persuade, and the semi-poetic, finely membered, freely soaring speech of a genuine Hebrew prophet, are two things which can hardly be combined; and at all events our orator has almost entirely failed to accomplish the task of combining them. Similarly his Greek language seeks occasionally to assume the peculiarities of the ancient Hebrew :* but even in this respect he only partially succeeds. The really prophetic elevation, according to which everything must be uttered as immediately as possible as a word from God himself, is barely attempted at the opening of the book;† from the beginning to the end the style is principally that of Greek oratory, and the weighty "thus saith God" of the Hebrew prophets nowhere makes itself heard.

And still this piece adheres in its course to a law inherited from ancient times, by which a Hebrew prophet's discourse so greatly distinguishes itself from every merely Grecian piece of oratory. It is at all events, as a whole, broken up into members after the ancient Hebrew manner, since it adheres to the measure of strophes of a medium length, and carries out this principle with regularity; indeed, it is the old sacred number of ten symmetrical strophes of this medium length to which the speaker binds himself. It is only by this means that the discourse in this instance finds the long, measured steps in which to move as it pursues the fundamental thought. For after the first strophe has presented briefly the fundamental thought, vv. 2-7, that proposition which as rising out of this contains the doctrine of the entire subsequent discourse is proved in the next three strophes: the proposition is that the idol-gods *must not be feared* because they are no-gods, and it is proved from what is most obvious, from their artificial origin and outward appearance. Then from the fifth to the last strophe what is less obvious is shown, namely, that they cannot be anything more than *no-gods*, and this is

---

* As in ἀφομοιωθέντες ἀφομοιωθῆτε, ver. 4, acc. § 312 c.

† *To proclaim to them as it was commanded him by God.* simply in the heading only. ver. 1.

done in very various ways, but particularly by a reference to their powerlessness and the treatment they receive from the priests themselves. But in each of these ten strophes is heard briefly at least once the general doctrine.

In the detailed working out of the thought Yéremyá himself in his individuality, and with his true contemporaries, vanishes more and more, and only the orator as such comes by degrees solely to the front: as is the case with Solomon in Ecclesiastes. Still, as in this book the king is, at all events at the commencement and once in the middle, somewhat brought forward in his historical individuality,* so is it in the piece before us. In the middle of the long discourse reference is for once made, vv. 40-43, with greater particularity to the peculiar gods of the Babylonians. But at the opening, where the time of Yéremyá and the possible occasion of such a discourse must more pointedly appear, the author has the opportunity to give, quite after the manner of the later prophet-authors, a hint with regard to his own actual time, at all events for intelligent readers, as will have to be explained further when we come to the Book of Daniel. That is, when he makes Yéremyá say, ver. 3, that those who are about to be carried away to Babel would be there a *long time*, namely, *until seven generations*, it is true he makes reference to that prophet's prophecy of the seventy years, but he quietly extends these seventy years to seven generations; and as a generation must necessarily extend over more than ten years, and can, according to Gen. xv. 13-16, in higher discourse, as after a divine measure, extend over one hundred years,† we find here that the seventy years become seven hundred. This is quite similar to the way in which in Dan. ch. ix. seven times seventy years have been

---

* Comp. *Dichter des A. B.*, II., 281 sq.

† Comp. *History of Israel*, I., p. 402 (I., p. 575). A special proof of the point that our author really had in his mind at these words ver. 3 the passage, Gen. xv. 13-16, with its plain numbers, is also implied in the fact that he borrowed the words *but afterwards I will lead you out from there in peace* without doubt from Gen. xv. 15, 16, in a free adaptation.

artificially derived from these seventy years of Yéremyá: and our author might have that prophetic literary process in the book of Daniel and the book itself already before him. But in that case we obtain a clear indication that the contemporaries for whom the author published this piece could not have lived earlier than some five or six centuries after Yéremyá. For the Messianic hope to which those words, ver. 3, at the same time point does not, it is true, come very prominently forward anywhere in this book: and the author could very well conceive the interval before its arrival as still more than another century. At the same time, the hope itself had not vanished either from him or his contemporaries; and a prophetic book had necessarily to refer to it and the interval before its fulfilment.

If these indications conduct us to about the beginning of the last century before Christ as the date of the origin of this piece, the same date follows from other signs. The Grecian kings had then already greatly fallen in estimation and power, vv. 18, 34, 53, 56, 59, 66, were easily deposed, and were so degenerate that there was a desire for some one who was somewhat braver and had ruled longer than the others. This which is here everywhere insisted upon with great emphasis points to the times of the last Seleukidæ and Ptolemies. The author may have lived in Egypt and have principally Egyptian Hellenists in his mind as his readers: though the descriptions of the gods, vv. 14, 15, 30-32, point rather to the Phrygian gods; and at that time there were many Hellenists living in Asia Minor also. Our book is alluded to as early as 2 Macc. ii. 2, those words particularly on account of the *adornment around the golden and silver images* referring too plainly to the beginning of our piece, vv. 3-9, and there is no reason why the writer of 2 Maccabees should not have been acquainted with our little book.

142   APPENDIX, 3. 1.—*THE GREEK YÉREMYÁ.*

1. *Copy of a letter which Yéremyá* sent out to those who were to be carried by the king of the Babylonians as prisoners to Babylon, to announce to them as it was commanded him of God.

1.

2 On account of the sins which ye committed against God, ye will be carried unto Babylon as prisoners by Nabukodrossor
3 the king of the Babylonians. Being come therefore unto Babylon, ye will be there many years and a long time unto seven generations: after this will I bring you out thence in
4 peace. But now ye will see in Babylon silver and golden and wooden gods borne upon shoulders, showing fear to the
5 Heathen: take good heed therefore lest ye also become more and more like the aliens and fear seize you on account of them,
6 seeing how people before and behind them worship them. But
7 say ye in your thought "thee must we worship O Lord!" For "my Angel will be with you," he himself also seeking after your souls.

2.

8 For their staff is polished by the artificer, they themselves
9 gilded and silvered; but are lies and are not able to speak! And as for a maiden loving adornment taking gold they prepare

---

1. *Carried upon shoulders,* ver. 4, after "Isa." xlvi. 1, comp. Vol. IV., 282. That in this position *they show fear to the Heathen,* is a concise way of saying that *show to them that they ought to be feared,* like יִרְאָת, Ps. xc. 11. But it is precisely only to *the Heathen* they show it, whilst our prophet at the end of each of the three next strophes, and then throughout the oracle, calls aloud to the people of God that *they are not to be feared.*—When they are moving amongst the Heathen, ver. 6, they shall, if not aloud, yet at all events *in thought,* constantly say *thee* (and not the idols) *must men worship, O Lord!* (δέσποτα instead of κύριε, as the LXX at other times translate Yahvé.) Moreover, they may always, acc. to the words Ex. xxiii. 20, have the word of God said to them, *My Angel will be with you!* and may know that he who said that is *also himself* always present *seeking after their souls,* never leaving them out of consideration and saving them when they deserve it, after 1 Chron. xxviii. 9, and so many other passages.

2. It ought to be obvious enough that γλῶσσα cannot here signify the actual tongue itself, but only, like *lingula,* a rod or staff rounded at one end so as to be similar in shape to a tongue, as the staff of wood round which the rich materials and the head of the idol-figure were fastened. The description

10 coronals for the heads of their gods: but it happeneth also that the priests taking away gold and silver from their gods employ
11 it upon themselves, but they will give it from them also to the harlots under the roof.—They deck them also as men with
12 garments, the silver gods and the golden and wooden gods: but
13 these save not themselves from rust and all manner of corrosion. They are hung round with purple raiment, people wipe their face on account of the dust of the room which lies thick upon them.
14 —And a sceptre hath he as a man a district judge, he who will
15 not destroy him that sinneth against him! he hath indeed a little staff in his right and an axe, but he will not deliver
16 himself from war and robbers.—Whence they are recognizable as No-gods: therefore fear ye them not!

3.

17 For as a man's vessel broken in pieces becometh useless, so are their gods If they are set up in the gardens, their eyes
18 are full of dust from the feet of those going in and out; and just as for an offender against the king the yards are closed or as

begins with this primary foundation of the manufactured god, with the *wood* which is always mentioned along with the silver and gold, vv. 11, 30, 39, 50, 57 sq.; it then refers to the abundance of gold and silver which has to be used upon the wood for ornament, particularly of the head, after that to the clothes, the costly materials of which are indicated more in detail subsequently, ver. 72, and concludes, vv. 14, 15, with the sign of power, staff (sword) and axe, which are placed in their hands. The picture of the preparation of such doll-figures is therewith finished in this strophe. It is evident that the speaker has primarily in his mind the small household gods which are ornamented like dolls, and on feast-days are borne upon the shoulder in public. In each particular it is the ridiculous element, *i.e.*, that which is at the very first sight comically opposed to what these gods are meant to be, which is brought out, and which, when it bears upon the action of the priests themselves, passes into bitter mockery. What could be worse than this? The priests steal from these gods at times much of their ornaments and give them to the *harlots under* (lit. *upon*) *the roof*, to the hidden harlots which dwell in the small garrets at the top of the houses.—The last words, ver. 8, that *they cannot speak*, allude to Ps. cxv. 5, it is true; but we must not on that account be misled to understand γλῶσσα of the tongue in the proper sense, which would here supply no meaning whatever; comp., on the other hand, ver. 50.

3. Though the third strophe starts, in the first instance, from the figure of the worthless vessel, which is a favourite one with Yĕremyá (comp. *Dichter des* *A. B.*, I *b*, p. 205 sq.), the attention is more particularly directed to the idols which are set up publicly in gardens and temples, in order to show

for one condemned to death, the priests fortify their houses with folding doors and locks and bars, that they may not
19 be stolen by the robbers.—They burn lamps and more than
20 for themselves, of which they cannot see even one.—They are as one of the beams from the room : but their hearts it is said are gnawed out by the creeping things of the earth which
21 eat up both them and their raiment.—They observe not how they are blackened in the face with the smoke which
22 burneth out of the earth; upon their body and their head fly night-owls swallows and birds of prey, as well as cats
23 likewise.—Whence ye will know that they are No-gods: therefore fear ye them not!

4.

24 For from the gold with which they are hung round for ornament, if one wipeth not off the rust they will surely not shine: they did not themselves even perceive it when they
25 were molten. At every price are they sold in whom there is

similarly their ridiculousness from their very outward appearance. There can be no doubt that ver. 17 the reading κήποις of the Alex. is preferable to οἴκοις: the verb εἰσπορεύεσθαι of itself points to gardens and not to houses; it is also reasonable to speak of this kind of idol; and, on the other hand, the closed houses (temples) in which other idols are placed are not referred to before ver. 18. In these often very dark temples (*adyta*) are found the numerous lights which are lighted from them, ver. 19; and there stands many an image on the wall, like a beam springing out of it, ver. 20, comp. ver. 55. At the close of the strophe the images placed quite publicly in the sacred gardens are again reverted to, the heads of which are *blackened by the smoke ascending out of the earth*, and upon which, furthermore, night-owls, swallows, and birds of prey, as well as cats, take their seat, all of them unclean creatures. It ought to be perfectly obvious that the words οὐκ αἰσθάνονται, ver. 20, should be connected with the following verse, and ver. 21 γῆς καιομένου must be read with the Alex. instead of οἰκίας; only we must understand by *the burning smoke ascending from the earth* every kind of smoke which is here described as arising from the earth simply in antithesis to the things which come from above.

4. This strophe primarily supplies further particulars which had been omitted, as regards their public appearance: what folly it is to buy at such a price things which never possessed any splendour of their own, and which have from the first been, and will always remain, inanimate, vv. 24, 25; and how ridiculous it is at public solemnities to carry upon men's shoulders such images, which thereby only the more display *their own dishonour* (their privy members) to men, and which men must carry as dead corpses without

APPENDIX, 3. 1.—*THE GREEK YEREMYÁ.* 145

27 no spirit!—Without feet they are borne upon shoulders, showing their own dishonour to men. But that they also perceive who serve them, because when they fall on the earth they do not arise of themselves, nor when anyone setteth them straight move of themselves, nor when they are bowed become straight:
28 but as to dead men they offer the shoulder to them.—Giving away their sacrifices their priests misuse them; as likewise also their women put in salt from them: lest they should impart anything to a poor or impotent person of their sacrifices, menstruous women and those in childbed touch them!—Knowing therefore from such things that they are No-gods, fear ye them not!

5.

30 Wherefore should they then be called gods? because women
31 make presents to silver and gold and wooden gods; and in their houses the priests drive round them having torn raiment
32 shaved heads and beards, keeping their heads uncovered, roar
33 and cry aloud before their gods as some people at the feast of the dead, because taking of their clothing the priests will clothe
34 their wives and children?—Neither when they experience evil from anyone nor when they experience good, will they be able

---

life or sense, vv. 26, 27. That is, the common reading at the end of ver. 27, *but as unto dead men they set gifts before them*, makes only seemingly a suitable transition to ver. 28, where the sacrifices are spoken of: in reality we are compelled by the connexion of the words vv. 26. 27 to read τὸν ὦμον instead of τὰ δῶρα, and then παρατίθενται, which readings are still discernable in the Vulgate, comp. *supra*, vv. 4, 26.—It is not before the end of the strophe that the sacrifices come in their turn to be

5. Proceeding from the sacrifices and feasts last mentioned, at which they ought most to show their power if they possessed any, the discourse now goes on further to develope its ridicule of them as *powerless* beings. The description of their numerous public sacrifices and feasts on great occasions,

scoffed at: but it is only the sacrifices of flesh which are here spoken of. The parts of them which fall to the share of the priests are misapplied by these, as well as by their wives, to the most unholy purposes: and these wives particularly, when they salt them down simply that they may not communicate of their abundance to the poor or sick, do not scruple to touch them even when in those states of uncleanness to which they are liable (comp. *Antiquities*, 208 sq. (178 sq.)).

vv. 30-32, which has been already referred to, p. 141, is historically very noteworthy: women place before them the sacrifices, the priests drive round them in the temples upon two-wheeled carriages, in profound mourning as regards their clothes and their whole behaviour, as well as their speech; but

to repay it; neither to set up a king are they able nor to
35 dethrone; likewise they will surely give neither riches nor
   a copper, when anyone hath vowed a vow to them and not paid
36 it will not call him to account, from death will save none nor
37 deliver a weaker from the stronger, a blind man will not
38 restore to sight, in need deliver none, upon no widow have
   compassion nor do good to an orphan.

6.

39   To the stones of the mountain are to be likened the wooden
40 and the gilded and the silvered ones: but they who worship
   them will be ashamed. How therefore can it be thought or
   proclaimed that they are really gods, since even the Chaldeans
40 themselves dishonour them? who when they see one dumb
   who cannot speak, bringing him before Bél, desire that he

after such great solemn occasions they give to their wives and children much of the ornament of the gods, which was undoubtedly fresh made every year for the feasts, ver. 33. But after all, of what use are they in all those cases in which they are usually most invoked at such annual sacrificial feasts? the cases being here enumerated in all their variety, vv. 33-38. This enumeration embraces exactly ten different cases; and this number is probably, acc. p. 139, not accidental. They can (1) neither make any recompense for either good or ill that is done to them (the words have a similar sound to those of Jer. x. 5, but their sense is very different); (2) neither either set up good kings nor depose bad ones (how suggestive that this point is very nearly the first of the long enumeration); (3) neither give much money nor even a farthing ($\chi\alpha\lambda\kappa\acute{o}\varsigma$ must here be equivalent to $\chi\alpha\lambda\kappa o\tilde{v}\varsigma$, which is often found on coins); (4) they cannot punish thoughtlessness in the matter of vows; (5) cannot deliver from death; (6) cannot assist the weaker against the stronger in the law-courts; (7) cannot heal a blind man; (8) can save no one from a sudden danger; (9) can show to no widow compassion; and (10) to no orphan a benefit.

6. From this central point of the whole discourse onwards it is really only the thought which has been just indicated that is further developed, namely, that they are totally useless, and if it is desired to compare them with other things, it is only the coarsest, or at all events the most useless, with which they are comparable; and all along the question recurs, how is it possible that, having such a nature, they should be *considered*, or *proclaimed* publicly, *e.g.*, in discourses and prayers, to be gods? The comparison with *the stones of the mountain*, and that their worshippers must in the end be *ashamed*, ver. 39, is moreover a re-echo of passages like Jer. ii. 27; iii. 9; Isa. i. 29; "Isa." xli. 11; xliv. 9, 11. But that the Chaldeans themselves do them dishonour is immediately shown, vv. 40-42, in the particular customs they observe

APPENDIX, 3. 1.—THE GREEK YEREMYÁ.

should then address him as if he could observe it: and they
42 cannot themselves observing it express this, indeed they have
43 no perception.—And the women putting cords around take
their seat in the ways, burning bran as incense: but when one
of them drawn away by one of those passing by is dishonoured,
she revileth her neighbour because she is not desired likewise
nor her cord broken.—All things that happen with them are
44 lies: and how then can it be thought or proclaimed that they
are really gods?

in their treatment of a dumb person. They cause such an one to enter the temple of their great national god, Bêl, conduct him to the image of the god, and beseech this (himself dumb) god, as if the dumb deity could understand them, to say a word to him: probably a priest then said it instead of him, and it was hoped that it would produce an effect upon the dumb man, and if he was able to speak again the cure was ascribed to the god. Similar deceptions occurred in the case of the priests of Isis in Rome: but it is here properly said further, they would themselves be unable *observing* it *to express what the priests desired of them, since they have no perception;* when the priests therefore thus act with regard to their gods, they themselves in the end simply bring shame to them. As this is plainly the meaning, we must (1) read πρὸς τὸν Βῆλον, ver. 41, since it would make no sense to say that they bring Bêl himself to the dumb person, and (2) καταλαλεῖν instead of καταλιπεῖν, ver. 42. If the latter reading were correct, the words ver. 42 would simply complain that although men observed it they nevertheless could not abandon these idols; but that would not suit either the αὐτοί nor the closing words which, like those of ver. 41, can only refer to the dumb idols; and it is not surprising that the discourse passes from Bêl, who was mentioned ver. 41

simply on account of one particular image, and reverts, ver. 42, to the gods in general. Further, τότε before φωνῆσαι is a good addition of the Alex. The word ἐνεός, which is often erroneously written ἐννεός, signifies, as derived from ἐν and ἔο, i.e. Sansk. *sva*, generally one absorbed *in himself*, as insensible men, and therefore not necessarily the dumb simply: as may be seen from Acts ix. 7 and this passage, inasmuch as it has to be further defined by μὴ δυνάμενος λαλῆσαι.—The speaker then adds, ver. 44, the disgraceful practice of the Babylonian women, of which Herod. I., 199, had previously reported fully enough: but our speaker describes everything by no means in such a way as to lead us to suppose he had first read it in Herodotus or some other Greek author. *The women place cords,* or wreaths in the form of cords, but of material which can be easily torn, *around* the head, as Herodotus more particularly describes: that is, as a sign that they are bound by an oath to this temple; they *sit* thus by *the ways*, close round the temple of Mylitta, *burning bran as incense,* presenting the daily sacrifice to Mylitta (those who are under obligation in fulfilment of a vow present simply what is absolutely necessary) in order that they may get free of their vow; it is a somewhat different thing which is referred to by Theokritos, *Idyls,* ii. 33, according to whom a love-charm was

7.

45 By artificers and goldsmiths they are manufactured: they
will certainly be nothing else than what the artists will they
46 shall be. They also who manufacture them will certainly
47 not be long-lived: how then shall the gods manufactured by
48 them be? they leave notwithstanding lies and insult to those
that come after.—For when war and evils come upon them,
the priests take counsel with one another how they may hide
49 themselves with them: how then is it not to be perceived that
those are not gods who cannot even save themselves from war
51 nor from evils?—For as being wooden and gilded and silvered
they will later be recognized that they are lies: to all the
nations and kings will it be evident that they are not gods but
52 works of men's hands, and no work of God at all is in them.
To whom then must it not be known that they are No-gods?

---

elsewhere made of the bran. As Herodotus narrates, a woman had often to sit thus for several days, until some one came to her and released her from her vow; this is presupposed here also, inasmuch as it is said further, *when one*, perhaps after many days and weeks, at last *drawn away by one of those passing by*, who brings an offering to Mylitta for her, *is lain with*, she reviles the other that she is not likewise deemed *worthy and has not broken her cord* as a sign that the vow has been redeemed. Instead of now going on to say that such a disgraceful custom can only tend to the reproach of the Goddess in whose name and at whose sanctuary it is carried on, the strophe is closed, ver. 44, in general terms, because the space allotted to it is nearly exhausted; and the following strophe

7. begins again, ver. 45, in the same way as the second, ver. 8: as the end of everything corresponds to its beginning, these gods also at last must be seen to be what they are—lying gods, because from the very first they have been dependent on the arbitrary human will, and were prepared by perishable beings, and because their own priests even are unable to save themselves in any mortal peril. Thus the strophe is pervaded by something of the Messianic spirit. It is possible that some images of the gods may last longer in point of time than their short-lived human makers; but should that be the case, it must still, unhappily, be said that such artists *left behind them only lies and reproach to those after them* (the Epigonoi), as these images can never become true gods and famous deliverers, but must always in the end be recognized as what they really are, lies instead of truth and disgrace instead of fame (comp. also vv. 27, 28). This thought is introduced with great brevity, but not unsuitably, ver. 47.—Ver. 52, the Alex. supplies the correct reading, τίνι οὖν γνωστὸν οὐκ ἔσται, but γνωστέον must be received into this reading from the other.

8.

53   A king for the country they will certainly not set up, nor give rain unto men; they will not carry through any cause of their own nor protect themselves from a wrong, being powerless:
54   surely they are as crows between heaven and earth.—For when
55   in a house of wooden or gilded or silvered gods fire should fall, their priests will indeed flee and escape, but they themselves
56   burn up as middle beams. Moreover a king and enemies they will certainly never withstand: how then should it be
57   supposed or thought that they are gods? certainly neither from thieves nor from robbers will wooden and silvered and gilded
58   gods ever deliver, they from whom the mighty ones will take off the gold and silver and the raiment put on them and go away therewith, and who cannot at all help themselves.—
59   So that it is better to be a king who showeth his courage, or a useful vessel in the house of which the owner maketh use, than the false gods; or else a door in the house protecting the things therein than the false gods; and a wooden pillar in the king's hall than the false gods.

8. The point which was referred to so significantly, ver. 34, that they will never give to a country the boon of a good *king*, occurs again at the commencement of this strophe, ver. 53; and it is added that, as a like great blessing, they can never give the boon of a refreshing *rain*, as this is expected from Yahvé, Ps. lxv.; Zech. x. 1; Isa. xxx. 23; Jer. v. 24; x. 13; it may be seen from Prov. xvi. 15 how easily these two boons may be looked upon as similar. In like manner they are able neither *to carry through their own judgment, i.e.*, to defend themselves when they are attacked with words, as is so vividly described "Isa." xli., nor *to save themselves* ($ρύεσθαί τι$ like $ἀμύνεσθαί τι$) *from a wrong* which might be done to them, *e.g.*, by maiming, but, on the contrary, appear only to hang like repulsive *crows* between heaven and earth, as belonging to neither, ver. 54, although as spirits ($δαίμονες$) men locate them in the former. For how little are they who can do no good service able to give protection against any calamity which befalls them or their worshippers, *e.g.*, against fire in their own house (on the contrary, they will in that case themselves burn *like* completely unprotected *middle beams*, ver. 20), against a bad king or enemies, against thieves and robbers, since they must themselves submit to be robbed by every mighty one! vv. 55-58. The conclusion from all that, that they are accordingly worse than any useful person or useful thing, is commenced ver. 59, in order that it may be worked out further in the last two strophes. This is done so that in the next strophe

9.

60 Surely sun and moon and stars, being shining and sent as
61 the need is, are obedient; likewise also the lightning when it
appeareth, is good to behold; in like manner also the wind
62 bloweth in every region; and when clouds are commanded of
63 God to go forth over the whole world, they fulfil the command; the fire also sent from above to consume mountains
and forests, doeth that which is commanded: but these are
neither in shapes nor in powers to be likened to one of them.
64 Whence it must not be thought nor proclaimed that they are
really gods, as they not able to judge causes nor to do good
65 to men. Knowing then that they are No-gods, fear ye them
66 not! for they will certainly neither curse nor bless kings,
neither show signs in heaven among the heathen, nor shine
like the sun nor give light like the moon.

10.

68 The beasts of prey are better than they, for they fleeing into
69 a covert can help themselves: in no wise therefore is it manifest to us that they are gods; therefore fear ye them not! For

9. they are compared, in language of special elevation, particularly vv. 60-64, with the vast heavenly powers, which are so clearly visible and yet so mysterious, which at all events rule over the earth in such a way that they can be considered as obedient to the divine will, as is here described after Job xxxviii. 12 sq.; in these powers also there is something divine, but nothing imaginary and deceptive as in the case of the idols, ver. 66. The *fire from above*, ver. 63, which the speaker does not take from that passage of the book of Job, he derives undoubtedly from Amos vii. 4. The *lightning* when it appears as commanded by God is *good to look upon*, presenting a pleasing appearance to men, because they think as they see it, acc. "Zech." x. 1, that God will be sure soon to send them again rain after long drought; just as Hindoo poets also sing.—It is true that the mention of the kings in their twofold aspect is again introduced, ver. 66; still the strophe concludes notwithstanding, after Jer. x. 2, with the mention of the celestial signs which *the Heathen* at all events fear, and of the sun and the moon, in order finally

10. to close with a numerous and various mass of other things which are better than idols, or with which they are comparable on account of their repulsive nature. To the latter class belong the three vv. 70, 71; a *scarecrow* in a cucumber-field which does not even perform its proper office, and which is itself often an old ugly idol, *e.g.*, a Pân, a *thornhedge in a garden* which is likewise intended to give protection and yet gives covert to all kinds of birds of prey, and an unburied *dead* man cast into a dark corner, a particularly

70 as in a cucumber-field a scarecrow which guardeth nothing, so are
71 the wooden and gilded and silvered gods. In the same manner to the thorn-hedge in the garden upon which every bird of prey alighteth, in like wise also to a dead man thrown into the dark,
72 are the wooden and silvered and gilded gods to be compared. By the purple and white silk also which rotteth on them will ye know that they are No-gods; and they themselves will at last be devoured and be a reproach in the land. Better therefore
73 is a righteous man who hath no idols: for he will be far from reproach, hoping in the Lord God.

repulsive object! There is once more at the end, ver. 72, in order to recur to the commencement ver. 12, inserted the rotting of the garments, although they are of purple and *white silk;* for the connexion of the words shows that μάρμαρος is not here really marble but a kind of white silk which was at that time so-called in those parts on account of similarity of colour; that such a silk then existed was shown above, Vol. I., p. 177. The *Pesh.* translates μάρμαρος correctly by *shērāyē*, silk. —But this last strophe is as it were bracketted between references to two better things: even the beasts of prey are better than they, because they are at all events able to save themselves in straits, ver. 68; but above all a man that cleaves to the true religion and can hope that he *will remain far from reproach,* particularly that which is mentioned ver. 47 and ver. 72; with which ver. 73 is briefly and fittingly closed, only the last words must be supplied from the *Pesh.*—

We have received this piece into this work for the reason amongst others that it has hitherto been so far from accurately understood, although it was from the first written in Greek. But we may also draw some important inferences from it from a purely historical point of view. If it originated at the end of the second or the beginning of the last century B.C., we can infer from it how certainly the two pieces now thrown together in the Book of Barûkh date back to the earlier age to which we have assigned them above. We can easily see that according to all indications of date centuries must have intervened between those pieces and this; so great is the distance of this piece from those, not only as regards the use of the foreign language, but also as regards prophetic, artistic, and literary characteristics. And although the piece falls far behind all prophetic writings from a purely prophetic point of view, including the Book of Daniel which has next to be treated, and scarcely any of the sparks of the genuine prophetic spirit are emitted from it, we must nevertheless remember that it required no little courage at that time to publish in the midst of the Heathen a work of this kind in the universally known language of the civilized world. In this respect it is very much like the Sybilline books, the origin of which dates back to somewhere about this time.

2. *The new prophetic writers of the more elaborate kind.*

The Book of Daniel.

It is far more agreeable to the entire character of these late writers of the semi-prophetic class that they pursue that method of description with an exclusive preponderance of the imagination which had been first adopted by Hézeqiél (Vol. IV., p. 12 sq.), and then by Zakharya (*supra*, p. 45 sq.). The reasons which led these prophets to adopt this method were now, after all public prophetic activity had entirely ceased, simply so much the more powerful and adequate. It is simply the imagination of a prophet-author of this kind which is at work within him as the creator and former of all his ways of treating things; before that imagination are constantly hovering angels and spirits in endless numbers, by whom the author who stands upon the earth far below feels himself from time to time elevated and enlightened; before it also crowd successive representative symbols regarding the matters which have really to be described, just as it everywhere seeks for the most figurative form of expression. But just in proportion as the pure symbols of the imagination are presented exclusively and unexpectedly and in a form needing explanation, is it the more necessary that the prosaic explanation of them should generally follow in some suitable guise, as soon as the attention has once been attracted to the strange forms presented. In this way the two component elements—symbol and thought,—which always appear so beautifully combined in the discourse of the earlier prophets, are separated. The commencement of this process is already discernible in Hézeqiél, comp. Vol. IV., p. 12 sq.

But in order correctly to comprehend this prophetic art of the new type in its extensive application and development, it is necessary particularly to observe that these later authors were very frequently unable to speak freely with respect to the depressing condition of things of their time, simply because they lived under the oppression of a foreign rule. Hézeqiél had made use of artificial means of designating the Chaldeans because he could not speak of them without disguise, as was shown Vol. IV., 181 sq.; and the subsequent form which this form of enigmatic speech soon assumed is explained *supra*, p. 2 sq. It was accordingly all the more natural that a prophetic author, who was desirous to speak of things of his time which could not be openly referred to, should choose some ancient prophet or saint, having as it seemed to him suitable characteristics, that he might speak from his elevation to the men of that time. But inasmuch as the true and anonymous author belongs to an entirely different and later age than that of the prophet in whose name his art requires him to write, he is obliged to speak not simply for his own actual contemporaries, but also to speak concerning the things of the future by the mouth and from the age of the personated ancient; he is obliged therefore to cause this ancient to speak in such a way that he, looking from his olden time into all the spaces of the future, and prophesying regarding them, shall at the same hit with special clearness that spot of the future which is also the actual future for the contemporaries of the author and first readers of the book. For he is unable, of course, merely to speak of the time which is the simple future to him and his contemporaries as the future: the intermediate period from the standpoint of the assumed author until the real author must also, if the artistic propriety of the work is to be kept up, necessarily appear as future. But inasmuch as the real author has already passed through this assumed future, and it exists plainly before him as the past in the strict sense, there is nothing left for him but to describe a past in the guise of a future;* the events which have already happened he seeks to group in pictures of a somewhat obscure and vague outline, giving them the appearance of really belonging to the future;

---

* As in a like case in the Purânas, *e.g.*, Vishnu-Purâna, p. 461 sq.

he does not like to speak of them quite undisguisedly and without any circumlocution, and in this particular also that skill in the employment of the imagination above referred to may produce its most various and greatest effects. Still, it is neither possible that what has already actually passed into the light of history should be so completely concealed by artistic description that that light should not gleam through the veils, nor is it either in reality the intention of the real author completely to conceal the light and destroy the true difference between the merely artificial and the actual future; on the contrary, he casts into the midst of the dark and obscure symbols and enigmas sufficient scintillations of the real meaning, indications and hints of the solution, so that at least no attentive reader amongst the immediate contemporaries could long remain in doubt. However, the prophetic element in the strict sense in such pictures does not commence before that half of the picture which was also the simple future of the author and his contemporaries: and with as much certainty as the first readers were able easily to solve these enigmas are we able, after examinations of penetrating thoroughness, quite well to distinguish the hidden half of the future described from the actual half. Indeed, as that first half properly sketches the past very accurately according to wholly terrestrial and historical features, whilst where this second begins suddenly everything passes into the absolute region of celestial foreboding and anticipations, we are still in a position also to distinguish very clearly the date of the authorship of such books precisely from those marked differences which crop up in the midst of the descriptions of the future.

It must be further added that the authors of such books had in the first instance no intention whatever of acting as deceivers, but intended simply to be authors in a special form of literary art, who selected this form of their art because it appears to supply them with the only means by which they could more powerfully and with least danger produce an effect upon their contemporaries. Their choice of this literary method may be compared with that of dramatic poets, who, going but a step further, summon completely back into life the venerable ancients who speak and act upon an artistic stage, in order that the contemporary spectators may be gratified and taught. Because they therefore in reality themselves wish that, at all events, the more intelligent readers should penetrate the historical veil which is thrown over the properly intended subject-matter of the book, and should find out the time and circumstances which they desired not openly to name, they supply in the book itself landmarks and hints regarding these, which it is only needful carefully to follow in order to discover what is really meant. It is therefore not their fault if such books are misunderstood.

These are the books which we may briefly designate *Apokalypses*, a name which has at last become customary. They may be thus designated, inasmuch as they by their peculiar art aim as it were at taking off the veil from the future, and uncovering with their powerful symbols and accompanying elucidations and hints the secrets of the future. As nevertheless the real author of such a work must at the same time examine more particularly the history of his hero, and adhere to it in the external description, and the history also serve, *per se* as such an unveiling, the purpose of instruction and admonition, it is not difficult to see how easily this class of literature can be blended with that class of prophetic legends above explained, p. 89 sq.

Of this mixed class, half apokalypse and half prophetic legend, but more the former than the latter, is this *Book of Daniel*. The narrative portion of it serves partly as merely an introduction of its various apokalypses, partly to instruct the contemporaries by presenting lofty examples and their plain antitheses. If we carefully note the separating line of the two halves of the descriptions of the future, which have been above described, it appears with perfect clearness that the veiled future extends to the years 168-7 B.C., *i.e.*, until a few years before the death of Antiochus Epiphanes; but from that point the pure prophetic anticipation commences. The book was accordingly written in that age of highly-strained relations and of genuine inspiration for brief intervals, when the persecutions of this tyrant raged most violently, the fidelity of very many and highly-esteemed Yudeans wavered, and when, though a small band of faithful ones had risen, resolved to find victory or death in opposition to Heathenism, the colossus of those centuries (ch. ii.), the impending struggle still seemed in the highest degree questionable and in its results doubtful. It was then that the author who is concealed under Daniel's name came forward in brief and hasty pieces, without close connexion, partly to castigate the pusillanimity of the multitude, and to show to all how they ought to conduct themselves with regard to Heathenism, how they ought to live and contend, and partly to promise the near overthrow of Antiochus, the certain collapse of that colossus, and the transcendent glory of the Messianic kingdom close at hand, in words which are in reality here and there animated even in this late age by a genuine breath from above.

It is, however, evident that the book was after all specially written for the sake of the more powerful men among the Yudeans of that time who stood in some closer connexion with the Syrian court; and after that for the sake of the younger men of the wealthier and more respected families who suffered themselves to be led astray by the seductive charms of heathen manners. This follows from the circumstances of those times themselves; for then the danger that was threatening was by no means from below, but, on the contrary, the more influential members of the chief priests and other powerful families had submitted to Heathenism; and it was particularly the younger generation which suffered itself to be misled by the Syrian court which had then been for a long time wholly corrupt. This follows also with equal certainty from the choice of the subject-matter: for if one asks why the author selected the name of Daniel more particularly as the centre of his book when such an endless line of great names of antiquity was open to him, it appears that no other reason can have determined his choice than that he suitably to his design sought exactly such an older sage or prophet as had from his early youth come into close association with a heathen court of great influence, but who had in the very midst of the highest heathen circles not only evinced his wisdom in matters of this world but also his faithfulness in the religion of Yahvé and his open confession of it, and that to the author in his circumstances no other tradition from the wide field of antiquity crossed his path which appeared so suitable as this of Daniel.

If we then keep close to the unambiguous indications which the book supplies as to the time in which and for which it was written, and if we read it from the standpoint of that time and of the object which the real author had in view, everything in it becomes perfectly clear, as will appear below in detail. Every little word in it and every peculiarity of style then re-lives for us again in its original force in as perfect clearness as the general subject-matter of all its sections and the arrangement and art of the whole book. In fact this holds so strongly that much in the book cannot be sufficiently accurately understood, so long as the time of its origin is resigned to but apparently smaller errors. But if any one follows here merely external appearance and does not attempt to penetrate the enigma of the book, or rather the art by the aid of which the author shapes everything, he will be unable to understand even the separate words of it in their full and living force. Moreover, all the other indications of the real time of the author accord completely in their various directions with those which must here be considered the principal ones; a fact which will also be variously attested below in detail, and need here be touched upon more particularly as regards some only of its aspects.

1. If we begin with the language as that which first presents itself, there is nothing in this respect which is at once more remarkable than the interchange of the Hebrew and the

Chaldee. The first begins and closes the book, but still does not predominate more than through about half of it. The latter is chosen, ii. 4, when the Chaldeans speak, but manifestly only as on the first opportunity which offered, and it is then kept up uninterruptedly as far as the close of ch. vii. The two languages, therefore, do not interchange with the original documents, or with the matters treated of, for instance, still less with a change of authors, inasmuch as the whole book is manifestly by the same author; for rarely has a book so plainly one author, and rarely has one been written so plainly as in one consecutive order, and in the strictest unity of rapid succession, as this book of Daniel. It is true a similar change from one language to another is also met with in the case of the Chronicler, in the book which is now named from Ezra: it is there also evident that the book was written for such as are masters of both languages, so that the rapid change from one to the other is not avoided even in narrative; at the same time, in that book really different original documents have more to do with the change. But in the case before us the change can only be explained if the Chaldee, or rather the Aramaic, was to the reader actually the language which he liked best and with which he was most familiar, so that our author, without doubt, would have used it alone, particularly as it was very suitable for the countries on the Euphrates and the Tigris where Daniel dwelt, if he had not preferred at least to begin and to close his book with the ancient Hebrew language on account of its prophetic subject-matter; in connexion with which consideration it is not without significance that the larger portion of the prophecies, ch. viii.—xii., appears thus written in the ancient sacred tongue, while the four narrative pieces, ch. iii.—vi., are all Aramaic.

The next point to observe is that the work was, beyond all doubt, written in Palestine. For if we leave out of view its artistic disguise, the whole subject-matter of it points, most particularly precisely where Palestine is spoken of, to the

conclusion that it can only have been written in and in the first place for Palestine. There is nothing which leads to the supposition that it was written in Babel or Susa at any time whatever; but if it is carefully noted how the history of the Syro-Egyptian wars is recorded in the long piece of veiled discourse, ch. xi., it is quite clear that the author wrote only in or near Jerusalem, and pre-supposed that his immediate readers were in the same locality; for in this chapter the course of those wars passes before the reader's eye as if he himself dwelt in or near Jerusalem, and all the other determinations of locality are also fixed so as to accord with that supposition. But inasmuch as the author of the Books of Chronicles undoubtedly wrote in Palestine, and the Aramaic which he used, not only in the documents but also in historical narrative, exhibits substantially the greatest similarity with that of our book, there is no room to doubt that we have in both works that peculiar form of Aramaic which became more and more the popular language in Palestine, and particularly in Yudea during the centuries of the Assyro-Chaldean, Persian and Græco-Seleukid rule. We possess from other quarters plain proofs of the existence of this south-western Aramaic, and of its difference from other Aramaic dialects,* although our knowledge of it from those earliest times down to the date of our book, it must be allowed, is as yet very limited. Moreover, we know that the Aramaic, from various causes, gradually during those centuries displaced the Hebrew in Yudea also, even as the language of literature, until, with the great success of the Makkabeans, the New Hebrew was raised to this dignity.†
When the Seleukidæ reigned over Yudea, it may have revived afresh as the literary language in those regions; and it is just

---

* What is known from other sources of south-west Aramaic has been touched upon in the *Gött. Gel. Anz.*, 1866, p. 642 sq., in a notice of Erizzo's *Evangeliarium Hierosolymitanum* (Verona, 1864). The oldest fragment of a south-east Aramaic work, Jer. x. 11, is remarked upon Vol. III., p. 141.

† Comp. *History of Israel*, V., 464 *note* (IV., p. 605 *anm.*).

those times to which our book belongs. And if it is remembered in addition that the mixture of Aramaic with Hebrew in the Book of Daniel is certainly much greater than in the Book of 'Ezra, it will not then be possible to doubt that our book cannot belong to an earlier age than that which we plainly recognized above in its subject-matter.

If we go on to compare the Aramaic of the Book of Daniel with that of the Book of 'Ezra, we can at all events plainly see, from the few pieces contained in the two books, that there is no unimportant difference, and one which can only be explained from the distance of time separating the books, the later age, according to all indications, falling to the pieces in the Book of Daniel. This difference appears particularly in two things. First, in the use of the *particles*, or the small pliant words, which in every language are most frequently recurring, and on that account are also most subject to change, and which everywhere most plainly mark the changes of every language as regards time and place.*—Second, in the introduction of foreign words. In the Aramaic of the Book of 'Ezra we meet with Persian words; in the Book of Daniel we meet with many Persian but also Greek words. Now, it is certainly not strange to find Persian words in the Book of 'Ezra; his Aramaic is not of an earlier date than the Persian period, in which Persian words found their way into Hebrew also. But whether in those times in which Daniel flourished Persian words had already found admittance into Aramaic, cannot be proved and is *per se* scarcely probable, for this reason among others, that

---

* In the Book of 'Ezra דָּךְ, i.e., Arab. *dhálika*, or fem. דָּךְ, is used for our *that one* in the Book of Daniel דִּכֵּן: the first is not some abbreviation of the latter, but the latter is a more recent compound from the former. In 'Ezra the pronominal suffixes to the nouns have still in most cases the forms ־הֹם and ־כֹם, but in Daniel ־תֹון and ־כֹון, the latter being clearly the later; the verbal suffix, which is ־הִמֹּו in 'Ezra, is in Daniel הִמֹּון, and if the latter form is in accordance with many indications equally old, it was probably considered in this Aramaic dialect more as poetical. In the Book of Daniel the particles כְּמָא and כְּעֶנֶת are not found at all, although so far as their force goes they could have been used.

most of these words are names of official dignities, which first received their significance by the Persian rule in the Aramaic countries.* On the other hand, Greek words are still not met with in the Book of 'Ezra; but that they are found in the Book of Daniel as already completely naturalized Aramaic words, accords quite well with the true age of the book. But to the extent to which these Greek words are names of musical instruments, it is natural to infer that they were only able to make their way to Jerusalem through Antioch, Tyre, and other great cities of this kind in connexion with Greek art generally, which was then held in such high estimation.†

The Hebrew, if the author of the book did not really write it before the year 168-169, is, for this late time, still handled with great skill, and the style is very clear, so that at first sight it might be conjectured that it was written at a much earlier date. But we must not here overlook the fact that facility in the use of ancient Hebrew modes of expression could all the more easily be kept up precisely until towards the beginning of the times of the Makkabeans, the more certainly the New Hebrew was not elevated to the dignity of being the language of literature until after their victories; nor may we forget that there might always be individuals who, by absorbing study of the acknowledged models of the ancient Hebrew literature, were able to employ the language quite appropriately and elegantly in the production of new books. But if we look more narrowly into the matter, it appears that it is, after all, particularly only certain pieces of the prophetic writings,‡

---

* Many of these words are explained below.

† The four Greek musical instruments are mentioned Dan. iii. 4, 7, 10, 15 in each case *after* the two which have Semitic names; if, however, סַבְּכָא as corresponding to the Greek σαμβύκη, as well as קִיתָרֹס, which is formed from κιθάρα, is originally Semitic (comp. *Dichter des A. B.*, I a, p. 218 sq), both were nevertheless only at that time afresh adopted with the ψαλτήριον and the συμφωνία from the Greek and cast into an Aramaic form. These instruments are further discussed in the *Gött. Gel. Anz.*, 1861, p. 1094 sq.

‡ As Isa. x. 22 sq.; lii. 13—liii. 12; comp. on the particular passages below.

then revered as sacred, which were before the eyes of our author as his guiding-stars, and of which he makes free use, but only in such a way as a later author does who likes to follow somewhat closely the words and images of a Scripture of long-acknowledged sanctity, in order by such means to deal effectively with the affairs of the present. This is a somewhat different case from that of the re-echoing of the notes of older lyrics in more recent ones, *e.g.*, in the most recent Psalms, or from the repetition by the Chronicler of words from the older historical works, or of the recurrence of single sentences or words of older prophets, as freely remembered, in the writings of later ones. For in the case before us the use of such older passages by a prophetic author is connected with the fact that to this author the older prophetic books, those that are still looked upon in our Hebrew Old Testament as the Kanon of the Prophets, already existed as a closed Sacred Scripture, which the moderns had only to read, apply to their own time, and from the correct understanding of which they might solve the dark things and enigmas of their present.* So far from the living laboratory of ancient prophetism was this age conscious of being; with which further harmonizes that it was the Biblical learning of the time only which appeared to be adapted to guide the nation spiritually.† If we are thereby brought down to the times after 'Ezra, we thus obtain an explanation of the fact that the author takes single passages of the Bible‡ of that day, particularly prophetic passages, as a foundation for the presentation of his ideas, and, as it were, works after their model.

The choice of peculiarities of Hebrew and the orthography points by some indications§ to such a later age, although the

---

* Comp. below the explanation of the piece ch. ix.

† Comp. below on xi. 33-35.

‡ Acc. § 2 and Bar. i. 3, comp. *supra* p. 113, and *Geschichte des V. Israel*, VII., p. 428.

§ As the use of אֲשֶׁר לָמָּה i. 10, comp. § 337 *b*, the orthography נבוכדנצר

author on the whole has taken the earlier form of the language as his model.

Finally, if we pay close attention to the age of the books which the author specially likes to follow, and which were before him as those most used in his time, we come upon not merely the oldest and the older basis of the present Kanon of the Old Testament, nor merely upon the rest of the most recent books which were received last into this Kanon, as the Books of the Chronicles, but also upon writings which originated later than these, or even such as did not get into the present Kanon. We shall see subsequently that the historical ideas about the last times before the destruction of Jerusalem, as well as those about the Chaldean and Persian kings, go back to writings which are more recent than the Books of Chronicles; and as regards the Persian kings, this has been incidentally shown above, p. 116. But the most remarkable thing is that our literary prophet uses the great prayer in the Book of Barûkh as a model, as will be further shown below on ch. ix.

2. If, on the other hand, we pay due regard to the historical aspect of the book, and get a closer understanding of it as regards its whole subject-matter, place, complexion, and age, the phenomena which present themselves on such an examination are not surprising, while they are wholly unintelligible if the age and the design of the author are not heeded.

If ch. xi. is accurately understood as the principal historical piece, and all historical notes and indications contained in the other pieces, we find especially the following facts. The author knows and describes no piece of history so fully and evidently after his own personal observation as that of Antiochos Epiphanes: but this history, be it noted, only to the year 168-167 B.C., a few years before his death. He knows accurately

---

instead of נבאצר—: this omission of the א is found in the Aramaic pieces of the Book of 'Ezra, but in Hebrew even the Chronicler always writes the name with א; the author of the Book of Daniel, however, writes it with א only i. 1, afterwards always without א both in Hebrew and in Aramaic.

enough also the history of his Seleukid ancestors, particularly that of the grandfather of this king, Antiochos the Great, as well as that of the contemporary history of the Ptolemies as far back as the origin of the Greek kingdoms from the kingdom of Alexander, and alludes, like a well-instructed man, to certain prominent events and strange things of this history: but the history of the Persian and the Chaldean kings, and of their time, lay evidently farther from the sphere of his vision. He communicates from those distant times to a good degree particulars which are historically well founded, but how few are they, precisely in respect of closer historical portraiture, as compared with the fulness and all-sided vividness of his communications as regards the life of Antiochos the Great and Antiochos Epiphanes! When a special design of his work requires it, he can also be accurate enough in the chronology of the centuries, as the great example (x. 24-27) proves: but when this design does not require it, he contents himself with the mention of the kings of ancient Israel, of the Chaldeans, and of the Medes and Persians, both as regards the chronology and also the less accurate ideas which were in vogue in his day concerning those distant kings and periods of time. We shall consider all this below at length; but there is one thing of general significance which we can best bring forward at once. If we compare the descriptions and allusions which he supplies with reference to the great kings, nothing is more remarkable than that not one Greek or Persian king appears to him to have been a man whom he could place in contrast with the contemporary king, Antiochos Epiphanes, from whom he expects nothing better as regards the future; but in his view the only king whose rebellious heart the course of divine providence gradually softened and opened for the divine truth and the true religion of Israel is Nabukodrossor. As compared with all the subsequent Heathen kings who ruled over Israel, especially as compared with those who ruled last, even the ancient king Nabukodrossor appeared then to have been a far better ruler, who at all events the longer he lived the more he received an open heart for the true God and the true religion. A general idea of Nabukodrossor of this kind had then been formed: and certain reminiscences which came to our author from this king's history appeared to him to confirm the idea.

The following indication as regards the profound depression and sultriness of the place and time in which he wrote is very instructive. It cannot be too carefully observed that this book was written just in that most depressed and downcast time preceding the rise and the victories of the Makkabeans: both its entire prophetic significance and our admiration of the human courage of the author are founded upon the certainty, that it was written in that time. If we now carefully attend to the manner in which the author speaks of his time and locality, it appears that he may not, as has been remarked previously, mention the affairs of the present quite without disguise, but only indicate them in accordance with the art and plan of his book. Of this, however, there are various degrees. He may not designate any one of the kings of the veiled past or present simply by his ordinary name: but the countries in which the events of which he speaks occur it is not so difficult for him to mention by name. Thus, ch. xi., he designates Egypt as *the land of the South*, Syria as *the land of the North* (that is from its capital, Antioch), in order primarily to keep up throughout his usual language of hint and indication: yet this method of bare hint is exchanged in the case of Egypt a few times for that of open mention (xi. 8, 42, 43). But Syria, *i.e.*, the kingdom of the Seleukidæ under which he was obliged to live, he never ventures to mention by name, just as he also constantly speaks of the Holy Land and Jerusalem by circumlocution only: so certainly did he live under the Syrian rule, and so great was the terror which this rule at that time caused everywhere where the faithful lived in the Holy Land.

But as regards the great importance of the thing itself, there is after all nothing of greater moment than the way in which the author looks upon and brings forward in this book the number and the order of succession of the great Heathen empires. From the time of Daniel downwards, as it is here conceived and described, there are exactly four great empires which are here constantly brought forward precisely in their proper order of succession: the Chaldean, the Median, the Persian, and the Greek. Notwithstanding all the difference of the various nations which rule in them, it is always Babel, as the great centre of Daniel's world and of the chief rule in Asia, around which all these empires revolve, and from which as a basis they claim to be the empires of the world. And however different in other respects they may be from each other, they have nevertheless something in common of higher moment in the fact that they are all in the bad sense world-empires, *i.e.*, Heathen empires without the true God, as if the great power of Heathenism had perpetuated itself in them in successive regeneration. The contemporaries of our author looked upon these successive universal empires, which, though different, were nevertheless in the main respect of their Heathenism completely alike, under whose yoke they felt themselves constantly oppressed since the destruction of Jerusalem under Nabukodrossor, as upon a Colossus, towering aloft into the clouds, which through the long centuries disappointed all hope of seeing it fall; as this figure is almost immediately so forcibly brought forward at the opening of our book, ii. 31 sq. If accordingly Daniel is introduced by our author as the man to whom it is given by God at once, from the first years of Nabukodrossor, even before the conquest of Jerusalem, to look forward into the long line of the centuries, a highly animated picture must be unfolded. Imagine a blameless man of Israel who is able before the destruction of Jerusalem to cast a steady glance into the coming four or five centuries. He can behold how the nation of the true religion, notwithstanding the restoration of Jerusalem from its ruins, will be subjected for such a series of centuries to the rule of

Heathenism, which does no more than change its colours. He must then, just on the horizon of a much more distant *final period*,* cast his glance into the horrible abominations of the reign of an Antiochos Epiphanes. O how must that man be the more overwhelmed with grief, indeed quite lose all possession of himself, in proportion as he is conscious of being a living member of his nation.† Neither can he feel himself properly prepared for the vision of the Messianic prosperity which follows at last after such a long series of centuries and so many mournful vicissitudes, so that the strongest proofs c the certain coming of the Messianic deliverance are needed to comfort him at least a little by such a final outlook.‡ A telling picture of the situation of an ancient hero of this kind may be thus sketched, and everything which tends to the enlightenment, consolation, and elevation of the contemporaries can be brought into it; and they, if they give due heed, must feel themselves placed much nearer than that hero to the final fulfilment of these divine words with regard to the approach of the Messianic age: for he must after all pass away, so far as this world is concerned, before he could even in the distance live to see the fulfilment of the final hope of Israel as shown to him, and had to count himself happy if he only received the certain divine assurance as regards the Messianic prosperity which was to come in the distant centuries.§ And we shall soon see that this is precisely the situation in which our author presents Daniel to us as the man of the ancient time.

But if this is the situation in which our author resuscitates Daniel for his contemporaries as the mouthpiece of prophecy, we get further an explanation of the manner in which he can both contract and expand, just as the object of his book demands,

---

* This *time of the end*, which is mentioned with increasing frequency and emphasis from viii. 17 onwards, is therefore the immediate present of the contemporaries of the author himself, until a brief period beyond it.

† As is often declared from vii. 28 onwards.

‡ ix. 2 sq.; x. 2 sq. § xii., li., 8, 12.

this whole framework of the four universal empires which the Messianic empire can only follow. To the contemporaries of the author who heard such words from the mouth of Daniel, it might also serve as consolation when they saw how, according to the divine will, all these four heathen empires must follow each other in this unbroken succession: there was now surely so much the greater deliverance to be hoped for if the entire Colossus, towering with its four parts high into the air, shall at last be all at once dashed in pieces! But certainly as the true glance into the vicissitudes, and also the connexion of the history of the world at large, must sometimes be opened to these contemporaries, it was of small importance, in the midst of the distress and oppression of their time, that they should have a knowledge of the way in which the earlier history from Daniel's day to their own had been unfolded: the immediate matter of interest to them was simply how the gloom and darkness of their own time would be scattered; and the author was obliged, in conformity with the design of his book, to make more and more clear from the mouth of Daniel himself that the matter of prime and indeed exclusive importance is their own time. Accordingly that framework of prophecy concerning the four universal empires is at the commencement greatly contracted, with a view to increasing expansion towards the end: and after there has been sufficient said about the four empires in ch. ii. and ch. vii., as early as ch. viii. it is only the last two or three which are spoken of, and in ch. xi. it is almost exclusively the last which is dealt with; and in the same proportion *the time of the end*, referred to above, is exclusively brought forward with increasing force and plainness as the true object of all prophecy and discourse, in order that the prophecy regarding the actual future may be connected with it.

The remaining observations which have here to be made concerning the four universal empires, conduct us with so much the greater necessity further

2. to a more particular consideration of the question of the historical character of Daniel himself, and of the time to which he is to be referred according to strict history. For at first sight it might seem as if the manner in which our author introduces the then ancient Daniel as acting and speaking, had the greatest similarity with that which we met with (p. 87 sq.) in the case of the ancient Yona. There is really a good deal of similarity in several respects. In that case, as in this, it is a more recent author who narrates much about an earlier prophet. And as in that case we saw that all that was told about Yona was but loosely connected in a series of short pieces of narrative, we find the same thing here in the case of Daniel, ch. i.—vi. At the same time, there is in other respects an observable great dissimilarity. Yona is not introduced that he may become the living mouthpiece of prophecy and admonition to the contemporaries of the author: and this renders the narrative of the Book of Yona of a much simpler nature. In the narrative of the latter work chronology is not deemed needful in any form; in the work before us it is found in each of the separate pieces of narrative. For in general the narrative in this book is meant to serve the higher, purely prophetic, purpose to which the entire book owes its orgin, the narrative standing in the closest relation with the subject-matter of the prophecy as its main element. And as moreover we have no information regarding Daniel from an older record in the historical books, as is the case with Yona, it becomes all the more difficult to form a well-founded opinion as regards the historical character of Daniel. Every step that a modern scholar ventures to take in this matter must be carefully considered, as it may so easily be, and so often has been, a false step. Still, a few things appear tolerably clear.

When, in the few passages in which Daniel is mentioned at an earlier date, this hero is spoken of by the learned prophet Hézeqiél, xiv. 14, 20, between Noah and Iyob, as a model of perfect righteousness (comp. Vol. IV., p. 83), and then, Ezek.

xxviii. 3, alone even as a no less exalted example of true wisdom, we learn from these passages more definitely what we might suppose without them from the whole character of antiquity, that Dauiel actually lived at some time, and at all events was deemed, as early as the beginning of the sixth century B.C., an historical example of the rare combination of the same two virtues for which he was still illustrious in the much more recent book now before us—of moral purity in life and wisdom. Together with this, Daniel may have also long supplied particularly the lofty model of a sage who was in his early youth highly educated and of great sagacity, and was greatly honoured even among the heathen, just as our book and the addition to the apokryphal Book of Daniel represent him.—We may also deduce from Hézeqiél with certainty the further important conclusion, that as this prophet places him, ch. xiv., between Noah and Iyob, he as a very learned and largely-read prophet drew his ideas of Daniel from some existing book, just as he speaks of Noah and Iyob only from the well-known books; but there can be no doubt, when the matter is carefully examined, that that book which Hézeqiél had before his eyes, or rather presupposed as long known to his readers, was a different one from that which did not come into the Kanon before some centuries after Hézeqiél. At the same time, important as this observation is with regard to our views of the former reputation of Daniel, we cannot nevertheless help seeing that that Daniel whom Hézeqiél presupposed as known to his contemporaries, belonged historically to an entirely different time and region from that Daniel who is described in our book. Hézeqiél looks upon Daniel, on that point we must not deceive ourselves, as just as much a perfect and long since departed hero of antiquity as Noah and Iyob; Daniel must therefore have lived, according to the historical range of view of the contemporaries of Hézeqiél, at latest in the Assyrian exile, more than a hundred years before Hézeqiél. The supposition that he as a descendant of the Kingdom of the

Ten Tribes lived probably at the court of Nineveh itself some hundred or hundred and fifty years before Hézeqiél, and acquired there reputation for the virtues mentioned above, is not only all that is required, but it is commended by the fact that in our book he still appears as living at a heathen court; and if Nineveh was the original scene of his noble career, he might also there become first the hero of a book which was in those very regions brought early under the notice of Hézeqiél and his contemporaries. In the present book, however, he is placed in the Chaldean exile; indeed, he is said to have lived until the first, acc. i. 21, and acc. x. 1, at least until the third, year of Kyros; and we understand very well the great freedom with which the author of this book handled the historical framework of his pictures.

If we now ask why our author supposes him carried as a youth into captivity as late as the time of Nabukodrossor, a very natural reason for this suggests itself. To the contemporaries of our author there was no one king of the Assyrian empire who was sufficiently well known. Nabukodrossor, on the other hand, stood from the very first in much closer relation to the Yudeans, and by the writings of Yéremyá and Hézeqiél he remained always to them the best known heathen king of the time previous to the destruction of Jerusalem. And without doubt there existed at the time of our author ample reminiscences and legends of his life such as he could easily use.

But the most noteworthy thing here is that, with this transference of Daniel from the Assyrian into the Chaldean age, a further sign of date of an entirely different nature fully accords. This indication is supplied by the constant, fundamental view of this book, as was above said, that the heathenism which rules in the world, until the coming of the Messiah, consists of four different and successive universal empires. For these four empires shall not, as wholly different according to the ruling nations, either entirely or in part, exist side by side, but follow each other in strict chronological order, the successor being always more corrupt, more cruel and merciless, than its predecessor. They then appear at once, ch. ii., under the figure of a monster, formed, as regards its four parts, quite differently; with the same meaning they are described, ch. vii., as four different mighty beast-like creatures, which come upon the stage in succession, of which, acc. ch. viii., manifestly one is intended always to destroy the other. But, as a fact, it cannot be said with strict historical truth that the Chaldean empire first made way for the Median, and then this to the Persian, but as is elsewhere always said in the Old Testament, Persians and Medes together, under Kyros as their true head, overthrew the Chaldeans and formed one kingdom; our author himself also still felt that, when, ch. viii., he comprehended the Medo-Persian empire under the one figure of a two-horned ram, the one horn of which, though grown later than the other, soon became higher than that. Everything becomes clear, however, if Daniel lived under the Assyrian rule, and an earlier book used by our author, dating perhaps from the time of Alexander or soon after him, understood by the four universal empires which he caused Daniel to foresee—the Assyrian, the Chaldean, the Medo-Persian, and the Grecian. If our author had not received the number of four empires as an existing tradition, he would, particularly according to the indication ch. viii., and others to be explained below in detail, manifestly (as nothing depends here upon the number) have counted only three from that of Nabukodrossor onwards.

In fact, the view that the great Colossus of the heathen rule of the world consists of just four such empires, and that the Alexandrine, *i.e.*, the Grecian empire, is the last of them, is so strongly held by our author, that he must necessarily have received the great conception itself from an older prophetic writer, as one which had been long in vogue. In our book there is no weight whatever laid upon the number *per se* as if there must be four precisely; still less is it communicated as something new, as yet never heard of, or mysterious, as for instance the number 490 in ch. ix.; it has the force simply of something which is taken as a matter of course, and on that very account can neither be enlarged nor diminished. The Seleukid and the other Grecian kingdoms had at that time become very different from that of Alexander, particularly in the direction of that development which our author had in his eye, and could therefore have been very well regarded as a fifth universal empire; and in fact our author, as we shall see below in detail, appears in some passages to be on the point of representing the kingdoms after Alexander as occupying a special age of the world; at the same time, he does not venture to go beyond the number four. But, as equally unable to reduce them to three, there is nothing left for him but to separate the Median from the Persian, just at those points where he speaks of the series and the number four, whilst on other occasions he also takes them together.—It is quite true that the older prophetic book, which must have in this case served as a model, does not now exist for us; still, there has been perhaps a trace of it preserved in the words xi. 14, as will be shown below.

Moreover, we know from many other indications that in writings of this kind belonging to the last two centuries B.C., the aim of which was to supply admonition and instruction rather than history, persons and times of the Assyrian and Chaldean empires were already very much confounded together, and that in general the earlier history of the heathen kingdoms was treated without much accuracy. If, *e.g.*, in the Book of Judith Nabukodrossor appears as an Assyrian king, we have but the reverse of the view which prevails in the present Book of Daniel regarding those more distant times. But just as in such books the authors themselves choose such historical framework and allusions simply on account of the prevailing taste of the time (whilst the Book of Yona proves how little they are fundamentally necessary), so we also must in reading them keep an eye upon things which are, according to their real significance, the important things, and in which the true meaning of such books is conveyed.

The plan and art of the book.

For the most important thing for us is that we now go on to understand the book correctly as regards its plan and artistic character, in order that we may afterwards the more correctly appreciate its subject-matter in all respects, as well as its true value. And for this there is nothing of greater importance than the recognition of the fact that this book, although written in a late age and in an age which was extremely depressed and calamitous, is exceedingly finished as regards its art and plan. Its arrangement in detail and its art in general is, it is true, very unlike that which had become customary in the previous centuries with the prophetic literature of the people of Israel; and in this also lies a further historical indication that it was not written before these later times. Still, the art of the book shows in its peculiar form such a finished excellence and beauty that it cannot be too highly valued, and we must be astonished that the ancient fine literary art of the prophets still in these wholly altered times put forth its energies in a way so worthy of its great past and in such depressing circumstances.

1. It has already been indicated that this book, in accordance with the necessities of the time for which it was primarily intended, was written for the prophetic consolation and encouragement of all faithful people, but also particularly to shame and threaten the powerful and at that time highly placed renegades, and to instruct and exhort the younger people. Whoever desires thus like our author to produce an effect upon his time by writing simply, may very well make it his object to promote at the same time the most different purposes of a book: and yet our author had but one higher purpose which combined all the rest. As now the various

objects which are pursued in the production of a book may be most easily attained by changing the manner of treating his subject, so an author may chose partly the narrative presentation of sublime examples and events from antiquity in order thereby to supply the more easily abundance of elevating lessons of the most varied kind to his contemporaries, partly prophecy in order from the consecrated voice of the same antiquity all the more powerfully to place before the eyes of his contemporaries the divine significance of their time and the time to come, sometimes using consolation and sometimes threatening.

A plentiful abundance of reminiscences and legends from their own antiquity was supplied to the people of those days; the people of this late time were always prepared and eager to hear of the men and things of that antiquity; and under the heavy pressure of the present to be entertained by elevating or even cheering narrations from a previous better time is exceedingly acceptable. Thus narratives, notwithstanding their deeply serious backgrounds, form the lighter side of this book; they open it accordingly, and pleasantly prepare for what is more difficult to understand.

The art of depicting the manner in which the human spirit can be touched by those spirits that reveal the mind of God, had made the most memorable progress between the time of Ḥézeqiél and Zakharya and the time of our author. For the prophetic spirit itself, separated in the course of time more and more from the public life of the nation, and thus getting continually more absorbed exclusively in its own efforts and unlimited endeavours, had since the days of those prophets learnt increasingly to have converse simply with divine spirits, had increasingly endeavoured simply to gain the proper state of mind in which it could feel most vividly that a new conception or a new outlook had been brought to it as it were by a divine spirit, or that a whole series of different conceptions and outlooks of this kind had come to it in the same way by a greater or smaller number of such ministering spirits. And then, in such cases as this, literary art could the more easily successfully present descriptions of such prophetic endeavours when the task was simply to describe with greatest vividness such revelations of the prophetic spirit and of the different divine spirits in contact with it from the standpoint of the time and position of an ancient prophet. It is precisely this kind of art which we meet with here at the highest summit of its development and at a degree of perfection far beyond those early stages in which we found it in the cases of Hézeqiél (IV., 12 sq.) and Zakharya (*supra*, p. 45 sq.). With the whole army of angels the daring of the prophetic imagination has established a personal friendship and become quite at home, has assigned to all its individuals their special positions, has given to them names and offices, and has worked everything out in this way in an original manner. That Gabriel and Mikhael are present, the former as the angel of the prophets more particularly, the latter as the angel of the people of Israel, is here rather simply presupposed as a long established conception. And from this fact also it may be inferred, in harmony with all previous phenomena, that a considerable time must have elapsed between Hézeqiél and Zakharya and our author, and that in the interim prophetic books must have appeared which had prepared for him this new way, and to one of which at least we were able above to point somewhat more definitely.

But the connexion between the narrative portion of the book above referred to and this prophetic portion must be supplied to the author in the character and work of Daniel himself, as he here once more revives this hero of the past. Just as the instructive narratives are connected with Daniel's life and times, so the states of mind preparatory to true prophecy are connected with him; and as the author in the first case translates himself in his narratives into Daniel's times, so in his prophetic mind he rises to Daniel's spirit and time in order to speak from the ancient prophet's position to his own contemporaries.

2. As the book was intended to consist of partly narrative and partly prophetic matter, it could not from the very first admit of any strict artistic unity, not even of such a unity as that of the Apokalypse of the New Testament, in which epistles and prophecy as its two constituent elements are welded together as closely as possible. It is true that here also the merely external uniting bond so far remains that, as the Apokalypse places the whole of the prophetic portion within the framework of an epistle, so this book places everything which Daniel has foreseen as regards the future within the framework of the narrative concerning him, the whole book obtaining thus the appearance of a book of narratives. It is also narrated, or rather simply indicated in a few words, under what circumstances, and particularly with what feelings and spiritual conflicts, everything originated which Daniel beheld regarding the future. At the same time, the instruction by means of simple narration breaks up of itself into a loosely connected series of separate pieces; in a similar way the fundamental matter of the prophetic element also is broken up into the various outward divisions of time and inward moods of spirit in which it dawned more and more perfectly and distinctly upon the mind of Daniel; and instead of comprehending all that has to be said regarding the future in one single, complex, but rigidly connected whole, which is supposed to have presented itself from one definite situation to the spiritual eye and ear of Daniel, as this is shown on a smaller scale in the piece containing the visions of Zakharya (*supra*, pp. 47-65), and on a larger scale in the Apokalypse of the New Testament, everything prophetic is brought forward more and more completely in one book in a series of pieces in accordance with the requirements of clearness or certainty. Small pictures of limited range, but the delineation of each executed with all the greater distinctness, animation, and richness of colour, must be thus

produced both in the narrative and in the prophetic portions of the book. We may say, therefore, that the author intended to draw a series of separate scenes as with the strong strokes of frescoes, on the one side for the purposes of instruction by history, on the other for warning and encouragement by prophecy. And in this respect all the separate pieces of the book show great excellence: indeed, it may be said that the same literary art as applied to prophecy which we found used by Hosea, Vol. I., p. 224 sq., is again met with here in an entirely new form of development. In this style of literary painting there lies also a peculiar charm. Every piece thus supplies a picture which can be looked at with satisfaction, in the contemplation of which it is possible to get completely absorbed. But how does this charm increase when the fundamental thought is seen to come out in each successive piece afresh in another manner and at the same time more and more fully and distinctly!

The book accordingly falls into various loosely connected scenes, each of which may be studied by itself with satisfaction. At the same time, these various pieces are not on that account by any means arbitrarily strung together: on the contrary, they are brought together in conformity with a higher thought which determines their closer relation to each other. Ultimately the pieces of both kinds have the same main object of raising the contemporaries out of the depressing present, and lifting them into higher and freer regions, although it may be but spiritually. Thus to the first piece, which conducts us into the elevating scenes of Daniel's youth, ch. i., there is immediately joined a second piece, which thus early plunges us into the midst of the grand subject of the prophetic glance into the future, ch. ii.: and the entire matter, in its twofold form, which the author desired to bring before the eyes of his readers, is therewith already presented in such a telling way, that it might be supposed the book could close at this point. But the author places this *first part* at the opening simply as a suitable introduction and preparation for the whole book, which he intends shall follow: accordingly, he goes on in a *second* part, ch. iii.—vi., to complete the didactic narratives in four pieces, following the thread of the subsequent life of Daniel, of the youth of whom and his friends we have beheld such an attractive picture at the opening. The piece at the end of the introduction, ch. ii., opened a prospect into a mysterious future, and that seems to have remained neglected: but now these prospects into a future of that kind are opened four times in the *third* and last part, ch. vii.—xii., in a new manner, and with all the greater frequency and vividness, until they exhaust all that remains to be said, and the book rapidly closes with them. But in this way all that the book offers to be beheld in the future is presented at the end with much greater significance, because it has become of much greater importance than its purely narrative communication; and just as the second half of the introductory portion, ch. ii., as containing prophecy, is even in extent much more important than the merely narrative half, ch. i., so the third part is still more lengthy than the second, whilst all three parts gradually increase both in point of intrinsic meaning and outward extent.

But just as the three main members of the book stand in such a mutual relation to each other that each succeeding part is of increased weight, so all the separate pieces composing each part hold a corresponding relation. The first part contains only two pieces, while the other two have four each: and the round number of ten pieces for the whole book is in this case plainly intentional, since it is of itself an outward sign of the certainty that everything will be finished with the tenth piece. But if the third part is thus on the same level as the second as regards the mere number of its pieces, its last piece, on the other hand, is made all the longer, ch. x.—xii., as if the weight of the whole book must after all fall at last mainly upon the revelation of the matters of the mysterious future. For within each of these two last parts, again, four pieces are arranged together, in each case by no means as by accident, in such a way that they might exchange places with each other in their respective parts: on the contrary, within everyone of the four pieces of each part both the main thought on which it rests and the subsidiary thoughts are expressed with gradually increasing completeness, until with the last everything is perfectly exhausted. Accordingly, it is particularly the picture of the actual present and future of the contemporaries which, with all that belongs to it, is gradually brought forward with growing completeness and distinctness in the four pieces of the last part, while in the last piece, ch. x.—xii., it comes out with such fulness and clearness, that it becomes at last, even as regards its external proportions, the most weighty of all, and weighs down the whole book with its closing gravity.

Further, every single piece also submits under the hand of our author to the ancient arrangement of poetic and prophetic art in *strophes*, having in the simple narrative pieces somewhat freer bounds, the purely prophetic pieces following the stricter laws which prevail in the older prophets. A great wrong would really be done to our author if we neglected to observe how in spite of his late age he still displays this elegance and care in his branch of literature. Indeed, he takes care to finish everything off so completely, that just as his whole book is composed of ten pieces, so the last of these, the peculiarity of which was mentioned above, itself falls into precisely ten strophes; and each of these strophes again is of the medium size, giving the appearance of great elegance.

But the elegance, regularity, and beauty of the whole discourse extends, in the last place, far beyond these limits: it penetrates even into the finest fibres of the style and description, even into the most telling form of every thought and of every situation described. Books of this kind, in which everything depends upon the propriety of the thought and the effectively telling charm of the discourse, must be more than ordinarily finished precisely as regards the force of expression and the beauty of treatment: and we may observe such excellences in our author, late as he is, whilst there is in this not the least trace of a foreign influence, but everything has in his case proceeded from the final forms of ancient Hebrew art and influences. We may here consider this one general example. As the book is so arranged that a fundamental thought shall be more and more perfectly presented in a series of pieces, similar, or even the same, phrases or sentences are often repeated, but this is only at the proper place, most frequently three times, and in this repetition itself with great effect, so that the feeling is produced that at last the thing has been said with sufficient plainness and force. It is particularly in the case of the decisive and characteristic expressions of the main thoughts and in the case of the mysterious, twilight hints which are thrown out, that this often produces the best effect with a few painter's strokes. And thus through these few leaves, which in their time winged their way through their world, there breathes a spirit which is gentle, and then again so weighty and telling, that they are in their peculiar form of art quite unsurpassed, and it becomes very intelligible how they came to produce such a powerful effect immediately after their first appearance.

3. However, the complete arrangement and art of the book only reaches its perfection in the fact that this fasciculus of excellently interwoven fly-sheets is intended to be heard, considered, and understood from the standpoint and the time and the lips from which it was delivered to the first readers. Just as a dramatic poet must make the hero whom he desires to bring before his audience or his readers speak and act entirely from his time and situation, so our author would have offended against his own purpose and art if he had caused Daniel to speak and act only partially or distortedly. And as the author has first of all transferred himself completely into the life and time of Daniel, that he may be able to speak from

that lofty standpoint both with greater personal safety for himself and his desired readers, and also with greater emphasis as regards his own present and future, he may accordingly expect and require all his readers with him to read and consider and understand everything he says from that standpoint exactly in the way he desires. A book of Daniel is meant to fall into the midst of the expectation and hope, the alarm and timidity, on the one hand, and of the indifference and irreligiousness, on the other, which prevail in this time, just as the ancient hero himself could have written and carefully hidden it so many centuries before if he had intended it for this very time; let, then, the reader suppose that he wrote it, vii. 1, that he carefully sealed and hid it, that it might not be found again and read until long after his death, viii. 26; xii. 4, 9, 13, that he composed it also quite in the form of a historical book with its dates; let the reader suppose this and study himself into the book as it is, witness the events of Daniel's life and time, and hear from the mouth of him and his Angel what will be the grand course of events which will befall mankind in the future; let him receive everything into himself most truthfully just as it is here presented, and permit it to produce its full effect upon him without any reserve. If he then find that it is his own present and future which is the chief matter concerned, and that all these narratives, and particularly these prophecies, come to him in this peculiar form simply because it might imperil life to present them in any other way, let him be all the more thankful to the author that he declined to supply his own name, and let him leave on one side the vessel when he has enjoyed its sweet and wholesome contents; or still better, let him value the vessel also, well remembering that its contents could not have reached him without its aid. Indeed, the author himself, while remaining modestly in his humble place, has supplied to the reader certain hints with a view to preventing absolute uncertainty as regards the outward origin of the book, if he has only the proper intelligence and the innocent desire to discover them: and no one, if a book-enigma of this kind is correctly solved, can be better satisfied or more pleased than the author must be.

That is the external finish and perfection of this book, without which it is, from beginning to end, quite inconceivable, and in this respect also the book is as elegant and beautiful as in all others. It is still more natural that the author should often vary the form of the discourse, in accordance with the great freedom of treatment which such writings allow. When it appeared to him that it would strike the reader more profoundly if he should hear Daniel himself narrate and speak of himself, he then introduced him as so doing, although the whole book appears as a collection of narratives concerning Daniel and his life. Accordingly the author does not introduce him as speaking of himself until the point when everything becomes much more serious and intensely interesting, and the reader can have become sufficiently attentive, that is, with vii. 1, 2, and then again with x. 1. But if he thus introduces him as speaking really only in the third part of the whole book at the head of the first three pieces and then of the last of them, and then makes the whole book, which commenced and is substantially worked out as a book of narratives concerning him, close with his immediate words, so that it does not finish as a historical book as it had commenced, there is conveyed by this fact a very plain hint to the reader that he must pay more attention to the words and thoughts than to the mere external aspect of a book which does not close as it began, and nevertheless, so far as its true object and real meaning is concerned, is so completely finished in itself that any further word would be in the highest degree superfluous for good readers such as the author desires to have.

The early history of the book.

It has already been shown that this book cannot be correctly understood, nor its value and early history properly appreciated, if it is not borne in mind that it was written before the actual outbreak of the Makkabean revolution. As a fact, it nowhere presupposes that a portion of the nation, then in such severe straits, had already made open resistance, neither does it advise that, and does not expect the Messianic victory from the use of weapons of war. On the contrary, according to the plain sense of its narratives concerning Nabukodrossor's conduct towards Daniel and his nation, it looks for the salvation immediately needed by Israel from an actual conversion of the princes of this world, as will plainly appear below, ch. i.—vi., particularly ch. iv. It is true that it cannot expect such a change in the case of an Antiochos Epiphanes, but prophesies for him near ruin; yet it is deserving of the greatest admiration that the author, in the very midst of the rage of the persecutions of a heathen king of this kind, expects also a salvation for Israel from an actual conversion of the foreign rulers, as far as men are able, before the great divine revolution of all things which the Messianic name stands for, to co-operate by their own endeavour towards the victory of better things. Now, that was in fact the expectation of all the nobler spirits in Israel before the outbreak of the Makkabean wars;* and the longing for such a change of things cannot be expressed in a more forcible way than that adopted by our author when he points back even to Nabukodrossor as a sort of model for heathen rulers on their gradual conversion to the true religion, and when he also in his book lays great stress upon this and makes it a chief subject of his narrative pieces.

Still, this book fell, nevertheless, like a glowing spark from a clear heaven, upon a surface which was already intensely heated far and wide and waiting to burst into flames; and its glowing descriptions of the divine rejection of the reigning Seleukid prince, accompanied by such mysterious and yet transparent hints with reference to a near deliverance from him, greatly fed and nourished, no less than his narratives of the divine deliverances of the faithful, the fire of the great

* It is only needful to compare, e.g., the poem of Phokylides, *Geschichte des Volkes Israel.* VI., 239 sq., 405, 412.

Makkabean attempt. If sixty or seventy years later it is narrated how the dying Matthias pointed his sons to the deliverance of the three friends of Daniel from the fiery furnace, and of Daniel himself from the den of lions (1 Macc. ii. 59, 60), we may find therein, as in other indications of the oldest Book of Makkabees,* a reminiscence of the first tremendous effects of this book, whilst the name of the author was either never properly known or soon forgotten. But we also know that the book was very early received into the Kanon of the Old Testament,† and that it soon called forth a number of similar works.‡

Of the uncommon zest and frequency with which the book was at once read in those first days, we have still a very plain proof in the book itself in the form in which it has been preserved in its original languages. It follows from all that has hitherto been said that, although the book falls into ten less closely connected pieces, it still possesses an original and decided unity and was written by one author: and on the whole it has come into the Kanon entirely as its author wrote it; which, as in the case of the Book of Ecclesiastes, is evidence also of the fact that it came into the Kanon soon after it was written. At the same time, as soon as ever we begin quite accurately to understand this Hebrew-Aramaic book in the sense of its author, we are irresistibly led to some smaller and greater *lacunæ* which it presents in the text which we now possess. The book has nowhere foreign additions, as such additions so often originate from other hands; but it presents instead of them *lacunæ* here and there, which prevent a correct understanding of it unless they are properly noted

---

* The expression Βδέλυγμα τῆς ἐρημώσεως, 1 Macc. i. 54, comp. iv. 43-46, is taken from Daniel, and shows that at that time this passage was still correctly understood, although the translation τῆς ἐρημώσεως, borrowed from the LXX, is too literal and too inaccurate.

† Comp. *Geschichte des V. Isr.*, VII., 480.

‡ Comp. the *Abhandlung* über das Æthiop. Buch Henókh entstehung sinn und zusammensezung. Gött. 1854.

and filled up. These *lacunæ* appear partly in the comparatively very old text from which the LXX translated; and they are all of that kind which easily arise through the haste of the copyists in the case of a book which is very largely read and very frequently copied; and precisely a work of the lighter class to which this belongs, which is more frequently devoured simply for its various descriptions, is particularly exposed to omissions which creep in unobserved, so long as it has not been received into a Kanon. We possess, therefore, in these *lacunæ* a sign of the frequency with which the book was read and copied immediately after it had been published. The *lacunæ* themselves will be noted as we go on.

Moreover, after the Makkabean period our book continued to be one which was most gladly and frequently read. The charm which pervaded it from the very first continued the more strongly to attract the readers of these times in proportion as it met the necessities and the taste of the last times before the second destruction of Jerusalem, and in a brief compass presented the richest contents. Its narrative pieces, in themselves so easily understood and, moreover, so captivating, became the models of martyrologies; and its enigmas of the future stimulated all those minds which longed for the fulfilment of the Messianic hope.* How popular the narrative portion was particularly, may be seen from the fact that it found early imitators on the one hand and enlargers and republishers on the other: as the form in which it appears in the LXX shows all this most plainly.†

It cannot, it is true, remain unperceived that the book owes the unusually high value attached to it by the faithful first and foremost to the circumstance that a main portion of the prophecies which it contains was fulfilled, even chronologically,

---

* Comp. the continuous chain of evidence which is presented in Matt. xxiv. 15; 2 Thess. ii. 4; the Apokalypse, and Josephus' *Antiquities*, XI., 8, 5, and other passages in this writer.

† Comp. *History of Israel*, V., 486 sq. (IV., 635 sq.).

so soon and so obviously with the death of Antiochos Ephiphanes: for only some three and a half years as the period of the *time of the end*, which it had fixed until the possibility of a great change for the better, elapsed before the overthrow of this tyrant, and by that time the first victories of the Makkabeans had been gained and the temple retaken and purified.* Still, the further course of the Makkabean wars showed immediately how little the Messianic hope which the book contains had been thereby attained. At the same time, these great wars and their results produced within a half a century, and, indeed, in a shorter time, such a serious disorganization and alteration of everything national and Israelitic, that it is not in the least surprising to find that the really original meaning of the enigmas of this book, easily as they were understood by the immediate contemporaries of the author, was gradually lost. Together with the fulfilment of the Messianic hope of the book, its enigmas regarding the future, with their mysterious hints regarding kings and numbers, seemed also to have been more and more deferred into a far off and dark future. It is true the art of shaping such enigmas of prophetic literature was long preserved by the authors of similar works in various ways:† nevertheless, the primary meaning of each particular enigma might easily pass from the remembrance of later readers, while the contents of such a book were for special reasons regarded with increasing attention. After the Book of Daniel had, as received into the Kanon, grown increasingly sacred, and its prophecies in very different historical circumstances stimulated curiosity constantly afresh, the enigmas of its names and numbers became of themselves a wholly new subject of thought and inquiry just in proportion as its original historical meaning had been lost; and when the Greek rule had been completely overthrown without the accompanying fulfilment of the Messianic prophecy of the book, the Roman

---

* Comp. on this point the notes below.
† As we saw above in the example of the Greek Epistle of Yéremyá, p. 140.

rule appeared to have taken its place as that which was intended by the book. With that the long representations of chap. xi. particularly became then quite unintelligible, because the key to their solution had been lost. Neither do we find that any learned Jew of the first centuries of the Christian era ever rediscovered this key. On the contrary, it was the new and free outlook which Christianity opened into the wide history of the world which in the case of some Fathers of the Church, especially Hippolytos, enabled them to see that the descriptions in chs. vii., viii., xi., had their immediate significance for the times of the Seleukidæ: with the perception of that fact the possibility at least was supplied of a rediscovery of the meaning of the book in the manner in which that has now been gradually more and more completely and certainly accomplished.*

I. *The introductory part.*

(I. 1.)

Description of Daniel and his friends in their youth.

Ch. i.

i.
1   In the third year of the reign of Yoyaqim king of Yuda came Nabukodrossor king of Babel to Jerusalem and besieged
2   it; and the Lord gave into his hand Yoyaqim king of Yuda *with the noblest of the land*† and a number of the vessels of the house of God: so he brought them to the land of Shine‘ar to the house of his god, but the vessels he brought into the
3   treasure-house of his god. Then said the king to Ashpenaz the chief of his eunuchs to bring of the sons of Israel both of the royal race and of the nobles youths quite spotless and fair
4   of form skilful in all wisdom full of knowledge and understanding science quite able also to attend in the king's palace

---

* Comp. on this point further the *Gött. Gel. Anz.*, 1859, p. 270 sq.; 1865, p. 352 sq.

† Inserted by conjecture.

and to teach them the writing and language of the Chaldeans;
5 and the king appointed them a daily allowance from the table
of the king and from the wine of his drinks, commanded to
educate them three years, and then certain of them should
6 attend before the king. Now there were among them of the
7 sons of Yuda Daniel Chananya Mishaêl and 'Azarya, and the
chief of the eunuchs gave them names, he called Daniel
Bêlteshazar, Chananya Shadrak, Mishaêl Mœshakh, and
'Azarya 'Abed-negó.
8 Then Daniel purposed not to be defiled by the king's table
and the wine of his drinks, and he besought of the chief of
9 the eunuchs that he might not be defiled. Now God caused
Daniel to find find favour and compassion before the chief of
10 the eunuchs: yet the chief of the eunuchs said unto Daniel " I
fear my lord the king who appointed your meat and your
drink might see your face more fallen-in than that of the
youths who are about your age, and ye might thus endanger
11 my head with the king." So Daniel said to the attendant
whom the chief of the eunuchs had appointed over Daniel
12 Chananya Mishaêl and 'Azarya "make now a trial with thy
servants for ten days, let there be given to us of the vegetables
13 to eat and water to drink, and then let our faces and the faces
of the youths who eat of the king's table be looked upon
before thee, and as thou shalt then see deal with thy servants."
14 So he gave ear to them in respect thereto and tried them
15 during ten days: and at the expiration of ten days their faces
appeared fairer and they themselves plumper in flesh than the
16 youths which ate of the king's table; and now indeed the
attendant took away continually their table and the wine of
17 their drinks and gave to them vegetables, and to these youths
God gave to all four of them science and skill in all writing
and wisdom, and Daniel became shrewd in every vision and in
18 dreams. But after the expiration of the days when the king
had commanded to bring them, the chief of the eunuchs brought
19 them before Nebukadnessar, and the king talked with them:
but among all there was none found like Daniel Chananya
20 Mishaêl and 'Azarya: they waited upon the king, and every
kind of shrewd wisdom concerning which the king enquired of
them therein found he them ten times surpassing all the
book-scholars and dream-interpreters which were in all his
kingdom.

So Daniel was *at the king's court** till the first year of the king Kyros.

It can hardly, in the form in which it is here narrated, be brought into harmony with the oldest documents, that Nabukodrossor besieged Jerusalem in the third year of Yoyaqim, led away captive to Babel this king with a great portion of the descendants of the royal house and of other nobles, deposited also a portion of the sacred temple-vessels at that time in the Belus temple at Babel as his choicest booty: on the contrary, we have here one of the narratives of those times which could not grow up until the third stage of narration had been reached, comp. the remark in *Hist. of Israel*, IV., 264 (III., 793). That is, our narrator drew his information in the first instance from the words of the narrative, 2 Chron. xxxvi. 6, 7, 10, but with a reference to the statement preserved in 2 Kings xxiv. 1, that it was the third year of the Chaldean vassalage of Yoyaqim in which the war of annhilation was commenced on the part of Nabukodrossor. The reason why the sacred temple vessels are here, ver. 2, purposely referred to so prominently, is evidently because it is intended to speak of them further subsequently, v. 2, 3.

However, this indication of the circumstances of the time, vv. 1, 2, is manifestly after all intended simply to serve as a foundation for the fuller description of that which is really the main matter in the entire narrative. The characteristics of Daniel and his three friends in their youth, of this subject an extremely lively picture is sketched in such attractive colours that it must of itself become an inspiring ideal for all such youths of high rank. How wrong and how debilitating is the life in which such youth are the more generally educated the nearer they stand to a royal court, to which they so readily accustom themselves, and in which they easily imagine lies the *summum bonum* of their existence, whilst really they waste in it all the best powers of body and soul! Not so Daniel, followed by his three friends. We see from Hezeqiel's words, xxiv. 21, 25, that the noble youths which Nabukodrossor took away with him after the first revolt were intended mainly to remain about him simply as hostages: it is in harmony therewith here narrated that he caused them to be educated at his court, indeed at his table. But in such cases it is natural enough to the conquerors and potentates of the earth, to think also of taking the most capable of them gradually into the service of their court, to estrange all of them as much as possible first from their own people by instruction and education in the sciences, arts, morals, and customs of the ruling nation, and then to select for immediate royal service the most capable of those who have been thus educated. That the education of such noble youths, the immediate oversight of whom and the final choice of the best the king always reserves to himself, is committed to the chief of the eunuchs, is founded in the high importance which that officer had as chief chamberlain in the royal courts in the ancient kingdoms (comp. *History of Israel*, III., 271 (III., 370 sq.)): and it often happened then that certain of such noble youths educated in this manner were themselves, when they appeared specially suitable, made eunuchs of, in order to fill the offices of such at the court. It appears plainly from

---

* Conjectured insertion.

2 Kings xx. 18 (Isa. xxxix. 7) and "Isa." lvi. 3-7, that it was precisely at the Assyro-Chaldean courts that this happened in the case of Jewish youths of noble family: this makes it all the more remarkable that in our narrative the possibility of it even is not presupposed. We are here involuntarily reminded of the fact that at the time of the Grecian kingdoms in Asia and Africa, low as they had fallen in other respects into the ancient evils ways of the royal courts in those parts of the world, and certain as it is that at the Egyptian court, *e.g.*, the ancient institution of eunuchs flourished again, it nevertheless appeared to be something impossible to educate at least Jewish noble youths in this way.

Accordingly the most capable of the noble youths shall be educated simply in all the manners, culture, and science of the Chaldean royal court. For this object a selection shall be first made amongst them, according to three points of view, ver. 4: (1) Only those who are *quite faultless in body and distinguished for beauty* shall be selected. But inasmuch as wisdom and science of every kind is the most indispensable requisite for the more immediate royal service, the Chaldean wisdom and science, moreover, was very different from that of Judea, and could not be easily appropriated perfectly, (2) only such shall be admitted as have already proved themselves in other ways in all kinds of *wisdom, knowledge, and science* as able and capable youths, as this may be sufficiently clearly discovered in youths who are educated in more elementary schools until about their fourteenth year. For the higher education in all the branches of Chaldean wisdom is intended afterwards to last only *three years*, pretty much as at the present time in our universities. But, again, education by means of the lower and the upper schools is not considered enough even in the case of physically faultless and fair youths, if (3) it is not attended by quick cleverness, skill, and faithfulness in office, a final series of virtues the foundation and capacity for which an apt teacher can likewise discover during the term of the lower stages of tuition, as is justly presupposed ver. 4. When the noble youths, who have been selected according to these three fundamental requirements, and presented to the king for supervision, have passed through this three years' course of higher education, they are presented to the king again for closer examination, who then, acc. vv. 5, 18-20, chooses for his special service those which are most pleasing to him. But at this third stage also a further distinction is possible amongst them: and in accordance with the peculiar Chaldean custom, acc. ver. 17, that man only was deemed the most distinguished who was most efficient in the secret arts of prophecy and the interpretation of dreams, just as Yoseph and Moses in their rivalry with all kinds of Egyptian sages were victorious only as they surpassed all the Egyptian interpreters of dreams and prophets, and just as the prophets in all nations take their position at the head of the clergy (comp. *Hist. of Israel*, II., 140 (II., 201)). It must, therefore, be said that in this entire description of the manner in which Daniel, with his three friends and the rest of the noble youths, is educated, is found a good acquaintance with the ancient art and science of education amongst the heathen nations most distinguished in it. Moreover, just as anyone who passes into a higher rank often receives a corresponding new name, so these four youths receive Chaldean names on their admission to the advantages of the higher Chaldean culture, ver. 7.

Still, after all, what is this course of education even amongst those heathen nations which are most distinguished for it, and in its most finished and severe forms, if that very thing is wanting in it which can alone conduct to the ultimately desired object! Daniel is conscious of that from the very first: here, too, close contact with heathenism and its customs can only have a prejudicial effect; but he is conscious of this simply as a youth, as by an instinct natural to him in the peculiar national community whose child he is, as this instinct had at that time developed itself. But we may most plainly recognize the writer of a particular age in the fact, that the one thing which so essentially separates Daniel from the highest culture and wisdom of the time, with all his zeal to share in it, is nothing other than the strict avoidance, accomplished by patient and prudent endeavour, of the luxurious diet of the court, that instead he may live upon vegetables alone. For, incontestably, there is at the bottom of this the view and the doctrine, that a good Jew, who will keep faithfully to his religion, should he be compelled at any time to live among heathen, would then do best to live upon vegetables and like pure fruits rather than to share in the foods and drinks prepared by heathen, inasmuch as it can never be certainly known how much of impure things may be mixed with them by such hands, a doctrine of the strict school which, though it could never find general acceptance, was the more readily nevertheless gradually taken up by Essenes and individual Pharisees, and met with the admiration of many and faithful adoption of not a few.* But that this doctrine and practice prevailed as early as the Assyrian, Chaldean, and early Persian times, we are not able at present to corroborate by any evidence: according to all that we are yet able to discern, it arose as one of the consequences of those strict ideas of purity and of the duty to avoid even the remote possibility of a heathen defilement which were developed in the centuries subsequent to Ezra and which logically conducted to Essenism.

However that may be, the love of sumptuous food and delicious drinks is never good, and with the use of the most temperate diet body and soul can flourish most admirably, as experience had at that time sufficiently taught. Accordingly it is here admirably related, first, how zealously Daniel sought to attain this object for himself and his three friends; he begs the chief overseer for permission to abstain from the royal diet, but this officer, although from the first showing him favour, fears by such a departure from the express will of the king to imperil his head, vv. 8-10. He then begs the subordinate overseer, or attendant, as it were privately and without the knowledge of the chief overseer, to make the trial with them for once, for ten days: † and the officer consents to do this; indeed, as the experiment is

---

* We have an entirely analogous, only a somewhat more marked, instance in the attendants of Josephus in Rome, acc. to his *Life*, ch. iii. How powerfully the commencement of the Makkabean times tended in this direction, is narrated 1 Macc. i. 62, 63; 2 Macc. v. 27; and similarly at the commencement of the great Roman war, the oil which had not passed through Jewish hands was forbidden to all, comp. *Geschichte des V. Isr.*, VI., 654. Our passage finds its first imitation in the Greek reproduction of the Book of Esther, v. 13, 46, 46. Further comp. Vol. IV. p. 44 sq.

† This number ten points to the ancient Persian custom which probably pre-

successful, he continues it from that time, vv. 11-16. In fact, there is thereby a good deal saved for this man which he can make use of! as is pretty plainly hinted ver. 16 a. In the second place, it is brought forward with equal emphasis, that these noble youths all four nevertheless lost so little, either bodily or mentally, that on the contrary it was from this time that the divine blessing appeared really to rest upon them, vv. 16-20.* And when of all the noble youths it is only the four who had steadily followed this stricter instinct of their mind, who, after the three years' higher schooling, quite successfully gain the highest confidence of the king; and when amongst them it is only Daniel again that attains to the acknowledged ability to work in the secret sciences, the entire series of the following narratives has been therewith sufficiently introduced, particularly the very next in which it is immediately clearly shown how much Daniel is able to do as the royal dream-interpreter. For the present, therefore, the conclusion is here, ver. 21, comp. ver. 17, made with the observation, that he now remained as one of the acknowledged masters in the highest science constantly at the court until the beginning of the reign of Kyros.

2. (I. 2.)

Daniel as interpreter of dreams and seer.

Ch. ii.

1.

1 In the *twelfth*† year of the reign of Nebukadnessar Nebukadnessar had dreams, | and his spirit felt much troubled and
2 his dreaming was gone for him. ‖ So the king commanded to call the book-scholars the dream-interpreters the astrologers and the Chaldeans, that they might tell to the king his
3 dreams: | and they came and waited upon the king. ‖ Then the king said to them "I had a dream: but my spirit was too
4 troubled to know the dream;" | and the Chaldeans spoke to the king in Aramaic. ‡ " O king, live for ever! say the dream to
5 thy servants, and the interpretation we will declare!" The king

---

vailed here and there in Babylonia also, comp. *Antiquities of Israel*, p. 131 sq. (112 sq.). We should use instead of it a *week* as in some measure equivalent.

* When, on the other hand, x. 3, it is presupposed that Daniel took the usual food and drink, it must be remembered that at this later period he was no longer living at the Chaldean court, still less under Chaldean training; further, that the strict avoidance of all ordinary foods in heathen countries appears, even according to the sense of this narrative, ch. i., rather as something unusual, and therefore as naturally attended by a special divine blessing.

† A conjecture instead of the *second*.

‡ The Aramaic portion is distinguished in this translation by a difference in the type and the numerals for the verses.—*Tr.*

answered and said to the Chaldeans "the matter is gone from me! | If ye do not make known to me the dream and its interpretation, ye shall be made into pieces and your houses be turned into dirt; | but if ye declare the dream and its interpretation, ye shall receive gifts offices and great honour from my part! | only declare to me the dream and its interpretation!" || They answered a second time and say "let the king say to his servants the dream, and the interpretation will we declare! || The king answered and saith "of certainty I know that ye bargain for time, just so as ye have seen that the matter is gone from me : | if then ye do not make known to me the dream, then is your sentence one

As according to the previous piece Daniel had passed through the four stages of all the wisdom which was inherited by Chaldeans, so the time now arrives when, by that divine power which surpasses all this wisdom, and which he knew from his early years how to keep and to increase, he climbs a fifth and at the same time the highest stage that is possible in that terrestrial and temporal sphere in which his life is cast. But that this took place in the *second* year of Nabukodrossor's reign, as we should have to suppose according to the reading ver. 1, is according to the plain sense of all the words of the narrator himself impossible to conceive. It is too plainly and circumstantially narrated, i. 5-20, that Nabukodrossor, who carried them to Babel in the third or fourth year of the (Chaldean vassal-) rule of Yoyaqîm, caused Daniel with his three friends to be educated for three years in the higher school, that Daniel then, ver. 21, remained at court where we find him subsequently also, ii. 49; and the house in which he meanwhile dwelt with his friends, acc. ii. 17, is but a part of the extensive royal castle. For its extent was without doubt sufficient to supply room for the whole society of the *savants* who had been appointed by the king, in order that, according to the royal will, they might always be at hand and could be appealed to when their counsel was needed; all of which is here, ch. ii., vividly enough described. It is also certain enough from the whole of the pieces which now follow, especially from vv. 13-18, that Daniel with his three friends already belonged to the fully-constituted and therefore responsible Masters in the strict sense (Doctors) of the sciences. We cannot therefore doubt that the reading *two*, ver. 1, offends too greatly against the proper meaning of the author; and if it is remembered that no year is more suitable to the whole narrative, in which Nabukodrossor is described as standing at the summit of his power, than the sixth before the destruction of Jerusalem, or the twelfth since the commencement fixed, i. 1, we may conjecture that the number *two* arose out of the number twelve. The earliest year which could suit the passage would be the seventh or eighth.

It is true the essential purpose of this piece is the prophecy, the subject-matter of which was explained more at length above, p. 171 sq. Still, since a man appears as its mouth-piece who, although holding a place in the society of the heathen sages at the same time, far surpasses them all by that which they lack, the description of the different

and a lying and pernicious thing have ye agreed to say before me, | till the time shall be changed; || only the dream say ye to me, that I may know that ye will declare to me its interpreta-
10 tion!" || The Chaldeans answered before the king and say "there is not a man on the earth who would be able to declare the king's matter, | just because no great and mighty king hath ever asked such a matter of any book-scholar or dream-interpreter
11 or Chaldean, | since the matter which the king asketh is difficult and there is none other who could declare it before the king

relation of both to each other and then of both to the king, forms likewise a chief subject. On the part of the heathen sages there is nothing but a nervously formal servility towards the king, pride of knowledge and yet complete helplessness in every case of real difficulty, mortal terror on account of the danger of their own lives; on the other hand, how prudent and calm in the hour of peril, taking every pains to remove every evil even from heathen companions, fearless in the presence of the king, does Daniel appear! Moreover, a king such as this, harsh and unscrupulous as he is, occupies nevertheless too independent a position amongst the various sets of the sages, and is too shrewd not to observe and to let all the world know upon which side he finds the real ability and wisdom. This entire description, with this meaning, is lively and humourous to a degree; and its real sense is almost entirely missed, unless this its "salt" is properly found and tasted. This appears forthwith

1. in the case of the relation subsisting between the whole of the members of the learned society, in the numerous body of whom Daniel with his three friends for a time almost disappears, and the king, vv. 1-13. The latter has in a night beheld a number of visions; but whilst in the morning he feels himself unusually disturbed by the collected impression which they have made upon him, and desires to recall precisely the separate representations, in order to hear according to custom from the interpreters their explanations, it happens that in his great excitement he has forgotten them, whilst he remains too disturbed to reproduce them. So this time he causes the sages to come, in order to learn from them not only the interpretation but also the dreams themselves, inasmuch as it seems to him that they who presume to be the only true interpreters of the dream of another ought also to know it independently of him. Indeed, if I presume to give counsel to a disquieted and anxious man who is well known to me as regards his whole position at a given time (accordingly to estimate and pronounce judgment upon his confused thoughts and dreams), it is not necessary that he should first make that position known to me. I can easily find it out and describe it to him exactly as he himself feels it in some indistinct manner. Those therefore particularly who pretend, like the heathen astrologers, to know everything, why should they not also know the dreams which one has had but forgotten? So the king, in his uneducated but straightforward mind, might suppose; and this is plainly the position of the matter which is here described, vv. 1-3, with which, however,

13 *

12 save the gods whose dwelling is not with mortals." ‖ Quite accordingly the king was very angry and wroth, and commanded to destroy all the wise-men of Babel ; | and a sentence went forth
13 and the wise men were to be put to death, | and Daniel and his companions were sought for to be put to death.

2.

14 Then Daniel made answer prudently and discreetly unto

it is well to compare the words below, vv. 28, 29, in order to get their sense more easily.

To none of these *savants* has such a case ever before occurred : so though, proud of their knowledge and their ability, they offer by all means to give the interpretation of the dream in question immediately, they require that the king shall himself first communicate it, ver. 4. Displeased at this refusal and suspecting something wrong in them on that account, the king declares once more that *the matter* in question has escaped him, but adds at once a severe threat in case of their further refusal, and on the other hand, the greatest promises in case of their compliance, vv. 5, 6.—As they then can do nothing else than repeat their previous declaration, ver. 7, the king considers that his first evil suspicion as regards the reason of their refusal is thereby confirmed, declares openly "men who are unable to find out the matter of the dream are also incapable of handling this matter and explaining it ; and, as they form a great society, they must have agreed to speak lying and therefore pernicious things before their king; only they will not confess this, and therefore only now act thus in order to gain time, supposing that there will probably another time come when they may be able more effectually to deceive and lie to the king ; once more I will

2. Not *one* wise man upon the whole earth, they had said before the king,

herewith call upon you to show your pretended art and wisdom !" vv. 8, 9. They are in fact, on the one hand, not clever enough to invent at haphazard the dreams which the king might have had, and, on the other, they must fear that if the invented dreams should not immediately recall to the king's mind in all its vividness the picture of those which he had seen, he will instantly have executed upon them the *sentence* with which he had just now threatened them in his highly excited speech, when he declared to them *then one is your sentence*, one single sentence (that of death) will be passed upon you equally! —They are thus then, thirdly, unable to help themselves further in any other way than by most humbly pretending that there does not exist on the broad earth one single man who could be equal to a demand such as was never before laid upon any sage whatever, even by the mightiest king, and would be too difficult for any one, save the spirits dwelling far off in the heavens, vv. 10, 11. But by this they simply excited only too surely the wrath of the king which had long been ready to break out : and they have hardly been dismissed, have hardly reached home, when that threatened *sentence* of the king overtakes them all, including, therefore, Daniel and his friends, vv. 12, 13.

would be able to fulfil his requirement ! So little do they know as yet of Daniel,

APPENDIX, 3. 2.—DANIEL, I. 2.—CH. II.

15 Aryokh the chief of the body-guard of the king who had gone forth to kill the wise-men of Babel, | he answered and saith to Aryokh the king's potentate "why doth the sentence go forth in such haste from the king?" ‖ Then Aryokh made known to
16 Daniel the matter, | and Daniel went in and besought of the king that he would give him time, | and he would declare the inter-
17 pretation to the king. ‖ Then Daniel went to his house, and to Chananya Mishaêl and 'Azarya his companions he made known
18 the matter, | and pity should they beseech from the God of heaven concerning this secret, that Daniel and his companions might not

although he is one of their number! But without questioning them much, he perceives what has to be done in this terrible position of mortal danger which has overtaken him and his friends as well as all his professional associates. Least of all does he despair in his communication with the chief of the royal guard, who is entrusted, according to ancient custom (comp. *Hist. of Israel*, III., 143 (III., 194 sq.), with the execution of those sentenced by the king, and is already on the point of collecting all the condemned: Daniel ventures boldly to ask this officer, *wherefore the sentence* of death is issued *in such haste from the king*, vv. 14, 15, an utterance which the narrative calls properly enough a *reply of counsel and understanding* to the requirement of the executioner to follow him: quick counsel with himself and prudent determination were needed to interpose this brief decisive word. The high officer (who was accordingly by no means a rude unfeeling man) then explains to him the whole position of affairs, that is, what had been resolved upon in the meantime by the king, and how little prospect there is that the king will depart from his resolution, ver. 15 b: nevertheless Daniel ventures, in the royal palace, to beg for a postponement of the sentence for *a* day (one night, acc. ver. 19) for himself and all his professional associates, promising to fulfil the king's requirement on the morrow, ver. 16. As one of the society of the *savants* (we must suppose) he enjoyed, according to the rules of the court, this permission to present a request immediately to the king, or at least to announce it at the court: and the request was heard. But what has he undertaken, before he had even in his own mind clearly enough recognized how he should meet in detail the king's requirement! Up to that point it had been in this most pressing moment not much more than a semi-conscious instinct which had guided him: but with rapid determination he withdraws alone into his own and his three friends' chamber, makes known to them that he has been granted a day's postponement, and calls upon them to turn with him in prayer to the true God, to see whether it is possible to obtain the divine compassion for this case, vv. 17, 18, just as below, ch. ix., a similar prayer on another occasion is given at length. Not from vanity and love of fame, only if possible to become an instrument in averting the great threatening calamity, does Daniel with all the deepest energies of his soul thus wrestle in prayer, to find the key of this mystery which weighs upon the king's soul; nor does he thus pray perish with the rest of the wise-men of Babel. ‖ Then unto Daniel in vision of the night was the secret revealed, | then Daniel blessed the God of heaven, Daniel answered and saith ‖

20
    Let God's name be blessed—from eternity to eternity,
      he whose is the wisdom and the might!

21 And he who maketh the times and the hours to change,
    maketh kings pass away and setteth up kings,
  giveth wisdom to the wise understanding to them of understanding,

22 he who revealeth the deep and hidden thing,
  knoweth what is in the darkness and with him dwelleth the light—

23   thee the God of my fathers I thank and praise
that wisdom and might thou gavest me—and now hast made known to me what we besought of thee,
that the king's matter thou madest known to us!

alone, but in common with his friends: accordingly, in this night, also in a vision, though the manner of it is entirely different from that which took place in the king's mind, it becomes manifest to him what the divine secret is which hangs over the head of this king, but of this king not merely as an individual man, but as the beginner of a great kingdom which is to endure long after him in many new forms. And as soon as on the morrow he has quite certainly and clearly perceived this secret, not as the creation of his own imagination, but as the truly divine, genuine secret of the great course of history, he cannot refrain from expressing his feeling of joyful thankfulness in a hymn of praise to that God by whose spirit he has perceived it, ver. 19.

This song of thanksgiving, vv. 20-23, is strictly simply a benediction, finding its expression most briefly first in general terms, ver. 20, then, at somewhat greater length and with greater particularity in reference to the present case, vv. 21-23, consisting of precisely ten longer lines. But as the poet who thus blesses the true God already speaks from a knowledge of the meaning of that secret, indeed, is in this hymn still quite carried away by the first feeling of joy at the happy burden of this prophecy, we find that there are here strictly but two great powers on account of which he blesses the true God as their sole and ultimate possessor: *wisdom* as to the wonderful destinies of mankind, into the secrets of which a glance is here given to the sage who submits to its instructions, and *might* which is sufficient to accomplish these destinies. It will sufficiently appear from the burden of the prophecy, vv. 31-45, and still more particularly subsequently, ch. vii.—xii., how truly it is the province of this wisdom and might to change *the times and the hours*, to cause at the right season conditions to pass away which have become insufferable through man's fault, and to create new and better times, also to change *kings* and kingdoms: and how gloriously *he that knoweth what is in the darkness and with whom the light*

24 Quite accordingly Daniel went in to Aryokh whom the king had appointed to destroy the wise-men of Babel; | he went and said thus to him || "The wise men of Babel do not destroy! bring me before the king, and the interpretation will I declare to
25 the king! || Then Aryokh brought Daniel with haste before the king, | and thus he said to him " I found a man of the Yudean exiles who will make known to the king the interpretation." ||
26 The king answered and saith to Daniel called Bêlteshassar | "art thou able to make known to me the dream which I saw and its
27 interpretation?" Daniel answered before the king and saith "the secret after which the king asketh can no wise-man dream-inter-
28 preter book-scholar astrologer declare to the king: | nevertheless there is a God in heaven who revealeth secrets; | he will make known to the king Nabukodrossor what will come to pass at the end of the days. || Thy dream and the visions of thy head upon thy couch is this: ||

dwelleth from the wealth of his wisdom *imparteth wisdom* which penetrates and reveals the divine secrets of the future to those who are the most capable of receiving it, so that by this work also God produces perpetually the result of *revealing all the deep and hidden things* which the ordinary mind is unwilling to see and utter,—this it is which Daniel must here dwell upon with greatest emphasis, not merely with reference to himself, but also to *all* the true members of that community in which such spiritual work is possible, vv. 21 c-23; for with great suitability the *I* changes into *we* at the end of ver. 23, comp. Rev. xix. 10.* And inasmuch as thus the order of the two powers, *wisdom* and *might*, ver. 20, is properly reversed in the special application, vv. 21, 22, the end reverts to the beginning, and the short hymn of thanksgiving is also made a complete and finished whole. When, moreover, Daniel gives thanks, ver. 23 b, for the *strength* received from God as well as wisdom, that is suitable inasmuch as he is conscious in this position of a sudden accession of higher strength such as he had never before felt, and which must at this moment still further enable him to accomplish the most difficult task which awaits him.

For in the consciousness of this strength he hastens to the chief executioner to beseech him not to execute the sanguinary sentence, inasmuch as he believes he possesses the certain means of meeting the king's requirements, infects this good man with a like enthusiasm, gets himself immediately admitted by and with him into the presence of the king, and begins to accomplish his task before the latter, first of all, however, as in the daring strength of a true prophet, remarking that this task could not be accomplished by any of the heathen sages, but only by a prophet of the true God, as he then forthwith begins to speak

---

* Hence the reading of the LXX and Theod., ver. 23, *ad fin.*, ἐγνώρισάς μοι is very unfortunate, as if they had read הודעתני.

3.

29 Thou O king—thy thoughts arose on thy couch of that which should happen after this, | and the revealer of secrets made known
30 to thee that which will happen. ‖ But to me not by a wisdom which I possessed above all living men was this secret revealed, | but for this that the interpretation may be made known to the king and thou mayest know the thoughts of thy heart. ‖
31 Thou O king wast seeing—and behold a mighty image : | this image was great and its brightness extraordinary as it stood
32 before thee, | and its look terrible. ‖ This image—its head was
33 of good gold, its breast and arms of silver, | its flanks and its haunches of brass, its thighs of iron, its feet part of iron and
34 part of clay. ‖ Thou wast seeing till a stone broke itself loose

only in his name, vv. 24-28. It should be carefully observed with what warmth of language, even in the simple narrative, vv. 14-19 and vv. 24-28, every-

3. In the discourse before the king there is nothing which is from the very first so remarkable as the manner in which Daniel commences his account of the dream : he does not at once, without any preface, begin it, but first of all, vv. 29, 30, presents a few remarks which, unimportant as they appear to be, contain the key to all that is to be revealed subsequently from the mysterious depths of the unfolding ages. A king who is thus powerful and thus independent, having fought his way upward by his own efforts, and who is conscious of being the head of a long line of similar monarchs of substantially the same empire, can, when he is tormented by the most uneasy thoughts and imaginations day and night, manifestly be thus tormented only inasmuch as he is precisely this king and in this peculiar situation ; and all such tormenting thoughts reach their climax ultimately in the one short, pointed question : *what will be after me?* Inasmuch as Daniel, with greatest acuteness,

thing is animated which refers to this undertaking and deed of a true prophet in a situation of this kind.

perceives this, and immediately makes reference to it briefly before the king, he obtains at once complete control over the true spirit of the monarch, relieves him forthwith of his own deepest thoughts and cares, and is able to construct before him *the thoughts* and images of *his heart* clearly and connectedly as they moved before his mind's eye in former moments of his own lonely meditation, although but dimly and disconnectedly ; and if every particular as it now comes to him from the lips of the true prophet was not quite the same, it still presents itself to him so vividly that he seems simply to see and hear again everything as he previously dimly beheld it and can now only distantly recall it. Thus Daniel supplies, at all events in the good sense, what the king found wanting, acc. vv. 8, 9, in the heathen sages, and their inability to supply which he was on the point, in a moment of displeasure at their want of skill, of making even a mortal offence. But when Daniel, after

not with hands, | and smote the image upon its feet of iron and
35 clay and broke them in pieces. || Then were broken in pieces at
once the iron the clay the brass the silver and the gold, | and
became as chaff of the summer threshing-floors, and the wind
carried them away, | so that there was no place found for them; ||
but the stone which smote the image became a great mountain |
36 and filled the whole earth. || This is the dream : | and its interpretation let us now tell before the king : ||
37 Thou O king, king of kings, | thou to whom the God of
38 heaven hath given dominion wealth might and honour, | thou
into whose hand he hath given everywhere where they dwell the
sons of men the beasts of the field and the fowls of heaven
and hath made thee to rule over them all; || thou art that
39 head of gold. || But after thee will arise another kingdom

this necessary preface, addresses himself to the fulfilment of the king's requirement, he does not forget to add, that he has not received this wisdom simply by his own wisdom, as if he were not a man like all men ; which could in other cases be presupposed as the feeling of a true prophet, but may be remarked with advantage in the presence of a heathen king, in order that he may perceive that the divine wisdom and true prophecy make themselves felt in the presence of such a king also, because they must make themselves felt, because it is well and a divine arrangement that the king *may know the thoughts of his heart.*

The details of the *dream* itself, vv. 31-35, are however such that the king might very well have dreamed it : for it consists of separate but very well connected pictures, each of which may, taken alone, easily force itself at some time upon a dreamer. Figures of gigantic size were least of all unknown to early antiquity, particularly in Egypt, Babylonia, and Assyria, as we now know so well : whatever exists in the actual world can easily present itself to the imagination in dreams, only in larger and more striking shapes ; and every immensely gigantic thing often produces, *per se*, the *feeling of horror*, as was the case with this confronting figure, although it was itself so splendid, ver. 31. What precisely this figure was intended to represent is not here told us by any one definite word : but from the whole description it appears that an animal is not intended as we might have supposed from ch. vii. and viii., but a man of such a gigantic form; nor were such Colossuses unknown to the ancients : although it is precisely a human Colossus which has naturally something in the highest degree offensive to the cultivated eye and the finer sense. It is also known that such immense works of art and architecture are not always finished in conformity with their original design, that many details which were at first intended to be formed purely of gold or silver are at last executed with poorer materials, and the material of the various members can thus be very different : moreover the mixture and the interchanged variety of the different materials may be carried too far and become the more fatal to the durability of the whole work in proportion to its size. Now, it is certainly strange that in this monster human

smaller than thou, | and another third kingdom of brass which
40 will rule over all the earth. || And a fourth kingdom will be
mighty as iron, just as iron crusheth and beateth down every-
thing, | and as iron breaketh in pieces all these things it will
41 break and crush in pieces. | —And that thou sawest the feet and
toes part of potters' clay and part of iron, || it will be a divided
kingdom; | yet there will be in it the hardness of iron just as
42 thou sawest the iron mixed with loam-clay. || And the toes of
the feet part of iron part of clay: | the kingdom will be half
43 strong and it will be half brittle. || That thou sawest the iron
mixed with loam-clay: | they will continually mix together by

figure gold, silver, brass, and iron-clay* vary according to the four quarters of the erect figure; and it is yet stranger that at last a stone from above, and no human hand is seen which could throw it, smites this giant-figure quite at the bottom at its feet, and from that blow, as indeed was to be expected from such clay-iron feet, the whole Colossus tumbles down, whilst the stone itself becomes a rock which fills the whole earth. With all this, curiosity is powerfully excited to inquire, How it is possible, and what it means? But dreams are the very things which the longer and the profounder they run on the more varied and extraordinary are their creations.

In the end, therefore, everything depends upon the *interpretation,* as was finally, ver. 24, 25, 30, said so emphatically and as it is here given without a break, vv. 37-45. That the interpretation is longer than the dream is natural enough; but when once it commences, it must forthwith touch upon three very different things, which are the essential matter here. Because, however, it must embrace such various things, the words and clauses which serve to introduce the explanation of the details grow gradually shorter and more broken, just as when a connoisseur, undertaking to explain all the separate parts of a great picture, can compress his remarks in proportion as he observes that his hearers are attentively following him through all the details: for thus this king also, the more he hears all these marvels explained, and particularly by this interpreter, the more quiet and attentive he becomes. There have to be explained, however,

(1) in the first place the four strange variations of colour and material in this gigantic body: this is, therefore, simply one continuous description, vv. 37-40, in which, however, it can suffice to explain only the first of these four stages from top to bottom in detail. What is the signification of *the golden head?* Thou art the head, thou king, not of the common kind, but thou *king of kings,* as the Assyrian king was first called, comp. Isa. x. 8, and after him the Chaldean king, Ezek. xxvi. 7, *to whom the God of heaven,* whom Daniel deems it is unfitting to speak of here in the presence

---

* We might conjecture that the Greek idea of the four ages of the world was present to our author's mind: yet this idea is not originally Greek, acc. to *Hist. of Israel,* I., 257 sq. (I., 368 sq.), and the mere comparison with gold, silver, brass, iron is too obvious to require that our author should borrow it from Hesiod.

the seed of men and yet not hold together with one another, | just as iron doth not mix with clay. ||

44 But in the days of those kings will the God of heaven set up a kingdom which will not be destroyed for all time | and of which the dominion will not be left to any other people, | which will crush and put an end to all these kingdoms and itself stand for

of the heathen king, as ver. 23, as the God of his fathers, has given the supreme power over all things living on this earth, as this is in still greater detail described according to court language, vv. 37, 38. But Nabukodrossor represents at the same time the entire Chaldean empire, which could the more easily be the case, inasmuch as his successors were all less famous and reigned for a much shorter time, and as this was also actually the case formerly, "Isa." xxiii. 15, and "Jer." l. 17; li. 34 (comp. *supra* p. 4). The discourse then passes the more easily with greater brevity to the rest of the four empires: *after thee will another kingdom arise*, the Median, which is intended, acc. p. 172, and is, therefore, immediately, at all events somewhat more particularly, designated as *smaller than thou*, corresponding to that *silver*, ver. 32; hence the others are dealt with more rapidly, *and another third kingdom, of brass*, that, acc. ver 32, *which*, as the Persian kingdom, *will rule over the whole earth*, as again more powerful than the preceding one, ver. 39. But here again, as in the pieces ch. vii., viii., xi., the fourth receives at once more attention than the third, as the Grecian kingdom which was existing at the time of the author; and in order first simply to complete the explanation of the brass with its declining value and rank, this only is mentioned, ver. 40, but mentioned with great emphasis even three times, that *it will be like iron, just as the iron crusheth and breaketh everything*, and then once more as a climax, *and as iron which breaketh in pieces all these* before-named metals *will it crush and break in pieces*. And it is easy to observe that this one aspect (which is certainly at the same time the most prominent in the main figure of the four metals) which may be presented by the clay-iron lowest quarter of the Colossus, is so prominently mentioned in this place alone, simply because thereby the Greek empire, as it appears in its immediate historical form, that is, the empire of Alexander himself, shall be indicated as that which shall crush everything.—But everything is not yet finished that the seer has to set forth from the main figure: just as in the dream itself, ver. 33, he had called the thighs iron simply, but the feet clay-iron. It is Alexander only who crushed everything to pieces as he strode along upon iron legs; but,

(2) with the *feet and toes*, ver. 41, *i.e.*, the principally two greater offshoots which will branch out of the Alexandrine empire, as the feet belong to the legs, namely, the Seleukid and the Egyptian, the case is somewhat different: their composition, partly of clay and partly of iron, signifies precisely that that mighty kingdom of Alexander will be broken and rent, primarily into the two great parts which are below, ch. xi., further distinguished; *a divided kingdom* is of itself weaker, but it is here, as if by way of supplementary remark, observed as a thing not to be overlooked, that there is nevertheless also *something of the dura-*

45 all time : || just as thou sawest how from the mountain a stone broke itself loose not with hands | and crushed in pieces the clay the iron the brass the silver and the gold.* || A great God hath made known to the king what will come to pass after this : | and sure the dream is and certain its interpretation. ||

bility of iron in it, that these two kingdoms have still much toughness and power of resistance, as in fact at the time of the author they were not anything like so fundamentally weakened and fragile as they were half a century or even a century later.—However, although the toes as well as the feet are also here unexpectedly spoken of, which was not the case ver. 33, as if these smallest and lowest little members would after all push themselves particularly forward at last, it becomes therefore necessary

(3) to speak of them further, in the first instance, as if to satisfy the curiosity which has been raised with regard to them. And the simple reader and student of the whole book may already at this passage infer that, as the ten separate toes, though at the bottom, push themselves most forward on the feet, so here those ten individual Greek rulers might be intended who most immediately concern Daniel's nation, and whose claws it felt so much, the Seleukid rulers : but inasmuch as these are intended to appear below, vii. 7, under another and nobler figure as the ten horns, the interpretation is here content to give simply two more general signs of the individual offshoots of the Greek power : (1) the indication that *the empire* will be *partly strong, partly broken*, i.e., fragile and weak, composed of strength and weakness, as of two wholly different constituents, or as of hard iron and soft clay, ver. 42; and (2) the individual representatives of this rule would, in order to put an end to the weakness mentioned, it is true, more closely associate and mix with each other by the strongest means possible, *by the seed of men*, that is, by marriage and procreation, but that will as little enable them to attain the designed object as if iron should attempt to mingle with clay, ver. 43. By this allusion to the intermarriage of the Seleukid and the Ptolemaic houses (allusions which are not explained until vi. 17), we come down plainly enough quite to later times : and as the thighs of the figure bring us to Alexander, the feet to the division of his empire, so the toes bring us into the circumstances particularly of the Seleukid kingdom, just as they actually were at the time of our author. And it is already time that this figure should now be quite abandoned, since at last, ver. 43, it had already become necessary to speak of the individual men, indeed, *the seed of men.*

But *in the days of those* last indicated, ver. 43, *kings* comes the end of this entire Colossus, of all heathen rule : it is time to interpret that stone whose sudden irruption had been beheld, vv. 34, 35. Yet as the discourse before the king has already been long, the unexpected, surprising, rapid coming of the Messianic age (as of all divine things when they become powerfully manifest) with the Messianic people as the true heirs of that kingdom, can now be indicated with all the greater brevity in a few strong outlines as the true meaning of the irruption of that stone,

---

* In the common text *the iron the brass the clay.*

4.

46 Then king Nebukadnessar fell upon his face and he worshipped Daniel, | and offering and sweet incense he commanded to be presented to him; || the king answered Daniel and saith
47 "Truly your God is a God of Gods and a Lord of kings and revealer of secrets, | in that thou couldest reveal this secret! ||
48 Then the king honoured Daniel, and many great gifts he gave him, | and made him ruler over the whole province of Babel and
49 chief overseer over all the wise-men of Babel; || and Daniel requested of the king and he appointed over the administration of the province of Babel Shadrakh Mæshakh and 'Abéd-negó, | while Daniel was at the king's court. ||

ver. 44: whilst in the repetition of the figure, ver. 45, which has to be interpreted a further small word is introduced as if furtively—*from the mountain*, which was needed to make the figure absolutely complete. For to be set in motion *without hands*, without human, visible effort, is part of the nature of this stone: still it must come from somewhere, and it can accordingly only come, like every other stone, from the quarter where its true territory is amongst thousands more; high above the highest human Colossus and human empire there towers aloft in the infinite expanse another Colossus, the rock and the mountain of the celestial Ssion: a stone rending itself loose *from* this highest *mountain* must when it falls with its marvellous energy strike and, if it is fragile, dash in pieces *that* which it strikes, whilst out of it as a pure celestial spirit and material, wholly new here below, a firm mountain, filling the entire earth, a new and better citadel of Ssion can arise. Thus we have here so early quite the New Testament imagery of the Church, particularly as the Shepherd of Hermas works it out.—But as the whole discourse began, vv. 29, 30, with the assurance of its certainty, so it here ends therewith, ver. 45 b, only with more emphatic brevity.

4. If the king has really listened to all this with attention, and has been gradually carried on by the charm of the prospect till he enters into the nature and the fulfilment of this great dream, it is not surprising that, in the first joy of his heart, he heaps honour and thanks upon Daniel after the manner in which a heathen king is accustomed to express his gratitude. He falls down in homage before him and causes offerings to be presented to him, as he is at other times accustomed to do to his gods, ver. 46 (as indeed a living interpreter of the mind of the true God appears to be infinitely more than a dead idol); and yet he does not merely then feel that there is here in this plain revelation more than a god as he had hitherto known them: he acknowledges this also and praises this God as he must praise him after the new knowledge of him which he has so certainly gained, ver. 47; but he also most handsomely keeps his promise, ver. 6, honours Daniel with public thanks, gives him great gifts of various kinds, and puts him in the two high offices of a chief administrator of

Babylon as the principal province and of a chief overseer of the court scholars, ver. 48. And Daniel has to submit to all that, but does not forget his three friends, and asks to have them made subordinate officers in the province of which he is chief administrator, ver. 49: with which this whole piece is more appropriately finished off, inasmuch as these friends are immediately to be spoken of again.

II. *The typically illustrative part.*

3. (II. 1.)

The sufferings and triumph of Daniel's three friends.

Ch. iii.

When in the second chief part the simple narrative is again resumed, and in the first instance with Nabukodrossor, it is still especially the relation of this king to faith in the true God as the great subject of the book which we here see further developed. According to the result of the former incident, ii. 47, Nabukodrossor had already advanced so far that he perceived that the God of Daniel "is a God of Gods, a Lord of kings, and a revealer of secrets." The following narrative shows how he was brought to confess that there is no other God at all than this one true deliverer and saviour of men. To learn by experience to know the true God as the deliverer from the deepest affliction leads both more and more irresistibly to the complete knowledge and worship of him than to know him merely as the inspirer of the true prophet. As we are here, therefore, no longer, as in ch. ii., concerned with the mere revelation of secrets and the antithesis between the genuine and all the innumerable kinds of false prophets, but with the marvellously protecting and delivering power of the true God, a great example and model of suffering for the sake of divine truth is depicted, out of which suffering the three friends of Daniel, as true heroes of endurance, come forth victoriously before the king's eyes. A man like this powerful king, being precisely at this moment at the summit of his power, must first come into personal contact with a perfectly clear instance of such profound sufferings for the sake of divine truth, of such divine security and joy in the midst of them, and of such a divine victory over them, in order to receive his first ideas of the wonderfully redeeming power of the true God. The true friends of a Daniel are faithful and God-fearing enough to stand the hottest trials.

I.

1 King Nebukadnessar had made an image of gold, its height sixty cubits its breadth six cubits; | he set it up in the valley of
2 Dura in the province of Babel. ‖ So king Nebukadnessar sent to assemble the satraps the presidents and the prefects the chief astrologers the chief chamberlains the chief judges the chief prophets and all the rulers of the provinces, | that they might come to the dedication of the image which king Nebukadnessar
3 had made. ‖ Then assembled the satraps the presidents and the prefects the chief astrologers the chief chamberlains the chief judges the chief prophets and all the rulers of the provinces to the dedication of the image which king Nebukadnessar set up; |

The occasion for such trials is supplied, as is here narrated, by a great feast which Nabukodrossor observes on a day of rare rejoicing (as we may suppose), after he has won all his greatest victories (long since destroyed Jerusalem also). As a heathen empire, notwithstanding all its numerous gods, generally worships one of them as the highest, and a king has one amongst them to whom he very readily ascribes his victories, and to whom he gladly gives special honour,* in like manner Nabukodrossor has erected for a god of this kind a golden image which is intended to be displayed on some suitable site as a lasting monument of the king's thankfulness, both in honour of this god and, at the same time, of the victories which he supposes he has won by his help. This (as it is here called) *golden* † image is intended to be erected in honour of the chief god of Nabukodrossor, whether this was Nabu from whom he derived his name, or Bél, chief god of the ancient Babylonians;

---

* There is no doubt but that there is only one statue intended here, and that the worship of the god represented upon it is what is alone implied; it is accordingly equally certain that the Massôra, ver. 14, has the correct pointing לֵאלָהִ֣י and must also, vv. 12, 18, have read לֵאלָהָ֣ךְ, or at least have thus understood the word, since in Aramaic and also elsewhere in this book of Daniel the actual sing. אֱלָהּ is used for *a* god. Another reason for this is mentioned below, for it becomes, if possible, more certain iv. 5.

† Which need not, in accordance with the usages of ordinary language, be more than an image overlaid with gold.

and they stood in front of the image which king Nebukadnessar
4 set up: ‖ and the herald called mightily "To you ye nations
5 communities and tongues it is said: | at what time ye hear the
sound of the horn the flute the cither the sambyke the harp the bag-
pipe and all kinds of instruments, | ye shall fall down and worship
6 the golden image which king Nebukadnessar set up; ‖ and whoso
doth not fall down and worship, | shall the same hour be cast
7 into the midst of the burning furnace of fire! ‖ Quite in accordance herewith at that time when all the nations hear the sound
of the horn the flute the cither the sambyke the harp the bagpipe

but its gigantic size is meant to correspond to the greatness of the deeds and victories of the king, who imagines that he has been favoured by this god, just as a gigantic statue of this kind had already been described in general terms, ii. 31: still, the detailed description of it given here, ver. 1, as sixty cubits high and six cubits broad is too brief to enable us to get thence an accurate idea of its structure; it would be most natural to understand by it a high column upon the summit of which was placed the proper image of the god, as the Romans subsequently constructed such columns: however, according to the ultimate purport of the narrative, very little depends here upon the mere form in which the image was constructed. We are equally unable at present to discover what induced the author to conceive this gigantic image, which was intended to be seen from a great distance, as erected by Nabukodrossor precisely in the plain of Dura of all the level country of Babel; but a special reason of some kind must have induced him to do this, as otherwise he could have supposed the extensive plain of Babel in general.

It follows, as a matter of course, according to ancient custom, that for the dedication of this monument when it had already been erected at the suitable spot, a great festival should be kept, and particularly that all the chief dignitaries of the empire and friends of the king should be gathered around it, in order to present their first homage, amid the joyful sounds of all kinds of musical instruments (what is called in these days *Janitscharenmusik*) to this chief god of their king who was being thus honoured. Boisterous Janizary-music (*Janitscharenmusik*) forms part of such a festivity, as is here everywhere, vv. 5, 7, 10, 15, described with graphic effect: for the specially-named six instruments are intended with *all* the instruments added as seventh in the list simply to signify in a round number all possible instruments. Whether there was to be singing at the same time is not indicated, and with such music singing would really be impossible according to the feeling of the ancients:* moreover, what place would there be here for the singing of a congregation, which was generally unknown in heathen worship? Instead of singing, simply *prostration* and *worship* shall be shown by all those assembled before this image and its god when the music strikes up; first the magnates and dignitaries who surround it immediately, then all the rest who stand behind, of whom, however, nothing is said here

---

* Comp. *Dichter des Alten Bundes*, I a., p. 217.

and all kinds of instruments, | will all the nations communities and tongues fall down worshipping the golden image which king
8 Nebukadnessar set up. || Quite in accordance herewith at the same hour came forward Chaldean men and accused the Yudeans, |
9 answered and say to king Nebukadnessar: || "O king, live for
10 ever! | Thou O king wast pleased to command that every one who should hear the sound of the horn the flute the cither the sambyke the harp the bagpipe and all kinds of instruments, |
11 should fall down and worship the golden image; || and whoso should not fall down and worship, | should be cast into the midst
12 of the burning furnace of fire: || there are Yudean men whom thou hast appointed over the administration of Babel, Shadrakh Mæshakh and 'Abéd-negó: | these men O king thought well not to regard thee, | thy god will they not serve nor worship the golden image which thou hast set up."

because according to the meaning of the discourse nothing depends on them. And in fact, where the singing of a congregation is absent, there remains nothing else than prostration and kneeling.

But while all the magnates of the kingdom, who are likewise here, vv. 2, 3, introduced with great emphasis as forming such a number *seven*, have already assembled themselves and are prepared to fall down upon their knees at the given sign, the enemies of the Yudeans, *i.e.* of the friends of the true religion, who are everywhere on the watch, observe with no small satisfaction that the three friends of Daniel, just raised to high offices, are nowhere to be seen: and as those who have received official appointments are generally placed on such occasions in their proper order, an absence of this kind could easily be observed. Accordingly they hasten, before the preparations for the solemn moment * are finished, to the king † as their accusers. It cannot be doubted that Daniel was also missing from these ranks, as also according to the following narrative, ch. iv., he is still found holding exactly the same post which is described ii. 48: however, his position is too high for these accusers to assail, and they are shrewd enough to perceive that if they only once succeed in destroying the friends of this high officer, he will then be unable long to keep out of their reach!

We have seen from ii. 47 that Nabu-

---

* For this is incontestably the meaning of the narrative in its general connexion; and accordingly everything is narrated, vv. 3, 4, also as still continuing, or unfinished, *i.e.* in the Aram. *part.*, instead of as simply having occurred as ver. 2 and ver. 8.

† It is impossible here to avoid recalling the similar splendid feasts which Antiochos Epiphanes arranged in the neighbourhood of Palestine, and at which guests were expected from the magnates of Jerusalem (*Hist. of Israel*, V., 294 sq. (IV., 383-5)): how may the friends of heathenism in Jerusalem have then suspected and accused all who took no pleasure in such feasts!

2.

13 Then Nebukadnessar in anger and fury commanded to bring Shadrakh Mæshakh and 'Abéd-negó, | then those men were
14 brought before the king, || Nebukadnessar answered and saith to them " Will ye seriously Shadrakh Mæshakh and 'Abéd-negó not

kodrossor had acknowledged and learnt to a certain degree to reverence the God of Daniel as a very special and high god: but it did not thence follow that he considered him to be the only true God, or the only God worthy of the name: on the contrary, he occupied, according to these narratives, no more than the position of an Alexander Severus, when he commanded the portrait of Christ to be placed with those of the rest of his gods. He had no intention of giving up his own god, whom he worshipped as the author of his victories and his royal power in Babylon, and who could seem to him, as well as to his whole people, to be the symbol of the glory of the Babylonian empire itself; neither had Daniel indeed required

2. appears to be the result: the king enraged at the three Yudeans, alone named to him, who could be at hand and yet are not occupying their proper places in the official ranks, commands them to come before him for a brief hearing, and threatens that he will be unable to exempt them from the extreme punishment which has been long prescribed; but when he concludes this threat, ver. 15, with the words *who is that God that can save you out of my hands?* he only says thereby what he must say in this situation, and may suppose he can safely say, but falls precisely with this closing word into the same self-deception as regards his own omnipotence, and into the same blasphemy of the true God which appeared formerly in the case

this of him; and that he should look upon Daniel's God as the only true one, none of his subjects could expect of him thus far even if what is narrated, ii. 47, was generally known. It would certainly have been by far too great a demand if the requirement had been that the officers holding the Yudean faith should worship *all* the heathen gods: but that they should worship simply the chief god of their king, and of the empire whose officers they are, does not appear to be an unreasonable demand. The accusers, as they themselves knew beforehand, must accordingly expect to find a gracious hearing of the king, particularly if they take care not to refer to Daniel. And in fact this immediately

of Sanherib, acc. " Isa." xxxvi. 20; 2 Chron. xxxii. 13-17, since acc. Hos. ii. 12; Deut. xxxii. 39 there is no one but the true God Himself who may thus speak and think with regard to the truly guilty. But in reality there is in this final sentence simply an expression of the same feeling which animates every tyrannical ruler, and with which he might conclude every one of his unjust commands; but the use of that passage of the Chronicles by our author proves beyond doubt how profoundly this expression had sunk into the souls of many, and how often it was gladly repeated.— The punishment of death at the stake, or in a furnace of fire, was an ancient custom in those districts, where offences against the supreme power of the State

now serve my god | nor worship the golden image which I have
15 set up? || Therefore if ye are ready at what time ye hear the
sound of the horn the flute the cither the sambyke the harp the
bagpipe and all kinds of instruments to fall down and to worship
the image which I made-- | but if ye will not worship it, ye will
in the same hour be cast into the midst of the burning furnace of
fire; | and what god is it who will save you out of my hand? ||
16 Shadrakh Mæshakh and 'Abéd-negó answered and say to king

were concerned;* and it was precisely thus simply designate) can also save
from those eastern regions that similar them from the extremest peril of this
narratives may at that time have mortal life as well as from the power
already got into circulation from earlier of the king; but if they are compelled
antiquity.† to speak more definitely (as without
While the king acts here as might almost doubt the intention is here to make
be expected from his situation and age, them), they can then (2) only openly
on the other hand, we hear the friends and boldly say that they are determined
of Daniel, vv. 16-18, thinking and not to comply with the requirement.§
speaking in his presence in the manner Thereby they as a fact assert neither
which is alone worthy of them. Their too little nor too much: they do not
reply to him is neither stubborn nor say, as in blind confidence, that their
angry, still less rude and discourteous:‡ God *will* without doubt deliver them
they simply declare firmly and confi- from this most extreme peril, they
dently what they are compelled to assert only that he can as far as his
declare as confessors of the true God. power is concerned, and therewith they
If the king's requirement is of such a do no more than feel and express what
kind that it is impossible that it should is quite correct, that no one who really
be fulfilled by such a confessor, they believes in the true God may, on
declare, because they know only too account of such threats, though they
plainly what is expressed in the last were ever so violent and ever so immi-
threat, with perfect calmness but with nent, shrink back and abstain from
determined mind (1), that they have no doing what is conformable to the
necessity to make any answer to this divine will, or when it becomes neces-
threat, because they believe that that sary to suffer for it. Even with
God whom they serve (and whom they the most imminent death in view, a

---

* Comp. Vol. III., 240.

† The question deserves further inquiry, whence the narrative concerning
Gámshîd in Tabari (I., p. 60, 97, ed. Dubeux) has its origin.

‡ This it would be if, ver. 16, the becoming and everywhere customary
address *o king* were wanting at the beginning of their reply, or if the present
accents were correct. But it is only the present reading which is doubly incorrect
in the ordinary text.

§ This alone is the correct meaning of all the words, vv. 16, 17: *we need not*,
i.e., we feel no inward compulsion because we have the faith, ver. 17; *but if* not,
if we are compelled from without, *let it be* herewith *made known*.

14 *

Nebukadnessar: O king* we need not concerning this answer
17 thee a word : | lo our God whom we serve is able to deliver us out
of the burning furnace of fire, and will deliver us out of thy
18 hand O king ! || If not,† be it known to thee O king that we will
not serve thy God | and the golden image which thou didst set
19 up will we not worship! ||—Then was Nebukadnessar full of fury
because of Shadrakh Mæshakh and 'Abéd-negó and the form of
his countenance was disfigured, he answered and said that the furnace should be heated seven times more than it seemed needful to
20 heat it, || and certain men of mighty strength which were in his
army he commanded to bind Shadrakh Mæshakh and 'Abéd-negó,
21 in order to cast them into the burning furnace of fire. || Then
were these men bound in their hosen hats cloaks and garments
22 and cast into the midst of the burning furnace of fire ; || quite in
accordance therewith because the king's word was so hasty and
the furnace was excessively heated | the flame of the fire slew
23 those men who had taken up Shadrakh Mæshakh and 'Abéd-negó, | and those men all three Shadrakh Mæshakh and 'Abéd-negó
fell bound into the midst of the burning furnace of fire.

man must not permit himself to be frightened from the right, and to fall away from God, even at a king's threat.

But the king is no longer able to listen with like calmness to such language of a calmly self-possessed spirit in reply to himself: accordingly his anger becomes all the more violent, as if the fire which he is now more than ever determined to prepare for the three men were about to blaze beforehand from the disfigured features of his own visage. The furnace he commands to be heated seven times hotter than is usual (thus the number seven recurs here once more!), and gives the commission to some of the strongest men of his guard to bind the three for execution. And they are still able while they are being bound to revoke their refusal; but they calmly allow themselves to be bound and cast into a furnace which, by the terrible haste to which the king's rage drove him, had been so unreasonably heated that the executioners themselves, who had by the aid of ladders to precipitate the three men through the open air-holes into the fire, could not escape being burned to death by the flames which suddenly shot forth out of them, as for a divine token that here something was about to take place which, if it should

---

* Added by the LXX.

† In the *Anhang* to the fourth edition of his *Hebräische Sprachlehre für Anfänger*, p. 235, Ewald has the following note on this passage: "Dan. iii. 16-18 may be best taken thus: "*We need not answer thee anything as regards this whether* our God is able to deliver us and will deliver us, *or not*." But then it must be allowed that the division of the verses is not correct."—*Tr*.

3.

24 Then king Nebukadnessar was amazed and rose up with haste, | answered and said to his court-chamberlains "did we not cast *three* men bound into the midst of the fire?" | They answer
25 and say to the king "certainly, O king!" || he answereth and saith "I see there four men unbound and walking without pain in the midst of the fire, | while the appearance of the fourth is
26 like a son of God!" || —Then Nebukadnessar approached the door of the burning furnace of fire, answered and saith | "Shadrakh Mæshakh and 'Abéd-negó, ye servants of the Most High God, come forth and hither!" || Then came Shadrakh
27 Mæshakh and 'Abéd-negó out of the midst of the fire, | and the satraps presidents and prefects and court-chamberlains of the king assemble together | seeing that over these men's bodies

really be completed, would cause the world death and destruction without end. But for the moment nobody attends to this token either: and the immense festival of joy may be quite happily completed whilst innocence seems to be compelled to be suffocated

3. But at this point everything must suddenly be reversed, unless the infernal fire which has been kindled by the utmost folly of men shall lay hold of everything: and this king, with all his extreme blindness and infatuation for the moment, has already been once brought too near to better knowledge, acc. ii. 47, and this moment is also itself one of too great decisiveness, whether for life or for death, that he should not precisely in it be transformed in his inmost nature and changed suddenly as into an entirely different man, in order to behold and comprehend what he never hitherto beheld and comprehended. He beholds suddenly four human forms in the fire, and they are not bound or seized upon and lamed by the fire, but are walking about as unrestrainedly as any unbound person can walk about without pain.

for ever in such burning heat, just as with great heathen festivals generally the most barbarous feasts of execution were often connected, and the one form of unreasonable heat was intensified to even higher degrees by the aid of other forms.

He is amazed, he rises hastily from his royal seat, hastens to the door of the furnace, still further convinces himself by closer inspection, and calls those who have been thus miraculously saved to come out to him, whilst all his magnates also collect before the door and convince themselves that not a hair upon them is singed, nor even the lower borders of their trousers burnt, nay, that they have not even smelt the fire, as we are accustomed to say. So he then, ver. 28, breaks into a much more enthusiastic laudation of the true God than before, ii. 47, is no longer angry, but glad that they did not obey his command in this matter, and issues an order for his empire, that no one whatsoever, under pain of severe punishment, may dare to use the words of blasphemy in the presence of that God *who alone can deliver* his worshippers in such a

no fire had gained the mastery, not a hair of their heads had been singed their hosen not altered and not even a smell of fire had
28 come upon them; || Nebukadnessar answereth and saith " Blessed be the God of Shadrakh Mæshakh and 'Abéd-negó that he sent his Angel and delivered his servants | who trusted in him and transgressed the king's word and gave up their bodies that they might serve and worship no other god whatever than their own
29 God!" And from me be published a decree that whoever of a nation or community and tongue speaketh a blasphemy against the God of Shadrakh Mæshakh and 'Abéd-negó, | shall be cut in pieces and his house be made a dunghill | just as there is no
35 other God who could thus deliver || —Then the king set Shadrakh Mæshakh and 'Abéd-negó again over the province of Babel. ||

marvellous manner, ver. 29. It is no more than proper that the three friends of Daniel should be fully restored to their offices, ver. 30: which is at the same time of itself the best punishment of their accusers and other enemies, of whom, as is due, not another word is said at the end. Thus this narrative, complete in three strophes, closes quite satisfactorily: and who could at its close, after he had followed its course, remain so dull as to misunderstand and misapply it? That an Angel attends the faithful and guards them, is acc. Ex. xxiii. 20; Gen. xxiv. 7 a good belief of early times; but certain as it is that the king beholds him here at the first moment, it is still not narrated that the others also saw him, still less that he walked forth with the three, and so became visible. With such perfection does the narrative, even when it expresses things which lie on the utmost limit of expression, everywhere preserve proportion and propriety.

4. (II. 2.)

Nabukodrossor's trials and conversion.

Ch. iii. 31—iv. 34.

By the immediate sight of the sufferings of innocence and its marvellous deliverance, this king has been brought a great step nearer to divine truth and reverence for it: and this greater perfection to which he is ripening is apparent in almost all that he thinks and says in the following narrative. Still, it is not by the mere sight of the divine sufferings and victories of others that the man attains the full perfection of the divine life: his own personal suffering he must also taste to its depths, and only he who is conscious of having been saved from these by divine grace alone can attain to the purest knowledge and to the most joyful praise of the true God. It is here that the third and final stage of the divine education of Nabukodrossor commences; but it is only when this point has been reached that in our book also the full picture of the great moral guilt recurs which, according to the earlier books, attaches to the memory of this powerful heathen king and this irresistible destroyer of Jerusalem and cruel persecutor of the confessors of the true religion. Such a mighty ruler may, by nearer contact with the sages and saints of the true religion, be seized by many profounder inklings, surmisings, and impulses, he may also be touched by feelings of benevolence towards the members of its community, he may become an Alexander Severus or even a Constantine; but from the profounder knowledge of the true God and his joyful worship he still remains far distant, unless in some way, and should it be but as the result of the experience of personal suffering of the most painful and protracted kind, the consciousness of his great sinfulness and actual sin overwhelm him, and the most sincere repentance transforms him into a perfectly new man according to the divine will. Hitherto we have in this book been made acquainted after all only with the good side of Nabukodrossor, notwithstanding all his strictness as ruler; but suddenly an abyss opens in the account of him which permits us to look quite deep enough into the dark side of his human nature also. Whoever as a man resists the divine will, is, after all, ultimately but as an animal (Ps. xxxii. 9, 10), and declines from the original elevation and glory of man, as God desires him to be, to the level of the animal; whoever, like Nabukodrossor, occupies the highest stage of all human power and glory, may fall all the more easily; and whoever, like him, already stands in some closer relation to the mystery of godliness by some occasional true conceptions and impulses, and yet remains in his inmost soul estranged from it, and permits himself to be again carried away by his pride,—he falls thereby to a still lower level; and one moment may suddenly degrade him still more, even lower than the basest and most unhappy of men. It is now narrated most vividly and tellingly in this piece how Nabukodrossor, because, in spite of all divine warnings, he still fails to come to true repentance and to perfect sincerity of life, becomes suddenly the most miserable of men—indeed less than a man; and how his sufferings are all the greater and more protracted in proportion as he had lived proudly as a king for a long period in his fleshly security, until at last, as if softened and transformed by these extreme sufferings, he attains to the true knowledge, indeed, to an unreserved and joyful confession, of the true God.

The sufferings of Nabukodrossor, as they are here represented, are unknown to us from any earlier narrative, nor are we able to trace the stages which the narrative of them may have passed through before it assumed the form which we see it taking under the hand of our prophetic narrator. That man may become like a beast, or even worse, by mental disorder, is unhappily still too certain; indeed, the fact forces itself upon us to-day in almost worse and plainer forms than ever: in myth and legend this phenomenon may easily be developed until it gives rise to more definite and lasting conceptions, and the ancient Germans were in the habit of repeating many stories of Werewolves, the Greeks of Lykanthropoi, and the Hindoos of men transformed into all kinds of animals.* It is at all events known to us from strict history that Nabukodrossor neither died a heroic death like a hero upon the battle-field nor an easy death, but had to contend with much sickness before his death.† A distant point of connexion for such a legend to get applied to him was the more readily supplied by the fact that he was early conceived

---

* Comp. amongst other illustrations, Wilson's *Vishnu-Purâna*, p. 401 sq.
† Comp. the remarks in *Hist. of Israel*, V. 1, 2 (IV. p. 4).

of as a true devourer of men.* The man that has himself
become as it were animal, that has found his satisfaction only
in the crushing and devouring of nations and men, let him not
be astonished if God at last makes him, in the midst of his
physical life, into a mere brute. However, we cannot, as we
have said, now trace the stages which this narrative, of the
mighty Chaldean king who had become an animal, had passed
through before our narrator took it up. But as he received it
here, it plainly fits most artistically into the whole connexion
of the powerful picture which is brought before us in this piece
of narrative.

There is, however, one thing interwoven in this form of
narrative also which is historically of greater importance.
That the degradation of Nabukodrossor lasted just seven years,
acc. vv. 13, 20, 29 (A.V. vv. 16, 23, 32), is plainly nothing
else than one of the lines of grand prophetic fresco painting
such as we have often observed above in the case of this
number. At the same time, it is not a matter of indifference
in what period of the life of this long-reigning monarch his
degradation to an animal is intended to fall; and here it
becomes obvious that according to the meaning of this particular narrative itself as well as of the connexion of all these
three pieces concerning Nabukodrossor's life, ch. ii.—iv., that
it must be placed in his later years, indeed as late as possible
before his death. As a fact, it is incidentally indicated in the
midst of the narrative, iv. 26, 27, that Nabukodrossor had then
finished all his magnificent buildings in Babel;† this points to
his later years. But this was manifestly not meant to be thus
merely incidentally indicated, but to be said plainly somewhere
in this piece. As a fact, sufficient reliable indications have
been preserved to show that a chronological note was found

---

* " Jer." l. 7 ; li. 34 with Ps. xiv. (lii.) 4.

† See especially Bérossos in Josephus, *Arch.* x. 11, 1 ; *against Apion* 1, 19, and the Babylonian cuneiform inscriptions as far as these have been trustworthily deciphered.

originally at the head of this piece; and it is represented, according to its most probable number, in this translation.

But the thing which makes this narrative so vivid is that it appears as communicated by Nabukodrossor to all his nations, indeed, to all men, without exception, in the form of a public royal proclamation. Late repentance is, in the case of this king, so true, and his joy to have arrived at last by his recent severe experiences at the full divine truth so great, that he cannot refrain from communicating it in this way quite publicly to all men, very much as the poet, Ps. xlix., feels compelled to proclaim to the whole world a profound truth which he has at length attained to. And thus the narrative of such marvellous personal experiences really assumes here, in four long strophes, the form of a much more vivid description than is usually found in royal proclamations and public documents, while it becomes most suitably at this point the true crown of all narrations about Nabukodrossor. Through the discovery and decipherment of the great inscriptions of Assyro-Babylonian and Persian kings, we know that the great kings of these countries had actually the custom of telling in such public documents the most memorable events of their own history as for all eternity: the model of such public records must have been before the mind of our author, although the discourse departs, in the whole of the first half of the fourth section, vv. 26-30, from the use of the *first person* of the king to that of the *third*. And if we should succeed some time in obtaining really a public record of this nature by this king, we should gladly submit ourselves to it as to every other obvious historical fact. At the same time, it is impossible not to perceive, and is not to be denied, that the linguistic and literary character of this piece is exactly the same as what we have elsewhere recognized as peculiar to the author of this book.

1.

In the twenty-eighth year of the reign of king Nebukadnessar king

Nebukadnessar wrote to all the nations communities and tongues which dwell upon the whole earth thus: | *

31 King Nebukadnessar unto all the nations communities and tongues which dwell upon the whole earth.
May your peace increase!

32 The signs and wonders which the most high God wrought on me it seemed good to me to make known.—His signs

33 how magnificent are they, and his wonders how mighty! | his kingdom is an eternal kingdom, and his power with generation and generation! ||

iv.

1 I Nebukadnessar was at ease in my house, | and feeling secure

2 in my palace: || a dream saw I and it affrighted me, and fancies

3 upon my couch, and the visions of my head confounded me. || And a decree was published by me to bring in before me all the wise-

---

1. It is not only surprising that this piece should, in the present Hebrew text, begin forthwith with the proclamation itself, and without any prefatory note, but it is also positively disconcerting and insufferable according to the plan of the whole book. We can, however, supply the few introductory words, which might easily be omitted by a copyist's error, occasioned by the great similarity with ver. 31, from the LXX, where they have only got incorrectly removed to the end in the freer treatment of the text, with the exception of the date, which still remains here in its proper place. But we must then make up our minds further to alter the eighteenth year of the LXX into the twenty-eighth. The eighteenth would be the year of the destruction of Jerusalem, but of this event there is here no mention, even when the sins of the king are referred to, ver. 24; and moreover, that year would be too early. The thirty-eighth would, on the other hand, be too late, on account of the seven years which still follow, as the king reigned altogether forty-three years.— It must further be carefully observed that the proclamation is by no means directed simply to the subjects of the king. His subjects he might not only command (as he has already done, iii. 29) to utter no blasphemy against the god of Daniel, but also to place no hindrance in the way of Israel's return, as Kyros subsequently commanded. But our author knew too well how little that was the case: and so the praise of the true God, which Nabukodrossor purposes here to proclaim, can only be directed to all the nations of the earth, and whatever inference they may eventually desire to draw therefrom must be left to them.

As in epistles of some length, or in public speeches, there is often added to the greeting, iii. 31 b, and to the general announcement of the matter which is to be spoken of, ver. 32, a further prefatory word of a general character, in the form of an exclamation or a wish, in case such a word is called for by the subject which has to be immediately

---

* Addition from the LXX.

men of Babel, that they might make known to me the interpre-
4 tation of the dream. ‖ Then the book-scholars and dream-interpreters the Chaldeans and the astrologers come in, and I say the
dream before them : | and the interpretation they do not make
5 known to me. ‖ But at last came in before me Daniel, | he sur-
named Bêlteshassar after the name of my God, and who hath
the spirit of a holy God in him : | and the dream I said before
6 him : ‖ " Bêlteshassar thou chief of the book-scholars, | who (as
I know) hast in thee the spirit of a holy God, and to whom no
secret is too difficult : | hear the vision of my dream which I
saw, and tell its interpretation !

2.

7 In the visions of my head upon my couch I was beholding, |
and lo a tree in the midst of the earth, and its height was great ; ‖
8 the tree grew and became mighty, | and its height reached to

dealt with at length,—so we find that is done here, ver. 33. In this way the very first words answer excellently to the very last which have to be spoken ; but it is observable in the complexion of these words, ver. 33, that the person who is here speaking has already, in accordance with the two former nar-ratives, experienced many and great wonders of God.

The king felt himself *at ease* and *secure,* thus the narrative begins, ver. 1 ; very much in the same frame of mind, as will be more specifically expressed just a year later, ver. 27 So much the worse, therefore, did he immediately feel the tremendous trouble and anxiety which the dream of a night caused him, ver.2, while if he had but properly under-stood it, or attended sufficiently to the instruction conveyed in it as he after-wards learnt it through Daniel, it might have been, and (we may say) should have been, to him a beneficial divine admonition. He has not this time as formerly, ch. ii., quite forgotten it in the trouble of the first moment, as if that kind of terrible commotion which he then felt had now already become observably less ; yet he again as formerly summons his wise men to interpret it, and is compelled at last, inasmuch as they, as might be supposed, do not understand the words and signs of the true religion, to trouble the chief-sage Daniel, who is already known to him as a better interpreter of the true divine wisdom, vv. 3-6. And when he asks him, ver. 6, to tell him *the visions of the dream* itself as well as its interpretation, we have before seen, ch. ii., that the true interpreter must, before all things, live in the dream itself, quite as if it were his own, if he will correctly interpret it, as if he him-self had had it : the heathen sages can do neither the one nor the other.

2. The dream itself, vv. 7-14, has as its centre but one image—the com-parison of Nabukodrossor to a *tree.* It would be more natural to compare a whole nation with a plant possessing greatest similarity by its character or its situation, as the people of Israel in Kanáan, a land of vineyards, with the

9 heaven, and its circumference to the end of all the earth ; ‖ its leafage was fine and its fruit abundant and nourishment it had for all, | under it the beasts of the field find shade, and in its branches dwell the birds of heaven, | and from it is fed all flesh. ‖

10 —I beheld further in the visions of my head upon my couch, and lo a never-sleeping holy one descending from heaven, | calling

11 mightily and saying thus : ‖ " hew down the tree and top its branches, | strip off its leafage and scatter its fruit, | that the beasts

12 may flee from under it and the birds out of its branches ! ‖ But the stump of its roots leave in the earth, yet in a girdle of iron and brass—in the green field, | and with the dew of heaven let it

luxuriant and noble vine, Ps. lxxx. 9-18. But as we know from ii. 37, 38, that Nabukodrossor represents in our book not only his own royal family, or his stem, but also the highest power of the Chaldean empire, he can the more naturally appear as a tree. If the delicate vine, modestly covering the ground far and wide, is peculiarly suitable as the symbol of Israel in its vine-clad land, still more is that of the high tree appropriate for Nabukodrossor whose realm towers aloft high and mighty. This tree appears, acc. ver. 7, *in the midst of the earth*, as representing a universal empire which aims at compassing the whole earth ; but, as it is here intended to indicate the destiny which awaits it as that is partly determined by its past history, there is unfolded before the eye of the dreamer at the same time the whole course of the growth of this tree until its highest development and end.* Accordingly this eye beholds it (1) *growing continually higher and mightier*, as if it intended to reach *heaven* with its proud crown and *the ends of the earth* with the broadest branches of its girth, ver. 8 ;—it then accordingly beholds it (2) in all its verdant splendour and glory (as it is at the present time) with the fairest foliage and the most abundant and nutritious fruits, so large, so cool, and so beautiful that all animals wish to house under its shade and all birds in its branches ; whilst it also presents nourishment enough to all people that seek protection near it, ver. 9 ; just as all men, over whom the peace and protection of a great empire are extended, particularly those who live by trade and commerce, and are thus not fixed to one spot, seek to sojourn in it and to enjoy its advantages ; and as that prophetic lyric, " Isa." ch. xlvii., expresses this only in another manner with reference to Babel. But in the midst of this picture of peace and happy prosperity, the eye suddenly beholds — (3), vv. 10, 11, an entirely different form *descending* from heaven, the form of a *never-sleeping* Holy-One, *i.e.*, of one of the seven highest Angels (and as Nabukodrossor has since ch. ii. become much more familiar with the words and symbols of the true religion, he is able to recognize and correctly name

---

* We have a perfectly similar prophetic vision of a form in all its successive stages of change, Gen. xlix. 9-12, comp. *Jahrbb. der Bibl. Wiss.*, II., p. 51 ; and the same succession may be observed still more perfectly in the prophecies of Bileam, comp. *ibid.* VIII., p. 25 sq.

be soaked, and like the beasts be his lot—on the herb of the
13 earth; ‖ let his mind be changed from being human, and let a beast's mind be given him, | and seven times pass over him! ‖
14 In the determination of never-sleeping ones lies the affair, and an utterance of holy ones is the matter, | to the end that the living may know that the Most High in the kingdom of men is ruler and to whom he will will he give it | and the lowliest man he
15 exalteth to it! ‖—This dream I king Nebukadnessar saw, but thou Bêlteshassar say its interpretation, | just as all the wise-men of my kingdom are not able to make known to me the interpretation but thou art able | because thou hast the spirit of a holy God in thee!" ‖

such a form with greater ease), whilst the ear of the increasingly eager beholder hears terrible accents proceeding incessantly from his mouth, words which remorselessly command, ver. 11, to hew down this entire tree and to put an end to its security, and at last growing more and more obscure they indicate that only a bare stump shall remain from the mighty tree, remaining firm with its roots in the deep earth (something like that stump, Isa. xi. 1, and yet at the same time how totally different!); yet if a stump of this kind must, in a perfectly dry, barren soil, devoid of all moisture, necessarily fall more and more to decay, this stump shall, at all events, be at the bottom encircled *by greening turf*, and at the top *soaked* by the rains and *dews from heaven*, in order that it may be preserved for some future time when it can shoot forth again and grow. But towards the conclusion of the enigmatical oracle so much must nevertheless transpire as shall indicate that this melancholy remnant of the mighty tree retains all along some human element, there must intrude into this series of mysterious words and signs the hint, that if the green turf round the body of a stump is a boon to it, that which surrounds the body of this stump is, it is true, but a *girdle of iron and brass*, by which a maniac driven from human society is secured by force, acc. ver. 30, v. 20, 21, that his *human mind* is transformed into an *inhuman* or *brutal* mind; and that if it is a boon for the stump to be soaked with the dew of heaven, which causes all green things to grow, the green which grows around this stump is only like the *herb* from which this man changed into a beast will, *like a beast*, still his hunger. So horrible is the condition of the remnant, although it is alive, and is possibly to be preserved for a better time! And with a similar meaning it is quickly added quite at the close, that *seven times*, *i.e.*, in the enigmatic language of prophecy, *years*, will *pass over him* in this condition, ver. 13, how terribly long and yet leaving some hope!

After such hints of increasingly weird mysteriousness, there follows, ver. 14, simply the assurance from the same voice, that this is the sure divine determination, as it has just been resolved upon in the council of the highest Angels and proclaimed by one from their midst; but with greatest brevity there is added further the purpose for which all that has been so determined. This must take place thus in order that once more it may be

3.

16 Then was Daniel surnamed Bĕlteshassar struck dumb almost an hour | and confounded by his thoughts. || The king answered and saith " Bĕlteshassar, let not the dream and its interpretation confound thee!" | Bĕlteshassar answered and saith " Sire, the dream be to thine enemies and its interpretation to thine adversaries! ||
17 —The tree which as thou sawest grew and became mighty, |
18 so that its height reacheth to heaven and its circumference to the whole earth, || whose leafage was fair and its fruit abundant and which hath nourishment for all, | under which the beasts of the field dwell and in the branches of which the birds of heaven
19 abide! || it is thou O king, thou who grewest and became mighty, | whose growth reached to heaven and whose power to
20 the end of the earth! || But that thou sawest O king a never-sleeping holy one descending from heaven and saying " hew down the tree and destroy it, | but leave the stump of its roots in

manifest to all the world (1) that above all earthly kings there is a still higher king as the only potentate, who will also punish this king and give the kingdom *to whom he will*, as was further said at greater length ii. 21-23, and will be more definitely shown below, vii. 13, 14 ; and (2) and that as pride is the error and the ruin of all human rule, God exalteth not the proud but *the humblest* to reign; and how true this last fact is will appear below, vv. 27, 28.—Thus the second section can close, ver. 15, with the words of the king himself, just as the first section, ver. 6.

3. Daniel discovers in a moment the true interpretation and application of this dream; but because he perceives that its meaning is so terrible and, moreover, is by no means so pleasant for Nabukodrossor to hear as that of the first dream, ch. ii., which contained nothing plainly unpleasant at all events for the reigning king (for he might, in the case of that dream, think, if everything remains quiet till my death, there is no need for me to be alarmed), he becomes for the moment as if confused in his thoughts, and remains as if dumb, so that an express encouragement from the king to speak openly and without fear must come to his aid. He then indeed begins to speak ; but his first word is a wish that the meaning of this dream may have reference to the king's enemies rather than to himself ! ver. 16, and not until he has spoken this exculpatory word does he calmly begin to give the interpretation. But as the substance of the dream is divided essentially into three parts, inasmuch as what is indicated with regard to the past and present can be easily brought into one, so it is observed (1) that the tree which had grown and now become what was seen in the dream is Nabukodrossor himself, vv. 17-19 ; next it is (2) explained in plain words that all the calamity which befalls the tree, and which is here repeated after the words of the dream with only a little abbreviation, signifies that the king will, according to divine decree,

the earth, yet in a girdle of iron and brass—in the green field, | and from the dew of heaven let him be soaked and like the beasts of
21 the field be his lot—till seven times pass over him!"—this is the interpretation O king, and the determination of the Most High is
22 it which went forth over my lord the king— | that thou shalt be driven forth from among men, and with the beasts of the field will be thy home, and with herbs wilt thou be fed as oxen, || and with the dew of heaven thou wilt be soaked, and seven times will pass over thee | until that thou knowest that the Most High in the kingdom of men is ruler and to whom he will will he give it. || —But that it was said the stem of the roots of the tree should
23 be left: | thy kingdom remaineth sure to thee as soon as thou
24 knowest that heaven is ruler. || —Only, O king, let my counsel please thee— | and redeem thy sins by righteousness and thy unrighteousnesses by doing good to the poor, | if so be there may be healing for thy lightness! ||

be driven from all human society as a man changed into an animal, that he will live as a beast in the open air and eat herbs like oxen, until after seven years he give up all pride of dominion in genuine repentance according to better knowledge, vv. 20-22; and it is (3) explained that the leaving of a stump of the tree signifies that the royal power itself will remain secured to him as something to be at once resumed as soon as he shall come to the better knowledge above mentioned, ver. 23. But since this dream-interpreter is, as a prophet of the true God, more than a mere dream-interpreter, and as every genuine prophet can and, indeed, must give the most salutary counsel at the right moment, he adds, ver. 24, the well-meant counsel, let the king *redeem his sins by righteousness* and in detail his *unrighteousnesses* thereby that he *show to the afflicted* and persecuted the more *mercy* and love. Every actual sin is like a personal possession, or a pledge, given away to the person sinned against; the sinner is therefore in the position of a debtor under a pledge to the person against whom he has sinned; but he can redeem his sins, when he has sinned against God, by repentance and righteousness, as well as by the works of love which flow therefrom: this is the profoundest conception of sin which finds expression, ver. 24. As early as Ps. lxxii. 4, 12-15, it was emphatically enough taught that to help with love and righteousness those who are afflicted and abandoned without their fault is the primary royal duty: and at the time when Daniel thus spoke there could be as little doubt as to what class of men were specially intended thereby as at the time of the actual author; it is here therefore presupposed without remark.

With the last words that has been said which cannot be freely said to a king without danger, and so as only a Daniel could well say it so openly. With all the greater brevity he can now rapidly add, let the king do this, *if so be there may be an amendment for his light-mindedness* in thought and action: for whether this is possible, as Daniel desires, is what has now to be shown.

4.

26 All this came upon king Nebukadnessar. At the end of twelve
27 moons as he walked upon the royal palace of Babel, | the king answered and saith "Is not this the great Babel which *I* built into a royal house by the might of my treasures and to the honour
28 of my glory?" || The word was still in the king's mouth, when a voice fell from heaven | "to thee it is said king Nebukadnessar,
29 the kingdom is taken from thee! || And forth from among men thou art driven, and with the beasts of the field is thy home, | with herbs like oxen thou wilt be fed, and seven times will pass over thee, | until that thou know that the Most High over the kingdom
30 of men is ruler and to whom he will will he give it!" || In the same hour the word was fulfilled concerning Nebukadnessar, and forth from among men was he driven, | and herbs like oxen must he eat and from the dew of heaven his body be soaked, | till his hair grew like that of eagles and his nails like claws. || — But after the end of the days I Nebukadnessar lifted up my eyes

---

4. What the king said in reply to this, and how he dismissed Daniel, is not narrated. The fact that it is not said in the prophecy *when* that terrible calamity, which is foretold as divinely certain, will *actually* take place; and the words of the last strophe, that God will see *whether* the lightness of the king can be healed, leave even the possibility open that all that is threatened may perhaps not take place if the king reforms thoroughly at once. It may therefore be conceived that the king, who had previously received so many admonitions to better knowledge, now sincerely endeavoured for a time actually to speak and act less thoughtlessly. But it is related with equal vividness, vv. 25-34, how nevertheless just a year later a single inconsiderate, frivolous thought to which he resigned himself drew upon him the whole divine punishment. A single ungodly word now sufficed, because he had now at last been warned distinctly enough for the third time: that is the meaning of this weird narrative.

He is just walking to and fro in the pride of his heart upon the flat roof of the palace which he has finished building, casts a glance round him upon Babel, which he has similarly rebuilt and enlarged in the noblest style, boasts that he has accomplished such great things *by the force of his treasures and to the honour of his glory*, boasts thus without remembering God of his own power and glory; but hardly has he done this, and it is as if his inmost soul must rise in remonstrance against it, as if suddenly all his thoughts are confounded and must turn against him, and he now actually becomes the prey of that horrible madness, the picture of which had previously been brought so close before his eyes, as is so graphically narrated vv. 25-30. For the actual thing itself is always in such cases so much worse than the presentiment, as appears here in these bristling hairs as were they *eagles' hairs*, in these long nails and toes as if they were *lions' claws*, and as if the nature of an eagle

to heaven, and my consciousness returned to me, | and the Most High I blessed and the Everliving I praised and extolled, | him whose might is eternal might and whose kingdom is with gene-
32 ration to generation; || before whom all the inhabitants of the earth count as nothing and who dealeth according to his will with the hosts of heaven, | but the inhabitants of the earth—there is not one who might strike upon his hand and say to him " what
33 doest thou ?" || At the same time my consciousness returneth to me, and even the honour of my rule of my glory and of my splendour returneth to me, | and unto me my chief chamberlains and my magnates seek, and unto my kingdom was I restored and yet greater glory was given to me. || Now I Nebukadnessar praise and extol and adore the King of heaven, | him all whose deeds are truth and whose paths righteousness, and who can bring down those who walk in pride. ||

or a lion, of which such kings boast in their arms and banners,* and to which unhappily they often make themselves so similar by robbery and plunder, must now for once become a visible reality in this most terrible and revolting fashion. Seven long years he remains thus, as if smitten by the divine curse, a madman, who finds satisfaction in the condition of a brute, whilst no one ventures to come seriously to his assistance and to show him if it were only human respect. The loftiest and proudest has now become the lowest, sunk below a beast, because he lacked that lowliness, that humility before God, which alone can preserve man from such debasement, and to which he had previously been brought so near by various experiences.

Still, a single glance to heaven of the right state and humility of mind, as if coming involuntarily from the depths of returning self-consciousness, one true aspiration and prayer and struggle upwards to the true God, as it is described vv. 31, 32, restores also to this king all his former truly royal glory and power in a still more glorious form, ver. 33, so that he now strikes up that hymn of praise to the true God, ver. 34, to which he intended, according to the opening of the entire proclamation, iii. 31-33, to give all publicity. But the necessity of true humility before God is at the same time, in accordance with the entire purpose of this narrative, once more most strongly dwelt upon at the close, ver. 34, corresponding perfectly with the closing words of each of the previous sections, vv. 14, 24. In other respects it is plain that the Book of Job was present to the mind of our author in the second half of the last section, the phrase *to strike anyone upon the hand* whom one has caught in the commission of an offence *and to say to him, " what doest thou?"*

---

* For the *eagle* as such a symbol, see Jer. xlviii. 40 ; xlix. 22 ; Ezek. xvii. 3, 7 ; for the *lion* and ox, Ps lxviii. 30: all three have now been vividly brought before us again by the colossal figures of Nineveh. We must, however, bear this in mind in the case of the figures of ver. 30, otherwise, they are not made quite clear.

ver. 32, is from Job ix 12, 33; that one who had been abandoned of all his friends on the turn of his bad fortune is again sought after by all his friends, and that he then attains still higher prosperity than before, ver. 33, are both from Job xlii. 10, 11. But the elevated phrase that *he before whom all the inhabitants of the earth are counted as nothing doeth also just as he will with the host of heaven*, i.e., with all angels, is from "Isa." xxiv. 21, 22, xl. 15, 17.

Lactantius' book, De Mortibus Perse-cutorum, and the recently published Syrian Church History of John of Ephesus, give very similar descriptions of Cæsar Maximianus and Justinos II, both books probably not being uninfluenced by the descriptions of the Book of Daniel, but in such a way that it is well to compare them. The first of them describes also the persecutions of the Christians in words and deeds which may remind us strongly of ch. iii. and ch. vi. of our book.

5. (II. 3.)

Overthrow of the Chaldean Empire.

Ch. v.—vi. 1.

The various delineations of the portrait of Nabukodrossor in these prophetic frescoes is now ended, as at the time of the author he might already be regarded as a figure of more distant antiquity and of a more venerated and elevated character. According to the popular idea of the numerous kings and rulers of those times, as this idea had then been developed and as our author makes use of it, he had but one son and successor to his empire, the same under whom Babel was taken by the combined Medes and Persians, and Nabukodrossor's dynasty overthrown, and who here bears the name Bêlshassar.* But of all events which at last brought on the inevitable fall of the Chaldean empire, there was none more memorable down to the later centuries than the manner in which the great, mighty Babel had fallen in one night, and, moreover, in a night which resounded with festive gaiety.†

---

* Comp. on all this *ante* p. 116, and further *History of Israel*, V., 52 (IV., 69 sq.)

† We may also infer from the fact that in the piece "Isa." xxi. 1-10 (Vol. IV., 233-6) precisely the conquest in a *night* is not brought out, that it had been composed and committed to writing *before* that event.

Nabukodrossor had just employed the treasures of all his immense wealth upon the building of the city, and had transformed it particularly into the strongest citadel and bulwark of the whole empire; he had further staked upon it as it were all the honour of his rule and power, as our author mentioned both these facts together just before, iv. 27. And now this sudden, terrible fall, by the conquest of such a mighty city in one night!

It is natural that thus the picture drawn in this narrative also should become under the hands of our author a true nightpiece, with all the colours of the dissolute, luxurious riot of extravagant passion and growing madness, of ruinous bewilderment, and of the mysterious horror and terror of such a night of revelry and death. Still, it is something of an essentially different character which is here brought forward from the very first as the only thing of importance. The drunken joy of the Babylonian royal and imperial feast, perhaps the celebration of the royal birthday and at the same time of the national god Bêl, from whom in fact Bêlshassar derives his name, is in no small degree increased by the fact that this king, who is no longer a Nabukodrossor, even causes the sacred vessels from the former temple of Jerusalem, which were mentioned i. 2, to be brought and then to be misused as common drinking vessels at the banquet: the mad intoxication and heathen profanity cannot become greater; and it is fitting that the divine punishment for this also should overtake the king in the same night, and the same lips which thus profaned the holiest things with this wine should on the contrary sip the wine of the divine poison-cup whose fierce heat must prove fatal to them in the same night. But even such sinners, drinking as it were over the pit of hell according to images used elsewhere (Ps. lv. 16), must still at the last moment be warned, according to the divine will, by a suitable divine sign, that it may be known whether they will give to truth the honour; and if Nabukodrossor, according to the foregoing narrative, ch. iv., was warned by a last divine sign before his grievous fall, and at last though late took warning from it so as not to experience the utmost punishment and lose everything eternally, a not wholly dissimilar issue is in this case just possible though very difficult. Bêlshassar in the midst of the riot of this nocturnal revel has still wits sufficiently awake and eyes sufficiently sharp to see how a mysterious, weird, divine hand is writing some letters on the white cement-wall of the splendid chamber opposite the brilliant chandeliers, as on a place which is high and yet light enough to be easily read; the letters he cannot read, but desires above all things in the world to have them decyphered, as if in the irrepressible presentiment of their great significance. There existed in these countries from early times written characters hard to read, *e.g.*, the various kinds of cuneiform character: but the famous Chaldean court scholars, at other times so skilful in decyphering all possible characters, cannot read these nor answer to the expectation of the king just when he most needs their help. Thus there is here repeated for the fourth time what we saw ch. ii. and ch. iv., that Daniel only is the true interpreter of divine mysteries regarding the condition and future of the empire: and it must here also be shown whether the counsel of the faithful man of God will be followed or not.

I.

1 Bêlshassar made a great feast for his thousand magnates, | and before the thousand he drinketh wine. || Bêlshassar commanded in the mirth of the wine to bring the golden and silver vessels which his father Nebukadnessar had carried away out of the temple in Jerusalem, | that the king and his magnates his prin-
3 cesses and his concubines might drink out of them. || Then were brought the golden vessels which had been carried away from the temple of the house of God in Jerusalem, | and the king and his magnates his princesses and his concubines drank out of them, ||
4 drank wine and praised the gods of gold and silver of brass iron
5 wood and stone. || In the same hour came forth fingers of a man's

hand and wrote over against the chandelier on the lime of the wall of the king's palace, | and the king saw the wrist of the
6 hand writing. || Then the king's features were disfigured, and his thoughts confound him, | and the bands of his loins are loosed,
7 and his knees knock one against the other. || The king calleth mightily to bring in the dream-interpreters the Chaldeans and astrologers, | the king answereth and saith to the wise-men of Babel || "any man who will read this writing and tell me its interpretation, | shall be clothed in purple with a gold chain of honour about his neck, | and as the third in the kingdom shall
8 he rule!" || Then came in all the wise-men of Babel | and they are unable to read the writing or to make known the interpre-
8 tation to the king. || Then king Bêlshassar becometh exceedingly confounded, and his features are disfigured, | and his magnates are bewildered.

1. The few but so much the larger and stronger strokes with which especially this fresco is drawn are forthwith sufficiently plain at the commencement, vv. 1-4. A night banquet for a thousand of the immediate servants and friends of the king, at which particularly the thousand royal *princesses* and royal *concubines* are not absent, as is three times, vv. 2, 3, 23, mentioned, forms the ground-work. But it is not until the increasing whirl of excitement has commenced that it occurs to the king to order the sacred vessels of Israel to be brought, acc. i. 2, from the temple of Bêlus, not merely to make a boast of them and show them to his guests, but to drink out of them and thus intentionally to profane them, whilst the drinking songs meanwhile resound to the honour of the idols, ver. 4.—Not less pictorial in the highest degree is then, ver. 6, the description of the king as he is suddenly seized with fear at the sight of mysterious powers which he wished not to see and still more on the consciousness of his own gross profanity, vv. 2, 3, 22, 23: and not only does his face assume unsightly colours, as in the case of Nabukodrossor, iii. 19; iv. 33, but also all the ligaments of his bones seem to be loosened as if he would immediately die in mortal terror.

In the case of the promised reward, vv. 7, 16, comp. ver. 29, vi. 3, the main thing is that he who can solve the enigma shall be *third-man ruler*, as it is most definitely said ver. 29. That does not mean that he shall have the third place in ruling the empire after the king and perhaps the queen-mother, who appears, ver. 10, as of great importance: for the dignity of the queen-mother cannot be regarded as perpetual in this sense. On the contrary, this designation and the more definite account, vi. 3, presupposes that in the Babylonian empire there existed an institution similar to that of the Roman empire from the time of Diocletian, according to which three Cæsars could exist under one Augustus, or as if the Roman Imperators had appointed three Consuls instead of two. Quite different is the ancient Egyptian institution presupposed Gen. xli. 43, 44, and elsewhere frequent in ancient monarchies, accord-

2.

10 The queen on account of the words of the king and his magnates entered the banquet chamber, | the queen answered and said " O king, live for ever! let not thy thoughts confound thee,
11 nor thy features be disfigured! || There is a man in thy kingdom who hath in him the spirit of a holy God, and in whom in thy father's days enlightenment and insight and wisdom as the wisdom of a God was found, | and whom the king Nebukadnessar thy father raised to be a chief of the book-scholars dream-interpreters
12 Chaldeans astrologers, || quite in accordance therewith that extraordinary spirit and knowledge and insight in interpreting dreams and revealing of riddles and untying of knots was found in him, in Daniel to whom the king added the name of Bêlteshassar: || now let Daniel be called and the interpretation will he
13 reveal!" || —Then Daniel was brought in before the king, the king answered and said to Daniel: | art thou Daniel who is of the Yudean captives whom the king my father brought hither
14 from Yuda, | and of whom I have heard that a spirit of God is in thee, and extraordinary enlightenment and insight and wisdom
15 is found in thee? || And now were the wise-men the dream-interpreters brought in before me that they might read this

ing to which the king can appoint a man as *second* ruler in the empire, or as his vice-regent; and inasmuch as the institution mentioned in the Book of Daniel is so peculiar, it rests according to all appearance upon an ancient genuinely Babylonian custom. A last trace of it has probably survived in the three men who according to Strabo's *Geographica* XVI., 1. 20, were at the head of the three Babylonian φυλαί. On the other hand, the investiture with purple and a golden necklace is rather a general distinction of men of princely rank, just as it is met with in the same way in the case of Yoseph, Gen. xli. 42.

2. *The queen,* who is thus plainly enough designated, ver. 10, and in distinct antithesis to the *princesses* (*i.e.*, the proper wives) and concubines of the king, is without doubt the same lady who might be yet more plainly called the *queen-mother*, inasmuch as this king could be still considered as in his youthful years. According to the venerated custom of those kingdoms (comp. *History of Israel*, III., 272 (III., (372)), the greatest respect is due to her even when she will interfere with the affairs of government: thus she who had kept quite aloof from the noisy banquet now enters the banqueting chamber only *over against the* wholly perplexed and helpless thoughts and expressed *words of the king and the magnates,* and gives the counsel which is alone worthy of her concern for the welfare of the empire and of her long experience. She still knows quite well how the father of the king would have acted

writing and make me know its interpretation : | but they are not
16 able to tell the interpretation of the word. || But I have heard of
thee that thou art able to give interpretations and to untie knots: ||
if then thou art now able to read the writing and to make known
to me its interpretation, | thou shalt be clothed in purple with
the gold chain of honour about thy neck, and shalt rule as third
in the kingdom!" ||

3.

17 Then answered Daniel and said before the king "let thy gifts
be thine, and thy high offices give to another! | yet the writing
will I read to the king and make known to him the interpre-
18 tation. || Thou O king, to whose father Nebukadnessar the most
High God gave dominion and greatness and honour and splen-
19 dour, | and before the greatness which he gave him all the nations
communities and tongues trembled continually and feared before
him; | whom he would he slew always and whom he would he
kept alive, whom he would he raised up and whom he would he
20 bowed down always : || yet as soon as his heart became too proud
and his spirit violent unto haughtiness, | he was hurled down
from the throne of his dominion and his honour was taken from
21 him, || and from amongst the sons of men he was driven and his
understanding made like that of the beasts, | and with the wild
asses was his home, with herbs they fed him like oxen, and with
the dew of heaven his body was soaked continually, | till he knew

in such cases, and has not forgotten Daniel, to whom the son has hitherto paid but little attention and from whom he has never asked advice. So she gives the reassuring counsel to let this wise man come and to expect the best from his unusual skill, vv. 11, 12: and

3. Another courtier than Daniel, feeling sensitively the long neglect which he had experienced from the new court, would probably have preferred to let the king feel his displeasure, or would have even quite turned away from him just now when, as he anticipates, the most extreme misery is threatening him close at hand. Not so Daniel. He does not deprive the king

as soon as he has been fetched and stands before the king, the latter explains to him particularly why he had summoned him into his presence, and what he may expect after the successful solution of the enigma, vv. 13-16.

of his art and his services, and is prepared at once to comply with his request. At the same time, as a man of great experience who had long ago rendered great public services, he now stands in a very different relation to this young king to that in which he stood to Nabukodrossor when he was called before him as a very young man; and if then he neither kept back the

that the most High God is ruler over the kingdom of men and
22 whom he will he raiseth thereto : ‖ —but thou his son Bêlsbassar
23 hast not humbled thy heart, | quite in accordance therewith that
thou knewest all this and yet thou showedst thyself haughty
towards the Lord of Heaven, | the vessels of his house were
brought before thee and thou and thy magnates thy princesses
and concubines drink wine out of them, | and the gods of silver
and gold of brass iron wood and stone which see not and hear
not and feel not thou didst praise, but that God in whose hand
is thy breath and whose are all thy ways—him thou honouredst
not! ‖

4.

24 Then was the wrist of the hand set in motion before him and
25 this writing was traced; | and this is the writing which was
traced:

NUMBERED NUMBERED
WEIGHED AND IN PIECES!

26 This is the interpretation of the word: *Numbered:* God hath
27 numbered thy dominion and ended it! | *Weighed:* thou wert

truth nor belied his own dignity before that king even, he is now in a position to speak from the very first with much greater freedom. Accordingly he first of all, ver. 17, at once declines beforehand the offered distinctions : indeed, he is no longer at that age when the pleasures of government are amongst the highest for those who are conscious of being equal to its duties. But as he has now cast a glance at the mysterious writing on the wall, it has sufficiently taught him what its real meaning is, he deems it particularly needful, in

order that he may in the end express himself with greater brevity, to prepare the king well for hearing the serious words of the divine writing by an important prefatory observation. With a skilful turn in his personal address to the king accordingly, he reminds him, vv. 18-21, of the bitter lot from which the father of the king was scarcely able to save himself by late humiliation and repentance, in order then to lay before him the grievous transgressions into which he has fallen by his pride, vv. 22, 23.

4. Is therefore deliverance possible in this case? Daniel passes by a rapid transition to the real matter, v. 4, he reads aloud to the king, who is now calm, the few short but infinitely significant words, which an Angel-hand has just now written on the wall of his

festive hall, in characters of light, opposite the king, during his last and most grievous act of insolent pride, and then gives a clear interpretation of them. These dark, weird words are short and disconnected: and yet they are not confused and of themselves

28 weighed in the balance and found wanting! | *Piece :* thy kingdom is broken in pieces and given to the Medes and Persians!" ||
29 Then Bêlshassar commanded and they clothed Daniel with the purple and the gold chain of honour about his neck, | and proclaimed concerning him that he should be ruler the third man in
30 the kingdom. || In the same night was Bêlshassar the Chaldean king slain, and Dareios the Mede received the dominion being about sixty-two years old. ||

meaningless; but on the contrary, as soon as their meaning begins to be discovered, they arrange themselves immediately in the form of a perfect quadrangle, with four words for its four sides,* and is moreover a brief oracle, intelligible and complete in itself, however enigmatical it may appear, consisting of two symmetrical members of a verse, ver. 25, so that their interpretation, when their structure and the position and connexion of each word has been correctly understood, is made the more easy and certain, vv. 26-28. *Numbered! numbered!* is the weird and mysterious sound of the first member: what can that mean but that the time has now gone by according to the most accurate reckoning, the time of the rule of this king and his house; and the most dreadful part of this is that this prophet can say that *God Himself has numbered and ended it*, brought it to its close. And when in the second member occurs the first of the side-words *weighed!* it may accordingly be surmised *who* it is that is here *weighed and found too little* upon the most accurate scales (it is the divine scales only which are the most accurate and trustworthy). But that the second side-word, *and in fragments!* (being in Aramaic but one word), or in the application, *fractured!* instead, refers to the division of the Babylonian empire between the two conquering nations, the Medes and the Persians, is precisely the true prophecy of this interpreter.

Yet perhaps the terrible divine catastrophe might pass by more gently if the king would at least now at this moment follow the hint plainly enough conveyed by this interpretation and the words introducing it, if he would abandon the utterly vain life in which he has lost himself, and give the honour to Him to whom alone it belongs. But as yet he does not know anything that he can do which could *help* him, and resolves to keep his promise to Daniel inasmuch as he raises him to the high dignity, ver. 29: it is indeed ancient sacred custom in those regions that the king cannot revoke what he has once publicly promised to another.† But *that* is not of great importance, nor now the most needful thing. If it has thus with all this now got past midnight, this night is still long enough to permit the enemies during its course to break suddenly into Babel, and in order that this entire royal house may be destroyed and another, that of the Medes, be set up, vv. 30, vi. 1. With such brevity can this narrative now close.

---

* We met with something similar, Vol. II., p. 109.

† What our narrator, vi. 9, 13, 16, and the narrator of the Book of Esther i. 19; viii. 8, says of the Persian king, in agreement with Greek historians, could in this case be applied to the Babylonian kings.

6. (II. 4.)

Daniel's sufferings and triumph.

Ch. vi. 2-29.

Thus far we have seen Daniel on the whole always prosperous, though at times neglected by the kings; indeed, he has been like a Yoseph of these later times, rising like Yoseph in Egypt from similar causes ever higher in esteem before the kings and in power in the empire. Nor under the entirely new reigning house which has now risen in Babylonia does he lose any of the consideration and influence which he enjoys in the empire ; he is, on the contrary, confirmed in the high position to which the last Chaldean king publicly raised him, acc. ch. v. ; in fact, he succeeds, simply because amid all the changes and revolutions of the kingdom he continues the same and true to himself, in soon obtaining so specially the favour of the new monarch, that he intends to raise him, acc. ver. 4, to the highest dignity which a man can reach after the king, and which Yoseph had once really reached in Egypt, acc. Gen. xli. 42 sq. This apparently highest prosperity a mortal can enjoy seems about to fall all the more easily to his lot, as the new Median king is himself the true antithesis of the last Chaldean monarch, partly as the beginner of an entirely different rule (and the Medo-Persian rule appeared to the people of Israel as in any case a more righteous one than the Chaldean), partly because this Median Dareios succeeded to the government as a man of years and experience, as is so expressly mentioned ver. 1, and which corresponds with other historical indications.*

---

* As regards the name and character of this Median Dareios comp. further *History of Israel*, V., 72 sq. (IV., 94 sq.) According to v. 28 our narrator considered him undoubtedly to be the king who reigned but for a short time and with Kyros conquered Babel, but in agreement with Kyros received only a part of the

But the man that occupies the highest place in the realm, be he who he may, may fall into the greatest temptation and the extreme of suffering, indeed, such a man most naturally and easily; and if it was Yoseph's lot to feel the sting of such trials in his youth, with Daniel it is so far just the reverse. So little is his position likely to free him from trials of this kind, that the special religion itself which he confesses is of such a distinctive nature that it presents readily the most various occasions to designing men for bringing suspicion and persecution upon those who desire to remain most faithful to it; and as acc. ch. iii. the three friends of Daniel had very early to suffer severely for such faithfulness, the same trial now befalls Daniel himself last of all and most severely, upon another occasion and in another manner, yet with no essential difference.

But if Daniel stands this trial and comes out of it triumphantly as a perfectly blameless man, protected by all powers of unseen good angels, as in the case of his three friends, the divine fruit of this triumph can be still more glorious. And as a fact, at the end of this trial so well endured, according to this narrative there occurs the most glorious and blessed thing which can happen in the historical development of the true religion upon earth, as long as the Messianic kingdom itself is not yet realized, *i.e.*, as long as the true religion has not been made more than the possession of one nation and one limited community in the midst of Heathen nations. This king, in whom generally, in contrast with Nabukodrossor's son, the best elements that strove more and more successfully to get the upper hand in Nabukodrossor's mind found their continuation and stronger expression from the very first, becomes, as touched by the wonderful sufferings of Daniel and his

---

whole Babylonian empire as his portion of the spoil (comp. *ante* on ii. 39), and dying bequeathed his kingdom to Kyros. On that account the Medes are named before the Persians, v. 28; vi. 9, 13, 16, also, quite contrary to the later custom prevailing elsewhere.

divine deliverance, not only himself the warmest friend of his religion, but also commands (acc. vv. 27, 28) in the whole territory of his rule that everyone shall hold it in high estimation and honour. This is more than that royal prohibition that none shall blaspheme it, iii. 29, more also than that public laudatory proclamation regarding it with which Nabukodrossor closes his life, ch. iv.; here then is everything that our narrator could possibly desire to be actually realized in his own time.

The great strong fresco-strokes which the narrator loves to use are here, if possible, at the climax of the whole series of pictures, still more forcibly employed, and yet nowhere so that they offend the eye or displease the spectator.

I.

2   It seemed just before Dareios and he appointed over the kingdom the one hundred and twenty satraps, | that they might be over
3   the whole kingdom, and over them three chief-princes of whom Daniel was one, | that these satraps might always give account to
4   them and the king never suffer damage. || Then this Daniel gained ever more a pre-eminency over the chief-princes and

1. According to the narrative vv. 1-4 it is not so much the hundred and twenty satraps set over the whole realm as the three chief-princes who are something peculiar to this kingdom, or rather still remaining, acc. ch. v., from the previous Babylonian kingdom. For the hundred and twenty satraps are here presupposed as something previously known, and their number is here undoubtedly connected with the hundred and twenty-seven provinces which the Persian kingdom contained, acc. to Esther i. 1; viii. 9; ix. 30, and which may also have been the correct number according to some narrative of the later period of this kingdom if the name of satraps was understood acc. Esther viii. 9 in the more general sense of the heads of all the three various kinds of provinces; the number of the original satraps was acc. to Herodotus III. 89, and the Bisutun inscriptions much smaller. The LXX at least also supposed that this number one hundred and twenty was a reduction of that of hundred and twenty-seven, and restored the latter accordingly; the view, on the other hand, that the number hundred and twenty is intended to represent the third of three hundred and sixty (after the number of the days of the Persian year without the intercalary days), as Josephus, *Arch.* x. 11, 4, read in our passage, is probably only allegorical. But we may also perceive from the fact that he considers the dignity of these three chief-princes themselves as liable to be abolished, ver. 4, how much the

satraps, just as an extraordinary spirit was in him, | and the
5 king thought to place him over the whole kingdom. ‖ —Then the
chief-princes and the satraps sought to find a pretext against
Daniel on grounds of the government : | but they were not able
ever to find any pretext at all or any fault, just as he was trustworthy and no error or fault could be found against him. ‖
6 —Then at last these men thought "we shall not find against this
Daniel a pretext unless we find it against him in the law of his

narrator regarded them as simply re-tained from the previous Babylonian empire: this king thought already of appointing Daniel as the only first administrator of the realm, just as such an officer appears in the Book of Esther x. 3.

But this very design of the king's provokes Daniel's enemies of high rank all the more against him, ver. 5 : and as on part of the realm, or (as we should now say) from a political point of view, much as they seek for it, they can find in him neither an apparent nor an actual *fault* (or as it is also here said, neither *pretext*, or *mistake*, nor *fault*), that they may make an accusation against him to the king, they seek to get a handle against him on the side of his peculiarities in religion, ver. 6, and for that object they plan, acc. vv. 7-10, with great craftiness a plot against him, of the success of which they may be beforehand assured, inasmuch as they well know Daniel's unbending faithfulness with regard to his religion. As the institutions of the Median empire are described more particularly in the whole of this piece of narrative, they differ much from those of the Babylonian empire, and approached more closely to what we should in these times call a government by the Estates. The Estates of the realm, in this case consisting, it is true, as in Europe in the Middle Ages, only of the occupants of the various imperial offices, assemble for consultation upon an important matter affecting the realm generally, and they form a resolution with regard to it which the king must confirm if he has nothing valid to say against it. For the king is himself strictly bound by the ancient laws of the realm, is acquainted with the limits of his power, and just as his magnates are constantly saying, *the law of the Medes and Persians let it never pass away!* so he also is absolutely bound both by these general ancient laws of the realm and by every new command or prohibition which is once issued with his sanction. It is really remarkable with what particularity this is here described ; and it cannot be disputed that many a reminiscence of the past institutions of the Median empire may have been here preserved. This is not contradicted by what we know from Herod. I., 95 sq. of the invincible love of freedom of the Medes. In our narrative the idea of this constitution, so rare in antiquity, is so aptly carried through that ver. 18 even the state seal appears as a double one, that of the king and that of his magnates. The unusual weight which is attached, vv. 9, 10, 13, 14, to the proper written publication of a valid law is also in harmony therewith.

When the party of these Estates which now prevails has agreed to lay before the king for his confirmation the draft of a law according to which it shall not be allowable for any one anywhere in the realm to request anything during

7   God." ‖ Then these chief-princes and satraps rushed before the king, and speak to him in this wise, "O king Dareios, live for
8   ever! | all the chief-princes of the kingdom the presidents and satraps and chief-chamberlains and sub-prefects have agreed in this counsel to establish a royal statute and to give a stringent prohibition that anyone who entreateth any thing from any God or man during thirty days except from thee O king shall be
9   thrown into the lion's den : | therefore do thou O king establish the prohibition and issue the writing, unalterable according to the law of the Medes and Persians which will never pass
10 away." ‖ Quite in accordance therewith king Dareios issued the writing and the prohibition. ‖

the next thirty days (*i.e.*, according to pp. 192, 237 within a month) from any God or man save the king, that may sound to us to-day stranger than it really is. For in reality nothing more is meant by it than what people call now-a-days a state of siege, a condition of affairs in which the ruling power presupposes the existence in the case of every man and every one of his actions an ill-will and rebellion against itself, and proceeds, whenever it imagines it has discovered anything of the kind, at once with the most rigorous measures and penalties. In such cases all and every movement and endeavour in which the ruling power surmises the possibility even of the prevalence of another will than that which animates it are by law suspected and hindered ; no one shall in all that he does, at all events, visibly and publicly think of and promote anything else than what it will and what it has prescribed ; the bearing of arms, public assemblies or domestic consultations when a number of persons are present, are forbidden ; and public religious exercises even may then be easily deemed suspicious, inasmuch as the mind may in them be directed towards something very different from what the reigning force desired (or as the phrase is to-day, political designs may be concealed under ecclesiastical forms); and what are the dragonnadings of Louis XIV. against the Calvinists, or (notwithstanding all other differences) the closing of the Roman Catholic churches at Warsaw in 1861-2, else than what we read here in the Book of Daniel ? We can say with perfect correctness that the will of neither God nor man shall be of any force, but the will of the prevailing power only, accordingly of no God or man shall anything be requested save of it. There are periods when the powers that be imagine that they cannot proceed otherwise if they will maintain their position in a nation: and when is such a period so likely to arise as when (as here) a new foreign rule has but just been set up ? But even such a condition seeks legal establishment in some form or other, and can never put on a legal form for longer than a fixed period (as here for one month). If the party which here prevails amongst the Estates of the empire, who resolve, and can so resolve by outvoting Daniel, to place such a draft-law before the king, should say to the king beforehand, that this law was ultimately aimed only at Daniel and men like him, the king would certainly

2.

11 But when Daniel knew that the writing was issued, he went home to his house : | now he had open windows in his upper-chamber toward Jerusalem, | and three times in the day he knelt now also upon his knees, and prayed and sang praises before his God, just the same as he had been used to do hitherto. || Then
12 these men rushed thither | and found Daniel praying and
13 beseeching before his God. || Then they came near and say before the king : "O king Dareios,* | didst thou not issue a prohibition that any one who should entreat any thing from any God or man during thirty days except from thee O king should be cast into the lion's den ?" | The king answered and saith " the word is true according to the law of the Medes and Persians which
14 will never pass away." || Then they answered and say before the king " Daniel one of the Yudean captives payeth to thee O king not confirm it; but the strategem in the matter is precisely not to say this beforehand to the king. So the king permits himself to be misled and confirms the law, ver. 10.

2. What shall Daniel do now that he has learnt that such a law has actually received the king's signature, and has been issued in the full legal form ? What we should call *domestic worship*, or private religion, could not possibly be forbidden to Daniel, if the newly coined law should be honestly interpreted ; and whoever shut himself in his chamber for the purpose of praying or prostrating himself before an idol unseen by anyone, he was let alone safely enough. But in Daniel's case there was something else upon which malicious intention could nevertheless fasten, as his enemies had reckoned beforehand cunningly enough. He had no idol to fall down before; but as a truly pious Israelite in exile he had a little chamber in his *upper-house* upon the roof, the windows of which are open in the direction towards Jerusalem : †
there he performs now also his devotions, and *three times a day*,‡ just as he had been used to do. If the law, as it had been issued by imposing upon the honest mind of the king, was in itself irrational, as Daniel could easily perceive it was from his high position as third in the realm, what could prevent him from devoting himself now also to his accustomed religious exercises, inasmuch as according to ancient use and wont they could only be regarded as domestic worship, and he does not invite the presence of even one more person ? But it was the open windows upon which his enemies had counted : spies could look in upon him from the neighbouring roofs. After the spies, therefore, have

---

* According to a better reading.
† Comp. *History of Israel*, V., 23 sq.; IV., 33.
‡ *Ibid.* VI., 166; comp. *infra* Dan. ix. 21.

no respect! nor to the prohibition which thou didst issue, | and
15 three times a day maketh his prayer." || Then the king as soon as he heard the word was greatly pained, and upon Daniel set his thought to save him : | and till the hours of the sunset he
16 employed himself unceasingly to deliver him. || Then those men rushed to the king and say to the king | "Know O king that the Medes and Persians have a law that no prohibition or decree
17 which the king may establish can be altered!" || Then the king commanded and they fetched Daniel and cast him into that lion's den, | the king answered and said to Daniel "thy God whom thou servest without ceasing may *he* save thee!" || and a stone was brought and laid upon the mouth of the cave, | and the king sealed it with his own seal and with the seal of his magnates, that nothing should be altered with Daniel. ||

3.

19   Then went the king unto his palace and spent the night

perhaps for a few days seen him three times a day praying and heard him singing to his God, they think they have witnesses enough to bring against him : they fall upon him unawares and find him in this attitude, vv. 11, 12. It is true the king feels great pain when the fatal accusation is brought before him, vv. 13, 14, because he saw himself doubly deceived, as is plainly insisted upon vv. 15 sq.: first, that the law should be thus applied, and, secondly, particularly that it should fall upon Daniel precisely with its severity. So he thinks the whole day long anxiously over the means of saving him : but kings, least of all men, when they have once made concessions to the aims of a party in the realm, are able to secure themselves from the most lamentable inferences ; and in a state of siege, moreover, judgments and sentences proceed with greater rapidity. He must therefore yield to the letter of the law before evening, alleviate his pain when the sentenced man is brought before him as much as he can with the hope that the God whom Daniel worships with such marvellous faithfulness, consistency and unwearied zeal will as marvellously save him, and must permit the punishment itself to take full effect and himself impress the double imperial seal upon the stone which covers the opening of the lions' den, vv. 16-18. It is still the custom in some districts of Africa and Asia that the lions or tigers which a king causes to be caught for his amusement and kept in a cage are also used for the destruction of criminals. But the stone which is rolled upon the mouth of that cave in which these savage creatures dwell looks like one that is rolled upon a grave, after the custom of Palestine ; and the seal is stamped upon it in order that *nothing may be changed with Daniel*, but that he may remain just as he has been thrown down the prey of the lions, and no one venture to roll away the stone again before the proper time and perhaps cause him to be drawn up.

3. But a king who is bound by the laws of the realm, and who binds him-

fasting, | dancing-women he summoned not before him into the
20 chamber, and his sleep fled far from him. || Then the king
21 would arise at the first dawn of the morning, | and with haste
he went to the lion's den ; || and as he came near to the lion's
den, he called to Daniel with a sorrowful voice, | the king
answered and saith to Daniel : " Daniel, thou servant of the living
God! hath thy God whom thou servest without ceasing been
able to save thee from the lions?" || Then Daniel spake with
22 the king : " O king, live for ever! | my God sent his Angel and
23 shut the mouth of the lions that they should not destroy me, |
just as that I was found to be guiltless before him; and also
24 before thee O king I committed no offence ! " || Then the king
was very glad, and Daniel he commanded to take up out of the

self by them conscientiously, does not so easily permit himself to be deceived by mere appearance, nor suffer it to stifle the doubts of conscience ; and if he has been compelled to concede something against his better judgment and foreboding, he still remains enlightened and attentive enough to do everything that a possible change for the better may be brought about. The whole evening the king finds no rest; he cannot eat anything, nor does he cause the dancing girls to come in, who at other times usually close the evening meal with their amusements, and is unable to sleep, ver. 19. So in the very earliest morning he feels irresistibly impelled to visit the cave again, and this time undisturbed by the slanderers, cannot refrain as soon as he has come into its neighbourhood from calling aloud to Daniel, as if he had a prophetic feeling that he was still alive, asking whether his God had been able to deliver him, and, as he now at last learns the pure truth of the matter in all respects in a simple sincere dialogue between himself and Daniel, is himself wonderfully affected by the glad tidings of the miraculous deliverance wrought by *faith* in the true God and by Him, vv. 20-24. It is not surprising that, as heaven itself has declared itself in such a manner against that party in the realm, he now commands Daniel to be set at liberty, and his enemies to be punished in the way which is usual in such cases,* vv. 24, 25; and the similar narrative of

---

* It was the feeling and the law of antiquity generally that those who endeavour to procure by judicial sentence the death of a person by the employment of intentional calumny and false witness, should themselves suffer the merited death as soon as their murderous intention is discovered and proved. But that the children and wives of a gross offender suffer with him, ver. 25, is according to *Antiquities of Israel*, p. 253, 416 sq. (2nd ed. 217 sq., 156 sq. Eng. Trans. 314) not a form of punishment sanctioned by the Old Testament at the time of our narrator, but occurs as legally allowable precisely amongst the Persians It was only as long as the *ban* was observed in its original rigour amongst the people of Israel (*Antiquities*, p. 103 (87)), that it was found amongst them also, acc. Jesh. vii. 24, 25.

den, | and thereupon Daniel was taken up out of the den and no hurt was found upon him, | because he believed in his God; ||
25 and the king commanded and they fetched those men who had used deadly slander against Daniel, | and into the lion's den they threw them their children and their wives, | and they did not reach the bottom of the cave before the lions got hold of them and crushed
26 all their bones.|| — Then king Dareios wrote to all the nations and communities and tongues who dwell on the whole earth
27 "Your peace be increased! | From me is a decree gone forth that in the whole territory of my realm there should be awe and fear before the God of Daniel continually, | because he is the living God and endureth for ever, | and his kingdom that which
28 cannot be destroyed, and his power is unto the end; || he delivereth and saveth, and doeth signs and wonders in heaven and on earth, | who delivered Daniel from the power of the lions!" ||
29 This Daniel moreover was reinstated during the reign of Dareios and the reign of Kyros the Persian.

the friends of Daniel, iii. 22, comp. "Isa." l. 11, showed that they whose hands bear the principal guilt in the reversal of all eternal divine justice are at the proper moment seized by the flame of the fire they themselves have kindled. But the best thing is that the king, seized by lasting admiration and complely converted, gives public expression to the deeper insight he has now gained, and does all that he can do as king in order that for the future it may be possible for a better condition of things to be lastingly established in the kingdom, vv. 26-28. It is not his design by the proclamation, as it is found vv. 27, 28, to compel forcibly any of his subjects to adopt the religion of Daniel, to build for themselves likewise such a little chamber of devotion with open windows towards Jerusalem, and so forth! he makes simply the reasonable requirement, that the God of this religion be not publicly slighted but held by all in that honour which, when it is directed towards God, becomes of itself awe and fear.

But when at the close, ver. 29, it is remarked that Daniel was reinstated in the high office which he held during the short reign of this monarch and that of his successor Kyros until his death (to which there is only once more an allusion, viii. 27), the historical section is therewith so completely brought to a close that nothing further remains than

III.—*The Messianic Part.*

7. (III. 1.)

The vision of the four empires and that of the Messiah.

Ch. vii.

1

1 In the first year of Bêlshassar king of Babel Daniel beheld a dream with visions of his head upon his couch; | then Daniel wrote down the dream, he told the chief matters. Daniel answered and saith: I was beholding in visions by night, and, see,

1. When it is said, ver. 1, that Daniel wrote down only a *short epitome* of all the wonderful visions which he had had, this might be inferred beforehand if only attention were paid to the great freedom with which the main lines of this history, drawn in the first two strophes of the piece, are then repeated in the following strophes in order to give their interpretation. But all the prophetic pieces of the book have substantially the same plan. It is moreover always for the reader's sake advisable to sketch simply the shortest, though the most lucid, outline of what one has personally experienced and beheld in vision, where the object is to give it a literary form.

To conceive of and to employ descriptions of animals as symbols of kings and kingdoms was a very early custom. This custom, however, attained to its true significance when animals were first used as well-known symbols upon banners, weapons (particularly shields), and in other ways upon lasting works of art and monuments; and the earliest picture-character in Egypt and Assyria then contributed to bring about the closest relation between the significance of a particular animal and a kingdom which should correspond to it. We now know that of the Twelve Tribes of Israel each was able from primitive times to bear a particular animal on its banner and arms: every representative of a Tribe could also carry such a symbol, and the king of Israel could elevate the symbol of his Tribe to the position of the ensign of the kingdom.* Such animals as the lion, the panther, the bull, were the first to suggest themselves; others could easily be added by way of contrast. But hardly anywhere did such animal-symbols receive so great significance as in the ancient Assyrian empire: we are very familiar with this fact in modern times from the circumstance that amongst other things the variously composed colossal animal-figures from the ruins of Nineveh have been brought to light, which were regarded as symbols of the power and glory of the Assyrian empire, *i.e.*, of its kings and gods. After Assyria and the other great powers of the ancient

---

* Comp. *History of Israel*, III., 250; II., 183 (III., 341, 849).

3   the four winds of heaven travailing in the great sea, ‖ and four immense beasts rose up out of the sea, | diverse the one from
4   the other. ‖ The first like a lion, and it had eagle's wings : | I was beholding till its wings were plucked off, it raised itself from the earth and it stood upon its feet like a man | and a man's
5   heart was given it. ‖ —And behold another second beast like a bear, | and it placed itself upon one side, having three ribs in its

world confronted the people of Israel from the eighth and seventh centuries increasingly as invincible, the poets and orators of the people became accustomed to represent them on suitable occasions under such figures, *e.g.*, to refer to Assyria as the *lion*, or the *bull of the reedbed* (by the Euphrates), to Egypt as the *crocodile* or *dragon*.* All this makes it more intelligible that here, ch. vii. and viii., animals appear as the symbols of the great empires of Assyria, Chaldea and their successors, although they are here freely selected symbols, because in this case there is added at the same time an entirely new idea. And the more animals as symbols of empires received a moral significance, the more easily could the imagination magnify the artistic representation of them beyond their actual forms and place them in new combinations; but our author avoids using purely mythical animals for these symbols, evidently because they appear inappropriate. For in this case the four metamorphoses of the great heathen empire, which were previously, ch. ii., introduced under the somewhat similar figure of a human monster, are represented with much greater reality and vividness by four wild, diverse beasts, each one of which is overcome by its predecessor in succession.

Yet these four must all equally become monsters beyond all the proportions and usual characteristics of such wild animals, becoming such as were never before seen, through the terrible imperial power which they contain within themselves: we accordingly see at the beginning, ver. 2, all *the four chief winds* roaring over and *travailing in the sea* itself, as if the sea only could as in travail give birth to and bring into the light of day such monsters from its dark, horrible depths (Job xxxviii. 16, 17).† And in fact all these four monsters now, ver. 3, appear rising together from the sea: but as on closer observation it appears very evident how *different* notwithstanding *the one is from the other*, it becomes at once, vv. 4-8, clear further that they acquire their power only one after the other and each in its fixed time and order, because the aim of each one is universal empire. Now, it is true each of the four worldpowers, as the prophet thinks of them, comprehends at the same time all the individual rulers who belonged to it and reigned successively or contemporaneously ; still, according to the nature of the image of such a monster, it is most natural to understand by each primarily only the powerful inaugurator, or the first most powerful founder, of

---

* Yesaya alludes once, xxx. 7, to Egypt under the image of a kind of dragon: to what greater length subsequent authors carried this I have shown in my notes on the passages, Ps. lxviii. 31; lxxiv. 13, 14, 19; comp. Vol. IV., 305; *ante* p. 32, and IV., 151.

† Comp. my Commentary on Rev. xii. 15.

mouth between its teeth; | and thus they say to it "Arise!
6 devour plenty of flesh!" || —After this I was beholding and, see, another like a panther, having four wings of a bird upon its back; | and four heads had the beast, and power was given to

such a world-empire, as is also plainly said in the interpretation ver. 17. On the character and the special peculiarities of the founder depends the entire future development, and indeed all the ultimate destiny, of an empire; and how much that is the case here becomes immediately evident

(1) in the instance of the first of the four, ver. 4. A monster *like a lion* but *with eagle's wings* points of itself, acc. p. 226, to the Assyro-Chaldean empire, but may refer primarily to Nabukodrossor, as has already been shown at iv. 30: that this king is really intended appears further when it is seen that this creature transforms itself into a man, that *its wings are plucked off, it raises itself from the ground and stands firm on its feet as a man.* We might really suppose that this long description was meant to signify nothing more than this, just as it is said, ver. 8, in the case of the horn representing an individual king, that (unlike a mere horn) it has a man's eyes and a man's mouth. Still, that this description is intended to denote something more than this appears quite plainly from the last thing which is added, that *a man's heart* also *is given to it:* that is as an outward thing hard to see, but it is true of the marvellous metamorphosis which Nabukodrossor underwent, iv. 13, 31, 33 (A.V., vv. 16, 33, 36); and as lion and eagle recur here from iv. 30 (A.V., ver. 33), there is the less reason to doubt it. There occurs once more here also the fundamental thought of the previous typical examples from Nabu-

kodrossor's life, that after all he became a good man before his death; and as this vision does not occur acc. ver. 1 until after his death, this retrospective reference is quite appropriate even from an artistic point of view. It was the less necessary, therefore, that it should afterwards be expressly said in the interpretation of the visions, vv. 17 sq., that here Nabukodrossor must be understood to be intended; and so much the plainer also is

(2) the next monster, ver. 5: *like a bear*, as the Median rule, referred to ch. vi., is so much smaller than the Chaldean as the bear is than the lion, as was previously implied ii. 39. But that this kingdom particularly is meant is at once more definitely indicated by the fact that this bear *placed itself upon one side*, as if it were powerful on this one side only: for the Chaldean kingdom is divided according to v. 28; vi. 1, between Medes and Persians, and though the Median represents in point of eminence the continuation of the great empire, it in fact gravitates as regards its power only towards the countries west of the Tigris and Euphrates; but if it thus embraces only the west, this bear has nevertheless precisely in this territory at least *three ribs in its mouth between its teeth* (i.e., at the time devouring them, after Numb. xi. 33; "Zech." ix. 7), namely, the three fine countries of Babylonia, Assyria, and Syria, which constitute generally, historically, and geographically an excellent trias.* And in any case this bear has seized so much of the rich spoil that it may be

---

* It is thus in every way safest to understand three countries by these three *ribs*.

APPENDIX, 3. 2.—DANIEL, III. 1.—CH. VII.

7 it. ‖ —After this I was beholding in the visions of the night, and, see, a fourth beast yet more terrible and powerful and mighty, | having immense teeth of iron and claws of brass, † devouring crushing and trampling the residue with its feet, as it is diverse

said to him *Arise! and devour human flesh in abundance!* But as this kingdom is represented only by the one king described ch. vi., it is distinguished thereby completely

(3) from the *leopard*, ver. 6, the Persian kingdom: this compound animal is distinguished very decidedly on the one hand from the previous one by the fact that it is not so limited and one-sided as that, but has *four wings of a fowl*, i.e., soaring wings, carrying it rapidly everywhere, *upon its back*, therefore moves easily and freely into any of the four quarters of the world, and by that power as good as possesses all four quarters of the world, i.e., is in the full sense of the term a world-empire, as this is claimed for it in another way viii. 4, 8. On the other hand, another marked distinction of it from the previous animal consists in the circumstance that it has *four heads*, namely, four kings who constituted in succession its power, as was narrated in the popular history of the Persian kingdom at the time of our author, and as he himself mentions it further xi. 2. And inasmuch as this kingdom is thus on the whole more powerful than the former one, the picture of it may be rapidly closed with the words that *great power (vollmacht) was given to it.* For the discourse hastens,

(4) ver. 7, to an animal which is not so much as compared with any other creature, because (as if it did not admit of any proper comparison with the foregoing) it manifested itself forthwith as still *more terrible, powerful, and mighty,* so that it is more particularly described only in so far as it has *immense teeth of iron and claws of brass* (comp. ver. 19), so that it not only *devours and crushes* like the former ones, but also proudly *stamps to pieces the residue with its feet, since it is* in fact, as is at last plainly remarked, *very diverse from all the former beasts.* If the Greek kingdom is thereby intended, it is as certain that it is primarily only Alexander who can be thought of, as clearly appears not only from vv. 17, 23, but also from the following piece, viii. 5 sq.—But when it is added quite at the end, ver. 7, that it has *ten horns,* it is true that ten successive individual kings of this empire are thereby intended, as was the case ver. 6 with the heads of the former empire; and without doubt these ten kings are to be sought in the Seleukid line, because they not only boasted of being the true continuation of Alexander's line, but this was also actually the case at the time of our author for the readers of the book in Palestine. Still, if one inquires further what historical kings are here meant, we must, as careful examination of everything shows, be on our guard against beginning the series with Alexander himself as the first of these ten and then proceeding, say,

---

which were only suggested by the image of the devouring mouth: if a great empire, comprehending many countries, is a great animal, its separate countries are its bones or ribs; and moreover such words as *side, stretch,* Lat. *costa,* of themselves yield readily a territorial sense. Under the third of these three countries Palestine may also be understood.

† Inserted here from ver. 19

8 from all the former beasts: | moreover, it had ten horns. ‖ I observed its horns further, and, see, another little one, ‖ which rose up among them and before which three of the former horns were

from Seleukos: for that the animal which *crushes the whole earth* can only be Alexander in the strict sense, and that the Greek kingdoms which arose out of that of Alexander are carefully distinguished, appears from the following piece, ch. viii.; and for none of these, not even for that of the Seleukidæ, could such a rule over the whole earth be claimed at a time when they existed side by side. In this first piece there is yet no mention, it is true, of a division of the empire of Alexander, as is the case ch. viii.; it is the Seleukid kingdom only which is referred to, partly because it boasted of being the true continuation of that of Alexander, partly and still more because it is principally it only which has to be further spoken of in this book, in order to conduct to Antiochos Epiphanes as the true object of the one-half of the prophecy. But here also the world-crushing kingdom of Alexander as the founder of the Greek rule is plainly enough distinguished, vv. 19, 20, 23, 24, from the ten horns as sprung from the *same dominion* (in other words *also of this dominion*), and the entire prophecy concerning the Greek rule passes in order to arrive at Antiochos Epiphanes through the three stages: (1) Alexander; (2) the ten kings; (3) Antiochos Epiphanes.

Now, from Seleukos I. to Seleukos IV. (Philopator) seven kings succeed each other in Syria: precisely this number seven may have been taken note of early in the reign of Antiochos Epiphanes as significant, and it might appear equally significant that this king was compelled to *overthrow* precisely three princes in order to pave his way to the throne; for that this is the meaning of the words regarding Antiochos Epiphanes' appropriation of the kingdom, vv. 8, 20, 24, admits of no doubt. Unfortunately we are not now in possession of any detailed narrative regarding the events in the Syrian kingdom between the death of Seleukos IV. and the acknowledged rule of Antiochos Epiphanes: still we know enough to save us from helpless ignorance. We know that Seleukos IV. died whilst his brother Antiochos, who had been in Rome a number of years as a hostage, was on his way home, and his eldest son, Demetrios, was on his way thither likewise as a hostage, that all the more easily a contention arose regarding the succession in the Syrian kingdom, Heliodoros sought to be made king,* and at the same time the rule over the whole empire, or at least over Phœnicia and Palestine, was claimed for the young Ptolemy Philometor on the side of his mother Kleopatra as daughter of Antiochos III.;† as a matter of course a party was also formed for the young king Demetrios, who had gone to Rome, as the legitimate successor. Thus there were three *horns* which Antiochos, who then named himself Epiphanes, must first hurl down if he intended to assume and maintain the government; Helio-

---

* Comp. *History of Israel*, V., 292 (IV., 380 sq.).

† With regard to the commencement of the reign of this king we are at present in a good deal of ignorance, as the history of Polybios is at this point defective, comp. however, *Polyb.* xxvii., 17; xxviii., 1, 2, 17. The Book of Daniel also alludes plainly to it below xi. 17, 21-23.

rooted out; | and, see, eyes as those of a man were in this horn, and a mouth speaking proud things, *but its look was bigger than that of the others."* † ||

2.

9 .... I was further beholding till thrones were cast and one ancient in days seated himself, | his raiment as

doros was really king for a time; but the conflict between Antiochos and the Ptolemy was for the immediate readers of our book so much the more important as on it centred essentially the question of the possession of Palestine, and the Ptolemy might be counted as belonging to the Seleukid empire by his mother. If that number of seven kings therefore made up a complete series, there was now added this smaller series of three whom Antiochos Epiphanes had first to remove before he could become king; and a larger completely finished series of exactly ten potentates, over whom this present Antiochos Epiphanes towers as an alien interloper not belonging to them, appeared therewith to be closed for all time.*—But this redundant king was the very one in whom just then centred all the calamity of the time for the community of the true religion and the enigma of the future which oppressed them. Therefore

(5) the eye and the discourse of the prophet linger at last, ver. 8, comp. ver. 11, quite specially with him. As it were unexpectedly, the eye falls finally upon *another horn, a small one:* for how small and helpless was this man

2. But if this proud speech against the holiest things is carried even to the mad blasphemy of the Holy One himself, to the attempt at the annihilation of all true religion with both its insti-

on the death of his brother, and how small and contemptible (comp. viii. 9; xi. 21) is he in himself! But this little horn is seen suddenly to be such an one as *has come up between the ten,* as if it had grown to an equal size, *and before which three of these former horns were uprooted,* or as it is said with like force vv. 20, 24, *fell,* so that it reigned instead of them; what a strange phenomenon! Yet something still more strange is revealed in this horn: if it is looked at longer, it is seen to have *human eyes,* to be really a man, but to have also *a mouth speaking proud things,* and what these proud things are is further touched upon ver. 25. Thus there are here brought into rapid review the three stages of this phenomenon up to the time when this was written: (1) his first insignificant appearance; (2) his increasing power as a ruler; (3) the proud and arrogant character which he then manifested more and more. But the idea of insignificance with which the whole description begins does not find its proper completion without the clause *and his look is greater than that of the others,* which stood here originally acc. ver. 20.

tutions and its community and the whole of its most devout members, and should this become finally the climax to which all heathen imperial power develops itself, then most likely everything

---

* All this is here explained with somewhat greater accuracy than in the *Jahrbb. der Bibl. Wiss.*, XI., p. 222 sq.

† Inserted here from ver. 20.

white snow, and the hair of his head as bright wool, | his throne
10 fire-flames, his wheels burning fire. || A stream of fire gleamed
forth and went out from him, | and thousand thousands serve
him and ten thousand ten thousands stand before him; | the
11 judgment was set, and books were opened. || —I was still
beholding how then on account of the loud proud words which

must at last take an entirely new turn, and at the same moment when the inspired eye beholds this it beholds also as the exactly opposite scene, the necessity, and the actual, certain, coming of the judgment of the world, of the overthrow of all heathen imperial dominion and the beginning of the Messianic age. The second strophe thus supplies in general the counter picture of the first: but it follows of itself from what has just been said, and is confirmed by the words which follow below, vv. 21, 25, that one or two verses are wanting at the beginning of the strophe, which must describe in the picture how Antiochos Epiphanes actually begins *war with the saints*, i.e., acc. Ex. xix. 6, the true members of the community of the true religion, and *overcomes them*, and how in connexion therewith he *presumes to change times and law*, i.e, the feasts and usages of the true religion, and supposes that he must do this. If such words had not originally formed the commencement of the second strophe, they could not have had any place at all in the interpretation below vv. 21, 25: moreover, the strophe thus only receives its proper length; and the LXX have in this passage at least a remnant of such words.*—The things which the seer beholds henceforth is a drama which reaches its climax by three stages:—

(1) vv. 9, 10, the commencement of the divine judgment of the world. He beholds *until thrones were cast*, were placed for judicial business, for the judges, that is, who are about to appear forthwith; and an ancient one in days *seated himself*, one who from his whole aspect appeared as if he must be old in days, a true patriarch, whilst *his raiment* particularly and the *hair of his head* shone with a bright white brilliancy, *like white snow* or *bright wool*: that is, the external appearance of him, as this prophet ventures to depict it with much greater boldness than any earlier prophet, not excepting Hézeqiél even, i. 26 sq.: and yet he ventures to do no more than depict what seems, only *how* he beheld him in vision, and leaves it to be surmised who he is, the Everlasting from of old who is dwelling in a light with which none can compare; for that there is something incomparable here notwithstanding the endeavour to make it as real to the imagination as is possible by comparisons, is quite obviously implied, since his garment is not compared with bright wool, his hair not with whitest snow, but the garment with the snow and the hair with the wool. But the lower portion of the appearance, all events, that which has in it as it were more of colour and of earth makes itself felt: *his throne like fire-flames, his wheels* on the Kerûb-chariot, after Ezek. i. 12 sq., *burning fire.*—And scarcely is he seated upon *his* throne and chariot (in heaven, of course) when *a stream of light*

---

* Namely, the words καὶ ἐποίει πόλεμον πρὸς τοὺς ἁγίους.

the horn was always speaking—I beheld till the beast was slain
12 and its body destroyed and given up to the burning fire, || but of
the rest of the beasts their dominion passed away, as a prolonging
13 of life was given them for a time and a period. || —I was still
beholding in the night visions, and, see, with the clouds of heaven
there came even as a son of man, | and up to the ancient of days

shines forth and issues from before him in that he commands that the judgment shall begin :[*] for his word is a shining forth of light, and proceeds thus from him according to the phrase which is customary in the case of human kings (as ii. 15; vi. 27, comp. ii. 6, 18; v. 24). And immediately the innumerable hosts of Angels *pay homage* to him, *waiting* for his commands (for the decisions of the court must be forthwith executed); the *court* of judgment (consisting of the highest Angels) seats itself, and *the books* in which all the deeds of men are recorded *are opened*, so that nothing is wanting to enable individual men to receive their divine final sentence.— But in this connexion there belongs,

(2) vv. 11, 12, nothing more than that the divine sentence should be delivered regarding the heathen world-empire, principally in that form of it in which it appears in the Greek kingdom of that last horn, or king. The seer beholds that this *horn*, which now, however, the better to suit the image becomes an *animal*, is condemned to death on account of its loud arrogant speeches and other bad deeds (which are here passed unmentioned for brevity sake, they being sufficiently plain from what has gone before), *its gross body destroyed and it is thus given up to the conflagration of fire*, not that fire from which, acc. ch. v., the faithful can be rescued even in the last extremity, but that which is described "Isa." l. 11; lxvi. 24, comp. Vol. IV., 304, 354. But if the horn is thus transformed into an animal, since by Antiochos Epiphanes the Syrian kingdom is meant at the same time, it follows as a matter of course that *the other animals* upon which the judgment now falls likewise are the remaining Greek or other heathen kingdoms of the same time, so that we see here also clearly that the animal representing Alexander does not appear here any more as such. All the other heathen empires shall also *lose their power, since*, as is most appropriately added, *a respite of life is given them* by God only *until a time and hour*, that is, not for ever.—On which side eternal life, on the other hand, is, appears,

(3) vv. 13, 14, most clearly for the first time. For another kingdom must then arrive : this kingdom can only be that of the perfectly true religion, which will rule uniformly over the whole earth and all nations, extending itself in the manner which was typically indicated previously especially in the last instance vi. 26, 27. But at this point, where the certain approach of this kingdom is foreseen only in general outline, where the ideal of its king and its nation is only put in contrast with that of those kings and empires, and only its highest characteristics and its consummation shall be made real to the imagination, the seer's eye immediately

---

[*] Comp. the Commentary on Isa. vi. 4.

14 he came, and right before him they brought him: ‖ and to him was given power and honour and kingdom, and all the nations communities and tongues will serve him, | his power is an eternal power which will never pass away, and his kingdom that which cannot be destroyed. ‖

3.

15 Pierced through felt the heart of me Daniel in the midst of its

beholds *one borne by the clouds of heaven* quickly into this celestial court of justice, who amid the purely celestial forms, who are by their wings or other shapes distinguished from men, has the appearance *as of a son of man*, and is also really a man,* only a man certainly of an absolutely peculiar kind, such an one as has never yet been upon the earth. For it is no other than the Messias, long ago foretold by ancient prophecy and particularly described, since then often so intensely longed for by thousands of the most devout, who still continues to delay his appearance, though he will surely appear in his time according to the divine will, who at the time of our author was conceived as already long since existing with God, and as it were preserved in heaven for the time of his terrestrial appearance.† Thus he can here be seen by the inspired eye as borne at the right time rapidly with the clouds of heaven from the place where he tarries in heaven to this spot of supreme decision with regard to the dominion of the world, *as arrived by the ancient in days and presented to him* by the ministering angels, so that it may appear whether it is he to whom,

3. The main burden of the dream is finished; but the seer still feels himself in contrast with all past heathen rulers of the world, the dominion of the earth can be transferred. Verily, when once at the right time the true human ruler comes, the divine grace, with dominion through it, is always secured for him; if it was so in the smaller cases of ancient history of which the Old Testament tells, it is most truly so in this highest instance which has not yet become actual, and is yet already here foreseen as so certainly coming. Thus the eye sees immediately how *power and honour and empire, i.e.*, the most complete *majestas*, as ruler upon earth, are *given to him*, since it is he whom, according to the ancient promises, *all nations* of every kind and tongue *will serve*, and *his empire* is the *imperishable and eternal* one by its origin and nature. What has been three times, iii. 33 (A.V., iv. 3) iv. 31 (33); vi. 27, said of the kingdom of God in a general sense, holds now of the Messianic theocracy with twofold force and truth, this twofold idea having been referred to most briefly in the introductory part, ii. 44, as the summit of all prophecy.

in the midst of its progress, and his spirit is as it were pierced through by

---

* That this is the true meaning of this phrase *one as a son of man, i.e.*, according to the Aramaic idiom *as a man*, and that the connexion in which it stands admits no other meaning, follows also from the exactly similar passages where, on the contrary, an Angel is spoken of, viii. 15; x. 16-18, see below.

† Comp. *Geschichte des Volkes Israel*, V., 139 sq.

16 sheath, and the visions of my head confound me; | I came nearer to one of those standing by, and the truth I begged of him concerning all this; | so he told me and the interpretation of the words maketh me to know : ‖ " These immense beasts which are four : | four kings will arise from the earth; ‖ yet the dominion will the holy ones of the Lofty One receive | and will maintain the dominion for all times, and till the eternity of the eternities." ‖

19 —Then I desired the truth concerning the fourth beast, which is diverse from them all, which is yet more terrible, | its teeth of iron and claws of brass, that devoureth crusheth and stampeth
20 the residue with its feet; ‖ and concerning the ten horns on its head, and another which rose up and before which three fell, | and

the tremendous and, from the first, mostly terrible scenes which it presented, so that it cannot remain like a sword quietly *in the midst of its sheath.* As the sword remains quiet in its sheath as long as it is therein, so a man usually feels his spirit quietly within him as long as he feels it enclosed by the coarse covering of the body; but there are moments when it becomes too disturbed for the spirit in the midst of this coarse covering, when it longs to burst the covering from impatience and to dare everything. The seer felt himself at that time in such a moment: and so he advances boldly to one of those who were still standing there from the scene just witnessed, one of the thousands of angels, in order to request from him the reliable interpretation of all that had been witnessed, vv. 16, 17. His request is also granted : the four animals are four kings of the earth, who rise in succession and always bring the heathen world-empire into a somewhat different form: but they are all of them *from the earth,* ver. 17, none of them from heaven like the Messias, acc. vv. 13, 14. Still, *the kingdom* in the purest and highest sense, the kingdom as God desires to have it, belongs to *the holy ones of the Lofty One,* the true members of the community of the perfectly true religion, and they *will* really *receive it* and then maintain it in conformity with its nature *unto all eternity,* ver. 18. When here, as likewise vv. 22, 27, the true members of this kingdom are immediately spoken of instead of the Messias, it is because the discourse in this manner condescends to a more particular interpretation of the great ideal picture which had been given. A kingdom and its king cannot exist without a people, but only become a reality by means of the nation; and if the kingdom and its king have a purely divine purpose, extending beyond both, and a law answering to this purpose, as is the case with the perfected theocracy and its Messias, the nation of such a king and kingdom must be accordant, it is only *the holy ones of the Lofty One* who are here suitable ; and if a people of this kind actually exists, it receives also that power and durability, that indestructibility and eternity, also that dignity and pre-eminence, which are implied in the nature of this kingdom and its Messias, as had already been more briefly said ii. 44. In the interpretation this *nation* is thus spoken of, and the previous ideal picture, vv. 13, 14, receives thereby an addition which, though necessarily involved, is not unimportant : still, the Messias, who is in

this horn as it had eyes and a mouth speaking proud things, |
21 and its look was bigger than that of the others of its kind; || I
was still beholding—and this horn beginneth war then against
22 the holy ones and overcometh them, | until the ancient in days
came and the judgment *was set and power** was given to the
holy ones of the Lofty One, | and the time arrived and the holy
23 ones received the dominion. || *Then he answered and†* thus he
said :

the first passage amply indicated, is not by any means identical with the nation which is added here at the close.‡ just as little as the description of the Messias there given, and not easily to be repeated in its sublimity, has any similarity with the words here used. It is only in the final results and aims, in the eternity and dignity of the kingdom itself, as is here and ver. 27 appropriately brought forward, that king and nation coincide; and yet even then the distinction is kept up, that the three things, *power, honour and rule, i.e., majestas* in its full manifestation and most magnificent acknowledgment, is assigned to the Messias only, ver. 14, but not to the nation, since even the three words for *power and greatness*, ver. 27, do not completely answer to those three, which acc. ii. 37; iv. 27, 33 (A.V., 30, 36) ; v. 18 also, are needed to describe fully royal characteristics.

Still, for good reasons the questioner is not satisfied with the general interpretation of the four empires and their opposite: he desires to learn fuller particulars especially as regards the fourth, as regards all the details of it, and as regards the Messianic kingdom which succeeds it. He now, vv. 19-22, causes all the various most marvellous features of this empire, just as he beheld them before as part of the great scene, to pass once more before his greatly excited mind, waiting most eagerly for the more special interpretation of them. It follows from this that in these simply repeated pictures, vv. 19-22, nothing may be mentioned which had not been already mentioned in the first two strophes, although it may have been not always in quite the same words. As a fact, the little clause *and the time arrived*, ver. 22, also occurs ver. 12, only it is more fully expressed in point of meaning. But by this long and yet appropriate repetition the space of this strophe has been already so completely filled up that the interpretation of this twofold section, which is for the readers the most important of all, does not follow until

---

* Supplied conjecturally. † Conjectured also.

‡ It was shown at length in the *Jahrbb. der Bibl. Wiss.*, III., 231 sq., that it is wrong and groundless to suppose that the *son of man*, ver. 13, is the nation. The proper order and division of the three connected ideas, corresponding to the high art and excellence of our book, is, on the contrary, this : (1) the *kingdom*, ii. 44 ; (2) the *king*, vii. 13 ; (3) the *nation*, vv. 18 sq. Further, as to each of the four world-empires, acc. vii. 17, there is a king who corresponds to it, so must there be above all things a king answering to this kingdom : God himself is alone not adapted for this ; he is adapted for it only until the proper divine-human kingdom

4.

The fourth beast : | a fourth dominion will be upon the earth, which will be diverse from all the dominions, | and will devour
24 break in pieces and crush the whole earth. ‖ —*And the ten horns :* | out of the same dominion will ten kings arise. ‖ And another will arise after them, he will be diverse from the former ones : | and
25 three kings will he smite down. ‖ And words against the Most High will he speak, and wear away the holy ones of the Lofty One, | will hope to change times and law, and they will be given
26 into his hand until a time and two times and a half. ‖ —*And the judgment was set :* | yet his power is made transitory, to annihi-
27 late and to destroy it unto the end; ‖ and the power and the dominion and the glory of the kingdoms under the whole

---

4. the main portion of the last strophe, vv. 23-27. And here the most important thing that remains is, (1) that as the distinction of the Greek empire from the three former ones is great enough in the bad sense, so that of Antiochos Epiphanes differs in the same way from all the former ten rulers of this special part of the Greek dynasty, vv. 23, 24. How true this is, is—(2) ver. 25 sufficiently explained when it is more particularly specified that the *proud* words of the man mentioned above, vv. 8, 11, 20 are directed *against the Highest* himself, but he will also *wear out* the members of the true community, or (as was said ver. 21) make war upon and overcome them, and in the bad sense *think* or presume *to change times and law ;* in what sense all this, which was at that time actual history, is to be understood has been explained in the *History of Israel*, V., 293-300 (IV., 381-390), as far as our present knowledge of it goes, and is somewhat more particularly touched upon below in our book itself, xi. 31 sq. *Times and law* refer in such a connexion to Sabbaths and feasts as well as to the remaining sacred customs as they were then in force according to the sacred law, *e.g.*, circumcision. But when it is here added, with reference to the then actual future, that they would be given *into his hand a time* (two) *times and half a time, i.e.*, three and a half years, this mysterious announcement is not meant to be explained until subsequently, ch. ix. But when finally—(3) the word *the judgment is set*, vv. 26, 27, shall be explained, the interpretation proceeds at once for brevity sake from

---

must on earth succeed the four world-empires; but God is not described as the king who will then follow. On the other hand, it is equally plain that, according to the idea of our book, the nation is not meant to be conceived as one man raised to heaven and to God: what a preposterous idea would then arise! For nobody would bring ἀπάντησις τοῦ κυρίου, 1 Thess. iv. 17, into this connexion, and it is not received in that Epistle on the authority of our Book of Daniel: the thought which it embodies could not arise before apostolic times.—There is, however, incidental allusion to the Messias, iv. 14 (A.V. 17) ; 22 (25), 29 (32), (comp. with עָנִי " Zach." ix. 9).

heaven is given to the people of the holy ones of the Lofty One, | his kingdom is an eternal kingdom, and all powers will serve and obey him." ||

28   Thus far is the end of the words.— I Daniel—my thoughts confounded me exceedingly at that time, and my features were disfigured upon me : | yet the word I retained in my heart.

that point where it was left ver. 25 : *and his* (Antiochos Epiphanes') *power shall be made transitory,* or perishable, *so that it shall be rooted out and destroyed unto the end, i.e.,* completely ; and still more rapidly the last thing follows : *and the full power* of all the previous kingdoms, of the heathen, that is, *is* thereby as good as certainly *given to the holy ones of the Lofty One,* so that *his kingdom,* that of his people, becomes an *eternal kingdom and all the powers* which shall then exist on the earth will *serve and obey him,* which is only the affirmative expression instead of the negative of ii. 44.

Thus far the end of the word of the interpreter, ver. 23, and therewith of the dream concerning all these things, is said ver. 28, at the close of the piece : and although the inward *thoughts* of this dreamer, as he adds, were still very much agitated when he at last became completely awake again after this gradually diminishing crowd of representations, and his outward *features* were disfigured, as any one might say to him whom he first met, he nevertheless *kept the word* and the matter of the dream in *his heart,* being unable to forget it as Nabukodrossor had forgotten his, ii. 1 sq.; Gen. xxxvii. 11.

8. (III. 2.)

The vision of the two empires of the world and the time of their end.

Ch. viii.

The Messianic piece just explained has thus, notwithstanding all the dissimilarity of its symbolic figures and their relation to each other, simply carried out further and more definitely the prophetic subject-matter of the introductory piece ch. ii. The distinctive feature of the Messianic piece is the marvellously glorious and inspiring picture of the divine judgment of the world and the arrival of the Messias : for although this had been more briefly sketched ii. 44, and in a third passage, xii. 2, 3, some additions will be made to it, what is all that in comparison with this magnificent passage in the middle of the book! Indeed, the beauty, and at the same time, the impressiveness of this description is so great, that any repetition of it, or of a portion of it, would only weaken its effect.

Still, anything which concerns the end of the heathen world-empire cannot be too fully and definitely delineated, inasmuch as it concerns precisely the actual present of the first readers of this book themselves, and the hints which refer to this great event cannot be supplied too abundantly. Accordingly, in the following piece, it is only the last of the four heathen empires which are again produced from other points of view, and, as it were, in other compartments and pictures, in conformity with the whole plan of the book, as explained *ante* p. 179 sq. In reality the first two empires in the previous piece, ch. vii., did little more than fill up the two stages which were involved in the fundamental thought of the four empires, whilst the third empire is too closely connected with the rise of the fourth to permit it to be quite left out when the design is to consider the latter at length, as will appear again in another way, ch. xi. It is particularly the comparison of the strength and military efficiency of these two empires which is here presented, and for the illustration of which they suddenly appear here under the new symbolic figures of a ram and a he-goat. Both were considered from ancient times as bellicose animals, each advancing boldly at the head of its herd; and although it was particularly the ram which had this reputation in Israel from earliest times,* they are still both very much alike; which then is the stronger?—But at this point the discourse is only once more brought to the same last offshoot of the Seleukid rule, who is indeed everywhere the real object of all such hints in this book, and who was for that time the subject of such inexhaustible discourse that in this second piece also fresh references to him can be made in abundance. And in the same way the

---

* According to the very ancient lyric Ex. xv. 15; repeated from thence later Ezek. xvii. 13.

question of relative size is applied to him also, and it is seen whether he is as great as the first founder of the Greek rule.

In other respects the plan of this piece is very similar to that of the previous one. As regards the space which it is to occupy, it is on a scale only a very little smaller than the previous piece, and falls likewise into four strophes, the first two of which supply the picture itself in its two halves, while the last two give its explanation and finish. It thus happens that precisely the second and the fourth are occupied almost exclusively with the symbols and hints as regards that king who is the true object of all the symbols and hints of the book which refer to the heathen world-empire. The glad tidings and certainty of the coming of the perfect kingdom of God is pre-supposed from ch. vii.: it is the period until its arrival which is dwelt upon with increasing plainness and emphasis, vv. 14, 17, 26.

1.

1 In the third year of the reign of king Bêlshassar a vision appeared to me Daniel, | after that which had appeared to me
2 at the first. || Thus I beheld in the vision—and then as I beheld I was in the castle of Shûshan which was in the

    1. The vision occurs before the end of the reign of the last Chaldean king, because it is intended to present the origin and nature of the last two heathen empires, and this is the more appropriate inasmuch as in these last two empires (as will immediately appear) that which is counted as the third ch. ii. and ch. vii., is at the same time included with them.—That this second vision is meant to be only like a resumption and continuation of the first, and to stand in close connection with it, is stated in the introduction of it, ver. 1, by the mention of that as the one *in the beginning*, i.e., the first or previous one (ix. 21): just as certainly as the similarly designated piece Hos. ch. i. ii., must be followed by the second piece ch. iii. sq. As now the first of these two pieces which are placed in the closest connection with each other is presented as a dream-piece, it follows that the above is intended to be the same. If, however, the word *dream* is not used ver. 1, the subject-matter of the piece is, notwithstanding, immediately indicated in the description of the place where this *vision*, or rather this series of several closely connected visions, is received by Daniel, as supplied by means of a dream. For *Susa* and, in the neighbourhood of it, the river *Ulâi*, vv. 2, 3, 16, and accordingly an entirely different place from that in which Daniel had hitherto moved as

province of 'Aelam, | and I beheld in the vision and I was by
3 the river-basin of the Ulái. || Then I lifted up mine eyes and
saw—and lo a ram, standing eastward of the river-basin, holding
up two horns : | and the horns were high, but the one higher
4 than the other, and the higher grew later. || I saw the
ram butting westward and northward and southward, | while
no beasts stood before him and none delivered himself from
his hand : | so he acted according to his pleasure and did
5 grandly. || —But I was considering further—and lo a he-goat
came from the west over the face of the whole earth without
touching the earth, | and the goat had as a horn to look upon
6 between his eyes. || So he came up to the two-horned ram

officer and prophet. *i.e.*, Babel, is here mentioned as the place where the vision forced itself upon his sight, because it is here especially that the collision of the Persian with the Greek empire is about to be beheld: not near Babel, but near this capital of the Persian empire beyond the Tigris, the great historic struggle must be decided between the two empires, as Daniel here beholds it. Therefore Daniel feels himself suddenly translated in spirit into the district *by the river-basin of the Ulái*, and the first object which he then beholds still *before* him, *i.e.*, to the east, is the ram, *i.e.*, the Persian imperial power, prepared for attack. But the manner in which he is translated thither, ver. 2, reminds us plainly enough of a dream : only in a dream could he in the first more active movements of it and the endeavour to put himself right *in that which he saw*, suppose that he was *in the castle of Susa*, and in the next moment *by the* near *river-basin of the Ulái*. It is only in a dream that the images and the places where one thinks one is are changed so rapidly: and only thus do the words of the extremely animated description, ver. 2, yield a meaning. We find ourselves in this dream at the Persian royal castle, beyond the Tigris, in the ancient province of 'Aelam, or rather by the neighbouring river-basin of the Ulái (called *Eulaios* by the Greeks): and we must then, acc. vv. 3, 6, 16, keep by this river-basin during the rest of the dream, because we are intended to take a glance into the great decision between the Persian and the Greek empires, and into the subsequent fortunes of the latter which are connected therewith. The Ulái, however, does not appear to be here so much a single river as a river-basin (*stromgebiet*), as in that district a number of great rivers meet :* hence it can afterwards, ver. 16, be said *between the Ulái.*

But the first more definite object which we notice in this locality is a

---

* It must not be overlooked that the Ulái, vv. 2, 3, 6, 16, is not designated as an ordinary river, but with the peculiar name אוּבַל, which has manifestly a much wider significance, and can be rendered *river-basin* (Germ. *stromgebiet*). With regard to this district and the names *Ulái* and *Shushan*, comp. Loftus' *Travels and Researches in Chaldea and Susiana*, London, 1857, and the *Gött. Gel. Anz.* 1857, p. 183 sq.

7 which I had seen standing eastward of the river-basin, | and ran against him in the fury of his strength. ‖ —And I saw him coming close to the ram : | then he embittered himself against him and smote the ram and broke in pieces his horns, so that the ram had no strength to stand before him ; | so he threw him to the ground and stamped upon him, | and there was no one who delivered the ram out of his hand. ‖

2.

8 But the he-goat did much too grandly : | and when he was full-grown the great horn broke in pieces, and there grew to

ram, ver. 3, *eastward of this river-basin standing* as already prepared for battle and expecting his enemy approaching in the distance : but as he symbolizes, as immediately appears from ver. 20, the Medo-Persian empire, or according to the previous images ch. ii. vii., the combined second and third empires together, he appears at once as *two-horned*, although it is seen that one of the two horns (the Persian one, that is) is really *the higher*, although the one *growing up last*. Thus skilfully does the author resume the thread of the history with the Median as the immediate successor of the Chaldean empire in point of time, which is in accordance with the two previous pieces, ch. ii., vii., and in fact with the whole of the previous pieces of the book, and interweaves all the most dissimilar symbolic pictures of the book together without confusing them.— Still, that which the seer further beholds, ver. 4, of the whole nature and expression of this double-animal, is nothing more than that he (as is known of the Persian empire) *butts* forcibly with his two horns *westwards* (beyond the Tigris into Europe) *northwards* (Scythia) *and southwards* (Egypt and Africa), whilst the east already belongs to him as his own possession ; that he thus like a true world-power ruled as with omnipotence and exactly according *to his* own *pleasure*, and in no small measure *doing grandly* after the manner of a heathen empire.

For the attention shall be directed far more to the *he-goat*, vv. 5-7, which *approaches from the sun-setting* (in order not again to say from the west as ver. 4) *over the entire surface of the earth* with the most marvellous rapidity *without even touching the ground* (as was said of Kyros, " Isa." xli. 4, comp. the note on this passage), and is externally distinguished only by the fact that he has *between his eyes* on his forehead only *one* thing which is *to look upon* like *a horn :* for it is, as is further indicated ver. 8 and ver. 21, strictly speaking only the *one* Alexander. But he comes up *in the fury of his strength* precisely against the place upon which this double-crowned one awaits him, ver. 6 : and already the seer beholds him when he has *arrived* near his antagonist, preparing himself for the decisive conflict with a final *embittering* of himself, and thus hurls him down beyond deliverance, as is described with great animation ver. 7.

2. It is not so very difficult to mortally strike an opponent under favourable circumstances : but what then becomes of the victor, and of this incomparably powerful victor ? Alas ! it becomes soon enough evident, ver. 8,

look upon four horns instead of it towards the four winds of
9 heaven. || But out of one of them shot forth a puny horn, |
   and became uncommonly great towards the south and towards
10 the sunrising and towards the Ornament; || became great
   unto the Host of heaven, | and cast down to the ground some
   of the Host and of the stars of heaven and trampled upon

that he becomes simply only so much the more *insolent* than his opponent had been, ver. 4: accordingly this *great horn* also is broken when it had grown sufficiently high, and in the room of it *four* horns are suddenly seen to grow up which divide from each other in the direction of *the four quarters of the heavens* or the world, as at the time of our author it could have long been said that Alexander's empire had fallen into four great parts, according to the four quarters of the world, the Syrian empire to the east, the Ptolemaic to the south, the Macedonian to the west, the Thracian-Pontic to the north !

But it is only of the Seleukid empire and of the last offshoot of this (Antiochos Epiphanes) that we are here to be told what the seer saw, and with the symbolic picture of it, vv. 9-12, the essential matter of this entire vision is brought to a close. It is particularly three things that are beheld with regard to it, just as its history, as far as it had then been unfolded, and was of importance for the readers of this book, could really be best reviewed in three stages: (1) the principal thing is, ver. 9, that this originally *puny*, wretched, helpless *horn* becomes nevertheless soon so *uncommonly great* and victorious, and *towards the south*, inasmuch as the king as soon as he secured himself on his throne began his wars in the first place against

Egypt,* *towards the east* against the disaffected nations in the east, particularly the Parthians, and (what is really the most important thing here) *against the Ornament*, or as it is somewhat more definitely named xi. 16, 41, *the land of the Ornament*, namely Palestine, which name at that time it had long been customary to use of Palestine in elegant or (as in this book) disguised language; the king began early enough the hostilities against Jerusalem.† As if, with these victories abroad and violent doings at home, his insolence must increase beyond all bounds, primarily against the community of true religion and its God, we see—(2) vv. 10, 11 a, his presumption madly aiming at *the host of heaven*, that is, the nation, duly organized in the community, which as the people of the God of heaven, ii. 18, 37; v. 23; Ezra v. 10, 11; vi. 9, 10; vii. 12-23, can also very well be called the host of heaven in lofty discourse and at the right moment ; and we see him *casting down and trampling with his feet*, treating most shamefully, *some of* this *host and* even some *of the stars*, those who among the innumerable members of this heavenly host can be counted as specially shining stars (xii. 3), yea, we see him even *insulting the prince of the host*, or, as he is designated ver. 25, *the prince of the princes*, the true God himself who exists as

---

* Acc. to *History of Israel*, V., 296 sq. (IV., 385 sq.).

† *History of Israel*, V., 299 sq. (IV., 386 sq.).—The origin of an expression like *ornament* refers back, acc. Ps. l. 2 ; Lam. ii. 15, to Jerusalem as the fairest city, but we are no longer able to trace all the intermediate steps.

11 them, ‖ yea unto the prince of the Host he did proudly, | and by him the daily was abolished and the place of his sanctuary
12 cast down, | and armed force is placed upon the daily by sacrilege, | and it casteth the truth down to the ground and it
13 beareth sway and prospereth. ‖ —Then I heard a holy one speaking, and another holy one said to the certain one who

the Most High above his own people and host, as well as above all that are called princes on earth or in heaven (ii. 47; v. 21). Precisely at the time of our author such lofty names for the members of the true community were in great favour, and were frequently used at least in higher discourse and also even in the headings of books;* if they were not here to be referred to again as in the last piece vii. 18, 22, 25, 27, as the *saints of the Lofty One*, or briefly *the saints*, and if the name of God was not again to be given in this piece by the same circumlocution as in the former one, for artistic reasons, the fundamental figure of the piece—*an army*—naturally presented itself, with all the other figures belonging to it, as more suitable in proportion to the frequent mention of martial matters in the piece; it is only in the explanation, ver. 24, that the words from ch. vii. recur with more freedom. But the extremity to which the king permits himself to be carried only now follows—(3), vv. 11 *b*, 12: *by him*, by the very man who was previously called the *horn, was the daily* (*das Tagtägliche*) the perpetually unchangeable, true offering in the temple (acc. to the *Antiquities of Israel*, p. 151 sq. (129 sq.)) *abolished and the place of his holy thing* (*i.e.*, sacrament, acc. to the *Antiquities*, p. 145 sq. (123 sq.)), *cast down*, the altar itself upon which alone the proper offering, or sacrament, can be presented, which is immediately, ver. 13 and below ix. 27*c*; xi. 31; xii. 11, in connexion with the heathen sacrifices forcibly introduced, designated as the most horrible abomination. For in closest connexion therewith is lastly *the compulsion*, ver. 12 (which he employs for no other purpose than the introduction of the heathen altar and sacrifice in the place of the true one overthrown, since it can only be carried out by his armed *host*), called here *host* according to the Hebrew expression, as apt as it is pointed, host against host, forced service against the true service (of God), compulsion against freedom! This compulsion *is laid upon the daily* in order that the true temple offering may not be brought, and *by sacrilege*, by the heathen offering substituted in its place, which is in one word nothing else than *sacrilege!* But hitherto this compulsion has been only too successful: *it casts the truth to the ground*, with the true sacrifice the true religion as it ought publicly to be acknowledged, *and has the sway and prosperity!*

And does the seer behold all that just as he beheld those bellicose animals with their horns? O how far is he already removed from merely beholding symbolic images, and now simply hears what is taking place, and taking place in such numerous and various ways! How truly is he all ear and has

---

* Comp. the heading of the first book of the Makkabees according to its proper meaning, *History of Israel*, V., 463 (IV., 604).

spake | "Till how long is the vision of the daily and the horrible sacrilege, that thus both the holy thing and Host are
14 surrendered to be trodden under foot?" || Then said he to him * "until two thousand and three hundred evening-mornings: | then will the holy thing be justified." ||

3.

15 And then when I Daniel saw the vision and sought to understand it, | lo there stood before me one to look upon like
16 a man, || and I heard someone between the Ulái speak aloud and call and say "Gabriel, explain to this one that which was

an ear only for learning ever and anon what lies hidden in the divine destinies of mankind, which perhaps an Angel tells to him, or of which the Angels discourse to each other! But he then hears, at the first moment when that discourse makes a pause, suddenly an Angel in conversation asking the other, as if it were the most intolerable thing merely to hear even a narrative of such calamities of the faithful and to be compelled to see them in symbols, *until how long the vision,* and therefore the condition of things into which a higher glance has just been opened, must last? the vision, that is (to repeat here briefly simply the most insufferable thing in it), *of the daily* which is suppressed *and of the horrible sacrilege* which is forced into its place, acc. ver. 12, *that both the holy thing and the army,* the sacrament with all other usages as well as his community and nation, *are made something to be trodden upon with the*

3. But if Daniel now longs for a closer understanding of the things beheld and heard, his longing shall now, during the continuation of this dream, be more decidedly rewarded even than in the former one: suddenly he sees (otherwise than vii. 15 sq.) one

feet? And who does not feel with what profound pain these half-finished words, hardly audibly uttered by reason of breaking sighs, are spoken!—But then the younger hears from the older, the inquirer from the better instructed, that that shall continue only *two thousand three hundred evenings and mornings*, i.e., only three and a half years (comp. below on ch. ix. and ch. xii.): then the violated *holy thing*, which is now so seriously compromised in the eyes of the world, will be *justified*, or again presented and acknowledged in the world by its divine victory as the only true and proper *sacramentum*, or, as is said Isa. v. 16, the holy thing shall be hallowed by righteousness, with which there is here expressed in a more solemn and definite form simply the same thing with which the picture of all the abominations closed in the previous piece, vii. 12.

who has *the appearance as of a man,* i.e., an Angel, who however, prepared to manifest himself to him in a kindly human manner, has put off his celestial distinction (his wings) *standing before him,* and *hears* a distant voice, becoming audible over the river-basin

---

* Amended for *me.*

17 beheld!" ‖ So he came beside my standing-place ; | but while he was coming I was terrified and fell upon my face. ‖ But he said to me : "Mark, son of man ! for unto the time of the end
18 is the vision!" ‖ But whilst he spake with me I fell upon my face to the ground overcome with sleep : | then he touched me
19 and caused me to stand where I stood, ‖ and said " Lo I will make known to thee what will happen at the end of the great
20 wrath, for it is for a fixed term. ‖ The ram which thou sawest,
21 the two horned—are the kings of Media and Persia ; ‖ and the shaggy goat is the king of the Greeks, and the great horn between his eyes is the first king.

4.

22 But that which broke in pieces and four (horns) came in its

and then quite intelligible to him as a *human* voice (of a yet higher Angel), as coming immediately from God, *call to this Angel of the name of Gabriel* (i.e., Man-god, a kindly god stooping to man), to explain to him the vision, vv. 15, 16. And it seems to him, indeed (inasmuch as he has never before been brought so near celestial beings), that he must perish even *whilst* the Angel *comes* and says to him, as formerly an Angel to Hezeqiél, *observe, thou son of man!* it is important that thou shouldst have the proper understanding of the symbols and the words, it concerns divine events which are the more decisive inasmuch as they have to do with the time of the end, a time when a great end of all the past must come, and therefore the most unusual things must happen in order that something absolutely new and better may arise, ver. 17. And he is still more on the point of perishing when he now actually hears him thus speak : but at the same moment when he is now really wholly moved by the divine illumination, when the Angel *touches him and causes him to stand firmly upon his own feet*, he is

4. to this time of the end, *i.e.*, to Antiochos Epiphanes, vv. 22-25. And

already conscious of a new and marvellous self-possession and power really to hear everything which is coming so close to him, ver. 18, inasmuch as it (as is once more beforehand, and this time still more emphatically announced) concerns *the end, i.e.,* the final period of the *great wrath* (ὀργὴ μεγάλη, 1 Macc. i. 64), or the extreme calamities which must come according to the divine will over the earth as from the angry God, *because* the vision, as was similarly said ver. 17, is *for the end-term,* has its most important meaning and bearing only for the (at the time of the first readers already commenced) final period of all the heathen past, vv. 18, 19. And in reality the interpretation of the two animals, which is now at first, vv. 20, 21, given with great composure, is extremely brief, although much plainer, and thus to a greater extent flooded with divine lucidity and certainty, than it was when supplied in the essentially similar cases ch. ii. and ch. vii. For the discourse and the interpretation hasten, as was already so emphatically announced, forthwith

then in the first instance (1) vv. 22-24a reference is made to the fact, that

stead: | four kingdoms will arise out of the people, but not with
23 his strength. || And at the end of their kingdom, when the
sacrileges come to the height, | a king will arise bold of visage
24 and versed in enigmas: | he will have mighty strength, but
not by his own strength. || And wonderfully will he destroy and
prosper and bear sway, | destroy mighty men and the people
of the holy ones, || and according to his cunning—deceit will
prosper through him : | yet in his heart will he do grandly and
unawares destroy many, | against the prince of princes contend

as none of the four Greek kingdoms which proceeded from that of Alexander equal Alexander's *in power*, so the kingdom of this last Seleukid will in no way (as many timid people might suppose) equal that of Alexander, of however *brazen face* (on account of the blasphemous words mentioned vii. 8 sq. sufficiently) and however *wise in enigmas*, i.e., in the solution of all kinds of difficult affairs which crowd upon him, or, as is indicated ver. 25, however *shrewd* and astute the king may be. But when he begins to be spoken about, ver. 23a, it is mentioned as a more particular explanation of the *last time* mentioned ver. 19, that his time coincides with the last days of *the rule* of the Greek kingdoms, ver. 22, which we learnt previously from another connexion vii. 12, the same time in which *the sacrileges* come to their climax and therefore also *to their immediate end*, as will have to be further said ix. 24. But with regard to the king himself—(2), vv. 24 b-25, it is then explained in a similar antithesis of his peculiarities and his abilities and fortunes,—that, on the one hand, he *marvellously destroys, is successful and does as he will*, as was previously said ver. 12, namely, *destroys* mighty men, princes, potentates of the earth, e.g., his three fellow princes vii. 8, 9, *and the people of the holy ones* too, as is here ver. 10 and again above ch. vii. further

said,—that further *in accordance with his shrewdness*, because he is so extremely clever and astute, *cunning prospers through him*,—but that, nevertheless, on the other hand, because *in his heart he does grandly* (and how insolent he is has been described ver. 10 and ch. vii.) and so *unawares* (as xi. 21, 24), or treacherously, by surprise, *destroys many*, yea even *uses up* and enters as it were into the lists against *the prince of princes*, i.e., against the true God, as was said very similarly ver. 11 a, as if he desired to destroy him also as he destroyed every one besides, *he will himself be broken without a hand*, not by a visible human hand, but immediately by God himself, with which this prophecy returns to the very first even as regards the figure, ii. 34. But we see that this whole interpretation, vv. 22-25, goes back but in a general way to the words which it is intended to interpret, vv. 8-12, and simply permits the great matter itself with which the book is concerned to come more and more fully and palpably to the front. However, that is implied in the plan and art of the whole book, acc. p. 174 sq., and in this respect also this piece in the middle, ch. viii., makes the transition from ch. vii. to ch. x.—xii.

Furthermore, it is here, ver. 26, remarked, as the only thing remaining to be said, that the number of the days also, but yet without a hand will he be broken in pieces. ‖

26 And the vision concerning the morning-evening which was spoken is true. ‖ — But thou—hide that which was beheld, because it is for many days!" ‖

27 And I Daniel was gone whole days and was exhausted: | but I arose and managed the king's business, | and I was silent concerning the vision for no one understood it.

of grace mentioned at the close of the first half, ver. 14, is correct: the mystery of them is left intentionally unsolved, and deferred for the present, as will be explained below. Accordingly the conclusion is here, ver. 25 *b*, for the first time, that Daniel may *hide the vision*, not publish it for his own contemporaries, because according to its subject-matter *it is for many days*, in fact, has reference to that time of the end which has been so emphatically mentioned vv. 17, 19, 23; and more emphatically and urgently still will this instruction, which is intended nevertheless ultimately to benefit the readers of this book, be repeated below, xii. 4, 5. As then, in accordance therewith, we are told in the postscript, ver. 27, that although Daniel on awaking, and with the gradual disappearance of the scenes of his dream gradually recovered himself from the first overpowering surprise in the sober occupations of his official duties, it was yet not very well possible for him to speak of the subject-matter of the piece because *no one understood* it. The readers may understand it and ought all the better to understand it!

9. (III. 3.)

The seventy years and year-weeks.

Ch. ix.

In the first of these pieces, vii. 12, there is a mysterious reference to *a time and season* which was set for all heathen governments by God, and in relation to the next government this fixed period is then in the interpretation, vii. 25, limited, still mysteriously enough, to the extreme sufferings of the faithful for *a time* (two) *times and a half*. It is somewhat more definitely fixed in the second piece, viii. 13, 14, as a certain number of evening-mornings, but at the end, viii. 26, there is nothing more than its truth emphatically affirmed. Thus far curiosity is excited more than satisfied: and the question regarding the duration of the *time of the end*, so significantly announced viii. 17, 19, 23, or of the final and most terrible sufferings of the faithful, must necessarily become more pressing after the revelations of the last two pieces. That the faithful must also endure the uttermost in divine patience, should this be their lot, at a time when the divine wrath rages as it were over the climax of all the wickedness which prevails in the earth at such a period, is not to be doubted; but then all the more does the question press for an answer, *how long* must this uttermost suffering last; the most faithful of the faithful will find it difficult to repress such a question entirely; and if, moreover, their thought has already in other ways so zealously striven to penetrate the secrets of the whole future so far as they can be opened to mortals, wherefore should not this faithful thought endeavour to fathom this special secret also, or, at least, to cast a distant glance into it?

The people of Israel at all events did not then for the first time pass through a period when all the energies of profoundest patience were tried in suffering, whilst with all the remaining noblest energies of its spirit it hoped for the Messianic consummation and wrestled for its approach; and the greatest prophets themselves had not hesitated in the times of the severest trials to meet by some special hints the wrestling longing to cast a chronologically limited glance into the dark future. We saw this in the case of Yesaya (Vol. II., 264 sq.); but it became far more significant and memorable from the time when Yéremyá had pointed his fellow-countrymen to a period of seventy years of great divine chastisements and sufferings (III., 219). Those seventy years had not then elapsed before Yéremyá's prophecy that the ruins of Jerusalem would not last for ever was fulfilled; forty-nine years after the destruction at all events a new Jerusalem as the sacred centre of the community of the true religion was restored,* and we saw above†

---

* *History of Israel*, V., 72 (IV., 94 sq.).

† *Ante* p. 35; the words Zech. vii. 5 should also be compared, as they are of equal importance here.

what greater hopes and endeavours were revived in this new Jerusalem precisely when the series of years foretold by Yéremyá was coming to an end, whether it might be possible then not only partially but completely to realize the fulfilment of Yéremyá's word. Nevertheless, this complete fulfilment came neither then nor in all the years afterwards, even down to the time when our author lived and wrote. But at this time a general and most severe fight of affliction had returned for all the faithful, such as had not been passed through since the days of the destruction of Jerusalem, then long since passed; and thus that most eager question about the duration of such extreme trials and the actual commencement of the Messianic age was again revived with quite a new force.

Without doubt there was no one at that time who strove with his whole soul more intensely and persistently to solve this enigma than our author-prophet: for as, according to his narrative here, Daniel contended with the profoundest energies of his spirit for a divine answer to the above question, so this man, who here conceals himself from his readers behind Daniel, does the same thing. As a genuine literary prophet he proceeded in this task from that piece of Yéremyá's, as, indeed, he took generally parts of the Bible of that time as the basis of his work,* and at its divine fire both kindles and warms, enlightens and clarifies the fire of his own soul; and there also he moderates that fire and keeps it within due bounds, that it may become neither too dull and dim nor too all-consuming. The task he had to perform, therefore, was to behold, as in a fresh blaze of light from this fire, thus to be enkindled, how the seventy years of Yéremyá, which had at that time long formed not only a well-known and established, but also a sacred number, still suited these late times, without losing their

---

* It is noteworthy that just before, viii. 24, 25, so many Hebrew words are repeated from "Isa." liii. 13—lii.; 9-12, although the application of them as regards their meaning is quite free, so that one is compelled to suppose that the author had read the piece shortly before and been deeply impressed by it.

original truth. Moreover, if the endeavour thus to kindle a new light from the sacred number was successful, our author-prophet obtained thereby at the same time a new and very efficient means of still more plainly assigning to its proper chronological position that *time of the end* to which he had already given much prominence for discerning eyes. For the hints which are conveyed in the order of succession of the great empires and in the number of the separate rulers of the last one when properly limited, are significant for those who carefully meditate upon them; but they may be a far safer guide if at the same time hints are given in definite numbers with regard to the entire chronology, such as the apt diviner needs only calculate to avoid error as regards the years in which that time of the end must really fall.

As now the problem was to find how that recognized term of seventy years, as a closed sacred period, was, without breaking it up, to be extended in such a way that it could embrace the divinely-intended and foreseen *end-time,* there were primarily two things which met the inquiring eye of our prophet which could serve as the proper points of operation for a final solution. This presupposes, however, that a chronology of these centuries from the destruction of Jerusalem onwards, perfectly reliable in its general outlines, was known to our prophet. For though he no longer observed the number of the kings of the empires which had long since perished, of Chaldea, of Persia, as was shown above, according to the strict order of history, it was at the same time not necessary, according to the design and plan of the book, to attach any importance to this; and we saw, p. 248 sq., nevertheless that he very well knew and observed that number of the kings of the contemporary Syrian empire, because it appeared to him more important in consequence of the artistic plan of his book. However, the chronology of the people of Israel itself is quite another matter; as long as an actual kingdom existed for the natives, its chronology had been accurately kept up ;* if the people had at that time in the new Jerusalem no longer kings, there still remained a kind of kingdom in the institutions of the High Priests and religious festivals ; and the Sabbatical year itself, which was at that time kept up,† required a continuous and careful calculation of the years. Neither were the nation and kingdom at that time so completely fallen into disruption as at the time subsequent to the second destruction of Jerusalem, when Josephus made in Rome his unsuccessful attempts at restoring a chronology. But the main thing is, that inspection will soon convince us how well founded this supposition is.

Presupposing this therefore, it might strike our prophet with surprise, that precisely the beginning and the close of this series of years with which he was here concerned showed, each of them with peculiar extension, the recurrence of the number seven. As the beginning of the series of Yéremyá's seventy years he placed, acc. ver. 25, the year of the destruction of Jerusalem, that is, the first that could be reckoned after that event: from that point to the year when Kyros gave permission for rebuilding the temple, exactly forty-nine years elapsed: therefore a series of 7 × 7 years, or of seven Sabbatical years, they could also upon the basis of the week be called *seven year-weeks*. But at the close of his own period he also observed similarly just seven years had elapsed from the commencement of the reign of Antiochos Epiphanes to that year when this monarch began his open hostilities against the temple and religion of Israel.‡ At the top seven year-weeks of a mysterious space of time, and at the bottom one year-week of an equally dark period ; what is the number of the years between these two *termini ?* From 538 to 175 B.C. there are

---

* Comp. *History of Israel*, I., 204 sq. (I., 294 sq.).
† *Ibid.* V., 166 sq. (IV., 215 sq.).
‡ From 175 to 168 B.C., comp. *History of Israel*, V., 297 sq. (IV., 381-88).

364 years or 52 year-weeks; if ten year-weeks, or seventy years are added to them, the result is 7 + 52 + 10 + 1, total seventy year-weeks, or 490 years. If now the Sabbath-year is a year of release and peace, but the seventy years of Yéremyá years of the trying toil and hard straits of life, may it not be presumed that these seventy years are not to be taken in their common meaning, but in a higher, divine sense, so that they are to be extended in their primary higher or divine relation to seventy year-weeks (490 years), but that seventy years, like the years of the release and of divine mercy, must be subtracted from the midst of them, so that in the case of the number here involved, it is 364 instead of 434? The flash of this thought must have suddenly illuminated the mind of our prophet in his struggles after divine clearness and certainty in this darkness, so that he felt himself sent as a Gabriel from heaven to hold the light firmly which may be conveyed in this thought, and to cause it to shine further.

The thought which was enkindled in the prophet's mind therefore was, that if the effort is made to harmonize Yéremyá's words, or the letter of Sacred Scripture, with actual fact, a divine measure of time may be discovered by which the apparent contradiction can be removed; and in the various members of this thought, which combined from every side in the result of a higher or divine measure to be presupposed, he found the divine attestation of it. If a thousand years are with God as one day, acc. Ps. xc. 4, it follows, since Sabbaths and weeks are the divine measures of time, that one year of human suffering may be lengthened in the secret divine idea to seven, from a simple year may grow a series of seven years; but if again, of seven years, according to the same divine idea, one is necessarily set apart as a release or year of grace, then the sixty-two year-weeks which lie in the long and weary interim between the seven year-weeks at the beginning and the one at the end may also be shortened by seventy-years, as from divine compassion for his people, and the entire long period, consisting of three such different stages, from the destruction of the first temple to the restoration of a more worthy one, may be counted as 420 instead of 490 years. It is true this calculation is based upon a "leap" in the logical process, that is, an interpretation of an utterance of Sacred Scripture which originates in certain presuppositions accepted as sacred and necessary, while the interpretation is not otherwise capable of substantiation; this is what we may designate by a better known word, *allegory*, and of which we have here probably the earliest instance that can be historically traced, possessing such importance and artistic perfection. Neither is it at all difficult to perceive how this may be historically explained from the age of the author as above described, p. 157 sq.

While the prophet of those days was endeavouring thus to solve the divine enigma of the time, the development of affairs had already got somewhat beyond those seventy year-weeks, in that Antiochos Epiphanes had already begun the open war against the temple and everything else most sacred, and therewith something quite new as well as the worst thing possible, merely to think of which appeared most horrible. Accordingly our prophet looks into this most oppressive *end-time*, in conformity with the fundamental thought and image, as into *half-a-week*, ver. 27, of such divine measurement and duration, or as into a short excess of the long dark time. Thus there may well be intruded between two long periods of wholly different character a short period of transition and extreme tension; and all the darkness, which it was foretold would hang over the nation as a divine punishment in the long period of those seventy years of Yéremyá, appears to compress itself till it becomes the deepest darkness for a brief waiting period in this half week, before the Messianic morning can shine forth all the more victoriously and brightly. With that the explanation also of the one, the two, and the half, *i.e.*, the three-and-a-half *times*, *i.e.*, years, is supplied which were first announced ch. vii. and viii.; and if Nabukodrossor had to endure in this sense an entire divine work of extreme darkness, acc. iv. 13, 23, 29, is not this half a week to be endured?*

We may accordingly give the calculation which is at the basis of this piece, with the addition of the *excess* just elucidated, in the following tabular form :—

Year-weeks.	Years.	Since 588 B.C.
7	49	587 to 539
62	434	538 to 105 less 70 = 175
1	7	174 to 168
70	490	
Excess .. $\frac{1}{2}$	$3\frac{1}{2}$	167 sq.

And with this calculation not only was the certainty attending his glance into the past, present, and future made complete for our prophet, but it also gave him the best means of enabling all who desired to follow his solution of this difficult enigma of the present to cast, on the basis of Yéremyá's sacred words, direct glances into this grand connexion of all history with that of the new Jerusalem and its community. He therefore slackens here the haste with which his work is about to close; and before he produces for the third and last time the different figures of the great drama before the beholder's eye, just as he had himself first beheld them in sacred extasy, he here opens a glance into a brief side-piece, in which nothing but numbers of days and years occupy the allotted space. He narrates that that number of the prophecy of Yéremyá occasioned Daniel the greatest anxiety, that in the

---

* The above view of the words vv. 24-27, explained in such innumerable ways, rests ultimately, it must be admitted, on the recognition of the fact that a few words, or rather verses, are wanting in the present text after ver. 27 ; but I have long ago come to the conviction that without this supposition the whole passage is left without its proper light and the author without his due. In fact, that these words have been lost follows not only from the ascertained sense of the words and sentences of this particular and most difficult piece, but also from that of all the other pieces of the book. The places where I have discussed this with increasing definiteness are indicated in the *History of Israel*, V., 302 sq. (IV., 394), and in the XIIth *Jahrbuch der Bibl. Wiss.*. p. 54.

growing earnestness of wrestling prayer he begged for a divine solution concerning that dark enigma, until the same human-divine Angel, whose coming he had for the first time experienced in the previous piece, viii. 15-19, and then in extreme agitation, descends to him a second time, from the very first more calmly, in order to bring to him the divine solution, vv. 20-23.

1 In the first year of Dareios son of Ahashverosh of the Median stock, who was set as king over the dominions of the Chaldeans
2 —in the first year of his reign, I Daniel gave heed in the Scriptures to the number of the years as Yahvé's word came to the prophet Yéremyá, that seventy years must be fulfilled
3 unto Jerusalem's ruins. So I turned my face to the Lord God seeking prayer and supplications, with fasting and sackcloth and ashes; and prayed to Yahvé my God and confessed and said:

"O now Lord, thou great and dreadful God, | who keepeth
4 the covenant and the mercy unto those who love him and keep
5 his commandments! ‖ we have sinned and done wrong and acted wickedly and rebelled, have turned aside from thy command-
6 ments and thy judgments, | and have not hearkened to thy servants the prophets who spoke in thy name to our kings
7 princes and fathers and to all the people of the land. ‖ Thine O Lord is the righteousness: but to us is the shame of face at this time, | to the man of Yuda and to the inhabitants of Jerusalem and to all Israel, to those near and those far off in all the lands whither thou hast driven them on account of their
8 treachery wherewith they betrayed thee. ‖ O Lord, to us is the shame of face, to our kings princes and fathers, we who sinned
9 against thee; | of the Lord our God is the compassion and the
10 forgiveness, because we rebelled against thee and hearkened not unto the voice of Yahvé our God, that we should walk in his doctrines which he put before us by his servants the prophets.

But all Israel transgressed thy law and turned aside, not
11 hearkening to thy voice: | so thou pouredst upon us the curse and the oath which is written in the law of Mosch the
12 servant of God, because we sinned against him; ‖ so he confirmed his words which he spake concerning us and concerning our judges who judged us, that he would bring upon us a

great evil such as hath not come under the whole heaven as it
13 now happeneth to Jerusalem. ‖ As it is written in the law of
Moseh, that all this evil will come upon us: | and yet we
appeased not Yahvé our God, that we turned from our misdeeds and gave heed to his truth. ‖ So then Yahvé watched
over the evil and brought it upon us, | because righteous is
Yahvé our God in all his deeds which he did and we hearkened
not to his voice. ‖

15 "But now O Lord our God who leddest forth thy people
out of Egypt with a strong hand and madest thyself a name
16 still at this time: | we sinned we did wickedly. ‖ O Lord!
according to all thy righteousnesses make thy wrath and fury
cease from thy city Jerusalem thy holy mountain, | for through
our sins and the iniquities of our fathers Jerusalem and thy
17 people are for reproach to all our neighbours! ‖ And now
hearken thou our God to the prayer of thy servant and to his
supplications, and cause thy face to shine upon thy desolated
18 sanctuary for the Lord's sake! ‖ Incline my God thine ear and
hear, open then thine eyes and behold our horrible things and
those of the city upon which thy name is called! | For not
upon our righteousnesses do we base our intercession before thee,
19 but upon thy great compassion. | O Lord, O hear! O Lord,
O forgive! O Lord, hearken and do! | defer not! for thine
own sake my God! | because thy name is called upon thy city
and thy people!" ‖

20 And while I was yet speaking and praying and confessing
mine and my people Israel's sins, | and presenting my intercession before Yahvé my God for the holy mountain of my
21 God, ‖ yea while I yet spake praying—the man Gabriel whom
I had seen in the vision before drew near to me in full flight
22 at the time of the evening sacrifice, | then informed me and
spake with me and said ‖ "Daniel! just now I come forth to
23 make thee wise for understanding. ‖ Hardly had thy supplication begun when a word came forth: | and I am come to
announce it, because thou art a dearly-beloved one. ‖ So give
heed to the word, and pay heed to that which was beheld:

24 *Seventy weeks* have been fixed concerning thy people and thy
holy city till the sacrilege is finished and the sins brought to
their height, till the iniquity is atoned for and eternal righteousness is brought, | till prophecy and prophet are sealed and

18 *

25 a most holy thing will be anointed. ‖ —And thou must know
and understand: from the time when a word was sent forth,
that Jerusalem should be restored and built unto an anointed
a high-prince are *seven weeks;* | and *sixty and two weeks* it
will be built again with street and trench,—but in the strait-
26 ness of the times. ‖ —And after the sixty and two weeks will
an anointed one be cut off and have no one, | and the city and
the sanctuary the people of a high-prince will destroy who
cometh with his army in a flood: | —but until the end of the
27 war is the decision concerning the horrible things. | And he
will conclude a covenant with many for *one week:* | but for *the
half a week* he will abolish the sacrifice and offering, and above
will be the horrible wing of abominations: | —yet until the
final punishment and decision will be poured out upon the
horrible one. ‖

According to vv. 1, 2 this vision of Daniel belongs to the commencement of the Median rule over Babel, after the Chaldean empire had just been destroyed: and a period of this kind, when, though the immediate cause of the desolation of Jerusalem and the temple had been removed, Kyros's command to rebuild it had still not been issued, demanded with quite a new motive the serious consideration of the question when and how Jerusalem should be restored and all the other Messianic hopes connected with this restoration could be fulfilled.—But if it is asked what particular passage in the Book of Yéremyá, which was then already reckoned among *the Books, i.e.*, *the Bible*, is here and accordingly ver. 25 also meant, care must be taken not to suppose that because the desolation of the land is spoken of Jer. xxv. 9, 11, 18 in connexion with the seventy years, therefore the fourth year of the reign of Yoyaqim must be reckoned, acc. Jer. xxv. 1, as the commencement of this desolation. The desolation of Jerusalem did not begin with that year: yet it is this desolation only which can properly form the beginning of the seventy years; and how certainly this had been the prevailing view from the very first can be most plainly perceived in the fact that the contemporaries of Zakharya, acc. p. 35, supposed that they only then witnessed the termination of the seventy years. It is true the Chronicler (2, xxxvi. 21-23) supposes this termination took place as early as the first year of Kyros: yet this is said by him only in a very general way, without any strict calculation of the chronology. But our prophet makes expressly, ver. 25, the first year of the actual desolation the commencement of the seventy years, because in this respect he takes as his basis more definitely the words Jer. xxx. 18, where the rebuilding of the city is promised. Although therefore the place of the promise of the seventy years in the Book of Yéremyá is between ch. xxv. and ch. xxix., our author, basing his view upon the words xxx. 18, nevertheless properly supposes that their commencement must be dated from the actual desolation of Jerusalem: only on this supposition can we plainly understand what he says subsequently, ver. 25.

The description of the way in which Daniel (so to speak) made all possible preparation to kindle the greatest fervour of prayer and confession and supplication, ver. 3, is remarkable: the only thing which is certain to him is that he must now pray with most intense earnestness; and he makes all the various and long preparations by *fasting*, by putting on *mourning garments* and by sitting in *ashes*, he disciplines himself first for the occasion and endeavours to *seek* the right prayer with heart and eye directed to God, until at the right moment the full stream of prayer pours from him with all possible power and fervour. The motive, however, which drove him to pray is scarcely indicated in the introductory narrative, vv. 1, 2, and must be supplied from the nature of the case itself. He had long been most profoundly troubled at the long duration of the times of the misery of his people, found and considered thus more particularly in the Bible those passages of Yéremyá's, felt then his trouble increased on account of the difficulty of understanding the divine meaning of the number, but perceived at once that if the divine period of punishment for Israel is so much prolonged, and this whole enigma is for himself and the entire nation so difficult to penetrate, the immediate cause of it can after all be simply the consequences of the grievous ancient errors and sins of the whole nation, and sought and found finally in this confluence of the most varied emotions the right word to utter before God. It is not to be able to solve this mere numerical enigma that he prays to him; of that there is no mention throughout the long prayer, and what is after all a mere number before God? It is really only on account of quite other grievous errors, obscurities and transgressions, as well as misconceptions and obliquities, that this enigma oppresses the heart of this individual praying for explanation as well as the heart of the whole nation; and only after this individual has wrestled with all the energies of his soul before God for the forgiveness of those general sins, can he hope that the immediate darkness under which he feels himself weighed down and tormented will also be perhaps cleared away by a gracious ray of light from the primal source of all light. Thus then the rolling stream of this prayer of profound emotion is poured forth from the midst of the fundamental feeling, that only when the deepest impulse of a new divine purification, pardon, and encouragement comes upon the whole nation can divine help arise for the "ruins of Jerusalem" also, for which Daniel really in the end prays in this special case also; and his word passes thus from the oppressive darkness of the present, as well as from the more extensive review of all the earlier history which is here concerned, in the first instance to true confession and then to true assurance and petition. It becomes on the basis of the present the most sincere confession, vv. 4-10, but then, vv. 11-14, still more so from the wider review of all earlier history, which is the more appropriate here, as the primary cause of this great and grievous destruction and ruin dates back into the earlier times; but then from stage to stage, vv. 15-19, believing petition and prayer for mercy grows more and more fervent, in the name of the whole nation, vv. 15, 16, and finally in the name of this praying man, vv. 17, 18, until, as in last broken moans, and in the final fervour of passionate desire, it exhausts itself and ceases, ver. 19.

It is true that the power and the

fervour of prayer were very great from the days of the destruction of Jerusalem, now long since past, and of the wide dispersion of the people, which is here, ver. 17, so appropriately referred to, as has been shown in *History of Israel*, V., 23 sq. (IV., 32, sq.). And who can help seeing that this long prayer, as it is finished in its three strophes of equal length, is all alive and aglow with a pure fire of genuine repentance, humbly assured faith, and most intense petition! Still, as the art, the external framework of the narrative and form of presentation adopted in this book implies, it cannot in this case either be doubted that the long prayer, both as regards its various phrases and thoughts and also its whole arrangement, follows earlier models. The invocation at the beginning, ver. 4, is from Neh. i. 5 ; ix. 32 ; the expression *our kings, princes, and fathers, and the whole people of the land*, ver. 6, from Neh. ix. 32, and as here, ver. 8, when it is repeated, the *people* is left out for the sake of brevity, so also there, ver. 34, only the contrast between the former time, with its kings, princes, and fathers, *i.e.*, elders, particularly also famous teachers,* and the present is plainer there than here ; and inasmuch as in Nehemya the priests and prophets are also named between the kings and princes on the one side and the fathers on the other, in order to put all the more distinguished persons together, and then the common people is added to them, the words bear the mark of the greater originality and completeness ; but from the fact that our author had just before mentioned the prophets in quite a different sense, it is easy to understand why he left them out with the priests in this connexion. The most remarkable thing, however, is how our author simply takes up substantially the words of the great confession of the Book of Barûkh, from i. 14 to ii. 19, precisely from the words ver. 6 which the prophet of the Book of Barûkh, i. 16, quoted from the Book of Nehemya: for that the words of the Book of Barûkh are more original than these before us has been already stated, *ante* p. 111, and will be proved in detail below, p. 321 sq. We can here only point out how appropriately our author casts that much more lengthy prayer into a shorter form, such as is all that is required here. But as this whole prayer took its origin from the desolation and ruins of the holy city and temple, so at the end, vv. 16-19, it is conducted back to the same subject with increasing emphasis ; the priest's blessing, *cause thy face to shine upon* . . . is also applied ver. 17, from Num. vi. 25, to the temple ; but in that there is further inserted with urgency, in the closing words ver. 19, the cry *O Lord, delay not!* from Ps. xl. 18 ; lxx. 6, at least one word becomes thereby audible which may call to mind the long delay of the fulfilment of the words of Yéremyá as regards the seventy weeks.

Just in proportion to the simplicity and truth, the depth and fervour with which this prayer for such a cause has been poured forth, does the Angel hasten, borne on celestial wings, to Daniel's side, bringing to him both for his hot desire the cool refreshment of the con-

---

* As the *fathers* signify more and more frequently in the times of the second temple, comp. my notes on Matt. v. 21, and the Talmudic *M. Abôth*. The word must originally mean this at least in the Book of Nehemya and Bar. i. 16. It is different when *the fathers*, standing alone in the sense of *forefathers* generally, are placed on an equality with those who are living at the time, as Bar. ii. 6.

soling assurance of the divine smile, vv. 20-23, and for his wrestling longing to penetrate the divine enigma of the time, the true solution, vv. 24-27. This refreshing answer to his prayer comes, acc. ver. 21, just at *the time of the evening sacrifice*, which had then long been considered as an hour most acceptable as it were to heaven,* while here it is for a special reason the only suitable one. For everything which happens here, ch ix., occurs in contrast with the experiences of the two previous pieces, not in a dream, but in the perfect wakefulness of life; and for this condition only has prayer its proper meaning. Still, on the other hand, inasmuch as the hearing of the prayer with the divine revelation falls in the twilight of the sinking day, there descends of itself upon the prophet, resting as exhausted from the fervour of his prayer, that higher repose and dreamful quiet which permits him the more easily in such a twilight between day and night to perceive the gentle approach and peace-bringing voice of Gabriel. How gracious are the very first words with which Gabriel arrives: *he was just going forth to teach him to understand* that which he desired, this is his first rapid word, ver. 22. But he then, ver. 23, adds in explanation, that even *at the beginning of his supplication,* i.e., from the words ver. 15 onwards, *a word* had gone forth, *or been uttered:* and what other kind of word can that be than a gracious one, and whence can it have gone forth but from the throne of God himself? *and he is come* at once *to announce* this word *to him,* because he is *a favourite,* a favourite above all to God himself, as this Angel is in a position to know. Let him therefore *give heed to this word, and pay heed to the vision,* i.e., the things which will be heard as in a dream-vision, as is said at last, ver. 23, with a pointed paronomasia, and in connexion with which it is carefully to be observed that the entire discourse at last draws to an emphatic point with the word *vision,* which cannot have any other meaning here than it has in the corresponding instances viii. 16, 27; x. 1, 7, 8, 16.

The subject-matter of the *vision* falls of itself, as soon as a detailed explanation of it is commenced, into three parts:

(1) For to touch in the first place only in general upon the chief matter, it is said at the very commencement with great emphasis, ver. 24, *seventy weeks have been determined concerning nation and city,* that is, not simple years as ver. 2 but seventy sevens, in which connexion years are as a matter of course supplied by the reader, since acc. ver. 2 it is the number of *years* only that is inquired about. And as their end three things are named, suiting perfectly the years 168-7 B.C.: (1) *until the crime be completed and the sins be brought to a head:* and such great crimes are always according to the view of this book the abominations which Antiochos Epiphanes and his adherents were guilty of, particularly in the temple, comp. ver. 27; viii. 12, 13, 23, and which had as a fact then been carried so far that nothing worse seemed possible. But that excess of heathen abominations is followed all the more necessarily by the speedy deliverance on the other side, therefore (2) *till the guilt* (of Israel) *is atoned for and eternal righteousness is brought* (by the Messianic kingdom), two cor-

---

* According to the observations of *History of Israel,* V., 23 (IV., 32), and VI., 166 (untranslated vol.).

relative ideas; and (3) the further consequence thereof, with which this sketch recurs to its commencement, *till prophecy and prophet* (e.g., in the first instance that very word of Yéremyá's about the seventy years) *is sealed* (confirmed by the result) *and a most holy thing* (which is still holier than the above-named holy city and the temple, named at the same time, ver. 26, that is, acc. 1 Macc. i. 54 the demolished altar (Ex. xxix. 37) *is anointed*, for temple and altar, as is said ver. 27 and often in this book subsequently, had been grievously polluted by Antiochos Epiphanes, and therefore needed anointing, or dedicating afresh.—But in order

(2) to go into details and thereby to show more particularly how surprisingly this number accords with the actual facts, a period of 7 × 7 years is first separated, ver. 25, as a space of time which elapses from the revelation of that word of Yéremyá's, that Jerusalem shall be rebuilt, until *an anointed a high-prince*; this person is not further designated, but from the double name of *anointed high-prince* alone, it can be inferred that he cannot be an ordinary king; for other kings, heathen and less powerful, are likewise called, ver. 26, either *anointed* or *high-prince* simply; on the other hand it is known from "Isa." xlv. 1, that Kyros is at the same time an *anointed* one in a much higher sense. But inasmuch as the rebuilding of Jerusalem has just been mentioned, as the subject of this oracle, we are still more plainly led to the conclusion that no one else but Kyros can be here intended, the famous prince under whom Jerusalem was rebuilt in such a way that Yéremyá's prophecy seemed to receive fulfilment in him, as is also really said 2 Chron. *ad fin.*—However, our author, departing therefrom in his detailed chronology, makes a further distinction in the larger period which he had adopted of 7 × 62 *years* in which Jerusalem was restored, it is true, but under such *straitness of the times* that the great Messianic restoration which Yéremyá intended cannot be supposed to be meant.

How little this restoration of Jerusalem can be regarded as the complete and satisfactory one, is still further specially indicated by the brief and significant additional clause, that it *will be only rebuilt with market and trench:* these two things are so indispensable that according to ancient ideas a city is inconceivable without them; still, what are they if they are all that is to be found in Jerusalem? Thus it is here that for the first time the thought finds utterance, that the existing temple in Jerusalem is of no account whatever, a feeling which gradually found more frequent expression, comp. *History of Israel* V., 432 (IV., 564); and as a fact in the view of our prophet it is only the Messianic temple which will be the true one.—But as vii. 7, 8, 24; viii. 8, 9, that period and that new heathen king in which and whom centres the most burning question of the book can only follow after the long period of the numerous heathen kings, there is here also

(3) quite a similar distinction made of what takes place after these sixty-two year-weeks with the shortening of them described above p. 272 sq., and this alone is touched upon vv. 26, 27. Afterwards, it is said ver. 26, *an anointed one will be cut off or slain and have no one,* have no direct successor or heir, namely Seleukos IV., Philopator, who was put to death in the year 176 B.C. by Heliodoros, while there was no son or relation about him who was his heir according to his desire. It is in no way indicated here that Antiochos Epiphanes put him to death: this also confirms the statements above made, p. 248. But it is

with this horrible event of a royal murder at the beginning of the terrible time that what immediately follows accurately accords: *and the city and the sanctuary will the people of a high-prince destroy who cometh,* the people of Antiochos Ephipanes, that is, who is not present at the time of the death of the prince referred to, but has first to come from Rome; and the manner of his coming is characterized in the few words, that he will *come overflooding with his army* the land, as the Assyrians Isa. viii. 8. But as soon as the discourse touches upon the man and his projects, it is at once irresistibly agitated as by the profoundest displeasure and wrath, so that, as if thrown back upon inward feeling and simply looking onward to the final issue of such crimes, without another word it at once adds, *until the end of the war,* which he will wage acc. vii. 21 with the saints, *is the decision concerning the horrible things,* the divine decision as it is due at the universal judgment, vii. 11, 12, for such horrible deeds and destructions. This sudden conclusion is likewise an oracle of Yesaya's concerning Sanherib, well-known to every one, and forming a brief, forcible paronomasia, Isa. x. 22, 23; xxviii. 22. Thus that *end* first indicated viii. 17, 19, 23 as so significant, is twice characterized with increasing definiteness.

But thus this time of the end has been spoken of almost too soon; and moreover, the seventieth year-week has in fact not been yet mentioned at all. In order, therefore, to complete the sketch of Antiochos Epiphanes, which has been given above only in general outline, and to complete also the chronology, the discourse commences once more, ver. 27: *And a covenant will he conclude for a week with* many, or rather, with *the most,* in the first seven years of his reign, acc. 1 Macc. i. 10, 20, first procure by the gentle means of seductive arts of all kinds the friendship of the majority of the influential and more powerful members of the nation, with regard to which there is much complaint elsewhere in this book as the commencement of all the most recent misery and one of the immediate causes of apostasy. But, it is said further, *the half week will he abolish sacrifice and offering,* completely abolish the temple-services: if, however, he lives the whole of the last week on the best terms with the majority, it follows of itself that this half week extends beyond that term; and simply because it had been mentioned above vii. 12, 25; viii. 14, 26, in another way, is it here at once designated briefly *the* half week. Only it is not enough that he simply abolishes the offerings appointed by the law, he also puts the abomination of the heathen sacrifices in their place, as this twofold sacrilege had been referred to above viii. 11, 12, and is again referred to subsequently xii. 11: *and above will be,* over the demolished true altar will project, *the horrible wing of abominations,* the head of the heathen altar placed thereon being here compared with a wing on account of its form no doubt, comp. *History of Israel* V., 299 (IV., 389). Still, the end is not doubtful, as has already been said, ver. 26, so that it is only briefly added in rapid discourse, but now with plainest allusion to the ancient words of Yesaya, that this after all will only last *until* the *end-punishment and decision shall be poured upon the horrible one* (Antiochos Epiphanes) with that deluge of divine righteousness already mentioned ver. 26.

With the last two great sentences, vv. 26, 27, the Antichrist has been afresh designated still more plainly than before: and as at the end of the previous piece viii. 23-25, the thoughts contained in this description had divided themselves for our prophet into two great sentences each of which closes with the echo of a member of the same consolatory meaning, so here also the last words of ver. 26 recur with a slight variation at the end of ver. 27. But it is impossible to avoid seeing that by the similar pulsation of the members vv. 25-27 the light of the movement of the whole increases, and thereby also sufficient light is thrown upon the dim course of the discourse.

It will appear more clear below, xi. 1, that a few lines have been lost after ver. 27, which contained especially the reduction of the number 490 to 420.

This fact may also be perceived from quite a different indication. For as the author always adds a suitable closing word to the other pieces of this part, vii. 28 ; viii. 27; xii. 8; indeed to those of the previous parts also, i. 21 ; ii. 46 sq.; iii. 34 ; iv. 34 ; v. 39 sq. ; vi. 29, a natural close, or a most appropriate recurrence to the commencement, being thus obtained, we naturally expect the same here after ver. 27. Further, it is true the plan of this piece is in so far different as it closes with only a short prophecy which is calculated to occupy one of the usual strophes : but for one strophe also the words are too brief.

Final explanations and final promises.

Ch. x.—xii.

After in the previous piece, however, the proper glance into the true present and future of the first readers of the book has thus been opened, as in a parenthetical piece, upon the basis of the simple number of the years of the great revolutions of general history, this same glance is for the third and last time directed back to the men themselves, whose fortunes in those times and whose connexion with their predecessors is after all the main matter with which the book is concerned. As early as the second piece of this series, ch. viii., he who can be regarded as the Antichrist and his first and subsequent deeds are characterized with much greater particularity than in the first piece, ch. vii. : but in this third piece, which corresponds to the two first, ch. vii. and, ch. viii., all the circumstances and situations, the deeds and the sufferings of the men not only of the real present but also of the real past, which is in closer contact with it, shall be brought forward as they present themselves to Daniel's seer's position and seer's eyes, in order that it may be more plainly perceived what is the nature of the actual future which must follow, according to divine determination, these times and particularly this time of the end, which has already been referred to as so incomparably important, ch. vii.—ix. For this purpose the framework of all the sketches is, on the one hand, still more contracted than in the previous piece, ch. viii.: if in that piece it was at the commencement so far limited that only the last two empires and their struggles were spoken of, here though the Persian kingdom forms the commencement, xi. 2, it is only in order to pass from it in rapid transition to the Greek empire and its forms, xi. 3, and then here also to linger, quite at the end xi. 21-45, all the longer over the portrait of Antiochos Epiphanes. On the other hand, in these so greatly restricted limits the various pictures of the men and the events are sketched with all the more numerous and finer lines, so that we have before us the most eloquent and distinct pictures that the plan and art of the book in any way admit of. The main thing in this delineation is that the general comparisons of the empires of the world and their representatives with animals, which had filled ch. vii. and recurred less prominently ch. viii., are not again made: these empires and their representatives present themselves at last in so far without any disguise, and the sketches of them are purely human, because they cannot be made too plain at this point. We thus get substantially a history of the Persian, or rather, after a few words concerning this kingdom, of the Greek and Seleukid kingdom, down to that moment of the reign and life of Antiochos Epiphanes, which for the author and the first readers of the book fell within their most recent experience; and the historical delineation is even from the last times of the father of this ruler so accurate that for many particulars it may serve as really a historical source. But as the whole sketch must be considered as spoken from the lips of an Angel, in the form in which it is heard by Daniel in a *spectaculum*, or a *vision*, of this Angel, the outward form of prophecy and all that this requires is accordingly retained, the historical narrative becomes, xi. 2-45, a description of the unfolding of future things as viewed from Daniel's time, and the peculiarities of treatment conform to this position of the seer. Amongst these peculiarities is this one, that the men and countries really intended are brought forward in the course of the description with the clearest indications possible, so that any one who will reflect a little cannot remain in doubt as to the persons and countries actually meant, while, on the other hand, the names at all events of the individual rulers and men are here also avoided, particularly as that of the contemporary tyrant Antiochos Epiphanes could not be mentioned on any account. As a matter of course, too, though the author was compelled to bring forward in the plainest possible lines and groups what he desired thus to present as in reversed historic pictures, so that no instructed reader could experience much difficulty in stripping off the last disguise from these enigmas, yet when that was done he need receive only as much of contemporary history into his book as appeared sufficient for his purpose. But this reversed historic narrative is most appropriately interlarded everywhere at suitable points with little words and hints which point as with an air of mystery to the great actual future of the time of the author and of the first readers,* inasmuch as to point to this future and give consolation is the ultimate object of the book itself.

As this piece supplies therewith the last explanations with regard to the times and situations and men intended by the whole book, as far as it could and would supply them, it embraces also the last hints with regard to the certainty and the glory of the actual future of the first readers. It was not intended, as was said above, to sketch a new complete picture of the Messianic age and its formation: but the artistic plan of the whole book permitted at this point a twofold addition with

---

* See the little clauses xi. 24, 27, 35, 36, 45, always at the end of the verses and in accord with the same mysterious final utterance vii. 12; viii. 17, 19, 26; ix. 26, 27; x. 14 a like instance at the beginning only xi. 40.

regard to it. First, the divine certainty of such a deliverance from the present straits and of the hoped-for Messianic future could not, according to the purpose of the whole book, be too emphatically brought forward: accordingly there follows here, as if intentionally (comp. the words at the beginning of x. 1), the last thing that after the words found here and there in the previous three pieces ch. vii.—ix., could be surely promised in human words and images, as regards that certainty, and in addition an inserted piece quite at the end, xii. 5-7, is devoted solely to this special purpose. Second, the incomparable glory of the Messianic times and the divine reward then possible of proved faithfulness in the extremest trials is sketched and assured towards the end in some new and most sublime images, xii. 1-3; and inasmuch as towards the end the preservation of faithfulness in the hottest fire of trial is pointed to in brief but most forcible words, xi. 35; xii. 10, this conclusion dealing with the pure future for the first time throws back the due light upon the corresponding narratives of the second part of the book, ch. iii.—vi. And as in general this piece is so planned that it shall close the entire matter of the whole book, all that has yet to be said concerning Daniel in reference to the book and its relation to the actual present of the author is plainly observed at the very end xii. 4, 8, 9, 13.

But a chief matter in this most characteristic piece, which is intended thereby to become the true closing-piece primarily of the whole book but also of its third main part, remains after all this, that its aim is to disclose from the point of view of Daniel's time and locality the secrets of the divine rule over all historical, *i.e.*, human, affairs with much greater particularity than this had been done in the two earlier pieces corresponding to it, ch. vii., viii. In human affairs nothing can take place without God; and even that which is to ordinary human experience and ideas the most surprising and wonderful (comp. xi. 36; xii. 6) has its divine possibility and truth preceding every part of it, is therefore, in accordance with its higher necessity, as it were noted in celestial books and recorded in divine handwriting before it takes place. This view, expressed incidentally as early as Ps. cxxxix. 16, had long been current at the time of our author; and is thus briefly indicated by him x. 21. Accordingly it is only Angels who stand nearest to those celestial mysteries that can disclose them to the true prophet: this is the view which underlies and controls the plan of the whole of this last chief part of the book, the corollaries of which appear nowhere so prominently as in this closing piece. For just as these secrets of the future themselves come forth only by degrees in the successive pieces of this last chief part and more and more plainly for human eyes and ears, so Daniel receives them in the first two pieces, ch. vii., viii., in a dream; but in the very next piece, ch. ix., the dream is changed for the half-dreaming condition, alternating between the darkening day and night; and in this piece, where everything shall be shown in greatest clearness, it is only the full day which is appropriate. But what is an angelic appearance, and, in addition thereto, this time such an elaborate revelation of divine secrets, in full daylight? It is only for dreams and dreamlike states of the mind of man that appearances and revelations of angels are primarily fitted (Job iv. 12—v. 1). Nevertheless, true as that is in general, both in the case of Daniel and also in that of the Angel, everything must here reach its highest climax. If in the first piece, vii. 16, it is only timidly in a dream that he approaches one of the thousands of Angels which stood nearest to him as by accident, and the Angel at his request acted as interpreter to him, in the second piece, towards the end viii. 13, 14, it is two Angels that he hears discoursing upon the things he has seen and adding to them, and quite at the end, viii. 15 sq., he hears an Angel, who had of his own accord as it were come to his assistance, giving the commission as from God to Gabriel, *i.e.*, to the kindly human prophet-angel, to instruct him more particularly with regard to the vision; but the closer an Angel comes to a man, the more must he tremble lest he should be unable to bear his near presence without being annihilated; even in a dream Daniel felt this in the former instance, yet he learnt to bear this near presence and communication and illumination. So he then, ch. ix., experienced the Angel's illuminating approach and words with more calmness after a true prayer in a half-dreaming state: but this time when this same Gabriel* appears to him for the third time, and now in full daylight, it is true the prophet is necessarily at first the more agitated by the most violent emotions, inasmuch as he had just been overwhelmed with long and dreary sorrow and humiliation, although this trouble had unmistakably arisen simply from the further consideration of the saddening meaning of the long and grievous sufferings of the holy city foretold in the three previous pieces, and the profound longing to penetrate still further into those secrets. But as Daniel now overcomes in the right way this extreme agitation and trembling at the approach of this Angel at such a moment, so he soon sees himself more and more clearly in broad daylight surrounded by the Angel-world, and receives from their lips words and hints as he had never done before. It is only that divine word which a man receives in broad daylight also which is the calmest, clearest, and in all respects most satisfactory that can be communicated to him.

In that now finally the knowledge of the things of the future which Daniel gains as the result of the toils and struggles of this final acquaintance with Angel-wisdom, shall, as the plan of the book requires, be described with this acquaintance itself, this closing-piece also becomes, in accordance with its most varied subject-matter, the longest and most weighty of all, and forms the most direct opposite particularly to the first piece, ch. i. Nevertheless, the very great variety of the matter it has to handle leads all the more necessarily to the division of it into a corresponding number of strophes; and

---

* It is the greatest mistake not to see that he is meant here, ch. x.—xii., also.

thus there are exactly ten strophes required to complete it, and these are so arranged that precisely the first three x. 1—xi. 2 *a* are devoted to the narrative introduction of the manner in which the final divine oracle came, while the oracle itself takes up seven strophes, the tenth pointing back at the same time to the beginning.

x.   1.

1   In the third year of the Persian king Kyros a word was revealed to Daniel surnamed Bêlteshassar, | with the truth of
2   the word and a great ministry. ‖ Therefore understand the word, as there is understanding of it in the vision! |
3   In those days I Daniel was sorrowful three weeks long : | sweet bread I ate not, and flesh and wine came not into my

1. When it is said, ver. 1, that this last thing which is to be narrated in the Book of Daniel happened in the third year of Kyros, *i.e.*, in the time when the Persian rule, in the strict sense of the word, was in existence, that accords with the subject-matter of the prophecy which, acc. p. 283 is intended to pass rapidly from the Persian to the Greek rule. But that at this time, acc. ix. 25, the first foundations of the new Jerusalem were laid, can the less suffice to make Daniel glad, as he considers, acc. p. 280, this entire rebuilding as incomplete. On the contrary, it was precisely this time which could incline him, in conjunction with other experiences, to that special profoundest sorrow and most serious self-humiliation which form the source, acc. vv. 2, 3, whence proceeds his elevation to the position of the divine seer of another future for Jerusalem.—It may be presupposed from vii. 1, that Daniel immediately committed to writing his experience and vision. There is the more reason why two things should be briefly referred to in this heading, ver. 1 : first, that the revelation which here follows makes its appearance accompanied especially also by its own *truth*; for although the truth of the revelation was formerly urged incidentally by angelic lips, viii. 26, it is nowhere else so frequently and solemnly asseverated as here three times, x. 21 ; xi. 2, and particularly at the close, xii. 7 ; and the fact that this revelation is thus three times given with the faithfulness of angelic lips, distinguishes it no less than that, secondly, it appears *with a great ministry*, in that here a number of Angels, as never before, are engaged in its ministration as servants of God, and with so much industry and care. But on that very account the author is quite unable to conclude this heading, ver. 1, without adding those words to the reader which he could just as well have placed at the opening of his book : *Therefore understand the word*, understand properly this symbolic and enigmatic word, *since there is understanding of it in the vision* which now follows ; since if there is only a desire to understand it, it is particularly here sufficiently intelligible. And how could the author point out everything that he really desired to show more plainly than he has done in this piece,

mouth, neither did I anoint myself | till three full weeks
4 were fulfilled. | But on the four and twentieth day of the
first month, whilst I was by the bank of the great river namely
5 of the Tigris, | then I lifted up mine eyes and saw and
lo! a man clothed with linen, his loins girded with gold of
6 Ophir, | his body like goldstone and his face like the appearance of lightning and his eyes like torches of fire, | his arms
and feet like a glance of shining brass, and the sound of his
7 words like the sound of a roaring. || And I Daniel alone saw

for readers who did not understand the previous pieces of prophecy, *e.g.*, ch. vii.—ix. ? Thus full of meaning is the great fresco-writing in this heading also of that piece which is the most important of all as regards the general design of the book.

The reason why Daniel, acc. vv. 2, 3, mourned more deeply than ever before can be inferred in general from vii. 28; viii. 27, and the whole meaning of the last two pieces, ch. viii., ix.: for a man like him it is verily painful enough to know that so many and such long calamities await his own people; but, moreover, acc. i. 21, he was no longer occupied and his attention diverted by the duties of a royal office, as was still the case viii. 27. If thus this state of mind and this time led him the more to incessant sorrow, they also still more urged him as a prophet to seek from God further explanation, and if possible comfort regarding such a future, as is also incidentally and as it were supplementarily mentioned x. 12. Accordingly he resorts to the same fasting to which he had resorted formerly before the last great experience of his life, ch. ix. 3, only that this time it is much more protracted and rigid; three whole weeks we see him here fasting, commencing with the third day of the first month, as the new moon might not, according to ancient custom, be a fast day, and its joy was readily extended to two days (acc. *Antiquities*, p. 461 sq.; 469 sq. (386 sq., 395)). But he cannot this time arouse himself from this profound mourning to fervent prayer, as he had done before, ch. ix.; and nevertheless he beholds himself, vv. 4, 5, on the twenty-fourth day of the month, as he was by the *Tigris*, suddenly wrapped in the blaze of a wonderful celestial light, as if a new revelation were about to come upon him before he anticipates or hopes for it. And the locality of the free wide stream of water is at all events in a heathen land the most suitable for this purpose, in this case not for the same reason as prevailed viii. 2 sq., but because, according to the custom of that time (*Geschichte des Volkes Israel*, VI., p. 407), such a spot was considered most suitable, for want of a better, for prayer and other sacred ceremonies.

This sudden appearance of light presents itself to his eyes, vv. 5, 6, immediately as a shining exalted Angel, as he appears before men in his kindly regard for them looking simply like a priest clad in white linen; yet still the brightness of his appearing and the sound of his voice, as both are described here in detail particularly after Ezek. ix. 2 sq.; i. 16, 13, 7, 27, 24, are so powerful that he does not at all perceive in this bright daylight that it is really the same Gabriel who had come so near to him twice before; so the spectacle, while the men which were with me saw not the spectacle : | on the contrary a great terror fell upon them, and they fled to hide themselves, ‖ and I remained behind alone.

2.

8 So I saw this great spectacle : ‖ yet no strength remained in me, my brightness changed unto me sadly into confusion and I
9 retained no strength. ‖ Then I heard the sound of his words : |
10 and as I heard the sound of his words, I was stunned in my face and my face came to the ground. ‖ Then behold a hand touched me and shook me upon my knees and the palms of my
11 hands, ‖ and he said to me " Daniel! thou dearly-beloved man! attend unto the words which I will speak to thee and place thyself upon thy place, | for I am just now sent to

great is the difference between the bright day and the night or the twilight. But in this case the first stage of further knowledge is for him precisely this, that he is not nevertheless at once terrified by the mere power of this brightness and this voice, as his attendants are who flee hiding themselves for overpowering terror, as if they were from the very first unable to have a really personal acquaintance with anything high and divine ; just as the same thing happened in Paul's history, *Geschichte des Volkes Israel,* VI., p. 376.

2. But though he stands thus alone confronting this bright appearance with its mighty voice, and can now the more calmly fix his gaze upon the former and listen to the latter, both primarily only make the more overpowering impression upon him, so that now, blinded for the first time by this light, and as if stunned by this voice coming upon him, he sinks quite to the ground, unable to keep his feet and to hold up his head, vv. 8, 9. Still, that is only the pardonable feeling of human weakness: so he feels himself in the next moment nevertheless touched by a hand not less powerful than kind, though his whole being is so shaken as by reproach that he already raises himself again upon his knees and hands, without venturing yet to lift up his face, ver. 10. In the next moment, ver. 11, he is already conscious of being addressed in the same extremely affectionate words which Gabriel had addressed to him in the previous revelation ix. 23, and which he subsequently addresses to him a third time, ver. 19, and of being encouraged to stand and hear the revelations which he is commissioned to communicate to him ; and he might now well understand that it is none other than Gabriel whom he sees before him, nevertheless it is only with trembling that he rises to his feet. So Gabriel admonishes him to dismiss all fear, inasmuch as he communicates to him as to an intimate friend an immediate glance into celestial things, vv. 12-14 : as early as *from the first day of his profound longing to understand* further the enigmas *and of his self-humiliation* in fasting, he has

thee!" | But whilst he spake with me this word, I stood
12 trembling; || and he said to me: "Fear not Daniel! for
from the first day when thou settest thy mind to understand
and to humiliate thyself before thy God, thy words were
13 heard, | and I came with thy words. || But the prince of the
Persian kingdom withstood me continually and for twenty
days : | then behold Mikhaél one of the first princes came to
help me, and I became there superfluous with the kings of
14 Persia; || so I came to instruct thee as to what will befall thy
people at the end of the days ; | for yet the vision is for the
times ! ||

3.

15 But whilst he spake with me such words, I turned my face
16 to the ground and became dumb. || Then behold one looking
like a man touched my lips : | so I opened my mouth and
spake and said to him standing before me : "My Lord, through

desired to communicate to him that same revelation concerning the things of the future, as he had been commissioned to do by God (so readily does Daniel therefore, and everyone like him, even when it does not seem to be so, find divine hearing, as was previously insisted upon ix. 23), and has been simply prevented for those three weeks from so doing by being compelled, as specially favourable to Daniel and through him to the people of Israel, to contend against the Persian kings and the Angel who defends their empire ; but inasmuch as just now *one of the first princes*, i.e., Archangels (one of the seven Archangels, comp. pp. 57, 176), as the special Guardian Angel of Israel, a much more powerful celestial prince, has come to relieve him in this severe conflict, he has for the moment *become superfluous there*, and accordingly has just come to communicate to him the revelation. Accordingly there are after all really celestial powers, who, exalted far above individual men, correspond to the high terrestrial powers or governments, the individual man may be convinced that he is represented or defended by them in the celestial council, and at all times, as he is a member of such a terrestrial government ; and also the people generally answering to such a government may have the same conviction ; there is a purely spiritual celestial history corresponding to the terrestrial human history, and behind all visible things stands an invisible higher necessity and concatenation of all human affairs. How consolatory is it to know that! But Daniel can at the same time foresee from that what long sufferings will await his people under the Persian rule which has only just commenced.

3. Since however Daniel notwithstanding all this does not yet venture to raise his face without restraint to Gabriel, the Angel having now become quite as a man, like all other men, graciously *touches his mouth,* in order to take from him, as in the case of Yesaya vi. 7, the last scruples hindering free conversation upon divine things ; and as Daniel, opening the divinely

the vision my features changed unto me and I retained no
17 strength; || and how should the servant of my lord here be able
18 to speak with my lord there, for from that time no strength
19 remaineth in me and no breath is left in me?" || Then one to
look upon like a man touched me once more and strengthened
me and said "Fear not, thou dearly beloved man! | peace be
to thee, be courageous and courageous!" || —And whilst he
spake with me, I recovered myself and said "Speak my lord,
20 for thou hast strengthened me!" || So he said "Knowest
thou why I am come to thee? | However now—I will return

consecrated lips and excusing his previous fearfulness, still feels too unworthy and overwhelmed to be able to speak quite freely from mouth to mouth in the presence of this higher being, the Angel touches him again with his own hand as a friend, and now for the third time speaks to him with such affectionate condescension and such effective encouragement, that really overcoming all further human fear and feeling himself able to listen to all the Angel may say, he begs him to impart to him what he proposed to communicate, vv. 15-19. Yes, if they are not otherwise too unworthy for such a distinction, men are able completely to overcome, stage by stage, all human timidity, diffidence, and shyness, so that they may become absorbed with collected energy, clear vision, and calm judgment in the contemplation of divine truths, make the certainty of them their calm spiritual possession, and shrink from no thought and no knowledge if they only know that they are of divine nature and origin. For the presentation of this great fact the length of this narrative, vv. 4-19, is not too great; moreover, Daniel must now be thus completely collected, assured, calm, and clear in his own mind, because Gabriel has such various things, and for the most part such calamitous things, too, to communicate.

Gabriel begins, however, ver. 20, with the confidential question, *knowest thou wherefore I am come to thee?* thou canst very well know this, as I told it to thee before, vv. 11, 12-14, and am unwilling to tell it again. But before he really begins thus to make himself in a long communication the mouth-piece of the revelation concerning the succession and the nature of the future events, he lets drop yet another word by way of further preface, vv. 20—xi. 1. That is, just as when he arrived he had immediately excused himself on account of the lateness of his arrival, vv. 12-14, so now he wishes to excuse himself beforehand if he communicates with greatest possible brevity what he is about to say. He has indeed said before, vv. 12-24, that he has come now for a moment only because Mikhaél has taken his place in the conflict with the Persian Angel: but as Gabriel, *i.e.*, as the Angel of the prophets, he also knows beforehand that the Angel of Yavan is likewise already going forth to contend against Israel, that Israel will very soon have two great enemies, the Greeks in addition to the Persians (who even if temporarily overcome by the Greeks will still remain in the Parthians). On that account he would prefer to go back immediately to the military post he left, in order there to contend by the side of the great Mikhaél for Israel:

to contend against the prince of Persia, so while I am going
21 forth the prince of Yavan will come! ‖ But yet I will
announce to thee truly what is recorded in writing, | though
xi. no one exerteth himself with me against these but your Prince
1 Mikhaél, | as I in the first year of Dareios the Median took
2 my stand as a support and protection to him. ‖ But now will
I announce to thee the truth.

and thus wavering between two services, for Daniel and for Israel, he falls into a dialogue with himself, loud enough for Daniel to hear. At first the powerful reason for not stopping here at all takes precedence: *and now I will return* whence I am come acc. vv. 12-14, that is, *to contend against the Persian prince, and whilst I go forth* to this war *the Greek prince will come:* so little is there here time to lose. Still, notwithstanding this hesitancy, he resolves *to communicate truly the things noted down in divine writing,* to execute his present commission. And then the subsidiary reason occurs to him which must urge him to a quick return thither: *although no one at all exerts himself with me against these* (all the enemies of Israel) *save Mikhaél,* a reason which is, however, somewhat weakened, inasmuch as he can hope that Mikhaél will, particularly just now, also contend the more assiduously against them, as he has put him under a special obligation by special assistance which he rendered to him only a little while previously *in the first year of the Median Dareios. And so he will* after these considerations *make the communication,* although in haste and on the point of starting to attend to his still more important ministry. But in this way Gabriel has opened at the same time to his Daniel an extensive glance beforehand into the position of the celestial powers, and into the great hostilities even of two great empires with which his nation will have to contend long and seriously.

What is here, xi. 1, said regarding the assistance which Gabriel had rendered to Mikhaél is in the highest degree obscure, in fact, taken alone quite unintelligible. At the same time, it is quite clear that these words must refer to something which had been said more at length previously in this book at the proper place: the first year of the Mede Dareios points us back to the last piece, ch. ix. Now, inasmuch as from quite another cause we were led above to the certainty that some words are wanting after ver. 27, we find here the confirmation of that conclusion, and indeed an indication also as regards the form of the matter which is now wanting there. And if we put everything together, we may complete that passage in the following manner. When Daniel had there heard of the long series of 490 years, he heard also how thereupon the Satan broke out into fearful derisive laughter against a highest Angel (Mikhaél, who, however, need not there be mentioned by name); and this Angel would probably have been hardly able to defend himself against the Satan (for seventy years longer might completely destroy a nation which was already weakened), had not Gabriel been quickly at hand to show that those 490 years are to be reduced according to the truest divine calculation to 420. All this could have been said in three or four verses.

4.

Behold yet three kings of Persia arise, and the fourth will have greater treasure than all: | yet when he hath become powerful by his wealth, all that will arouse the kingdom of Yavan; || and a hero-king will arise, | will win great dominion and bear sway after his pleasure. || But when he standeth, his kingdom will be broken and divided according to the four winds of heaven, | yet not for his posterity and not in such wise as he had a dominion: | but his kingdom will be rooted up and fall to others besides those. || And the king of the south becometh powerful: | yet one of his princes—he will be still more powerful and will rule, a great kingdom will be his dominion. || —Yet towards the end of years they will make alliance by marriage, and the daughter of the king of the south will come to the king of the north to make a fair

4. After the hearer has been thus reassured, and at the same time his attention has been excited by the glance, which has been incidentally granted to him by anticipation, into celestial occurrences and preludes, the revelation of the impending destinies follows on the part of the revealer with the greater calmness very nearly to the moment of the actual present of the author and his readers, vv. 2-43. It is precisely the five middle strophes of the whole piece, and accordingly the broad calm central portion of the angelic revelation, which are occupied with this subject; and in conformity with the importance of these events and destinies precisely from the standpoint of the actual present, all that has to be presented here as in winged haste is arranged as follows in the five strophes: this picture with its dark shadows, and here and there its brief luminous points, brings together in the first strophe everything down to the death of Seleukos Nicator, in the second everything down to the death of Antiochos the Great; but in the three next, after the life of his successor has been drawn with a few strokes, the time of Antiochos Epiphanes is handled according to its three great phases; and it must be said that the division into these five compartments is very appropriate, and answers to the design of the great picture in general.

The representation of the Persian period is accomplished, ver. 2, with the fewest strokes. Kyros, then reigning, is followed by three more kings, the last of whom (perhaps Artaxerxes I.) is uncommonly covetous and rich: accordingly *all this*, the extensive dominions and particularly the great hoards of money of this king, rouses all the more the Greek kingdom against him, so that Alexander, ver. 3, undertakes his campaign against the Persians. This was undoubtedly the brief, popular notion of that entire Persian rule, as it had already taken shape at the time of our author; and by the four kings Kyros, Dareios, Achashverosh (Xerxes) and Artaxerxes, whose names are elsewhere most frequently mentioned, were probably understood; comp. the comment on vii. 6, *ante* p. 247.

The exceedingly powerful rule of

arrangement : | but she will not retain the strength of arm, neither will its arm either last, | and she will be given up with those who brought her, and he who begat her and sustained
7 her in the times. || Yet one from the offshoot of her roots will step into his place : | he cometh to the army and cometh into the fortress of the king of the north, and will do his will with them
8 and prevail ; || and their gods also together with their molten images, with their dearest vessels of silver and gold, he will bring captive to Egypt : | yet he will for years stand off from
9 the king of the north. || Thus he cometh into the kingdom of the king of the south, | and returneth into his land. ||

Alexander, which was, however, so brief, and for his own house so exceedingly unhappy, is described, vv. 3, 4, likewise with only a few, though far more historical, lines : whilst he still *stands* in all his might, his kingdom is divided into four kingdoms according to the four quarters of heaven, none of which equals in power that of Alexander ; these two main features were before prefigured in a symbolic way, viii. 8, 22, 23.—But the discourse hastens now, from ver. 5 onwards, solely to the history of the two kingdoms of the *south*, i.e., of Egypt, and of the *north*, i.e., Syria : and then the rise of the kingdom of Seleukos, this man who was originally only one of the numerous *princes*, i.e., military commanders, of Ptolemy I., is amply indicated, ver. 5, by this one characteristic which is in the highest degree distinctive of the Seleukid family, though it does not add to their renown.

For the discourse now makes a leap intentionally (which is indicated by the words *and towards the end of years*, i.e., after several years had passed) of a considerable space of time, in order, vv. 6-9, to touch upon the tender place which really reveals the first more decisive cause of the weakening and final dissolution of the Seleukid empire. As early as ii. 43 there was a reference to the unhappy marriage alliances between members of the Seleukid and Ptolemaic houses : the first and worst instance happened under the third Syrian king, Antiochos Theos, who married the daughter of Ptolemy II., Berenike : but whilst this queen was made to advance towards the *north* (Syria) with a great retinue, *in order to effect a reasonable arrangement,* so that she might patch up again the interrupted peace between the two kingdoms, and serve as the pledge of a fair arrangement between them, nevertheless neither did she *retain the power of the arm*, i.e., the power of the strong military force attending her, so that they might have availed to protect her from the spies of the king her husband and the mortal plots of the Syrians, nor did *the arm of* this *arm*, the king her father and *protector in the* evil *times remain* firmly established, but died, so that almost at the same time she, with her whole retinue (which she had brought as a bride to Syria) and her sick father, was *given up, i.e.,* was hastened to death or violently slain. How her death was soon revenged by Ptolemy III. to the greatest disgrace of Syria, is described vv. 7, 8 : *one from the shoots of her roots, i.e.,* a young Ptolemy, as one from the green shoots of her stem (after Isa. xi. 1), who *steps into the place* of his father,

5.

10 Yet his sons wax war-furious and assemble a multitude of many armies: | that then cometh further and further overflowing and overwhelming, turneth round and warreth unto
11 his fortress; || and the king of the south will embitter himself, will march forth and fight with him with the king of the

but, in contrast with the effeminate Ptolemy II., *comes to the army* himself, takes part himself in the campaign, *comes into the strong fortress of the Syrian king, i.e.*, takes and holds Seleukeia in the Mediterranean, not far from Antioch, and *brings* back from his victorious campaigns in the countries of Seleukos II. (Kallinikos) even *the gods with their molten images* (as is here ingeniously said), once carried out of Egypt by Kambyses, with so many other precious vessels *as spoil to Egypt*. It thus appears as if he could have destroyed the Syrian kingdom entirely, and have restored again a complete Alexandrine kingdom: nevertheless, that shall not take place, as was said ver. 4, in accordance with higher destiny, so that this division closes almost ludicrously: *he*, the Egyptian king, *stands off*, notwithstanding all his victories, *some years from the Syrian king*, leaves him alone; but when the latter king now on his own acccount *comes to Egypt*, he also soon *returns again to Syria:* with such miserable marches hither and thither do they mutually weaken each other! Comp. *History of Israel*, V., 283 (IV., 368).

5. A new *warlike* life, full of commotion, now comes into the Syrian kingdom through the two sons of Seleukos II., namely, Seleukos III. (Keraunos), who however reigned only a few years, and particularly Antiochos the Great; *they collect immense armies, overrun* with them the northern countries, and suddenly turn back again and reconquer *the great Syrian fortress* (Selenkeia), which the Egyptians had held until then, ver. 10, comp. ver. 7. On the possession or surrender of this fortress the conflict of the two kingdoms and the honour of the Syrian power hanged at that time for twenty-seven years, so that the great emphasis which is here laid upon it, vv. 7, 10, is quite intelligible. Now, it is true that through the further advances and victories of the Syrian king Antiochos the Great the young Egyptian debauchee Ptolemy IV. (Philopator) feels *himself embittered* at last to war, collects once more a great army, and this *is also given into his hand*, in that as formerly, ver. 7, his father puts himself at the head of the army; this army also becomes excessively domineering, and at the great victory of Raphia, on the borders of Egypt and Syria, *throws down tens of thousands;* but nevertheless this king becomes no true conqueror, vv. 11, 12. For the Syrian king collects afresh a much larger army still, and *towards the end of the times, i.e.*, after his long victorious campaigns in eastern Asia as far as India, repeatedly *inundates* Palestine *for years* therewith, ver. 13. But at this point of the history of the Syrian kingdom, when Jerusalem became permanently Syrian, not without the complicity of a dominant Yudean party who in the dislike of the Egyptian rule welcomed the Syrian, the Angel cannot refrain from making, for the first time, reference to the domestic condition of the Yudeans in Palestine

north, | will set up a great battle-host and that will be given
12 into his hand; || and the battle-host will wax proud of heart
and cast down ten thousands, | and yet not become powerful. ||
13 For again the king of the north will set up a war-multitude
greater than the former, | and towards the end of the times
for years will he come repeatedly with a great army and much
14 war-material: || yet in those times will many stand up against
the king of the south, | and young high-handed men of thy
people will lift themselves up to confirm an oracle and meet
15 their fall. || —And the king of the north will come and cast
up a rampart and take a strongly fortified city, | and the
arms of the south will not stand, his most chosen nations also
16 —have no strength to withstand: || so he that cometh against
him beareth sway after his pleasure in that no one withstandeth him, remaineth in the land of the Ornament, and it

and raising the complaint that precisely *in those times many would stand against the king of the south*, and exactly *the most violent* fellow-countrymen of a Daniel would *show themselves* thus *lifted up*, which they would subsequently, after the Syrian rule had been further confirmed, have bitterly to repent of, as the last words indicate *and will meet a fall*, comp. *History of Israel*, V., 284 sq. (IV., 369 sq.). When it is incidentally remarked that they would be thus highminded *in order to confirm a vision, i.e.*, an oracle, or that an oracle uttered concerning them may be fulfilled, this remark is so far from clear from the immediate context, or from anything said in the book elsewhere, and stands moreover generally so completely detached in this discourse of the Angel, that we shall do best to suppose that it is an allusion to a special prophetic book of that time. In what way this is to be more definitely conceived has been previously indicated, *ante* p. 173.

Just as the whole description of the Seleukid - Ptolemaic relations is the result of an exceedingly accurate knowledge of the historical events themselves, so there is also communicated a very good general view of the history of Antiochos the Great, in that our description points out the turning point where, in spite of certain advances which he continued to make, his fortunes began to decline. He conducts another successful war in Palestine, besieges a *strongly fortified city*, namely Sidon, into which the Egyptian armies had flung themselves, *and takes it*, neither can the *choicest* Egyptian *troops* any more *stand before him*, and he remains thus *in the land of the Ornament, i.e.*, in Yuda and Jerusalem, as acknowledged conquerer, in that this land comes *completely into his hand*, vv. 15, 16. Comp. *History of Israel*, V., 284 (IV., 370).—But when he now proposes *to come into the possession* of the *entire* Egyptian *kingdom* thereby that he *concluded an arrangement* with the young king Ptolemy Epiphanes and *gave him a daughter of women, i.e.*, a young wife, namely, his own daughter Kleopatra, in the hope of through her reigning over Egypt and being able

17 falleth wholly into his hand. ‖ So he setteth his face to enter into the possession of his kingdom, and an agreement with him—that will he negotiate, | and a young wife give to him
18 to work its ruin : | yet will it not abide nor become his. ‖ So he turneth his face towards the coast-lands and taketh many : | yet will a potentate quench his scorn, only his scorn pay back
19 to him; ‖ and he turneth his face to the fastnesses of his land, | but will stumble and fall and be not to be found. ‖

6.

20 Then cometh in his place he who causeth an exactor to pass through a most glorious kingdom : | yet in a few days he will
21 be broken, but not by wrath and not by war. ‖ Then cometh in his place a reprobate and upon him shall not be set the

gradually to get complete possession of it, accordingly gave her to him *in order to destroy* the land, he commences therewith simply a series of totally wrong undertakings, as immediately appears in the fact that the land nevertheless does *not remain* to him *nor become his own*, ver. 17. He therefore now *sets his face in another direction*, forms another plan, namely, to conquer *many coastlands* in Asia Minor and Europe; but after he has already *taken* many of them, a potentate, namely, the great Roman Lucius Scipio, *quells for him his scorn*, as he had with insolent scorn declared he would overcome the Romans also ; yea (as the unusually resilient language adds) *nothing but his scorn does* this Roman *give him back*, ver. 18.

Once more, therefore, he proposes something new: *the fortresses of his land* in the east and the west he determines to make secure against future enemies (which our author undoubtedly knew from trustworthy recollection), but in doing that *meets* unexpectedly (by murder) in the distant east his *fall*, and although desired and wished for again by many friends, *is nowhere to be found*, being lost for ever, ver. 19. And with great effect the restlessness which overtook him precisely as he had . taken possession of Jerusalem, and which drove him continually from one great but vain undertaking to another, is thus depicted in animated words in these three sentences, vv. 17, 18, 19, all beginning with the same words.

6. His successor Seleukos IV. Philopator, who in exact contrast with his father sought to have the most quiet reign possible, is characterized, ver. 20, by that one feature by which he established such an evil reputation among the Yudeans of Palestine : *he causes an exactor*, tax-collector (Heliodoros), *to pass through a splendour of a kingdom*, i.e., a most glorious kingdom, adorned

above all others as with the highest royal crown, namely, Jerusalem with the Holy Land as the seat of the Theocracy, to exact as many taxes as possible and to plunder temple and land, comp. on this point *History of Israel*, V., 292 (IV., 380). And as he did not reign long, the conclusion follows forthwith *yet in a few days he will be broken;* as this points to a

splendour of a kingdom : | he cometh unawares and seizeth the
22 kingdom by flatteries ; || yet the overflowing wings will be
overflown before him and broken, | and even a covenanted
high-prince—from the relationship with him will he also work
23 deceit. || So he will grow and become strong by few people,
24 unawares even into the fattest districts will he come, | and do
what neither his fathers nor his grandfathers did : | plunder
and booty and baggage will he scatter to them, and against
strongholds devise his plots : | but unto a time. ||

violent death, the particular manner of it is somewhat more definitely indicated by the addition *but not by wrath*, in that some one of his magnates had suddenly turned against him in a sudden burst of anger and slain him, *and not by war*, but by the poison which Heliodoros administered to him. The fact that he died without an heir near him, so that three persons are now proclaimed whom Antiochos Epiphanes must first overthrow, has less to do with this connexion than with vii. 7 ; ix. 26, where the author most appropriately introduced it.

But as the discourse thus passes at once at this point to Antiochos Epiphanes, it cannot find sufficient words to describe his very first arrival, insinuation, and establishment of himself, vv. 21-24, as devoid of all royal characteristics. The first word with which he is here designated, *a reprobate* before God and man, expresses exactly the opposite of his surname Epiphanes, *i.e.*, the Illustrious; and that he reigned without having *placed upon him the splendour of a kingdom*, *i.e.*, a crown, becomes thus a sign of his own depreciation of true royalty. In reality we have no cause to doubt the fact itself, that he despised the old and customary ceremony of coronation ; he had learnt in Rome to despise the royal crown as such. Instead of royally *he comes* from Rome *unawares and seizes* as a usurper *the dominion by flatterings*, by the arts of flattery in every form learnt in Rome ; in which he is also so successful that *powerful* hostile *armies* which might have been in a position to overwhelm him from all sides are on the contrary *before him overflown and broken*, vv. 21, 22, which manifestly refers to the three princes whom he was obliged, acc. vii. 7, 20, first to overthrow before his own reign was secure. But at all events of one of these three it is considered proper that something further should be said here, namely, of the Ptolemy Philometor above mentioned, p. 248, who played such an important part also in the subsequent history of this king. The much younger Ptolemy Philometor was through the Kleopatra alluded to ver. 17, the nephew of Antiochos Epiphanes ; and that he now *even from the relationship with this high-prince*, who was thereby *confederated* with him *wrought deceit*, pretended to desire to protect him but therein simply deceived him, is a fact which it was important to mention here as the Syro-Egyptian events generally belong particularly to this long discourse.—But this whole description of the first times of the king is concluded with the words : *So he will grow and become strong by few people*, as at the beginning, having just come from Rome, he could not at that time have many soldiers about him,

25   Then he rouseth his strength and his heart against the king of
the south with a great army, and the king of the south heateth
himself to the war with an exceeding great and numerous
army : | but he will not stand because they devise plots against
26   him; and they who eat of his table will break him | whilst his
27   army overfloweth and many slain fall. || And the heart of both
kings is to do evil, and at one table they will speak lies : | but
it will not succeed, because yet the end is for the set-time. ||

7.

28   Then he returneth to his land with great movable wealth
whilst his heart is against the holy Covenant, | and beareth sway

will come unawares also into the fattest districts of the land, e.g., into fat Galilee, there first to obtain a secure footing, *and do what neither his fathers nor forefathers did,* namely, bestow *plunder and spoil and movable property,* which he has taken from others, upon *them* with a *liberally scattering* hand, simply in order to gain friends; while at the same time he will also thus early *form plans* of all kinds *against fortresses, e.g.,* against Pelusium on the Egyptian border, vv. 23, 24. And if we are not in a position to confirm this in detail by other historical authorities, everything has nevertheless too definite a character to permit us to suppose that it is not perfectly historical.—But this description of his first overbold appearance on the scene is also closed with the brief, expressive word which follows limpingly at the end : *but for a time!* verily not for ever will he be able thus to act !

After preparations of this kind he begins in the first instance a great war against his nephew : and although his nephew raises against him *an exceedingly*

great army, he is nevertheless betrayed by the people of his own court in accordance with the device previously prepared in conjunction with the Syrian king, ver. 25: in which treachery the most disgraceful thing is that the nephew is betrayed by those who are *eating his bread at his own table,* by the meal itself, whilst his army is in the raging battle and many are falling on both sides, ver. 26. But the two kings, uncle and nephew, stand at first in a perfectly friendly relation to each other, as it appears, and agree in common as to the many evil things which they propose to do to the people of Israel (comp. *History of Israel,* V., 296 (IV., 385): yet in this section of the great picture also the word limps up at the end : *yet it will not succeed; for still an end hath the set time!* the appointed period in which such things can take place has still an end, will not last for ever; still, at the time when this was written, despair is not permissible. The late closing word this time only puts on a somewhat different form !

7. If the king this year in his march through the Holy Land and *return* to Antioch conceives so much evil suspicion against the *holy Covenant, i.e.,* the whole constitution and basis of Israel's existence, it is not so very surprising that on the first occasion he casts off all consideration, ver. 28.

29 and returneth to his land. ‖ At the set time will he return and come into the south : | yet it will not be as the first so the second time also ; ‖ for Kittite ships come upon him and he
30 despaireth, | turneth back and is exasperated against the holy Covenant and beareth sway, | turneth back and payeth atten-
31 tion to those who forsake the holy Covenant. ‖ Yet troops will remain from him and desecrate the Sanctuary the Fortress, | and remove the daily and set up the horrible abomination. ‖—
32 And those who outrage the Covenant he will make profane by flatteries : | yet people who know their God will hold fast and
33 do well. ‖ And wise teachers of the people will bring understanding to the multitude : | yet they will fall by sword and by
34 flame by captivity and by spoiling for days, | and when they

At the time, i.e., the next year at the time when it is customary to begin military operations, *he returns* therefore once more *to the south* to recommence the Egyptian war ; but because this campaign is not so successful as *the former*, inasmuch as *Kittite, i.e.*, in this instance Rhodean and Roman, *ships* arriving on the Egyptian coast contravene his intentions against Egypt by their negotiations and threats, and he thus withdraws *in despair* and extremely displeased from the Egyptian frontier, he accordingly *returns enraged against the holy Covenant and does what he will*, takes wholly new measures against it, that is, in the first instance, shows special *attention to those who forsake the Covenant*, to the apostates in Israel, rewards and encourages them in his way, vv. 28, 29, but causes *strong troops* of his soldiers to *stand* in the Holy Land and particularly in Jerusalem : and they then at his command carry out those terrible things which formerly chaps. vii.-ix. brought so prominently forward, *they desecrate the Sanctuary, the Fortress,* as the temple was at the same time the strongest fortress, *remove the daily*, the proper sacrifice, and *set up* instead *the horrible abomination,* the heathen sacrifice, ver. 31, as is here said for the third time after viii. 11, ix. 27. As to the historical events to which all this refers, see *History of Israel,* V., 297 sq. (IV., 387 sq.).

The second half of this strophe gives a vivid picture in three sentences of the manner in which the various parties of the people of Israel meet these greatest abominations and of the immediate consequences connected with them. It is true *he makes those who do outrage to the Covenant profane, i.e.*, heathen, by the arts of *flattering* further mentioned vv. 21, 33 : *but people who know their God,* who know what they possess in the true religion and the true God, *they hold fast*, do not suffer themselves to be thus seduced to faithlessness, *and do well*, adopt in action also the proper means of guarding themselves against it, ver. 32. It is true *wise popular teachers bring understanding to the multitude* who are willing to learn, whether it be by written or oral teaching and admonition, as our author himself with his book might be counted amongst them : but it cannot be denied that *they fall* frequently for their daring and sincerity, in consequence

fall meet with little help: | for many will cleave unto them
35 with flatteries. || Yet of the teachers some will fall in order to
melt among them and to purify and to refine | till the time
of the end : | for yet is it for the set-time. ||

8.

36 So the king doeth according to his pleasure, and exalteth
himself and magnifieth himself above every God, | above the
God of Gods also he will speak wonderfully and succeed | till
the indignation cometh to an end because the decision is
37 taken. || Unto the God of his fathers also will he pay no
regard, and unto the desire of women or any God whatsoever
38 will he pay no regard, | but will magnify himself above every
one : || the God of fastnesses however will he honour upon his
place, and the God which his fathers knew not will he honour

of secret accusations to the rulers, *by the sword or by flame, i.e.,* at the stake, *by deportation* or *by plunder* of their goods *for days* (for no short period), *and* unfortunately *when* they thus *fall* persecuted by the ruling power of the day *find* but *little help because many* do not show themselves seriously faithful under all trials, and some also even *cleave to them* only *with flatteries* in order as spies and informers to betray them, vv. 33, 34. *Yet,* although this is lamentable, it is still on the other hand true that in accordance with the higher divine necessity *some* of them thus *fall* in order that precisely they of all men may as is just be *purified* in the great trial most severely in every way like metal in the heat of the crucible, to test whether they are really faithful, ver. 35, comp, xii. 10 : and the best supplement of this is supplied by the declaration xii. 3. But nowhere else is the conclusion with the brief words both so true and so rapid as here, that all this shall continue thus only *until the time of the end,* which will soon, ver. 40, xii. 1, be more particularly described, *because* the oracle *is yet for the set period,* as is here repeated from viii. 17, 19.

8. But from this glance at the conduct of the various parties in Israel the discourse reverts to *the king* again, with the view of describing in this strophe his conduct quite down to the actual present of the author. And with regard to him there is in the first instance nothing so important and so closely connected in point of significance with what had been last said, vv. 36, 37, as that he in conformity with his peculiar character despises both the God of Israel and all other gods, as is at first, ver. 36, quite generally expressed but at the same time by the phrase which is re-echoed from the end of the previous strophe, that although he utters *marvellous* (to say in this case the least) and extraordinary speeches *against the God of gods* (after Ps. l. 1) *also and* in doing that *has* all along *success*, this after all will last only *until the indignation comes to an end* (from Isa. x. 25 *because the divine decision will*

with gold and with silver and with precious stones and with
39 costly things; ‖ and he dealeth with the strong fastnesses as
with the strange God: | he who acknowledgeth them to him
he giveth much honour and causeth them to rule over the
multitude, and land he divideth as price. ‖
40 Yet in the time of the end will the king of the south thrust
with him, | and the king of the north storm up against him
with chariots and with horses and with many ships, | will
41 enter into the lands and overflow and overwhelm, ‖ will enter
into the land of the Ornament, and chief-teachers will fall, |
yet these will escape out of his hand: Edóm and Môab and the
42 flower of the children of 'Ammôn. ‖ Then he stretcheth his
hand over the lands, and the land of Egypt will not be to be
43 spared, | and he reigneth over the treasures of gold and silver
and over all the costly things of Egypt, whilst Libyans and
Kushites follow his footsteps. ‖

then be *taken* against him, as is here repeated from ix. 26, 27. But in order to show somewhat more particularly how much he despises all other gods also, reference is made, ver. 37, to the fact that he does not pay any regard even *to the God of his fathers*, *i.e.*, the Hellenic Zeus, *and to the desire of women*, *i.e.*, Adonis; for by this desire of women undoubtedly Tammûz-Adonis (comp. Vol. IV., 59) is understood, and these two divinities were at that time with certainty the gods then most celebrated and beloved by the people among the Syrians. On the contrary, it is only one God, the discourse continues, vv. 38, 39, in language of increasingly biting satire, whom *he honours upon his place* where he has set up a statue to him, namely, *the God of fortresses*, *i.e.*, Jupiter of the Capitol (of the Roman fortress), that God whom *his fathers did not know* and to whom he nevertheless has just now erected a statue in Antioch and dedicated all manner of precious things; but as he in addition *loves the fortresses themselves* only as much as this God (comp. ver. 24), so he loves and honours and endows with high offices or valuable lands only such men as acknowledge the fortresses as gods. On the historical facts here referred to comp. *History of Israel*, V., 298 sq. (IV., 389 sq.).

With this the discourse passes to the last great undertaking of the king, which came down close to the actual time of the author, indeed was scarcely properly finished in it, so that this present is here at the beginning, ver. 40, itself treated as *the time of the end*. That undertaking is the last war which he ventured against Egypt, and in which he supported his attacks by land with *many ships*, acc. ver. 40. According to ver. 40 Ptolemy Philometor would have been in this case the first to attack: and this is not at all improbable, as this king had then dissolved the alliance with him and reconciled himself with his brother as well as with the Egyptians themselves. It is also very easy to perceive why our author, ver. 41, particularly mentions that the tyrant now upon his march to the south comes first *into the land of the Ornament*,

9.

44 Yet rumours will terrify him from east and from north, | and he will march out with great fury to destroy and to ban
45 many. || Then he pitcheth his tent of state between the seas and the mountain of the holy Ornament : | yet will he come to his end in that none helpeth him. ||

xii. And at that time will Mikhaél stand forth, the great prince
1 who standeth forth for the sons of thy people : | and it will be the time of a distress such as never hath happened since a people existed until that time, | yet in that time will thy

i.e., Yudea, and now *chief-teachers* (who had been previously designated by another term vv. 33-35) *fall* as men who had got into disfavour with him, and no one *is* here *safe from his violence save Edóm and Móab and* the firstborn, or as we should say, *the bloom of the children of 'Ammón:* and as here it is only his conduct towards Israel which is spoken of, it follows that only those of the Israelites disposed to heathenism can be meant by these three names long known in their prophetic significance, the same people who had been above designated as heathen, ver. 32 ; indeed, the satirical name *the bloom of the children of 'Ammón* points to this : if the children of 'Ammón are the model of heathenish people, what must then the flower of them be !—But further *he stretches* next *his hand over the countries, and Egypt cannot escape him,* indeed he has already robbed all *its treasures and costly things,* since he now comes as the enemy of both brothers, and already he counts *Libyans* and *Kushites* as Egyptian deserters in his train, vv. 42, 43.

9. But nevertheless just then he finds himself suddenly compelled to abandon all his Egyptian spoil: *rumours of* great commotions in the more distant parts of his kingdom *from east and from north alarm him,* he *marches out* of Egypt, comes now all the more enraged to Yudea *in order* once more *to destroy and put under the ban many,* and already he *pitches his* royal *tent of splendour between the seas, i.e.,* on the eastern border of Egypt *and the mountain of the holy Ornament, i.e.,* the temple hill of Jerusalem, vv. 44, 45.— But this was the very last thing which had taken place in Jerusalem when the author closed our book ; and it has been shown *History of Israel,* V., 302 sq. (IV., 394 sq.) in what sense all this from ver. 40 onwards is to be understood historically and chronologically.

Accordingly the conclusion is here rapidly made, for the fifth time, after vv. 24, 27, 35, 37, with the slowly following sentence *yet he will come to his end in that no one helps him!* And the angelic feature of the discourse can once more become more prominent, as it must recur to its commencement : but at present in looking at the actual future it is mainly only happy promises for the faithful who still further stand the test of intensified and extremest trials, together with some side-glances at the opposite, which occupy the discourse. And as at the commencement x. 13, 21 ; xi. 1, Mikhaél was twice spoken of as the great guardian Angel

people escape as many as are found written in the book. ||
And many of those who sleep in the earth of dust will awake, | these to eternal life and those to scornings to detestation for ever. || And the wise teachers will shine brightly as the firmament shineth, and they who justify the multitude as stars for ever and ever. ||

4 But thou Daniel! hide the words and seal the book till the time of the end, | that many may read the lines and the knowledge be increased! ||

of Israel, so it is now, xii. 1, for the third time said, that *he will at that time make a stand for his beloved nation;* and if that time should also bring for it *a distress the like of which no nation ever before witnessed*, nevertheless *as many* of it *will certainly be saved as are written in the book*, that book which was similarly mentioned Isa. iv. 3 and the fellow of which is met above x. 21. But still higher and more definite things can be added in the course of these promises, vv. 2, 3: if it is profoundly to be lamented that, acc. xi. 33-35, many of the most faithful fall as martyrs, it is at the same time equally certain that *many of those who already sleep in the dusty ground will awake*, yet those who are here intended are spoken of as *many* only in comparison with the still more innumerable heathen. For the question is not here touched on, whether also a resurrection to judgment is to be expected for the heathen: the only thing that has here to be insisted upon is, that in the case of Israel a resurrection will certainly not fail to come, yea, will be general in its case, so that *these rise to everlasting life, those*, described sufficiently in our book above, only *to be eternally scorned and detested*, to serve as ever living examples of a life which none ought to live, as this had been said in another form "Isa." lxvi. 24, compared with lxv. 14, 15. And as in the times of our author when the prophets had ceased, according to xi. 33-35, 41, it is only *the wise teachers* who were famous through their unwearied care for the preservation of the light and the faith of the true religion, so this beautiful picture is suitably closed with the hint, that the few who enlighten *the many* by their true doctrine and *justify* (after "Isa." liii. 11) them by an immovable faith, befitting their doctrine, and faithfulness to death, *will* also *shine eternally like the most brightly shining heaven*.

But how far is Daniel from this present and this future, and how little is this book, now coming to an end, intended to be read by his contemporaries, and how certainly only by those of this late time relatively to him! Thus the last word of this long discourse of the Angel is simply the short instruction to Daniel, ver. 4, that he may so far as his own time is concerned *hide these words and seal this book* (as a book intended for later times is sealed, laid by, and shut up) *until the time of the end, in order that many may* then *read it carefully line by line and thus the knowledge* of the divine secrets and certainties *be increased!*

10.

5   And I Daniel saw—and behold two others standing there, |
    one on this side the bank of the river, and the other on that
6   side the bank of the river; || he said to the man clothed in
7   linen who was high above the water of the river " Till when
    is the end of the wonderful things ?" | then I heard the man

10. Were it necessary the book might close here, and it is chiefly one thing which on account of its importance delays somewhat the conclusion and deserves more particular attention. There was nothing which was more painful and horrible to behold in the view of the faithful of the actual present of the author than the "horrible abomination" in the temple, which was mentioned for the second time xi. 31, after ix. 27, and has here at the conclusion, xii. 11, to be mentioned for the third time : neither is there anything more horrible to hear than the open, and moreover in the highest degree coarse, insults which the king had accustomed himself in these last times to pour forth against Yahvé. To blaspheme the God of a community is of itself highly ignoble and unkingly : and to blaspheme this God, whom all former heathen kings had acknowledged and honoured, if only by the temple sacrifices which they ordered to be presented for them in Jerusalem ! * As if to avoid the constant repetition of the first most severe words which he had used vii. 8, 20, our author had expressed himself mildly when he just before, xi. 36, named these speeches of the generally *marvellously* outrageous king, viii. 24, *marvellous* ones : he here, ver. 6, designates them and the deeds corresponding to them still more briefly as *marvels* or *marvellous things ;* and how often had the faithful groaned most profoundly on account of them and longed for the final cessation of these things, yea, had undoubtedly in their prayers anxiously asked *when* they would cease ! In connexion therewith it was of special moment, however, that it was after all mainly only the Yudeans in the Holy Land who were compelled to see and hear such things : for beyond the Tigris this king had already but little to say, as those countries had by this time been almost lost for the Seleukidæ. If now our author here transplants himself for the last time into the situation and feeling of Daniel, it seems to him, vv. 5-7, as if this prophet by the Tigris, where he is placed acc. x. 4, has at the very close *seen two other* Angels like the previous ones, therefore acc. x. 5 likewise *clothed with linen* but standing *on this side* and *on that side* close by the river and thus towering with their mighty forms as it were *high above the water ;* and what can they be but the spirits of the two great countries and of the two halves into which the community of the true religion was then divided on this side and on that side of the Tigris ? He first sees the one on the nearer side, then the one on the further side : but he *hears* the one on the further side anxiously cry *until when is the end of the wonderful things ?* ver. 6. But immediately he hears also the other

---

* Comp. *History of Israel*, V., 113 sq. (IV., 147 sq.; VI., 663 sq.)

clothed in linen who was high above the water of the river, |
and he raised his right hand and his left hand to heaven and
swore by Him that liveth for ever, that it is for a set-time and
(two) set-times and a half; | and when the shattering of the
hand of the holy people shall be accomplished, all this will be
accomplished. ||

8 But I heard it and I understood it not, | and said "my
9 lord! what is the last end of this?" || Then said he "go,
Daniel! for the words are hidden and sealed till the time of
10 the end. || Although many be purified and refined and melted
and although the outrageous commit outrage and all the

Angel, who is standing nearer to him, affirm, as if he desired to reassure his colleague, under the most sacred oath conceivable, *by Him that liveth for ever* (that the true God should live for ever and eternally impose upon evil its limitations, is especially appropriate in this connexion), that *it* shall last only for the *three and a half periods* which have before been twice mentioned, vii. 25; ix. 27, and appear here so significantly for the third time, and that when *the shattering of the hand, i.e.*, the power, *of the holy people shall be finished* all these things which have been foretold in the book will also *be finished*, or in other words that the great change for the better will not come before the community of the true God has become completely powerless in the earth and as good as destroyed, so that the only question is whether it shall be really annihilated for ever or whether in this profound disorganization a new resuscitation securing reform and perfect life will all the more necessarily be granted to it; a Messianic outlook which had been uttered as early as Deut. xxxii. 36, although in quite another connexion.

Thus that dialogue which we saw first started, only on a larger scale, above. viii. 13, 14, recurs here again, and upon the same ultimate question.

But here this interlude must quickly pass over; for here Daniel stands at last quite confidentially by the side of that Angel only who had condescended so far to him and had promised to reveal everything to him. Accordingly, *he hears* it is true what those two Angels say to each other, and things which certainly concern the same all-important subject, but he does *not understand* any the better what they mysteriously hint with regard to such distant things; on the contrary, he turns back to his Gabriel, addresses him, as x. 16-19, confidentially with *my lord!* and asks, therein agreeing with that Angel, ver. 6, *what is the final end of all this?* ver. 8. Accordingly Gabriel's mighty voice replies, and that is the very last thing which he can say and which has a place in this book: *Go, Daniel!* ask no further, which would be quite in vain; *for hidden and sealed* are *the words*, all those contained in these prophecies, *until the time of the end!* then they will easily be unsealed and deciphered ver. 9. Therefore, once more to repeat this only from xi. 35 and the whole subject-matter of the book, as the great main point, although *many are then purified* in all ways, acc. xi. 41, *and although the outrageous commit outrage*, as they have their freedom of action, *and although even all the outrageous* fail to

20 *

ontrageous understand it not: | yet the wise will understand
11 it. ‖ —And from that time of the removal of the daily
and the setting up of a horrible abomination are a thousand
12 two hundred and ninety days: ‖ happy is he who holdeth out
and attaineth unto a thousand three hundred and five and
13 thirty days. ‖ —But thou go thou till the end, | that thou
mayest rest and stand to thy lot till the end of the days!" ‖

understand this whole book and divine things generally, that cannot be helped: but it is equally certain that *the wise men*, those intended xi. 33-35, 40; xii. 3, *will understand* it! ver. 10.

But one thing more by way of final farewell! In order that no one may suppose that those three and a half years, which are after all only intended to refer to great general conditions, must be understood in quite a slavish sense in the expectation of their fulfilment, let it be taken note of, that that period may very well be somewhat shorter or somewhat longer, and let no one be specially alarmed if it should last somewhat longer! Indeed, ultimately so much does not depend on *days*: profoundly tried faithfulness counts anxiously from one day to another: but let there not be too much anxiety in this respect! As now our own author adopts in this book, acc. p 237, a year of 360, or rather, with the five intercalary days, of 365 days, so he had already, viii. 14, mysteriously pointed to 2230 *day-nights*, *i.e.*, 1115 days, *i.e.*, three years and one month,* as if even this period of three and a half years could be somewhat reduced, as the 490 years were above, ch. ix., reduced to 420. Yet inasmuch as the contrary is also possible, the period is now, ver. 11, extended to 1290 *days*, *i.e.*, to half a month above three and a half years, and somewhat further still, ver. 12, to 1335 days, *i.e.* to two months above the three and a half years, and he also is pronounced blessed who *waits* for them.— But thus the number of the days also is three times fixed, as anything of prophetic importance is repeated three times; and every one will understand the freedom observed in fixing the numbers!

Therefore finally, ver. 13: *but go thou into thy grave until the end*, then to be awakened, acc. ver. 2: but inasmuch as the eternal blessedness cannot well be promised to any one before the final judgment, this is most appropriately expressed thus: *that thou mayest stand to thy lot*, the lot which shall then fall to thee, mayest wait for it and receive it *at the end of the days*, at the general judgment!

And now not a further word in this book! any further word would after all be useless for indolent and dull, or for illwilled readers. Nor would any closing word of a narrative character, such as closed all the previous pieces, be here so suitable, partly because all that would have to be said by it has already been amply said vv. 4, 8, 12, partly because the author does better to leave the reader at the end to ask himself why the book closes thus and not like an ordinary book of narratives.

---

* There appears to be here a slight error in Ewald's figures, though it does not materially affect his exegesis. "2300 day-nights," and "1150 days," and "three years and a little more than two months" are the numbers required.—*Tr.*

I have elsewhere* shown, following the Books of the Makkabees, in what way the prophecy of this book received at all events an approximate first fulfilment, precisely as regards the period which is so emphatically dwelt upon in these last words: just three years after the introduction of the idol sacrifice the true sacrifice was restored in the temple by the Makkabean conquerors; this could be regarded as a pledge of the further fulfilment; and it has been already mentioned, p. 183 sq., that thereby our book rose with great rapidity in the popular estimation. It is an error to which our own times first gave rise,† that our book was not written until *after* this restoration of the true sacrifice in the reconquered and purified temple in the year 165 B.C. and *after* the death of Antiochos Epiphanes in the year 164, and that the numbers of three and a half years as well as of 1115,‡ 1290, 1335 days, refer to three or four purely historical events of this kind. Even if this opinion had any foundation in the book itself, it would not accord with the actual history, nor could it be established from it. How little it has any foundation in the book itself, and how completely its meaning and immediate subject-matter as well as its true date are opposed to this opinion has been sufficiently shown above. In fact, it must be said that the pure meaning of our book does not admit of a greater misconception, nor its value a greater detraction, than this view of it would give rise to; a view which is not at all better, indeed strictly regarded is worse, in point of perversity and perniciousness, than any of those which formerly prevailed regarding it. Let only a serious attempt be made to apply this view in the interpretation of the prophetic portion of the book, and it will appear how absolutely wrong it is.

---

* *History of Israel*, V., 312 (IV., 406). Only in the last line 5 *jahre* is an *erratum* for 3 *jahre*.

† Most recently by Stähelin in his *Einleitung in die Bücher des A. Ts.*, p. 339 f.—What Josephus says in the *preface* to his *Jewish War*, § 7 of the three and a half years, he gets from a superficial explanation of the Book of Daniel, and what he says in his *Antiquities*, xii. 7, 6 of the three years, he gets from the Books of the Makkabees: he ought not therefore to be appealed to at all in this matter.

‡ Comp. note on previous page.—*Tr.*

NOTES ON THE HEBREW TEXT AND THE LANGUAGE.

As Nabukodrossor's name is, acc. p. 162, written according to the earlier orthography in i. 1 only, the difference is represented in the translation by the adoption, after this verse, of the Massôretic form *Nebukadnessar*.

As the Hebrew words i. 2 stand at present, they supply no sense. The LXX, who dealt generally very freely with the Book of Daniel, already omitted therefrom the words אֵת הַכֵּלִים entirely, in order so to make some kind of sense. But these words have a proper place in the context. We may conclude from ver. 3 that, on the contrary, the error lies in the omission of some words, and the words which are here wanting may be supplied with great certainty from ver. 3. At all events, the *nobles of the land* must have been mentioned here; but probably the captives were here referred to as ver. 3 according to the three ranks: (1) *sons of Israel*, i.e., common people; (2) *nobles of the land*, פַּרְתְּמֵי הָאָרֶץ, a Persian word also after the Book of Esther; (3) such as were of the royal stock; and if these were called מִזֶּרַע מַלְכֵי יְהוּדָה, it is explained how easily these words could be omitted after מֶלֶךְ יְהוּדָה by an error of the copyist. The nobles of royal blood formed, according to all appearances, a distinct order of themselves; and the number of them had gradually become larger in the course of the centuries, but not precisely to the strengthening of the kingdom, inasmuch as the pretensions and arbitrariness of many of them appear clearly enough from Jer. xli. 1 sq.; 2 Kings xxv. 25. Still, it must not be inferred from ver. 3 that Daniel and his three friends belonged to those of common rank, and that the narrator could the more easily have briefly so designated them, as is done ver. 6; for the words *of the sons of Yuda* are intended simply to denote the particular tribe to which they belonged, and which it must be allowed is in this book almost the same as Israel.

Neither do the words i. 21 yield any sense as they at present read, and in this case also the cause is to be found in the omission of a few words in consequence of too rapid copying. For it admits of no doubt, from ii. 49 alone, that the words בְּשַׁעַר הַמֶּלֶךְ have been omitted after דָּנִיֵּאל, and they just furnish what is required. Among the endless buildings of which the king's court consisted in Babel, there was one set apart for the royal Akademy (as we should say): in this Daniel dwelt with his friends; and while they, acc. ii. 49, could not after their promotion to the position of deputy-governors of the province of Babel continue to dwell there, he remained there constantly *until the first year* of the reign of *king Kyros* over Babel, because with this king, as it was long remembered, great internal changes were made generally, with which agrees what is subsequently announced ix. 1; x. 1 sq.

ii. 1. עָשָׂה must be inserted after שָׁרְתִים, just as 2 Kings xvii. 1, acc. p. 194 sq. Here also it is only too hasty copying which is the cause of the error, but in this case the error has already crept into the text of the LXX.

The meaning which the Persian word כִּבְזָּה, ii. 6, is intended to bear in this verse particularly can be gathered from a careful comparison of all the words of this verse with those of ver. 18 and v. 16, 17. The court distributes three kinds of marks of high favour: (1) *honour* by new titles, or by public commendation in the state annals, or in many other forms suggested by the custom of the land; (2) *presents;* but they were acc. v. 16, 17 not such as large gifts of money, but particularly costly garments and ornaments of very various degrees of value; (3) *offices*, also of very various degrees; and that נְבִזְבָּה must signify primarily an office follows clearly both from ver. 48 and the words v. 16, 17. The word was originally, however, probably written נְבִזְבְּה, inasmuch as from that vocalization the form of the plural נְבִזְבְּיָת, v. 17, is most easily explained. It is of first importance to remember the correct meaning of the word if it is wished to determine its derivation. Having ascertained its meaning, we are in a position to maintain with tolerable certainty that the word is originally Persian and signifies the *induction* into an office, comp. the Sanscrit word *nïvïshṭăh*.

That לָהֵן, ii. 6, 9, is meant to have an essentially different meaning from that which it has elsewhere, acc. § 270 b, is of itself improbable. It is true that at first sight the meaning *therefore* appears very suitable both here and iv. 24; it would then be rather a Hebrew than an Aramaic particle, either from לָכֵן by a consonantal change, or corresponding to the לָהֵן of § 217d *ad fin*. But as a fact it is really the meaning *only* which suits these three passages admirably; in all three places, although it stands at the close of a long sentence and introduces the final clause of them, it does this in such a way that it adds what the speaker demands by way of reservation as that which alone meets the case; just as the Arabic *inna-mā* is similarly used. Theodotion very appropriately uses in this passage ii. 6 πλὴν, whilst the LXX make shift with οὖν in these passages ii. 6, 9; in the other passage, iv. 24, Theodotion uses διὰ τοῦτο, but neither in this place is that meaning required.—Similarly כָּל־קֳבֵל must be everywhere taken as *wholly before*, i.e., (appearing) *as*, comp. לִפְנֵי § 217 l.—בֵּאדַיִן differs from the simple אֱדַיִן only as the Arabic *thumma inna* from the simple *thumma;* that is, it is somewhat more emphatic, as the German *alsdann* compared with *dann*.

In ii. 45 *the clay* in the present Hebrew text in the midst of the four metals appears in the wrong place, as according to the previous descriptions also it is not expected in this position. However, in the LXX it still retains its proper place as the first in order. On the other hand, in ver. 35 the position of the word between iron and brass is not so objectionable after the previous words ver. 33.

We must, however, more particularly consider, in connexion with ch. i. and ii., and also the following chapters, especially the meaning of the designations of the various kinds of scholars and sages into whose guild Daniel is received and all of whom he nevertheless far excels because he possesses something wanting in their case, which though apparently of little importance is essential. Usually four kinds of them are found together, when they are to be enumerated in all their different classes, ii. 2, 27; iv. 4 (7); v. 11; where only three, ii. 10, or two, i. 20, are enumerated, it is simply because this long series has been abbreviated; and it lies likewise in the nature of the enumeration of similar names of this kind that in the brief lapidary style of our pieces the conjunction *and* is as if intentionally left out between them, even when merely two of them are enumerated; v. 7, where the LXX have still four instead of three classes, the four in fact suit the context best. Where the fewest words suffice, they are all comprehended under the common name of *the wise-men of Babel*. The special meaning of each of the four names is at the present time somewhat uncertain. Historically considered, however, there is nothing of greater importance here than the fact that the name *Chaldeans* denotes one of the four classes of the wise-men, ii. 2, 10; iv. 4 (7); v. 7, 11; that also is an indication of the true date of this book. For this book is quite alone in the Old Testament in such a use of this word; and not before the Chaldeans had ceased, after Kyros' conquest, to be the ruling people in Babel, could they endeavour to maintain their influence at least as scholars, in that they got completely into their hands the scientific institutions, the chief management of which without doubt fell to them as early as the reign of Nabukodrossor. The earliest evidence of this is supplied by Herodotus, i. 181, from his own time. According to him, they were regarded as the philosophers of Babel in the most general sense, just as they also appear in the Book of Daniel, at all events ii. 4, 5, where their language shall be introduced in this most general sense; but ii. 27 the name *wise-men* in conjunction with the other three is substituted for that of the Chaldeans. But inasmuch as they are mentioned only as one of the four guilds, whether under the name of Chaldeans or wise-men, they must necessarily prosecute mainly one particular art or science; and acc. to Curtius Alex., v. 1, that was undoubtedly astrology and the care of the Calendar, the mastery of which sciences might very well give them as *mathematici* the first place amongst the other four. Nevertheless, in our book, except ii. 27, the חַרְטֻמִּים *the book-scholars* are placed first, and iv. 6 (9) they stand briefly for all the *savants*, without doubt in accordance with the Egyptian incident in the Pentateuch, from which the word is borrowed. —Next to these book-scholars are always placed the אָשְׁפִין, a pure Aramaic word, answering to the Syriac *ashŭph*, with which through Aramaic influence אַשָּׁף in the Book of Daniel only interchanges, i. 20; ii. 2 (it is also strange to meet the word pointed אַשָּׁף, ii. 10, in the midst of the Chaldee section). The Syriac word denotes, acc. *Js. carm.*, ver. 47 ed. Knös, a magician that employs his voice and words in his art: but as this meaning is less appropriate in this connexion, we have used for it a somewhat different word. This word is at the same time a very clear illustration of the great difference there was between the numerous ancient Hebrew words for the arts and sciences of this kind and those of the Aramaic dialect: and the same phenomenon meets us further in the case of the last of these four names. This name occurs, it is true, once in the genuine ancient Hebrew form מְכַשֵּׁף, ii. 2; and as the arts of a man of this kind were practised with the hand, acc. Mic. v. 11, we are led to think of something like the augur's wand (*lituus*) in the hand of a person inquiring, it may be, after celestial omens; and if the Syriac word *ethkashshaph*, derived therefrom, signifies to *intercede*, this office was undoubtedly originally connected with priestly arts of this kind. But that the word had actually such a meaning, follows from the word גָּזַר, ii. 27; iv. 4; v. 7, 11, which always corresponds to it in the Chaldee section: for the latter without doubt signifies, acc. "Isa." xlvii. 12, 13, the augur *dividing*, or *cutting* into sections, the heavens with his wand.*

The correct view of the גָּזְרִין, as the *heaven-watchers*, stargazers, astrologers

---

* The following note on the word מְכַשֵּׁף is added by the author in his last work, *Die Lehre der Bibel von Gott*, I., p. 245.

"I look upon מְכַשֵּׁף as the ancient name of the magician, in the first instance (as we may briefly render it), helps us very much when we attempt to understand the long list of the high state dignities iii. 2, 3. As in the former case the various kinds of *savants* were reduced to a series of four, falling again into two and two, in the same way the chief state officers are classified, when possible, in a still more constant series of seven, falling (as will appear) into three and two and two. Thus the list is repeated without variation twice iii. 2, 3 : and if the number is a little shortened iii. 27, or also a little altered vi. 8, that cannot signify much ; on the contrary, we may make inferences from the fixed order of the enumeration with regard to the meaning of the individual names, if this should in some cases be doubtful. A second assistance to the correct understanding of the terms is to be found in carefully distinguishing the origin of each. It is a mistake to derive them all from the Persian as if they had all found their way into the language of this book through the Persian rule. On the contrary, it is only the two which are of a perfectly similar formation, in addition to the *Satraps* mentioned first, which are of Persian origin : (1) גְּדָבַר, iii. 3, 4, with which הַדָּבַר, or rather הָדָבַר, iii. 27 ; vi. 8, plainly interchanges with only a slight change of sound. This word when it occurs not in the series appears as the designation of such magnates as are at the immediate call of the king, and whom he employs as his nearest and highest officers, iii. 24 ; iv. 33 ; there is the less need to doubt that it corresponds completely to the Persian *khudāvar*: this word signifies a *potentate* (for the Persian *khudā*, *God* means strictly self-sufficiency, absolute power), hence a high state magnate, and must particularly designate the highest officers who are always about the king and in the first instance execute his commands; the passage iii. 24 is plainly in favour of this meaning, and this meaning also suits equally well iv. 33, as well as the context, as will soon plainly appear. To connect the word with the half-Persian and half-Semitic גִּזְבַּר, *treasurer*, Ezra i. 8 ; vii. 21, is quite wrong and cannot be justified, as the consonants themselves are against it, and the treasurers are here everywhere out of place. (2) דְּתָבַר, as *chief judge* (lit. representative of the law), is more easy to understand, as the Persian דָּת is

---

of the magician who operates with his hands by using a magical wand, or in some similar way, in accordance with Mic. v. 11. The word is found Deut. xviii. 10, 11, " Isa." xlvii. 9, 12, in conjunction with חֶבֶר, which bears a similar meaning ; moreover, the constant plural form of both words, כְּשָׁפִים and חֲבָרִים, is the same (comp. further Ps. lviii. 6) and quite analagous to such Latin words as *præstigiæ* (irritations, magical arts, so-called from the root meaning to *irritate*, *excite*, comp. *instigare*). The primary meaning of the word points to the same conclusion : just as certainly as חָשַׂף, *to lay bare*, is the same as the very common Arabic word *kashapha*, which while originally it signified *to pull off* (and *to empty*), it could also mean *to attract to itself* and *to excite ;* and the Aramaic *ethkashshaph, to beseech,* formed like הִתְרַחַנֶּן, would accordingly be literally *to endeavour to draw another to oneself.* In the technical sense of *to enchant,* the word easily passed by means of the verb חָשַׁף into the Syriac *eschaph ;* and as the meaning of these two verbs is throughout the same, it is best to suppose that מְכַשֵּׁף in conjunction with the Aramaic אָשַׁף, Dan. ii. 2, is nothing more than a name placed by the side of the latter by the later author on account of the similarity of its meaning and which therefore is absent in the book of Daniel in the corresponding passages : this note is supplementary to the comment on the passage in Daniel."

itself often found in the books of the Old Testament written after the time of Kyros.—On the other hand, except the well-known פֶּחָה and תִּפְתָּיֵא, *chief judges*, the next two words must be derived from the previous Assyro-Chaldean time: (1) סָגָן which Ḥézeqiél introduced into Hebrew and which signifies "Isa." xli. 25 as well as "Jer." ch. l., li., the most powerful governors of the provinces, but acc. the Books of Chronicles and Dan. ii. 48, however, could also denote the governors or magistrates of smaller provinces, and in New Hebrew often stands for the superior, *e.g.*, of the priests (as *M.* שקלים iv. 4, אבות iii. 2). This word is, according to the consonants with which it was received into the Arabic, *shiḥnah*, purely Semitic, and as connected with the Syriac *shĕgan, to change*, may from the very first designate the office of the *vice-regent* (*statthalter*), and then similar offices also. Finally (2), אֲדַרְגָּזֵר is, according to what we have seen above, plainly our *chief-stargazer*, chief astrologer, or one of the highest officers of those learned guilds; for it follows from § 270 c, that a compound word of this description was possible in Aramaic.—If the seven words have these respective meanings, it follows that the order in which they appear is very appropriate: (1) to the ancient high offices of the governors of the provinces of the first and the second ranks were now added the new Persian *Satraps*; these three classes of officers are immediately followed (2) by two others, consisting of such officers as are always about the king, of the ecclesiastical and the secular order, chief-astrologers and chief-chamberlains; next (3) the *chief-judges* and *chief-prophets* (as the highest instances of appeal), the two heads of the judicial power, form the conclusion of the series. The *rulers of the provinces* who follow in addition are the heads of the military power, the generals as we should say.

A third long list of similar names is found in the enumeration of the musical instruments iii. 5, recurring with unimportant variations vv. 7, 10, 15. A seventh member, as comprehending all the rest, here closes the series, and three pairs are mentioned, evidently in such a way that the pairs follow in the order of the age of their introduction into use. First appear *the horn* and a kind of syrinx or *flute*, being by their names alone very ancient Semitic instruments; next *the cither and the sambyke*, by their names likewise two very ancient Semitic wind-instruments, which must, however, have at that time undergone some reconstruction after the Greek manner, as the fresh transformation of the first word קִיתָרֹס proves; finally the *psaltérion* and *symphonia*, both name and thing purely Greek, though here in an Aramaic dress; and inasmuch as thus a kind of *harp* and *bagpipe* are mentioned last, we see again very plainly that the list does not follow in the order of the materials or the kind of music but in that of their introduction into Syria; and we know from Polybios' *Hist.* xxvi. 10; xxxi. 4* that the instrument which was at that time called *symphonia* in Syria was a favourite one precisely with Antiochos Epiphanes. These instruments have already been referred to also *ante* p. 161. The only other point with regard to them which is remarkable is,

---

* Unfortunately, we possess these passages of Polybios only in the later extracts in Diod. Sik.'s *Hist.*, xxix. 31, and in Athenæos' *Deipnosophistæ*, v. 21; x. 52; a κεράμιον, or rather κεράτιον, which can be simply a wind-horn, is here placed beside the συμφωνία; and when the latter is found alone it must be understood in this sense.

that the Semitic name in its new Greek form קִיתָרֹס and the purely Greek names פְּסַנְתֵּרִין and סוּמְפֹּנְיָה, or acc. ver. 10 shortened סִיפֹנְיָה, do not appear once in the *st. emph.* which is required by the context: the longer Greek names and those formed afresh on a Greek model have remained at all events in Aramaic too recent and too inert to permit such changes.

As a fourth series of similar names we have in the piece of long-winded narrative, ch. iii., the *nations, communities, and tongues*, vv. 4, 7, 29, repeating itself ii. 31; v. 19; vii. 14: and it is observable that each of these three names must in the stricter sense be distinguished somewhat from the others. The first name *nations* has the most general meaning; the second אֻמָּה is like the Arabic *ummah* more our *community* (Germ. *gemeinde*), can therefore denote also, acc. Ezra iv. 10, rather a fraction of the nation, which must have however at all events a certain independent existence, and serves therefore in particular also to designate the separate community in a religious aspect; but both in a nation and in such a community different *languages* may prevail, especially according to the wide meaning of the word *tongue*, which includes also the smaller differences of dialect.

Also the clothes are finally enumerated iii. 21, comp. ver. 27, in a long list of this kind of four names: and it is also quite observable in their case also, as in that of the musical instruments, that many new kinds and new names creep in with the new times. For it is only at the end that the ancient Semitic לְבוּשׁ occurs, in order to embrace under one name all other kinds of garments: the first three names are new and come into Palestine from abroad. For even פְּטִישׁ is hardly Hebrew or Aramaic; and the meaning of the Syriac *petshā*, here retained by the Pesh., cannot be discovered from the ordinary Syriac. But inasmuch as it can hardly be doubted that סַרְבָּל, a word very well known and extensively found in Asia, signifies the *hosen*, trousers, we naturally expect in the position of פְּטִישׁ either the *shoes*, which would accord with the hosen (yet whether even a Rabbinical פשוט with such a meaning occurs is as yet uncertain), or the *hats*, and then it would be derived from the Greek πέτασος. It is not to be expected according to the context that it should mean an over or an under garment, whilst it is not easy to accept the absence of hats or shoes.

The orthography אֱלָהָיךְ, iii. 12, 18 in the *K'thîb*, has, according to the note p. 207, crept in in the course of time under the influence of the Hebrew form of the word, but as far as we can see it was late hands which introduced it. We must therefore be on our guard against ascribing to our author a blending of both languages, a fault of which he is nowhere guilty in such matters. It is in such cases as iv. 5, 6, 15; v. 11, 14 only, that אֱלָהִין is found according to the Hebrew form.

iv. 1 רַעֲנָן, *green*, would have to mean pretty much the same as *living flourishingly*, or *prosperously*: nevertheless, although the Greek translators had already this reading before them and endeavoured to interpret it as best they could, the original text would require, corresponding to the sense itself and the previous member, without doubt such a verb as שַׁאֲנָן, as the repose and security must here as elsewhere denote at the same time the forgetting of God.

הַרְהֹרִין iv. 2 is manifestly intended to be equivalent to שַׂרְעַפִּים, Ps. cxxxix. 23, comp. Job iv. 13; xx. 2, that is, dreamings, imaginations; the root הור may be ultimately related to the Arabic root *khyl* in the signification of *thinking*, but the intensive stem expresses a restless and therefore fanciful thinking. In the whole connexion in which it is found, however, it appears most natural to make it depend on חָזֵה, but in such a way that with the following verb another distinct clause is formed, in that the added clause *and the visions of my head* does not correspond, acc. § 339 a, to our *with the visions*, etc. (for this mode of connecting it suits ii. 28; vii. 1 only), accordingly forms as vii. 15 a clause by itself. These constructions alone bring out the proper movement of the members, which in accordance with the bounding animation of this narrative has in fact already, ver. 1, commenced.

The word *hear!* before the words *the visions of my head*, |iv. 6, might appear to be a late addition in Theodotion (the LXX is here imperfect), added in order to soften the somewhat blunt character of the king's language: but as it follows from ver. 4 (7) and ver. 15 (18) that the king is quite ready in this case to tell his dream, there exists no reason to leave his language blunt and abrupt, and indeed to cause him to suggest another meaning than that which he intends to express.

iv. 7 the words *and the visions of my head upon my bed* in this form are so far from yielding any sense that one might conjecture that they do not belong here and have got misplaced from ver. 2 : the LXX appear to have omitted them entirely, Theodotion at least has simply *upon my bed was I beholding*. But they can quite well remain if בְּחֶזְוִי is read: and we are justified in making this emendation by the recurrence of the same phrase vv. 10, 15; vii. 13, and similarly ii. 19.

The word חֲזוֹת, iv. 8, 17 must evidently be equivalent to the *breadth*, circumference, an entirely different word from the pure Hebrew חֻזְרָה, viii. 5, 8; and appears to differ from the usual פְּרִי, iii. 1, only as it expresses more the breadth of a living thing. As this breadth is shown most at the breast, it can be allowed that the word is connected with חָזֶה *the breast*, although the latter word has the form of חֲדִי in the Aramaic of our book also, acc. ii. 32: at the same time the meaning itself ought not to be misunderstood.

The complicated figures vv. 12 (15), 20 (23) will not be understood until it is borne in mind that אֱסוּר, according to the dialect of this book, is the same as אֵזוֹר, *girdle*, which is sufficiently confirmed by Job xii. 18. It must be allowed that the expression retains at first sight something to our minds surprising in this connexion : it is therefore probable that there is an allusion to some passage in a book much read at that time, and was accordingly more easily understood by the first readers. This supposition is the more probable as this whole phrase which is of itself strange and surprising is nevertheless here supposed to be familiar to the reader, and is not, as our author is on other occasions accustomed to do, further explained in what follows.

As in this piece ch. iv. a note of time must be restored at the commencement, according to the remarks *ante* p. 219, the question arises whether we ought not also, according to the LXX likewise, to read at the head of ch. iii., *In the eighteenth year* (very suitably as the year of the destruction of Jerusalem), and at the head of ch. v., *On the consecration-day of his reign*, with which the return of this day in a subsequent year is undoubtedly meant, as the Greek kings were accustomed to keep the anniversaries of their ascension. Still, if one were disposed to say that the author placed a note of time before each of his ten pieces, that assumption would not be found correct in the case of ch. vi. even according to the LXX. It is true that in the case of this chapter such a note could most easily be dispensed with, as this Median king of the age of sixty-two years did not reign long. And at all events it must be said that this Greek translator, according to the freedom which he everywhere allowed himself, supplemented the plan of the book in this case very successfully, if he made these additions at his own suggestion.

The king's name, בֵּלְשַׁאצַּר, constantly occurring ch. v., was, it is true, acc. p. 116, early confounded with the name of Daniel, בֵּלְטְשַׁאצַּר: but it is of itself improbable that both names were originally either the same or confounded together. In what way both names are different as regards their composition and meaning we are, it is true, still not in a position to determine with sufficient certainty, because we have not at present a sufficiently complete knowledge of the Assyro-Babylonian language generally. It would be natural to suppose that they differ simply therein that the first part of the first word is formed by the masculine *Bêl*, and the first part of the second by the feminine *Bêlt:* it is true we should rather expect the orthography בֵּלְתִּ־, and from iv. 5 we might suppose that Daniel received his name rather from the masculine *Bêl* as the chief god of Babel and of Nabukodrossor himself. Still, the difficulties which we at present feel in inquiring into the original meaning of the two proper names cannot after all lead us to consider them as originally entirely the same. The source of the confusion of the two names, or rather of their confluence in the erroneous (acc. to the clear evidence of iv. 5) orthography Baltasar of the Hellenists, which appears in the first part of the compound, we are at present unable to trace, as at all events in the Chaldee copies of ch. v. בלשאצר and not בלטשׁ is always found.

I have given sufficient proof in notes on Judges v. 30; Ps. xlv. 10, that שֵׁגָל, vv. 3, 23, is the true name for the wife of the prince or king. Perhaps the name was not in this sense of it ancient Hebrew, but rather Aramaic, or North-Palestinian, as the passages from Judges and the Psalm may show, and as the name occurs here in the Chaldee. Nevertheless I have preferred to translate it here *princess*, or *high-princess*, which would be better, in order to distinguish more clearly these women from her who is called *queen* in the higher sense ver. 10.— On לְחֵנָא, ver. 3, comp. *Antiquities*, p. 265 (229).

v. 21, the reading שַׁוִּי is in any case wrong: it could only be the act. perf. of the intensive stem *he made like*, but to think of God as the agent in this case is quite foreign to the context. And if such a reading as שֻׁוִּי were adopted, corresponding to the previous טְרִיד, the pass. perf., with the meaning *it was made like*, that would also be wrong, because the meaning *to make like* requires an intensive stem. Now, it is true that in later Aramaic the passive verb is apparently constantly distinguished by the prefix אֶת־, acc. § 123, but as this prefix appears only before the passive stem which has undergone internal vowel change,* so again there exist still, here and there, numerous remnants of the earlier simpler formation by means of purely internal vowel changes. It is true that this vowel-change itself is on the decrease in the Aramaic: it has been preserved in the later Aramaic only in the last syllable, and disappears where it was originally

---

* This phenomenon, confirmed also by the Ethiopic, is very important. The Syriac form *ethkĕthēbh* is correct because it is founded on a passive *kĕthebh*, the form *ethkattabh* because it is founded on a passive כְּתַב.

318   APPENDIX, 3. 2.—DANIEL.

very audible in the first syllable;* nevertheless it has been preserved in this oldest form of Aramaic, at all events in the perf., in many formations. Now, if הֵיתִי *he was brought*, iii. 13; vi. 18, was formed together with הֵיתִי *he brought*, and הֵעַל *he was led in*, v. 13, 15, together with הַעֵל or הַנְעֵל *he led in*, it was undoubtedly possible to make the form שֻׁוִּי for *he was made like*, although as an imperf. of it the form יִשְׁתַּוֵּה iii. 29 already exists. In fact, we might read שַׁוִּי simply, on the supposition that the passive vowel was already wanting in the first syllable in this case as in later Aramaic, because הַצְלַח, vi. 29, must have a passive force: yet as we find elsewhere הָרְקַן, iv. 33, and הָחְרַב, Ezra iv. 15, it is better vi. 29 also to read הַצְלַח.—But that we have preserved here throughout perfectly genuine remnants of the ancient Semitic passive formation, it is not possible to doubt. Let the exceedingly peculiar form הֵיתָי *to be brought* by the side of הֵיתִי † *to bring* be alone considered. The perf. of the simple stem, again, by which this Aramaic even is so greatly distinguished from the Hebrew, is not borrowed from the *part. pass.*, for instance, as in Syriac the personal pronoun can be more closely connected at all events with the active participle. The most that could be produced in support of such a notion would be the form תְּקִילְתָּא *though art weighed*, v. 27, as תְּקִלְתְּ is expected: but that in this Aramaic the final *a* of the ancient *atta* (*thou*) could still make itself audible, is proved by the orthography אַנְתָּה which only the Q'rî desires to change into אַנְתְּ; the orthography with י can alone prove nothing.

It cannot be denied that the pointing of the Chaldee in the Book of Daniel is very defective, just as the Massôretic treatment of some of the books of the *Kethubim* generally is less than usually painstaking. The division of the verses also is in case of ver. 22 very bad.—Finally, the connexion of the long address of Daniel's to the king will be greatly misunderstood until it is borne in mind that all the words vv. 18-23 form but one long, many-membered and much-involved sentence. A similar long sentence was met with above ii. 21-23, even in a lyric; and it is necessary to become more and more accustomed to acknowledge that the Hebrew admits of such long sentences, and that they are frequent, particularly in certain pieces.

The pointing of the word פַּרְסִין, v. 25, also is doubtful. If one were to proceed from a rigidly literal application of the explanation of the word given ver. 28, one might conjecture it would be better to read פָּרְסִין, *they divide*, or *men divide*. As a fact the author quotes the word, when he comes to explain it, ver. 28, not as פַּרְסִין but as פְּרֵס, which might also signify *divided* like the foregoing תְּקִל *weighed*, as if *men divide* were the same as *divided*. In that case the only ques-

---

* The instance mentioned above shows that this is the case not only in the pass. part. *mĕbharrakh* as compared with the active part. *mĕbharrēkh*.

† In the passive vocalization הֵיתַי every trace of a *u* seems to have disappeared from the beginning of the word: but הוּבַד and הֻסַּק, iv. 33; vii. 11, suffice to show how decidedly it once existed in all these cases. As the *u* sound is flattened to *o* in the closed syllable in the case of this Southwest Aramaic, the transition to *a* is thereby made possible, and *ae* has at all events a deeper sound than the *ai* of the active form הֵיְתִי. Similarly though the *ai* remains in הֲוֵית *thou wast*, it is deepened into *ae* in הֲוֵית *I was*, on account of the closed syllable in which at the same time the *i* at the end has coalesced.

tion is wherefore this shorter וּפָרֵס is not written also in the short lapidary inscription. To this question, however, the answer can be made that the oracle is meant to supply in its strict form in the first instance the exact words *they divide*, because this points more to something still impending (they are about to divide), as in fact this division has not taken place at that moment; whilst the explanation ver. 28 could be shortened as much as was found desirable. At the same time, we cannot after all lose sight of the fact that a word like *they divide* does not accord well with the brief incisive series *Numbered Numbered! Weighed and* . . . . , because the series does not then close symmetrically, and is not of itself sufficiently clear. As one expects at the end a brief incisive word, clear in itself, the pointing וּפַרְסִין is after all probably the best. This word *parts* might be equivalent to *lots*, as the Syriac *pessā* appears to have been contracted from it, since it has hardly been taken from πεσσός. Yet neither would a closing word *and lots!* or *and divine destiny!* be sufficiently clear. It is therefore best to take it as meaning *and to fragments!* or *into ruins!* which is in this connexion sufficiently forcible, and at the same time carries its meaning clearly with it. The explanation can then run thus : *fragment*, as being more briefly uttered and forming a good transition to *fractured is* . . . . The LXX shows in v. 5, 17, 26-28 how very differently the ancient readers already interpreted the words. There is no indication that פַּרְסִין is intended to allude to the Persians who are mentioned after the Medes ver. 28, although the originally quite long *ā* of *Pārs* appears as shortened in the pointing פַּרְסָיָא, vi. 29, contrary to all Eastern custom and only after the Greek fashion.

This instance v. 25-28 may, moreover, also serve as a proof of the high state of development to which the art of the *Exegetai* or *Hermeneutai* (as the Greeks say) had already in these early times been carried. This art had already its fixed methods and habits.—The interpreter selected in the presence of his auditors and eager pupils a distinct piece or word of the whole thing which he proposed to expound, repeating it in its detached form with a loud voice, or pointing to it with his hand : then making a break he added immediately, with a somewhat altered voice, the explanation, without inserting anything like a *that is*. It is evident that this custom had been thus developed in the exposition of monuments, when the instructed priest had to explain the separate portions of one of them ; and it was then applied by linguistic scholars similarly in the explanation of the obscure words of a book. In the Book of Daniel this established method appears ii. 37, 43; and below it is repeated in several examples in ch. vii. and viii. It is necessary to realize this distinctly, or otherwise the manner and the whole pregnant sense of all these passages cannot be understood with complete accuracy.

In vi. 13 the words "they speak before the king *concerning the interdict of the king*" are in the highest degree inappropriate and superfluous, whilst a fitting address of the king is felt to be wanting. We do best therefore to read with the LXX דָּרְיָוֶשׁ instead of עַל אֱסָר and to connect מַלְכָּא with it, which is confirmed by ver. 7.

The meaning of the word דַּחֲוָן, vi. 19, was as early as the LXX so obscure that they omitted the whole sentence ; the ἐδέσματα, *foods*, of Theodotion are plainly a guess from the context, and after the foregoing clause very superfluous, and moreover not very well accordant with הַנְעֵל, *to introduce*. According to the whole context and the sense of this word there is nothing more suitable than to understand by the word *dancing women*, if that can be done : and at all events the Arabic root *zakhkha to leap* (as *saltare* from *salire*) may lead to the idea of such women.

In order correctly to understand הַצְלַח, vi. 29, it is necessary to remember that the same word signifies in the peculiar usage of this book *to re-instate a person* in an office, iii. 30 compared with ii. 49, which after the observations made on Ps. xlv. 5 is not surprising ; for if the Arabic *aṣlaḥa* also signifies *to improve* and *to restore* (to cause that which was spoilt to sit well again, to be well arranged), it is easy to perceive that when applied to high imperial matters it could receive the above special signification. But in that case it is precisely here, vi. 29, that we must read acc. p. 318 הַצְלַח. In general the conclusion of this narrative resembles that of ch. iii. as regards the public office ; and in both cases it would be incomplete if it were not at last said that the brave men had been restored to the offices which bad men had deprived them of.

בְּחֶזְוַי, vii. 2, would be *in my beholding*, or when I beheld, *by night*, as if it were equivalent to the Hebrew בְּרֹאתִי, viii. 2, 15. But it follows from ii. 28 ; iv. 2, 7, 10 ; vii. 1, 13, 15, that when the word is used of spirit-visions it is found only in the plural, as the singular acc. vii. 20 designates rather the physical aspect, or the external appearance of a body. Inasmuch as furthermore vii. 13 חָזֵוי לֵילְיָא is exactly the same as what is here עִם 'ח 'ל in a somewhat more extended shape, more after the Aramaic style, there can be no doubt but that בְּחֶזְוַי must be read here. Only ii. 19 would בְּחֶזְוָא דִי לֵילְיָא actually be said in the singular: but there also the original reading will have been either בְּחֶזְוַי or בְּחֶזְוָיָא, since the supposition that the *stat. constr. pl.* had been written accoording to the recent Phœnician manner חָזְוָא would be too doubtful.

vii. 10 it is most likely better to read נְגַר וּנְפַק instead of נְגַר וְנָפֵק : the enumeration of what the seer beheld successively, surely advances here, and the description of the appearance of the *Ancient of the days* was finished ver. 9.

vii. 22 יְתִב וְשָׁלְטָנָא has been omitted acc. vv. 10, 14 and vv. 26, 27 before יְהַב : the sense requires this supplement ; and it is obvious how easily the eye of the copyist could stray from יְתִב to יְהַב ; that the hiatus appears in the Greek translators is not decisive. With a little reflection it may be perceived how greatly the sense of the whole passage is changed by this suppletion, a point which I will not pursue further here with regard to the New Testament : and it will be found that the original propriety of the thoughts and the true progress in the unfolding of the many things beheld is similarly increased thereby.

viii. 5 חָזוּת can in this connexion only signify *a horn of beholding*, i.e., to be beheld, something which was like a horn to look upon ; and on that very account it can also, ver. 8, be placed before the noun in the const. st. in a somewhat different manner, inasmuch as this better suits the connexion, in which case it is simply somewhat stronger than כְּ, *as*, which is so general in such instances. Everything which is thus beheld can present itself to the eye at first only *as if it were* this or that.—But elsewhere than in these two passages חָזוּת does not occur in the book.

With regard to מְצִעִירָה, viii. 9, enough has been said § 270 *b* ; according to what has been there said it ought to be of itself obvious that the whole word answers to the Aramaic זְעִירָה, viii. 8, and must be read מְצִעִירָה

If one were determined to retain viii. 11 the *K'thîb* הָרִים, and then read accordingly וְהִשְׁלִךְ, it would have to be supposed that the preceding *from him* was meant simply to refer back more emphatically to God himself: *from him he abolished the daily and cast down his holy place*, which would be equivalent to *he abolished* His, etc. The sense would be the same, the form of expression simply more unusual.

viii. 14 all the Greek translators read correctly אֵלָיו; the same error which has crept into the Hebrew "Zech." xii. 10, acc. Vol. III., p. 53.

viii. 25 it appears that בְּשַׁלְוָה can be understood as meaning "*in godless security* he will destroy many," the sense in which the word is found at all events in the Aramaic of our author, iv. 1, 24. However, the words xi. 21, 24 point precisely in the case of Antiochos Epiphanes to another signification; and when it is closely considered, it appears that the above meaning is in fact too feeble for this case.

If it is desired to perceive how certainly the long prayer in ch. ix., according to the extent assigned to it above, follows the course of the prayer in the Book of Barûkh, and is almost verbatim taken from it, the question must be examined from the two sides which it presents. A piece of writing derives its significance, on the one hand, both from the single words and sentences which it contains, and from the order and the whole connexion in which they are found. Examined from this point of view, the claim to originality is manifestly due to the Book of Barûkh. For if one compares

Dan. ver. 5, 6	with	Bar. i. 13.	Dan. ver. 14	with	Bar. ii. 9, 10.
„ „ 7, 8	„	„ „ 15, 16.	„ „ 15	„	„ „ 11, 12.
„ „ 9, 10	„	„ „ 17, 18.	„ „ 16	„	„ „ 13.
„ „ 11	„	„ „ 19-22.	„ „ 18	„	„ „ 19.
„ „ 12, 13	„	„ ii. 1-7.	„ „ 19	„	„ „ 14, 15,

it appears clearly (1) that the words in the Book of Daniel are in the main simply an extract from those in the Book of Barûkh: the completeness and originality of the composition belong plainly to the Book of Barûkh; all that the Book of Daniel contains in addition or different is either short additions from earlier sacred books which answer the special purpose of this discourse (and to the most important of these detailed reference was made above), or simply unimportant modifications in the connexion of the sentences. But it appears further (2) that the abbreviations which are found in the Book of Daniel point back in part by their proper meaning to the fuller form of the prayer in the Book of Barûkh as the original. The most important instance is that it is quite impossible to see why in the Book of Daniel, ver. 12, merely the ancient *judges* of the nation are mentioned, although vv. 6, 8 the ancient kings had been spoken of, and the mention of them is far more natural here in this connexion than there: but if the words, ver. 12, are simply abbreviated from Barûkh ii. 1, we can very well understand this; for in Barûkh, after the general review of this history in the form in which such a review could be made at the date of the origin of this book, the judges, the kings, and the princes of the people (simply princes as ruling over the new Jerusalem) are correctly distinguished. Another portion of the abbreviations, as well as of the other small alterations in the Book of Daniel, can be explained, when it is remembered that that which is the prayer of the community in the Book of Barûkh must become in the Book of Daniel particularly the prayer of an individual, as appears most plainly by the turn given to ver. 17. But it appears (3) that notwithstanding all these small differences it is certainly the same prayer in both books from its commencement throughout its entire course and the connexion of all its thoughts, only that in the Book of Barûkh it is continued much further, with an entirely similar arrangement and manner. But a further continuation of it in the Book of Daniel would have been in the highest degree unsuitable to the plan of this book as a whole as well as that of all its pieces: it is accordingly discontinued earlier in the Book of Daniel and finished with suitable turns of thought; but even ver. 19 the author uses the words of Bar. ii. 14, 15, as if turning back from ii. 19 to pick them up.

On the other hand, however, a concurrence of this kind in the case of two books, which is at first sight doubtful, must also be looked at quite independently of the separate words and their connexion, and according to the peculiar general characteristics of both books. Regarded from this point of view, it appears obviously that the prayer which is common to both is in the Book of Barûkh the one chief thing, while in the Book of Daniel it is only of secondary importance. If, therefore, the author of the Book of Barûkh had taken the long prayer from the Book of Daniel, or had even only worked with it as a model, he would have presented nothing at all of a characteristic nature, inasmuch as it was above, p. 108 sq., proved that the life and soul of that little book rest entirely upon this prayer. The author of the Book of Daniel, according to his entire purpose and the plan of his book, placed elsewhere the stress of his representations and his words, and for him the production of this prayer was a matter of secondary importance. It was all the more easy for him to design it according to the best model which presented itself in his time; and that he could find in this very Book of Barûkh.—As now this proof, which is of an entirely different character, conducts to the same result, the fact may be considered to be all the more certain; and we can maintain with confidence that the author of the Book of Daniel was indebted here to the Book of Barûkh. Finally, it is obvious how distinctly this result confirms the conclusions above explained as regards the dates and the authors of both books.

ix. 24 the *Q'rî* has correctly הָתֵם, as viii. 23; a double לַחְתֹּם *to seal* would also be in this verse not very poetical, the instance ver. 27 being of quite a different kind.

ix. 25 in the case of וּבְצוֹק the peculiarity is to be noted with which our author in the oracles of artistically brief and mysterious composition, uses also the simple וְ *and* antithetically; the same usage occurs again vv. 26, 27 and xi. 24 in the case of a closing clause which may be said to lag behind, and produces the more striking effect precisely through this concise brevity.—This is also of special importance on account of the words with which ver. 26 is closed, which are very obscure owing to וְקִצּוֹ. If this word is taken so that it signifies *and his end*, we shall be obliged to begin the antithesis thus early in the verse: *yet his end is with overflowing*, this idea of overflowing would then refer to the final overflowing of the righteous punishment of God and be abbreviated from שׁוֹטֵף צְדָקָה Isa. x. 22 comp. below xi. 45. Nevertheless, appropriate as the echo of a word from the passage Isa. x. 22 would here sound, inasmuch as that entire passage was evidently vividly present to the mind of our author according to the end of this, ver. 26 and of the following ver. 27, the simple word *overflowing* in this sense would after all remain here too vague; and on the other hand the author enables us to infer from his subsequent words xi. 10, 22, 26, 40, first, that in the case of the often repeated שֶׁטֶף he has in view the passage Isa. viii. 8, and secondly that he wishes to have it everywhere, in accordance with this last-named passage, understood of the overflowing of hostile heathen armies. But from the whole manner of the discourse in these last times it must be inferred that the great antithesis is not intended to begin so early as these words but with the following וְעַד: and three times it concludes with this slowly appearing but terrible and, which is in all cases followed by but a few words; and whoever understands the complexion of the discourse and the various feelings of our author will not consider this a small point. In fact, the pointing appears to have some sense of this, as it connects the words וקצו בשטף with those preceding. If we could read וְחַיִל instead of וקצו, as the reading really is xi. 26, the sense would be more certain, inasmuch as our author could, with that use of וְ mentioned above under iv. 2, connect the words in the sense of *who cometh with his army in an overflow*, while the only passage that could be quoted for the meaning of קִצּוֹ *his end* is xi. 45, where the word however is found in another connexion. But if one may suppose that this קִצּוֹ (perhaps to be pointed קָצוֹ) is equivalent to חָצוֹ "his line," *i.e.*, his line of battle (acc. Prov. xxx. 27), the word would give the same sense as חַיִל and would have been used in this passage probably on account of the paronomasia with the following קֵץ.

It ought to be obvious that וְאֵין לוֹ, ver. 26, cannot supply any other sense than that above ascribed to it; and הַגְּבִיר, ver. 27, has been sufficiently explained in the notes on Ps. xii. 5: it ought never to be forgotten that in Arabic *jabara* is the opposite of *kasara*.—נֶחֱרָצֹת is in the *st. const.* (comp. נֶחֱרָצָה, ver. 27), lit. "decision of what is terrible," or of "terrible things, punishments;" for the latter is no doubt the meaning of שֵׁמֵם, or rather מְשֹׁמֵם, ver. 27, xi. 31 (comp. § 160 *a*) both here vv. 26, 27 three times and when it occurs elsewhere in this book as an adjective, viii. 13; xi. 31; xii. 11, comp. the verb in the meaning "to be astounded, horrified," viii. 27; and the plur. fem. is in form and significance the same as נִפְלָאוֹת viii. 24; xi. 36, comp. פְּלָאוֹת, xii. 6; even ix. 18 it is sufficient to understand שִׁמְמֹתֵינוּ as "our terrible things, our punishments," comp. xii. 6.—The only further difficulty is the עַל ver. 27. If it were allowable to understand it in its Aramaic signification of *and will enter, i.e., be brought* into the temple, as was supposed in the *Jahrbb. der Bibl. Wiss.*, III., p. 230 sq., that would suit this connexion pretty well: but we are unable to find any proof of this use of the עַל in the Hebrew of our author. It is less difficult to take it acc. § 220 *a* (comp. further Hos. xi. 7), which is quite allowable in poetic language.

x. 6 כֶּתֶם אוּפָז is exactly like *gold of Uphaz*, Jer. x. 9: and אוּפָז, which occurs in these two passages only, is either an orthographical error for אוֹפִיר, acc. Vol. III., 141, in which case one would have to suppose that our author had only copied this error from the book of Yérèmyá; or we have here an actual interchange of the sounds *r* and *z*, which is not wholly impossible in these languages also, acc. § 51 *d*; in this case we should be obliged to assume that the word had been preserved in various dialects; for that they were two wholly different places is most improbable. If the word occurred elsewhere than in these two passages, or if אוֹפִיר were found as well in either of these two books, we should be in a position to form a more decided judgment.

xi. 1 עָמְדִי yields in this connexion no sense whatever; and the LXX in their time could not understand it: Theodotion, on the other hand, has ἔστην, and though he may have guessed it merely, there is no doubt that the word is simply an orthographical error for עָמַדְתִּי.

xi. 10 the *Q'ri* מָעֻזּוֹ, *his fortress*, would refer to the Syrian king, ver. 7: but the *K'thib* מָעֻזָּהּ, *her fortress*, can equally well refer to Syria as a land, comp. ver. 19.

With regard to the unusual construction בְּנֵי פָּרִיצֵי עַמְּךָ, xi. 14, comp. § 289*c*.

תְּקֹף, xi. 17, can the more easily signify also the *possession*, as being the *power* over something, since, as originally a genuinely Aramaic word, it is different from the Hebrew תֹּמֶךְ only in sound.

xi. 22 is unfortunately divided from ver. 23; ver. 26 also the members require to be better divided than the present accents permit.

The words xi. 39, *he doeth to the strong fortresses with*, i.e., the same as *to, the strange God*, do not admit in this connexion of any other meaning than that above given: they simply introduce what follows, inasmuch as they refer back to the last words of ver. 38. That עִם should simply express a more emphatic כְּ *as* is also met with elsewhere.

The formation רַבּוֹת, xi. 41, is remarkable: the word can in this connexion of the whole discourse, and in this construction with יִכָּשְׁלוּ, only signify the *chief-teachers*, much the same as those who vv. 33-35; xii. 3 are called מַשְׂכִּילִים. The formation of the word and its usage is plain from § 177*f*: but in this signification it occurs here for the first time, which is historically instructive in many respects, and may serve at the same time as a sign that this book was not written before the time of Rabbinism.

A very recent word is שׁוֹטֵט also, xii. 4, which in this connexion, where nothing but books are spoken of, can express nothing else than to go *from line to line*, i.e., much the same as our *read accurately*, derived from the subsequently much-used שָׂפָה (שִׂיטָה), שִׂטִּים *lines*, which itself answers to the Arabic *khaṭṭ straight line* (linea), with the change of letters explained § 58 *b*. It is very intelligible that the author should desire a minute reading of his lines, particularly of those on the prophecies; but in this reference to his readers expressed at the end of the book, he is very much like the author of the book *Qoheleth*.

For the benefit of those readers to whom perhaps the peculiar literary art of the Book of Daniel still remains somewhat obscure, I may remark at the close, that a comparison of the similar books, which are not explained in this volume, is very useful in assisting the attainment of a more certain understanding of it. I refer therefore to my work on the *Apokalypse*, which appeared in the second edition, entirely rewritten, 1861, to the *Abhandlung über des Æthiopischen Buch Henokh entstehung sinn und zusammensezung*, Göttingen, 1854, to the essay on the *vierte Ezrabuch*, Gött., 1863, to that on the *Zweite B. Barûkh* in the *Gött. Gel. Anz*, 1867, pp. 1706 sq. (on the third Book of Barûkh I intend to publish an essay immediately*), to the essay on the *Book of the Ascension of Moses* in the *Geschichte des Volkes Israel*, V., p. 73 sq., and to many other remarks in various places in the volumes of the *History of Israel;* the essay on the origin, contents, and value of the *Sibyllischen Bücher*, Gött., 1858, also contains much that belongs to this subject. When the other literature of this kind has been compared, it will be perceived that in all the books of this kind which have been perfectly or partially preserved, we possess merely the remnants of a most rich and varied literature, which was in continued growth through some centuries, and which had its own special conditions and laws, and became one of the most productive and also most characteristic branches of the whole later literature of Israel. It may be seen particularly from Dillmann's essay on the *Æthiopische Clemensapokalypse* in the Göttingen *Nachrichten*, 1858, pp. 185 sq., that it was long continued, even into the Middle Ages, after it had passed into the Christian Church.

---

* See *Geschichte des Volkes Israel*, VII., p. 183.—*Tr.*

INDEX TO THE PROPHETIC WRITINGS IN THE FIVE VOLUMES.

		Vol.	Page.		Vol.	Page.
Isa.	i.	II.	118-132	Jer. xlvi.-xlix.	III.	195-218
,,	ii.-v.	,,	18-52	,, xlvi. 13-28.	,,	299-302
,,	vi.	,,	62-72	,, l., li.	V.	1-18
,,	vii. 1-ix. 6.	,,	72-111	Ezek. i.-xlviii.	IV.	26-224
,,	ix. 7-x. 4.	,,	50-60	,, xlvi. 16-18.	,,	214
,,	x. 5-xii.	,,	225-242	,, xlvi. 19-24.	,,	205 sq.
,,	xiii. 1.	I.	97	Hos.	I.	210-304
,,	xiii. 2-xiv. 23.	IV.	237-244	Joel.	,,	107-142
,,	xiv. 24-27.	II.	246 sq.	Am.	,,	143-209
,,	xiv. 28-xvi.	,,	132-150	Ob.	II.	277-288
,,	xvii. 1-11.	,,	111-116	Jon.	V.	96-107
,,	xvii. 12-xviii.	,,	243-9	Mic. i.-v.	II.	289-322
,,	xix.	,,	266-276	,, vi., vii.	,,	333-339
,,	xx.	,,	249-253	Nah.	III.	1-13
,,	xxi. 1-10.	IV.	233-236	Hab.	,,	26-48
,,	xxi. 11-17.	II.	150-156	Zeph.	,,	14-26
,,	xxii., xxiii.	,,	158-177	Hag.	V.	37-44
,,	xxiv-xxvii.	V.	23-34	Zech. i.-viii.	,,	45-70
,,	xxviii-xxxii.	II.	178-224	,, ix.-xi.	I.	305-333
,,	xxxiii.	,,	253-261	,, xii. 1-xiii. 6.	III.	49-55
,,	xxxiv., xxxv.	V.	19-23	,, xiii. 8-9.	I.	327 sq.
,,	xxxvii. 22-35	II.	261-265	,, xiv.	III.	55-59
,,	xl.-xlvi.	IV.	257-354	Mal.	V.	75-86
Jer.	i.-xxiv.	III.	93-195	Dan.	,,	152-324
,,	xxv.-xxxvi.	,,	218-275	Bar. i. 1-iii. 8.	,,	114-123
,,	xxxvii.-xliv.	,,	276-299	,, iii. 9-v. 9.	,,	127-137
,,	xlv.	,,	275 sq.	Jer. Epist.	,,	137-151

www.ingramcontent.com/pod-product-compliance
Lightning Source LLC
Chambersburg PA
CBHW021205230426
43667CB00006B/570